POEM
FOR
THE DAY

Two

Also edited by Nicholas Albery

Poem for the Day One

Poem For The Day

Two

366 poems, old and new,
to learn by heart

Edited by

Retta Bowen
Nick Temple
Stephanie Wienrich

and

Nicholas Albery

Chatto & Windus
LONDON

Published by the Nicholas Albery Foundation
in association with
Chatto & Windus 2003

8 10 9 7

Compilation copyright © The Nicholas Albery Foundation 2003
For copyright of individual poems, see the acknowledgement pages

All royalties from this book are going to the Nicholas Albery Foundation, registered charity
no. 1091396, which runs the projects the Institute for Social Inventions, the Natural Death
Centre, the Poetry Challenge, the ApprenticeMaster Alliance and www.DoBe.org. The
Nicholas Albery Foundation gratefully acknowledges the generosity of poets, publishers and
agents who gave permission for poems to be published.

First published in Great Britain in 2003 by
The Nicholas Albery Foundation, 6 Blackstock Mews, Blackstock Road, London N4 2BT
(tel 020 7359 8391; fax 020 7354 3831; e-mail info@alberyfoundation.org)
in association with
Chatto & Windus, Random House
20 Vauxhall Bridge Road, London SW1V 2SA

Random House Australia (Pty) Limited
20 Alfred Street, Milsons Point, Sydney,
New South Wales 2061, Australia

Random House New Zealand Limited
18 Poland Road, Glenfield,
Auckland 10, New Zealand

Random House South Africa (Pty) Limited
Eudulini, 5A Jubilee Road, Parktown 2193, South Africa

The Random House Group Limited Reg. No. 954009

www.randomhouse.co.uk

A CIP catalogue record for this book
is available from the British Library

ISBN 0 7011 7401 3

Papers used by Random House are natural, recyclable
products made from wood grown in sustainable forests.
The manufacturing processes conform to the environmental
regulations of the country of origin.

Printed and bound in Great Britain by
Mackays of Chatham PLC, Chatham, Kent

Foreword

Andrew Motion, Poet Laureate

This anthology is founded on a very simple but salubrious premise: poetry is a part of daily life. But it also proves in heartening and exciting ways that it's also a part of everyday life. It celebrates the ordinary as well as the exceptional, the familiar as well as the remarkable, in language that is at once recognisable and wrought. In the process it reminds us that poetry is an essential thing, appealing to what is primitive and fundamental in all of us, no matter how elaborate our response to it might be. This is why, among other things, we often feel compelled to commit poems to memory – not in the dusty sense of 'learning by rote', but in the true deep sense of 'learning by heart'.

It's the range of the selection, not just the quality of the writing, which makes the case. Crossing continents and centuries, the editors have found a way of establishing the differences between individual voices while at the same time exploring continuities and resemblances. They have made a book of poetries which celebrates poetry itself, and reaffirms the means by which it puts us most deeply in touch with ourselves as it strengthens our connection with the world. The book is a treasure-trove, an adventure trail, and a cabinet of wonders. Just what it should be, in fact.

Introduction

If you are familiar with the first volume of *Poem for the Day*, the concept of this book should not need further explanation – we have tried, as far as possible, to keep with the spirit of the hugely popular original. If you have not come across this title before, it is perhaps easiest explained as a Book of Days with a memorable poem for each day, and a note or two about the poet or the poem for additional enjoyment. The idea is that you will feel inspired to learn at least some of these poems by heart – perhaps even all of them over the course of a year or more. This was the idea – and the claim – of the book's original editor, the late Nicholas Albery, our colleague and founder of the projects of the charity which now bears his name, the Nicholas Albery Foundation. All royalties from this book go directly to the Foundation to support its work (see page 399 for more information).

Nicholas liked to serenade us, and encouraged us to serenade him, with poems, old and new, after lunch each day – and indeed, that is how we came to choose the 366 poems for this present collection. We were looking for that certain 'heat' or 'magic' that becomes particularly apparent in recital. Whilst reciting, one could invariably tell from the others' reactions how well a poem was faring under this form of exposure. Some of the poems had the power to lift us immeasurably, others provoked furious argument or hoots of laughter; all those we finally decided upon delighted us. We will certainly miss this much-loved ritual of post-meal poems and would recommend it to anyone.

You may find, however, enough joy in just hearing the poems ringing around your own head throughout the day, and not feel inclined to inflict them on others (although we do still feel that that is a great part of the pleasure, and the reward of learning them). If you are not able to find a willing and attentive listener and would like an audience, we would recommend the annual Poetry Challenge, another Nicholas Albery invention. This involves reciting your hard-learned poem to an audience, large or small, in order to raise money for a charity of your choice. The Challenge takes place in London on the first Sunday in October each year; and there are co-ordinated Challenges taking place in schools all over the country every autumn term (see page 398 for more details).

The selection has, inevitably, a different feel from the first. Instead of one editor, there are four; this means four sets of favourite poets, four opinions to be reconciled, four different people with different likes and dislikes. There are more contemporary poems, more from Eastern Europe and America, and more women poets, but there are still many well-loved classics by Keats, Shakespeare, Yeats, and others. Indeed, we would argue that, rather than weakening the selection or dissipating a sense of a singular point of view, the four-way editorial process has strengthened and unified it, as poems had to be truly special to be agreed upon by all involved.

This book has been very much a labour of love, and lies very close to its editors' hearts. For some time now we have been carrying around with us a good proportion of these

366 poems – in our heads and in our hearts – and so it is with a mixture of joy, relief and a little trepidation that we now release them into your hands, with the hope that you might take some of them into your heart too.

We are very grateful to all those who kept us invigorated with new suggestions for possible inclusions, most especially to John Stammers, and for all the help we received from our volunteers, who so kindly dedicated their invaluable time and energies to collating dates and information for the notes. We are also delighted that so many poets took the time to write comments to accompany their poems.

Poem for the Day Two is dedicated to the memory of Nicholas Albery, who died part way through the process of compiling the book. He was a veteran of the pleasures of learning poems by heart as his poem (featured on July 28th) makes clear: 'to know a poem / by heart / is to slow down / to the heart's time'; 'to pay homage to intensity' and to have 'a poem at your side / through the valley and the shadows / in the day, in the night'.

Retta Bowen, Nick Temple, Stephanie Wienrich, Co-Editors

January 1

• Poet Arthur Hugh Clough born in Liverpool January 1st 1819
• Petofi Sandor, Hungarian lyric poet, born January 1st 1823
• Donagh McDonagh, poet, playwright and balladeer, died in Dublin January 1st 1919
• Scottish poet Iain Crichton Smith born January 1st 1928
• Cecil Day Lewis was named Poet Laureate January 1st 1968
• Carol Ann Duffy, 'the Queen of modern poetry', was appointed CBE in the New Year's Honours List, January 1st 2002

New Year Snow

For three days we waited,
a bowl of dull quartz for sky.
At night the valley dreamed of snow,
lost Christmas angels with dark-white wings
flailing the hills.
I dreamed a poem, perfect
as the first five-pointed flake,
that melted at dawn:
a Janus-time
to peer back at guttering dark days,
trajectories of the spent year.
And then snow fell.
Within an hour, a world immaculate
as January's new-hung page.
We breathe the radiant air like men new-born.
The children rush before us.
As in a dream of snow
we track through crystal fields
to the green horizon
and the sun's reflected rose.

Frances Horovitz
(February 13th 1938 – October 2nd 1983)

Frances Horovitz read English and Drama at Bristol University and trained as an actress at RADA. After graduating, she concentrated mainly on reading poetry and only began to write herself following her marriage to the poet Michael Horovitz in 1964. Her first pamphlet was published in 1967, followed by The High Tower in 1970. Her son Adam, now also a poet, was born in 1971 and the Horovitzs moved to a remote off-shoot of the Slad Valley in Gloucestershire which became a source of inspiration for many of the poems in her third book. It is from this book that 'New Year Snow' is taken. She married Roger Garfitt shortly before her early death in October 1983.

- *Roman poet Ovid died in exile January 2nd 17 AD*
- *Philip Freneau, poet of the American Revolution, born in New York January 2nd 1752*
- *American poet Robert Nathan born January 2nd 1894*
- *Christina Rossetti buried at Highgate cemetery January 2nd 1895*
- *Prolific poet and novelist Peter Redgrove born January 2nd 1932*

Remember

Remember me when I am gone away,
  Gone far away into the silent land;
  When you can no more hold me by the hand,
Nor I half turn to go yet turning stay.
Remember me when no more day by day
  You tell me of our future that you planned:
  Only remember me; you understand
It will be late to counsel then or pray.
Yet if you should forget me for a while
  And afterwards remember, do not grieve:
  For if the darkness and corruption leave
A vestige of the thoughts that once I had,
Better by far you should forget and smile
  Than that you should remember and be sad.

Christina Rossetti
(December 5th 1830 – December 29th 1894)

Christina Rossetti suffered ill-health for most of her life. At the time her illness was unexplained, although it was probably what would today be called acute anxiety. One physician defined her as "an hysteric", and a friend later described her illness as "religious mania bordering on insanity". When she returned to health Rossetti became shy, restrained and highly-principled. On her death in 1894, Beatrice Rosenthal wrote that her "whole life was marked with self-effacement".

January 3

• Tennyson's beloved Hallam was buried in Bristol January 3rd
  1834 ("if any man was born for great things he was")
• Poet Padraic Fallon was born in Athenry, County Galway,
  January 3rd 1905
• Poet and biographer Anne Stevenson born in Cambridge,
  England, January 3rd 1933
• Edwin Muir died in Swaffham Prior January 3rd 1959

The Confirmation

Yes, yours, my love, is the right human face.
I in my mind had waited for this long,
Seeing the false and searching for the true,
Then found you as a traveller finds a place
Of welcome suddenly amid the wrong
Valleys and rocks and twisting roads. But you,
What shall I call you? A fountain in a waste,
A well of water in a country dry,
Or anything that's honest and good, an eye
That makes the whole world bright. Your open heart,
Simple with giving, gives the primal deed,
The first good world, the blossom, the blowing seed,
The hearth, the steadfast land, the wandering sea,
Not beautiful or rare in every part,
But like yourself, as they were meant to be.

Edwin Muir
(May 15th 1887 – January 3rd 1959)

'The Confirmation' appeared in the collection *The Narrow Place* in 1943, and forms part of a trilogy with 'The Annunciation' and 'The Commemoration'. Despite the religious titles, the poems are all concerned with fulfilled *human* love – that of Edwin Muir's marriage to his wife Willa.

'The Confirmation' was written during the Muirs' stay at St Andrews in the period 1935 to 1942, during which time Edwin discovered Christianity. In her memoir *Belonging*, Willa wrote that the poem "sent me into a passion of tears, because I knew too well that I was only a botched version of what I was meant to be." Edwin commented, however, that, "My marriage was the most fortunate event in my life".

• A(lfred) E(dgar) Coppard, clerk, athlete, writer and poet,
  born in London January 4th 1878
• T. S. Eliot died of emphysema in London January 4th
  1965 and was buried in Westminster Abbey

January 4

La Figlia che Piange
O quam te memorem virgo . . .[1]

Stand on the highest pavement of the stair—
Lean on a garden urn—
Weave, weave the sunlight in your hair—
Clasp your flowers to you with a pained surprise—
Fling them to the ground and turn
With a fugitive resentment in your eyes:
But weave, weave the sunlight in your hair.

So I would have had him leave,
So I would have had her stand and grieve,
So he would have left
As the soul leaves the body torn and bruised,
As the mind deserts the body it has used.

I should find
Some way incomparably light and deft,
Some way we both should understand,
Simple and faithless as a smile and shake of the hand.

She turned away, but with the autumn weather
Compelled my imagination many days,
Many days and many hours:
Her hair over her arms and her arms full of flowers,
And I wonder how they should have been together!
I should have lost a gesture and a pose.
Sometimes these cogitations still amaze
The troubled midnight and the noon's repose.

T. S. Eliot
(September 26th 1888 – January 4th 1965)

'La Figlia Che Piange' ('The Weeping Girl'), was one of the poems copied carefully by Eliot into
a leather notebook between 1910 and 1911, which established his reputation. His contemporar-
ies, reading them before publication, were staggered at their assurance.

F. R. Leavis believed the poem came "from somewhere very deep in Eliot", and there has been
much speculation over the identity of the mysterious girl. There was some suggestion that she was
Emily Hale, whom Eliot courted at Harvard, but the description of her is ill-fitting. Others have
suggested that the poem is about a fictional painting brought to life by the poet, and is therefore
not at all autobiographical.

1. 'What shall I call thee, O maiden?'; from Virgil's *Aeneid*.

January 5

- First World War poet Humbert Wolfe born January 5th 1885
- On January 5th 1898, William Cowper said of John Dryden: "Never, I believe, were such talents and such drudgery united"
- Poet W. D. Snodgrass born in Pennsylvania January 5th 1926
- Informed of the death of the taciturn US president Calvin Coolidge on January 5th 1933, Dorothy Parker replied, "How can they tell?"

Requiem: The Soldier

Down some cold field in a world unspoken
    the young men are walking together, slim and tall,
and though they laugh to one another, silence is not broken:
    there is no sound however clear they call.

They are speaking together of what they loved in vain here,
    but the air is too thin to carry the things they say.
They were young and golden, but they came on pain here,
    and their youth is age now, their gold is grey.

Yet their hearts are not changed, and they cry to one another,
    "What have they done with the lives we laid aside?
Are they young with our youth, gold with our gold, my brother?
    Do they smile in the face of death, because we died?"

Down some cold field in a world uncharted
    the young seek each other with questioning eyes.
They question each other, the young, the golden-hearted,
    of the world that they were robbed of in their quiet Paradise.

Humbert Wolfe
(January 5th 1885 – January 5th 1940)

Humbert Wolfe was born Umberto Wolff in Italy to a German Jewish father and an Italian Jewish mother but the family moved to Bradford, England, shortly afterward. He spent the war years working in the Ministry of Munitions and the Ministry of Labour, and was respected as a courageous mediator. At the end of the war, when disgruntled soldiers would arrive at the War Office to air their complaints, they often shouted, "Bring out your German Jew!", and Humbert would be sent out to calm the crowds. He twice tried to enlist himself, but was rejected because of a weak heart.

His civilian war efforts were rewarded in 1918 with a CBE, though he did have to anglicise his name following objections to the honouring of men with German names. He began publishing poetry after the war, in the 1920s, and *Requiem* (1927) was a highly acclaimed bestseller. He died in 1940, on his 55th birthday.

- Sir Walter Raleigh was knighted by Queen Elizabeth and made Lord and Governor of Virginia on January 6th 1585
- Poet Carl Sandburg born to Swedish immigrant parents in Illinois January 6th 1878
- Kahlil Gibran born in Besharri, Lebanon, January 6th 1883
- Ivor Gurney escaped from his mental hospital and fled to London, January 6th 1923
- Poet P. J. Kavanagh born January 6th 1931

His Pilgrimage

Give me my scallop-shell of quiet,
  My staff of faith to walk upon,
My scrip of joy, immortal diet,
  My bottle of salvation,
My gown of glory, hope's true gage;
And thus I'll take my pilgrimage.

 Blood must be my body's balmer;
  No other balm will there be given:
Whilst my soul, like quiet palmer,
  Travelleth towards the land of heaven;
Over the silver mountains,
Where spring the nectar fountains;
      There will I kiss
      The bowl of bliss;
And drink mine everlasting fill
Upon every milken hill.
My soul will be a-dry before;
But, after, it will thirst no more.

Sir Walter Raleigh
(c.1552 – October 29th 1618)

Explorer, courtier, poet, wit, and consummate womaniser, Walter Raleigh was greatly favoured by Queen Elizabeth, the Virgin Queen – after whom he named the US State of Virginia. But he fell from grace when his clandestine marriage to one of the Queen's maids of honour was discovered. When James I succeeded Elizabeth to the throne, Raleigh was sentenced to death on charges of treason; but following an eleventh hour reprieve, he was imprisoned in the Tower of London instead. He remained there for 12 years, during which time he wrote prodigiously and produced, amongst other works, *The History of the World*. The first volume reached only as far as 130 BC. In the preface he thanked his enemy for incarcerating him: "For had it been otherwise, I should hardly have had the leisure, to have made myself a fool in print."

January 7

• French poet and patriot Charles Péguy born January 7th 1873
• On this day in 1890, A. E. Housman wrote in his diary only:
  "I heard he had married". 'He' refers to Moses Jackson, whom
  Housman loved without reciprocation until his death
• John Berryman leapt to his death from the Mississippi bridge
  January 7th 1972

The Ball Poem

What is the boy now, who has lost his ball,
What, what is he to do? I saw it go
Merrily bouncing, down the street, and then
Merrily over—there it is in the water!
No use to say 'O there are other balls':
An ultimate shaking grief fixes the boy
As he stands rigid, trembling, staring down
All his young days into the harbour where
His ball went. I would not intrude on him,
A dime, another ball, is worthless. Now
He senses first responsibility
In a world of possessions. People will take balls,
Balls will be lost always, little boy,
And no one buys a ball back. Money is external.
He is learning, well behind his desperate eyes,
The epistemology of loss, how to stand up
Knowing what every man must one day know
And most know many days, how to stand up
And gradually light returns to the street,
A whistle blows, the ball is out of sight,
Soon part of me will explore the deep and dark
Floor of the harbour . . I am everywhere,
I suffer and move, my mind and my heart move
With all that move me, under the water
Or whistling, I am not a little boy.

John Berryman
(October 25th 1914 – January 7th 1972)

John Berryman was born John Alleyn Smith Jr. His father shot himself when John was 12, and his mother hastily remarried Mr Berryman just two months later. From his early life it would seem, Berryman was 'afflicted by a sense of total L O S S' as his alter ego Henry would later claim in *The Dream Songs*.

As a professor, Berryman was flamboyantly erudite and gregarious, but the terrible melancholy and lacerating humour of *The Dream Songs*, for which Berryman won the Pulitzer Prize, reveals the reach of his despair. He married three times and severely tested his wives with repeated bouts of hospitalisation for alcoholic exhaustion. From his hospital bed he pronounced that "the artist is extremely lucky who is presented with the worst possible ordeal which will not actually kill him. At that point he's in business."

• French poet Paul Verlaine died in poverty January 8th 1895
• Harold Monro opened The Poetry Bookshop January 8th 1913
• Walter de la Mare declined the offer of a knighthood on January
  8th 1924; a repeated offer in 1931 was also declined
• Poet and artist Charles Tomlinson born January 8th 1927
• American poet Kenneth Patchen died January 8th 1972

January 8

Against Extremity

Let there be treaties, bridges,
  Chords under the hands, to be spanned
Sustained: extremity hates a given good
  Or a good gained. That girl who took
Her life almost, then wrote a book
  To exorcise and to exhibit the sin,
Praises a friend there for the end she made
  And each of them becomes a heroine.
The time is in love with endings. The time's
  Spoiled children threaten what they will do,
And those they cannot shake by petulance
  They'll bribe out of their wits by show.
Against extremity, let there be
  Such treaties as only time itself
Can ratify, a bond and test
  Of sequential days, and like the full
Moon slowly given to the night,
  A possession that is not to be possessed.

Charles Tomlinson
(January 8th 1927 –)

Charles Tomlinson writes: "This poem sprang from my distrust of extremism, of which our era has had its share, following the lengthy aftermath of revolution and two world wars. On a more domestic level, the legacy of violence was turned in upon the self. This occurred in the self-destructive urge that lay behind much 'confessional poetry' in the 1960s and '70s. Three Americans, Sylvia Plath, Anne Sexton, who are both in the poem, and, to some extent Robert Lowell, embodied that destructive urge. The English critic A. Alvarez acted as publicist for their angst and also wrote a book on suicide.

"What I was advocating, when this form of excess was at its height, was the need for a human balance and a suspicion of the ego which had played such a self-regarding role in the drama. Of course, the poem is not simply the history of an era, but a plea for reciprocity, both between people and between people and the non-human world, the ecological extension of human life."

Charles Tomlinson has published over twenty volumes of poetry. His most recent book is *The Vineyard Above the Sea* from Carcanet, who are also in the course of publishing his prose. The first volume bears the title *American Essays*. The second, *Metamorphoses* (2003), explores the history of the translation of poetry.

15

January 9

• Futurist and avant-garde critic and poet Giovanni Papini,
  born in Florence January 9th 1881
• Poet William Meredith born January 9th 1919
• Acclaimed poet of the Harlem Renaissance Countee Cullen
  died January 9th 1946
• Scottish poet W. S. Graham died January 9th 1986

I Leave This at Your Ear

For Nessie Dunsmuir

I leave this at your ear for when you wake,
A creature in its abstract cage asleep.
Your dreams blindfold you by the light they make.

The owl called from the naked-woman tree
As I came down by the Kyle farm to hear
Your house silent by the speaking sea.

I have come late but I have come before
Later with slaked steps from stone to stone
To hope to find you listening for the door.

I stand in the ticking room. My dear, I take
A moth kiss from your breath. The shore gulls cry.
I leave this at your ear for when you wake.

W. S. Graham
(November 19th 1918 – January 9th 1986)

Agnes (Nessie) Dunsmuir first met W(illiam) S(ydney) Graham in 1938, at a residential adult education college near Edinburgh. Graham had been training to become a journeyman engineer like his father when he was awarded a bursary to study literature and philosophy at the college.

After the war, the couple lived together for most of Graham's life, having married in 1954. Dunsmuir strongly supported Graham's desire to be a poet, and she often supported him financially too, at least until 1974, when he was granted a Civil List Pension.

The title of Graham's third collection, *2ND Poems* (1945), was a coded dedication 'To Nessie Dunsmuir'.

- *Poet and playwright Richard Savage born January 10th 1697*
- *Reclusive poet Robinson Jeffers, who built his own 40 foot tower in Carmel, California, born January 10th 1887*
- *Poet Philip Levine born in Detroit January 10th 1928*
- *T. S. Eliot married his private secretary, Valerie Fletcher, January 10th 1957; he was 68 and she was 30*
- *Black Mountain College director and poet Charles Olson died January 10th 1970*

From Sonnets from the Portuguese
VII

The face of all the world is changed I think
Since first I heard the footsteps of thy soul
Move still 'oh, still' beside me = as they stole
Betwixt me and the dreadful outer brink
Of obvious death, . . where I who thought to sink
Was caught up into love & taught the whole
Of life in a new rhythm. The cup of dole
God gave for baptism, I am fain to drink,
And praise its sweetness, sweet, with thee anear!—
The names of country, Heaven, are changed away
For where thou art or shalt be, there or here =
And this . . this lute and song . . loved yesterday, . .
(The singing angels know!) . . . are only dear,
Because thy name moves right in what they say.

Elizabeth Barrett Browning
(March 6th 1806 – June 29th 1861)

In December 1844, Browning chanced to see Elizabeth Barrett's latest collection of poems and was deeply impressed. On this day in 1845 he wrote the poet a letter famously declaring "I love your verses with all my heart, dear Miss Barrett," and concluded, "I love you, too." Thus began the relationship that in all likelihood prolonged Barrett's life by over a decade.

At this time, Barrett was suffering from an undiagnosed ailment which kept her weak and bedridden in a darkened room and dependent on opiates. Browning was keen to pay a visit, but Barrett did not feel well enough to receive him until late May and even then she feared she would disappoint him: "There is nothing to see in me ... If my poetry is worth anything to any eyes, it is the flower of me." But Browning was undeterred: his visit was the fulfillment of many months of waiting and longing. He meticulously logged the date and duration of this and every subsequent visit and was delighted to discover that his weekly visits were having a restorative effect on Barrett's health.

January 11

- On January 11th 1804, the Sussex Examiner *reported that William Blake was acquitted of sedition and assault, having said* "Damn the king and damn his soldiers"
- *Thomas Hardy died in Dorset aged 87, January 11th 1928*
- *Naomi Mitcheson, poet and author of over 70 books, died in Scotland January 11th 1999, aged 101*

The Self-Unseeing

Here is the ancient floor,
Footworn and hollowed and thin,
Here was the former door
Where the dead feet walked in.

She sat here in her chair,
Smiling into the fire;
He who played stood there,
Bowing it higher and higher.

Childlike, I danced in a dream;
Blessings emblazoned that day;
Everything glowed with a gleam;
Yet we were looking away!

Thomas Hardy
(June 2nd 1840 – January 11th 1928)

Hardy's mother, a domestic servant, fell in love with his father, a stonemason whose chief passion in life was music, when she saw him playing violin in the local church at Stinsford. A frail child, Hardy said he was "extraordinarily sensitive" to music. He learned the violin at a young age and would play alongside his father at country dances and weddings.

On this day in 1928, Hardy's heart was buried beside his parents and his first wife in Stinsford Churchyard. His ashes were interred in the Poets' Corner of Westminster Abbey.

- On January 12th 1795, Burns scandalised Mrs Dunlop by writing of the execution of King Louis and Queen Marie-Antoinette of France: "What is there in the delivering over a perjured Blockhead & an unprincipled Prostitute into the hands of the hangman..."
- Robert Browning Hamilton born in Kentucky January 12th 1880
- American Beat poet Bob Kaufmann died January 12th 1986

Along the Road

I walked a mile with Pleasure;
She chattered all the way,
But left me none the wiser
For all she had to say.

I walked a mile with Sorrow
And ne'er a word said she;
But oh, the things I learned from her
When Sorrow walked with me!

Robert Browning Hamilton
(January 12th 1880 – October 4th 1974)

Robert Browning Hamilton was raised as a farm boy in Lexington, Kentucky. He studied law at Harvard and eventually became Vice President of the American Surety Company. 'Along the Road' was first published in *Century* magazine in 1913, the month his daughter, the poet Virginia Hamilton Adair, was born. She has spoken of being read *The Iliad* by her father when still a toddler, and published her first collection of poems, *Ants on the Melon* (1996), at the impressive age of 83.

Of her grandfather, Kappa Waugh writes: "He was a witty and acerbic man and a life-long learner. He made us copy passages of literature for payment to improve our handwriting, though it was intended to develop our writing styles. He could quote poetry by the hour from memory and encouraged us to learn poems and recite them by heart."

January 13

• W. B. Yeats attended a meeting which established the Irish Literary Society in London, part of a move towards an Irish cultural revival, January 13th 1892
• Edward Thomas' final, unfinished poem for Helen ('The sorrow of true love is a great sorrow / And true love parting blackens a bright morrow') was probably written January 13th 1917

The Gods Do Not Consent

The gods do not consent to more than life.
Let us refuse everything that might hoist us
    To breathless everlasting
    Pinnacles without flowers.
Let's simply have the science of accepting
And, as long as the blood beats in our fountains
    And the same love between us
    Does not shrivel, continue
Like window-panes, transparent to the lights
And letting the sad rain trickle down freely,
    At the hot sun just lukewarm,
    And reflecting a little.

Fernando Pessoa
(June 13th 1888 – November 30th 1935)

translated by Jonathan Griffin

Fernando Pessoa was born in Lisbon, but was brought up and educated in South Africa, where he learnt to speak English fluently. He returned home in 1905 and earned a modest living as a commercial translator, writing controversial articles for avant-garde reviews in his spare time. His poetry, at first written in English, and only later in Portuguese, attracted little attention until after his death. Pessoa is famed for his exuberant use of literary personae, which were quintessential to his restless innovation as a writer and "nomadic wanderer through ... unconsciousness".

In a postscript to a letter of January 13th 1935, Pessoa wrote of his belief in "the experience of various degrees of spirituality, becoming more rarified until we arrive at a Supreme Being ... I do not believe in a direct communication with God". Pessoa was deeply interested in the occult, practised astrology, and corresponded with Aleister Crowley, a prominent witch. Though he felt an obligation to be religious, Pessoa found himself incapable of committing to any single belief.

• Pastor Martin Niemöller born in Lippstadt, Westphalia,
  January 14th 1892
• Lewis Caroll (the pseudonym of mathematician Charles
  Dodgson) died January 14th 1898

January 14

In Paris in a Loud Dark Winter

In Paris in a loud dark winter

        when the sun was something in Provence

when I came upon the poetry

        of René Char

I saw Vaucluse again

        in a summer of sauterelles

its fountains full of petals

        and its river thrown down

through all the burnt places

        of that almond world

and the fields full of silence

        though the crickets sang

with their legs

        And in the poet's plangent dream I saw

no Lorelei upon the Rhone

        nor angels debarked at Marseilles

but couples going nude into the sad water

        in the profound lasciviousness of spring

in an algebra of lyricism

        which I am still deciphering

Lawrence Ferlinghetti
(March 24th 1919 –)

Ferlinghetti studied poetry at the Sorbonne in Paris before joining the Beats in San Francisco. He
established the now famous City Lights bookshop, which published the landmark Pocket Poets
series, including Allen Ginsberg's *Howl*, for which Ferlinghetti was tried on obscenity charges.

January 15

- Osip Mandelstam born in Warsaw January 15th 1891
- Turkish poet Nâzim Hikmet born in Salonika, now Thessaloniki, January 15th 1902
- Gillian Allnutt born in London January 15th 1949
- Leo Marks, code poem writer and First World War cryptographer, died January 15th 2001

This is what I want most of all

This is what I want most of all:
With no one on my track
To soar behind the light
That I couldn't be farther from;

And for you to shine in that sphere –
There is no other happiness –
And learn from a star
What light could mean.

A star can only be star,
Light can only be light,
Because whispering warms us
And babbling makes us strong.

And I would like to say to you,
My little one, mumbling:
It's by means of our babbling
That I hand you to the light.

Osip Mandelstam
(January 15th 1891 – December 27th 1938)

translated by James Greene

Osip Mandelstam became famous in Russia as one of the Acmeist school of poets, of which Anna Akhmatova and her husband were also members. The Acmeist ideals, of compactness of form and clarity of expression, are embodied in Mandelstam's early poems, collected in *Stone* (1913) and *Tristia* (1922).

In 1934, Mandelstam was arrested for writing a mocking epigram about Stalin, and was exiled, first to Cherdyn, and then Voronezh. Whilst there, he composed a long cycle of poems, known as the *Voronezh Notebooks*. Mandelstam had been back in Moscow for just a year when he was arrested again in May 1938 for 'counter-revolutionary' activities, ostensibly poems criticising Stalin, and sentenced to five years in a labour camp. He barely survived the journey to the camp, and died there near Vladivostok at the end of December that year. He was buried in a communal grave.

• *Edmund Spenser died January 16th 1599*
• *'Canadian Kipling', Robert W. Service, born January 16th 1874*
• *Laura Riding born in New York January 16th 1901*
• *Anthony Hecht born in New York January 16th 1923*
• *Thomas Hardy's funeral at Westminster Abbey on January 16th 1928 was "a chaos of wrong invitations and uninvited gatecrashers"*
• *Translator and poet Robert Fitzgerald died January 16th 1985*

January 16

Sonnet LXXV

One day I wrote her name upon the strand,
But came the waves and washed it away:
Again I wrote it with a second hand,
But came the tide, and made my pains his prey.
"Vain man," said she, "that dost in vain assay,
A mortal thing so to immortalise,
For I myself shall like to this decay,
And eek my name be wiped out likewise."
"Not so," quoth I, "let baser things devise,
To die in dust, but you shall live by fame:
My verse your virtues rare shall eternise,
And in the heavens write your glorious name.
Where whenas death shall all the world subdue,
Our love shall live, and later life renew."

Edmund Spenser
(c. 1552 – January 16th 1599)

Whilst living in County Cork in Ireland, Spenser fell in love with Elizabeth Boyle, who became his second wife on June 11th 1594. The year after the marriage, Spenser published 89 love sonnets and a wedding poem, the *Amoretti* and 'Epithalamion', in celebration of the successful match. The above sonnet is the 75th poem of the sequence.

January 17

- *Poet William Stafford born in Hutchinson, Kansas, January 17th 1914*
- *Sylvia Plath gave birth to Nicholas Hughes January 17th 1962*
- *Sylvia Plath's semi-autobiographical novel* The Bell Jar *published January 17th 1963, under the pseudonym Victoria Lucas*

Ask Me

Some time when the river is ice ask me
mistakes I have made. Ask me whether
what I have done is my life. Others
have come in their slow way into
my thought, and some have tried to help
or to hurt—ask me what difference
their strongest love or hate has made.

I will listen to what you say.
You and I can turn and look
at the silent river and wait. We know
the current is there, hidden; and there
are comings and goings from miles away
that hold the stillness exactly before us.
What the river says, that is what I say.

William Stafford
(January 17th 1914 – August 28th 1993)

As a child William Stafford showed a prescient appreciation of nature and books, and a high school Indian vision quest during which he camped out near the Cimarron River made a lasting impression upon him: "That encounter with the size and serenity of the earth and its neighbours in the sky has never left me. The earth was my home; I would never feel lost while it held me."

During the Depression the family moved again and again as Earl Stafford searched for jobs. William helped to support the family by delivering newspapers, working in the fields and growing vegetables. Later in life, he was a conscientious objector during the First World War and worked in the civilian public service camps, an experience he documented in his prose memoir *Down In My Heart* (1947). He was said to have written a poem a day.

- *Oscar Wilde visited Walt Whitman on January 18th 1882*
  and said of him: "He is the grandest man I have ever seen ...
  [the] strongest character I have ever met in my life"
- *Poet Jon Stallworthy born in London January 18th 1935*
- *Rudyard Kipling died January 18th 1936*
- *Poet Grace Nichols born in Guyana January 18th 1950*

January 18

Praise Song for My Mother

You were
water to me
deep and bold and fathoming

You were
moon's eye to me
pull and grained and mantling

You were
sunrise to me
rise and warm and streaming

You were
the fishes red gill to me
the flame tree's spread to me
the crab's leg/the fried plantain smell
         replenishing replenishing

Go to your wide futures, you said

Grace Nichols
(January 18th 1950 –)

Grace Nichols has written a number of poems celebrating the nurturing spirit of her mother, Iris, and says, "One of my favourite [poems] is 'Praise Song for My Mother' who died when I was 21. I particularly like [it] even though it's a small poem, but the images came out of a deep focusing on my mother and a reconnecting with her memory. It's a very personal poem and does capture for me something of her spirit".

• Edgar Allan Poe was born in Boston January 19th 1809.
When 'Annabel Lee' was posthumously published, a number
of women claimed to be Poe's 'Annabel'

Annabel Lee

It was many and many a year ago,
   In a kingdom by the sea,
That a maiden there lived whom you may know
   By the name of Annabel Lee;
And this maiden she lived with no other thought
   Than to love and be loved by me.

She was a child and *I* was a child,
   In this kingdom by the sea,
But we loved with a love that was more than love –
   I and my Annabel Lee –
With a love that the wingèd seraphs of Heaven
   Coveted her and me.

And this was the reason that, long ago,
   In this kingdom by the sea,
A wind blew out of a cloud by night
   Chilling my Annabel Lee;
So that her highborn kinsmen came
   And bore her away from me,
To shut her up in a sepulchre
   In this kingdom by the sea.

The angels, not half so happy in Heaven,
   Went envying her and me:
Yes! that was the reason (as all men know,
   In this kingdom by the sea)
That the wind came out of the cloud, chilling
   And killing my Annabel Lee.

But our love was stronger by far than the love
   Of those who were older than we –
   Of many far wiser than we –
And neither the angels in Heaven above
   Nor the demons down under the sea,
Can ever dissever my soul from the soul
   Of the beautiful Annabel Lee:

For the moon never beams without bringing me dreams
   Of the beautiful Annabel Lee;
And the stars never rise but I feel the bright eyes
   Of the beautiful Annabel Lee;
And so, all the night-tide, I lie down by the side
Of my darling, my darling, my life and my bride,
   In her sepulchre there by the sea –
   In her tomb by the side of the sea.

Edgar Allan Poe
(January 19th 1809 – October 7th 1849)

• John Ruskin, author, art critic and poet, died January 20th 1900
• Robinson Jeffers, US poet and playwright, died January 20th 1962
• First World War poet Edmund Blunden died January 20th 1974

January 20

Sic Vita

Like to the falling of a Star;
Or as the flights of Eagles are;
Or like the fresh spring's gaudy hue;
Or silver drops of morning dew;
Or like a wind that chafes the flood;
Or bubbles which on water stood;
Even such is man, whose borrowed light
Is straight called in, and paid to night.

The Wind blows out; the Bubble dies;
The Spring entombed in Autumn lies;
The Dew dries up; the Star is shot;
The Flight is past; and Man forgot.

Henry King
(c. 1591 – September 30th 1669)

Henry King and his younger brother John were matriculated at Christ Church College, Oxford, on this day in 1609. Henry went on to progress through the ranks of the church to become Bishop of Chichester in 1642. In December of that year, he was taken prisoner when the cathedral city surrendered to Cromwell's Parliamentary army, though he was later released. On the restoration of the monarchy in 1660, he returned to his bishopric until his death in 1669.

As a poet, King is best remembered for his elegy to his wife, 'The Exequy', and for the elegy he wrote to John Donne (for whom he was an executor) which appeared at the front of the 1663 edition of Donne's poetry.

January 21

• Henry Howard, Earl of Surrey, executed at Tower Hill on January 21st 1547
• Keats composed 'The Eve of St Agnes' on January 21st 1819, the Feast Day of Agnes, virgin and martyr who chose to be tortured to death rather than be married
• Richard P. Blackmur, American poet and critic, born in Springfield, Massachusetts, January 21st 1904

The Snow Man

One must have a mind of winter
To regard the frost and the boughs
Of the pine-trees crusted with snow;

And have been cold a long time
To behold the junipers shagged with ice,
The spruces rough in the distant glitter

Of the January sun; and not to think
Of any misery in the sound of the wind,
In the sound of a few leaves,

Which is the sound of the land
Full of the same wind
That is blowing in the same bare place

For the listener, who listens in the snow,
And, nothing himself, beholds
Nothing that is not there and the nothing that is.

Wallace Stevens
(October 2nd 1879 – August 2nd 1955)

Wallace Stevens struck an imposing, if not austere figure: huge, dressed in uniform steel grey suits, he spent most of his working life as Vice President of an American surety firm. Each day he would forgo lunch and walk three or four miles, jotting down words and lines of poetry on scraps of paper which his secretary typed up for him. An intensely private man, Stevens very rarely received guests to his home, and even he and his wife lived in different sections of the house. Though he would send his employees to the library to look up the definitions of words he wanted to include in his poems, he rarely mentioned his work, and maintained that it was not necessary for anybody to understand it. About 'The Snow Man', Stevens simply said: "I shall explain it as an example of the necessity of identifying oneself with reality in order to understand it and enjoy it."

From Childe Harold's Pilgrimage
Canto IV, verses 178 & 184

There is a pleasure in the pathless woods,
There is a rapture on the lonely shore,
There is society, where none intrudes,
By the deep Sea, and music in its roar:
I love not Man the less, but Nature more,
From these our interviews, in which I steal
From all I may be, or have been before,
To mingle with the Universe, and feel
What I can ne'er express, yet cannot all conceal.

. . .

And I have loved thee, Ocean! and my joy
Of youthful sports was on thy breast to be
Borne, like thy bubbles, onward: from a boy
I wanton'd with thy breakers — they to me
Were a delight; and if the freshening sea
Made them a terror — 'twas a pleasing fear,
For I was as it were a child of thee,
And trusted to thy billows far and near,
And laid my hand upon thy mane — as I do here.

George Gordon, Lord Byron
(January 22nd 1788 – April 19th 1824)

It was Byron's belief that "a man must travel, and turmoil, or there is no existence." Thus, Byron and his friend Hobhouse set out on their 'pilgrimage' across southern Europe, with the express intention of gaining writing material. Their route deviated somewhat from the traditional tour, as their journey was dictated by the (still raging) Napoleonic wars. The pair followed in the wake of the British Army, picking their way across recently deserted battlefields. But the foreign air was as inspirational as Byron had hoped.

He returned to England with 'Childe Harold' but was hesitant about submitting it to his publisher. Byron was also reluctant for his name to appear on the poem, fearing readers would confuse the protagonist's character with his own. The poem's working title was in fact 'Childe Burun'.

'Childe Harold' was, in the end, well received. Only Coleridge ungraciously questioned whether Byron "could not lift up his leg six times at six different Corners, and each time piss a Canto."

January 23

• Poet Katharine Tynan born January 23rd 1861
• Poet Louis Zukofsky born in New York January 23rd 1904
• Robert Graves married Nancy Nicholson January 23rd 1918
• Poet Vernon Scannell born in Lincolnshire January 23rd 1922
• Nobel Prize-winning West Indian poet and playwright Derek
  Walcott born in Castries, St Lucia, January 23rd 1930

Love After Love

The time will come
when, with elation,
you will greet yourself arriving
at your own door, in your own mirror,
and each will smile at the other's welcome,

and say, sit here. Eat.
You will love again the stranger who was your self.
Give wine. Give bread. Give back your heart
to itself, to the stranger who has loved you

all your life, whom you ignored
for another, who knows you by heart.
Take down the love letters from the bookshelf,

the photographs, the desperate notes,
peel your own image from the mirror.
Sit. Feast on your life.

Derek Walcott
(January 23rd 1930 –)

The elder of twins, Derek Walcott was born in St Lucia, West Indies, to an English father and African mother, and originally trained as a painter. Walcott self-published his debut collection aged just 18, using a loan from his mother. Since then he has written more than twenty collections of poems and plays, including the acclaimed epic poem *Omeros* and, most recently, *The Bounty*. He received the Nobel Prize for literature in 1992. Walcott is widely recognised as one of the finest poets writing in English, and the foremost Caribbean poet of his (and any other) generation.

• *William Congreve, poet and playwright, born in Bardsey, near Leeds, January 24th 1670*
• *James Collinson, Christina Rossetti's fiancé, died in Camberwell January 24th 1881*
• *Poet Keith Douglas born in Tunbridge Wells January 24th 1920*

Before the Beginning

Before the beginning Thou hast foreknown the end,
  Before the birthday the death-bed was seen of Thee:
Cleanse what I cannot cleanse, mend what I cannot mend.
  O Lord All-Merciful, be merciful to me.

While the end is drawing near I know not mine end:
  Birth I recall not, my death I cannot foresee:
O God, arise to defend, arise to befriend,
  O Lord All-Merciful, be merciful to me.

Christina Rossetti
(December 5th 1830 – December 29th 1894)

Christina Rossetti was engaged to James Collinson, a painter member of the Pre-Raphaelite Brotherhood, between 1848 and 1850. Collinson ended the engagement when he reverted back to the Roman Catholic faith (having previously converted to the Church of England in order to be Rossetti's fiancé). He resigned from the Brotherhood at the same time.

Collinson died of pneumonia on this day in 1881.

January 25

• *John Donne ordained by the Bishop of London, most probably on January 25th 1615*
• *Robert Burns born in Alloway, Ayrshire, January 25th 1759*
• *Dorothy, Wordsworth's sister and lifelong companion, died January 25th 1855*
• *Poet and novelist Sasha Moorsom born January 25th 1931*
• *Irish poet and critic Tom Paulin born January 25th 1949*

Up in the Morning Early

Up in the morning's no' for me,
　Up in the morning early;
When a' the hills are covered wi' snaw,
　I'm sure it's winter fairly.

Cauld blaws the wind frae east to wast,
　The drift is driving sairly;
Sae loud and shrill's I hear the blast,
　I'm sure it's winter fairly.

The birds sit chittering in the thorn,
　A' day they fare but sparely;
And lang's the night frae e'en to morn,
　I'm sure it's winter fairly.

Robert Burns
(January 25th 1759 – July 21st 1796)

Although Burns claimed "the great misfortune of my life was never to have *an aim*", he became Scotland's best loved and most prolific poet. At the age of 15, Burns was the family's principal farm labourer, his life described by his brother, Gilbert as "the cheerless gloom of a hermit with the unceasing moil of a galley slave". It was this miserably hard labour which Gilbert believed "was in great measure the cause of that depression of spirits with which Robert was so often afflicted through his whole life afterwards."

Winter always held a particular attraction for Burns: "There is scarcely any earthly object gives me more – I don't know if I should call it pleasure, but something which exalts me, something which enraptures me – than to walk in the sheltered side of a wood or high plantation, in a cloudy, winter day, and hear a stormy wind howling among the trees and raving o'er the plain – it is my best season for devotion ..."

32

- *Ugo Foscolo, Italian poet and patriot, born on the Greek island of Zakynthos January 26th 1778*
- *Thomas Lovell Beddoes, Victorian poet and physician, swallowed poison on January 26th 1849*
- *Australian poet and novelist Amy Witting born in Sydney on Australia Day, January 26th 1918*
- *W. H. Auden and Christopher Isherwood arrived in New York during a snow storm, January 26th 1939*

Peace

At the ship's bow. It was my eye that drew
the perfect circle of blue meeting blue.
No land was visible. There was no sail,
no cloud to show the mighty world in scale,
so sky and ocean, by my gaze defined,
were drawn within the compass of my mind
under a temperate sun. The engine's sound
sank to a heartbeat. Stillness all around.
Only the perfect circle and the mast.
That moment knew no future and no past.

Amy Witting
(January 26th 1918 – September 18th 2001)

Amy Witting is the pseudonym of the Australian writer Joan Levick. She is best known for her second novel, *I is for Isobel,* which was published when she was 71. Its success prompted a revival of interest in her work, and a backlog of accumulated stories and poetry were published. Her *Collected Poems* was published by Penguin in January 1998 to coincide with her 80th birthday.

It is believed that Levick chose the surname 'Witting' for her pseudonym because of a personal promise she made to herself to never be *un*witting, to always remain conscious of everything in her life.

January 27

• Lewis Carroll (the pseudonym of Charles Dodgson) born
January 27th 1832

The World's A Minefield

The world's a minefield when I think of you.
I must walk carefully in case I touch
some irretrievable and secret switch
that blows the old world back into the new.

How careless I once was about this ground
with the negligence of ignorance. Now I take
the smallest delicate steps and now I look
about me and about me without end.

Iain Crichton Smith
(January 1st 1928 – October 15th 1998)

Iain Crichton Smith, whose Gaelic name is Iain Mac A'Ghobhainn, was born in Glasgow on New Year's Day 1928, and was brought up on the island of Lewis. After two years' national service, Crichton Smith was a teacher for 25 years, before devoting himself fully to writing in 1977. He died at the age of 70, at home in Taynuilt, near Oban.

During his lifetime, Crichton Smith published nearly 30 volumes of poetry, five plays, 14 novels and several short story collections. His poetry, written in both Gaelic and English, is marked by its lyricism, passion and candour, and has assured his reputation as one of the 20th century's finest Scottish writers.

• Canadian poet John McCrae died in France January 28th 1918
• W. B. Yeats died of heart problems on January 28th 1939
• Patric Dickinson, poet and playwright, died January 28th 1994
• Joseph Brodsky, Nobel Prize-winning Russian poet who studied
  under Anna Akhmatova, died in Brooklyn January 28th 1996

January 28

These Are the Clouds

These are the clouds about the fallen sun,
The majesty that shuts his burning eye;
The weak lay hand on what the strong has done,
Till that be tumbled that was lifted high
And discord follow upon unison,
And all things at one common level lie.
And therefore, friend, if your great race were run
And these things came, so much the more thereby
Have you made greatness your companion,
Although it be for children that you sigh:
These are the clouds about the fallen sun,
The majesty that shuts his burning eye.

W. B. Yeats
(June 13th 1865 – January 28th 1939)

The 'friend' in this poem is Lady Gregory, with whom Yeats had a long and mutually beneficial friendship; she provided him with patronage; he introduced her into literary circles in London and Dublin. Written during Lady Gregory's illness in 1909, the poem was undoubtedly intended to cheer her up by praising her accomplishment, even as it speculates as to whether her 'great race were run'. The poem appeared in *Green Helmet*, a collection which coincided with Yeats' increased responsibilities as a director of the Abbey Theatre, and the more public role he chose to play in Ireland's political controversies.

Yeats died at Cap Martin on this day in 1938 and was buried in Roquebrune, France. It was only in 1948 that he was reburied in Ireland according to his wishes.

January 29

• *Edgar Allan Poe's 'The Raven', caused a sensation when it was published on January 29th 1845*
• *Edward Lear, nonsense poet and limericist, died in San Remo, Italy, January 29th 1888*
• *American poet of passion, Sara Teasdale, committed suicide on January 29th 1933*
• *Robert Frost died January 29th 1963. His tombstone reads: "I had a lover's quarrel with the world"*

Fire and Ice

Some say the world will end in fire,
Some say in ice.
From what I've tasted of desire
I hold with those who favor fire.
But if it had to perish twice,
I think I know enough of hate
To say that for destruction ice
Is also great
And would suffice.

Robert Frost
(March 26th 1874 – January 29th 1963)

A distinctly American poet, Frost was discovered in England, where *A Boy's Own Will*, his first collection, was well received. On his return to the States he was hailed as a new talent, and swiftly established himself as America's most popular poet. Indeed, he became a de facto poet laureate, reading at J. F. Kennedy's inauguration and receiving birthday greetings from the US Senate. In addition, he won the Pulitzer Prize an unprecedented four times and was awarded 44 honorary degrees. At his 80th birthday celebrations Frost confessed: "All I've wanted to do is to write a few little poems it'd be hard to get rid of. That's all I ask."

Frost wrote this poem in Amherst, where he was studying, during the summer and autumn of 1920. He returned three years later to teach as a professor of English.

• Walter Savage Landor born January 30th 1775
• Arthur William Edgar O'Shaughnessy died January 30th 1881
• Yeats first met Maud Gonne, "a great red-haired yahoo of a woman", January 30th 1889
• Asked in an interview about writing free verse on January 30th 1956, Robert Frost retorted: "I'd just as soon play tennis with the net down"

somewhere i have never travelled

somewhere i have never travelled,gladly beyond
any experience,your eyes have their silence:
in your most frail gesture are things which enclose me,
or which i cannot touch because they are too near

your slightest look easily will unclose me
though i have closed myself as fingers,
you open always petal by petal myself as Spring opens
(touching skilfully,mysteriously)her first rose

or if your wish be to close me,i and
my life will shut very beautifully,suddenly,
as when the heart of this flower imagines
the snow carefully everywhere descending;

nothing which we are to perceive in this world equals
the power of your intense fragility:whose texture
compels me with the colour of its countries,
rendering death and forever with each breathing

(i do not know what it is about you that closes
and opens;only something in me understands
the voice of your eyes is deeper than all roses)
nobody,not even the rain,has such small hands

E. E. Cummings
(October 14th 1894 – September 3rd 1962)

On January 30th 1960, Cummings wrote to Hildegarde Watson, the wife of his Harvard friend James Sibley Watson, saying [idiosyncratic punctuation is Cummings' own]: "you certainly are a very great & generous dear,to tell me about your early morning reading. I had no notion that any poem of mine could affect someone – so vividly:& even now am amazed that the fortunate poem should be <u>somewhere i have never travelled</u>."

January 31

Robert Burns became founder member of the Royal Dumfries Volunteers January 31st 1795
• Nâzim Hikmet married Piraye, the long-suffering "red-haired woman" of his prison love poems, January 31st 1935
• Derek Jarman, filmmaker, painter and poet, born in Middlesex January 31st 1942
• Canadian poet F. R. Scott died January 31st 1985

Caring

Caring is loving, motionless,
An interval of more and less
Between the stress and the distress.

After the present falls the past,
After the festival, the fast.
Always the deepest is the last.

This is the circle we must trace,
Not spiralled outward, but a space
Returning to its starting place.

Centre of all we mourn and bless,
Centre of calm beyond excess,
Who cares for caring, has caress.

F. R. Scott
(August 1st 1899 – January 31st 1985)

F(rank) R(eginald) Scott was born in Quebec City, the sixth of seven children. He was a Rhodes scholar in Oxford, before returning to McGill University in Montreal to study (and later teach) law.

He married Marian Dale, an artist, in 1928, and the two were still together when Scott died at the age of 86. Even in 1981, the couple were described as "holding hands and swinging them, like happy children", while a friend described their marriage as "something very different – something creative in the art of living".

38

- Elkanah Settle, poet and dramatist who feuded with Dryden, born in Dunstable February 1st 1648
- Lord Byron's The Corsair sold 10,000 copies on the day of publication, February 1st 1814
- Langston Hughes, known as 'O. Henry of Harlem', born in Missouri February 1st 1902
- Galway Kinnell born in Rhode Island February 1st 1927

From When One Has Lived
a Long Time Alone
9

When one has lived a long time alone,
and the hermit thrush calls and there is an answer,
and the bullfrog head half out of water utters
the cantillations he sang in his first spring,
and the snake lowers himself over the threshold
and slides away among the stones, one sees
they all live to mate with their kind, and one knows,
after a long time of solitude, after the many steps taken
away from one's kind, toward these other kingdoms,
the hard prayer inside one's own singing
is to come back, if one can, to one's own,
a world almost lost, in the exile that deepens,
when one has lived a long time alone.

Galway Kinnell
(February 1st 1927 –)

Galway Kinnell writes: "It is true that on several occasions in my life, I have spent a 'long time alone'. Of course time is a flexible material: what seems an endless stretch of months to one person may be merely a somewhat protracted number of weeks to another. And I suspect my long times have been shorter, measured by the calendar, than the periods of time other people mean when they speak of spending 'a long time alone'.

Galway Kinnell is the author of ten books of poems. His latest book is *New Selected Poems* (Bloodaxe Books, 2001). He teaches part of the year at New York University and the rest of the time lives in Sheffield, Vermont. His poems have won the US National Book Award and the Pulitzer Prize.

February 2

• Novelist and poet James Joyce born February 2nd 1882
• Whilst reading Ovid's Metamorphoses on February 2nd
  1922, Rilke was seized by "a hurricane of the spirit", a creative
  frenzy which lasted for three weeks, during which he produced
  some of his finest poems
• American poet James Dickey born February 2nd 1923
• Moniza Alvi born in Lahore, Pakistan, February 2nd 1954

A Bowl of Warm Air

Someone is falling towards you
as an apple falls from a branch,
moving slowly, imperceptibly as if
into a new political epoch,
or excitedly like a dog towards a bone.
He is holding in both hands
everything he knows he has –
a bowl of warm air.

He has sighted you from afar
as if you were a dramatic crooked tree
on the horizon and he has seen you close up
like the underside of a mushroom.
But he cannot open you like a newspaper
or put you down like a newspaper.

And you are satisfied that he is veering towards you
and that he is adjusting his speed
and that the sun and the wind and rain are in front of him
and the sun and the wind and rain are behind him.

Moniza Alvi
(February 2nd 1954 –)

Moniza Alvi comments: "There was a newness in the air at the time of writing, as I was setting up home with Bob, who is now my husband. It was 1995, and apart from this new life, I was hoping there would soon be a change of government after many years of the Conservative Party. 'A Bowl of Warm Air' represents a slight departure in style for me – the poem took its own dreamlike course, and for that I'm grateful!"

Moniza Alvi has published four collections of poetry, the most recent being *Carrying My Wife* (Bloodaxe Books, 2000) and *Souls* (Bloodaxe Books, 2002). In 2002 she received a Cholmondeley Award from the Society of Authors.

• Augustan poet George Crabbe died February 3rd 1832
• Austrian Expressionist poet Georg Trakl born in Salzburg
  February 3rd 1887
• Sandor Csoori, major Hungarian poet, born February 3rd 1930

February 3

Jenny Kissed Me

Jenny kissed me when we met,
   Jumping from the chair she sat in;
Time, you thief, who love to get
   Sweets into your list, put that in!
Say I'm weary, say I'm sad,
   Say that health and wealth have missed me,
Say I'm growing old, but add,
   Jenny kissed me.

Leigh Hunt
(October 19th 1784 – August 28th 1859)

On this day in 1813, Leigh Hunt and his brother Robert were fined and imprisoned for two years following a slander against the Prince Regent in their liberal weekly, the *Examiner*. Whilst in prison, Hunt transformed his cell in the prison infirmary into a bower of bliss with blinds, rose-trellised wallpaper, busts of poets and flowers. Here, as the self-proclaimed "amazing prisoner", Hunt entertained swarms of revellers and members of the literati including Byron, Moore and Swinburne, swiftly establishing his prison cell as the fashionable place to be seen in reformist circles. These parties became the feeding ground for the group who came to be known as the Cockney School.

When Hunt sickened during a flu epidemic, Hunt's friends Thomas Carlyle and his wife Jenny feared he might not survive. On his recovery he paid them an unexpected visit and Jenny, delighted to see him alive and well, leapt up to kiss him, thus prompting the poem.

February 4

• *Paul Napoleon Roinard, French anarchist poet, born in Seine-Maritime, Normandy, February 4th 1856*
• *Gavin Ewart born in London February 4th 1916*
• *Beat poet Neal Cassady died in Mexico February 4th 1968*
• *Louise Bogan died in New York February 4th 1970*
• *Poet Edgar Bowers died in San Francisco February 4th 2000*

Song for the Last Act

Now that I have your face by heart, I look
Less at its features than its darkening frame
Where quince and melon, yellow as young flame,
Lie with quilled dahlias and the shepherd's crook.
Beyond, a garden. There, in insolent ease
The lead and marble figures watch the show
Of yet another summer loath to go
Although the scythes hang in the apple trees.

Now that I have your voice by heart, I look.

Now that I have your voice by heart, I read
In the black chords upon a dulling page
Music that is not meant for music's cage,
Whose emblems mix with words that shake and bleed.
The staves are shuttled over with a stark
Unprinted silence. In a double dream
I must spell out the storm, the running stream.
The beat's too swift. The notes shift in the dark.

Now that I have your voice by heart, I read.

Now that I have your heart by heart, I see
The wharves with their great ships and architraves;
The rigging and the cargo and the slaves
On a strange beach under a broken sky.
O not departure, but a voyage done!
The bales stand on the stone; the anchor weeps
Its red rust downward, and the long vine creeps
Beside the salt herb, in the lengthening sun.

Now that I have your heart by heart, I see.

Louise Bogan
(August 11th 1897 – February 4th 1970)

Louise Bogan considered the male modernist poets W. B. Yeats, T. S. Eliot and, later, W. H. Auden as her main influences. She first met Eliot in person in November 1948, ("So I shall at last behold Him in the flesh: yellow eyes and all!"), and was quite taken with his "physical beauty" and "perfect humility". "Well, it is all too late and too sad – but I must love him," she said at the time. After the meeting, Eliot went to Sweden to collect his Nobel Prize and Bogan returned to New York, where she proceeded to write 'Song for the Last Act'.

• Poet Henry Crabbe Robinson died in London February 5th 1867
• Nicaraguan poet Salomón de la Selva died February 5th 1959
• American poet Marianne Moore died February 5th 1972

Recuerdo

We were very tired, we were very merry—
We had gone back and forth all night on the ferry.
It was bare and bright, and smelled like a stable—
But we looked into a fire, we leaned across a table,
We lay on a hill-top underneath the moon;
And the whistles kept blowing, and the dawn came soon.

We were very tired, we were very merry—
We had gone back and forth all night on the ferry;
And you ate an apple, and I ate a pear,
From a dozen of each we had bought somewhere;
And the sky went wan, and the wind came cold,
And the sun rose dripping, a bucketful of gold.

We were very tired, we were very merry,
We had gone back and forth all night on the ferry.
We hailed, "Good morrow, mother!" to a shawl-covered head,
And bought a morning paper, which neither of us read;
And she wept, "God bless you!" for the apples and pears,
And we gave her all our money but our subway fares.

Edna St Vincent Millay
(February 22nd 1892 – October 19th 1950)

This poem first appeared in Harriet Monroe's *Poetry Magazine* in May 1919 and later served as one of the opening poems in Millay's 1920 collection, *A Few Figs From Thistles*. The Spanish title of the poem means 'remembrance' or 'souvenir'.

According to Millay's biographer, Miriam Gurko, the poet is remembering a date with the young Nicaraguan poet, Salomón de la Selva, whom she had met during her first summer in New York in 1913. In Millay's time, the Staten Island ferry was steam-powered, and it cost just five cents to make the five-mile trip across the bay.

February 6

- *Christopher Marlowe born February 6th 1564*
- *Canadian poet Louis Dudek born February 6th 1918*
- *James Merrill, prize-winning American poet, died in New York February 6th 1995*

Lady 'Rogue' Singleton

Come, wed me, Lady Singleton,
And we will have a baby soon
And we will live in Edmonton
Where all the friendly people run.

I could never make you happy, darling,
Or give you the baby you want,
I would always very much rather, dear,
Live in a tent.

I am not a cold woman, Henry,
But I do not feel for you,
What I feel for the elephants and the miasmas
And the general view.

Stevie Smith
(September 20th 1902 – March 7th 1971)

Despite a proposal or two in her youth, Stevie Smith never married and never had children. She once said: "I thought [marrying] was the right thing to do. One ought to … but I wasn't very keen on it." She turned down one of her beaus, Frederick 'Eric' Armitage (who appears as 'Freddy' in her writings), because she felt she would be stifled by a conventional marriage and the "suburban scene". After Smith died, Armitage, who had long since married another, confessed that he didn't much care for her poetry.

Smith's spinster aunt, Margaret Spear, with whom she lived for most of her adult life, and to whom many of her friends considered her 'married', was born on this day in 1872. Smith was devastated when she died at the age of 96: "People think because I never married, I know nothing about the emotions," she told a friend. "When I am dead you must put them right. I loved my aunt."

• Mersey poet Brian Patten born February 7th 1946
• José Garcia Villa, Filipino poet, critic, short story writer and
  painter, died February 7th 1997

February 7

The Bee's Last Journey to the Rose

I came first through the warm grass
Humming with Spring,
And now swim through the evening's
Soft sunlight gone cold.
I'm old in this green ocean,
Going a final time to the rose.

North wind, until I reach it
Keep your icy breath away
That changes pollen into dust.
Let me be drunk on this scent a final time,
Then blow if you must.

Brian Patten
(February 7th 1946 –)

Brian Patten comments: "It's about the hope that there will always be a final journey possible."
As well as publishing numerous books of poetry for both adults and children, including the much-loved children's collection *Gargling with Jelly*, Brian Patten has written for radio, stage and television. He received the Freedom of the City of Liverpool in 2001 and a Cholmondeley Award in 2002.

45

February 8

• *John Ruskin, the greatest art critic and social commentator of the Victorian Age, born February 8th 1819*
• *Elizabeth Bishop born in Worcester, Massachusetts, February 8th 1911*
• *American poet Lisel Mueller born in Hamburg, Germany, February 8th 1924*

Sonnet

I am in need of music that would flow
Over my fretful, feeling finger-tips,
Over my bitter-tainted, trembling lips,
With melody, deep, clear, and liquid-slow.
Oh, for the healing swaying, old and low,
Of some song sung to rest the tired dead,
A song to fall like water on my head,
And over quivering limbs, dream flushed to glow!

There is a magic made by melody:
A spell of rest, and quiet breath, and cool
Heart, that sinks through fading colors deep
To the subaqueous stillness of the sea,
And floats forever in a moon-green pool,
Held in the arms of rhythm and of sleep.

Elizabeth Bishop
(February 8th 1911 – October 6th 1979)

Elizabeth Bishop was often lonely as a child and learned to appreciate music at a young age. After her father's death and her mother's permanent hospitalisation for insanity, Bishop lived in Nova Scotia with her maternal grandparents who were all musical. She was later uprooted and sent to live in the emotionally stifling and unhappy atmosphere of her paternal grandparents' house. It was not until Bishop moved once again to live with her aunt, herself a lover of literature, that she began to write. This sonnet, one of Bishop's earliest poems, was written while she was at boarding school in Natick, Massachusetts.

Bishop briefly considered a career in medicine, but was encouraged in her poetry by the influential poet Marianne Moore, who swiftly became both friend and mentor. Moore once remarked of Bishop's work: "There are in her shaping of a poem curbs and spirits that could be known only to a musician."

46

• Amy Lowell, American poet, critic and spokesperson for the Imagist movement in the States, born February 9th 1874. Pound eventually referred to the hijacked movement derisively as 'Amygism'
• Oscar Wilde's The Ballad of Reading Gaol published under the pseudonym Sebastian Melmoth February 9th 1898

From The Ballad of Reading Gaol
V

I know not whether Laws be right,
    Or whether Laws be wrong;
All that we know who lie in gaol
    Is that the wall is strong;
And that each day is like a year,
    A year whose days are long.

But this I know, that every Law
    That men have made for Man,
Since first Man took his brother's life,
    And the sad world began,
But straws the wheat and saves the chaff
    With a most evil fan.

This too I know – and wise it were
    If each could know the same –
That every prison that men build
    Is built with bricks of shame,
And bound with bars lest Christ should see
    How men their brothers maim.

With bars they blur the gracious moon,
    And blind the goodly sun:
And they do well to hide their Hell,
    For in it things are done
That Son of God nor son of Man
    Ever should look upon!

Oscar Wilde
(October 16th 1854 – November 30th 1900)

Sentenced to two years' hard labour for "homosexual acts", Oscar Wilde was sent first to Pentonville prison, then Wandsworth, and finally to Reading. This last move proved to be the single most humiliating experience of his life. He stood handcuffed in prison clothing on the platform at Clapham Junction between 2 and 2.30 pm as a growing crowd jeered and laughed at him. "For a year after that was done to me, I wept every day at the same hour and for the same space of time," Wilde wrote in *De Profundis*.

Wilde was released in 1897 and went into exile in France, where he lived under the alias Sebastian Melmoth. *The Ballad of Reading Gaol* was published on this day the following year and was described by Wilde as "Terribly unrealistic for me ... a sort of denial ... of my philosophy of art."

February 10

- *Alexander Pushkin died in a duel February 10th 1837*
- *Dante Gabriel Rossetti's wife, Elizabeth, died from a self-administered overdose of morphia, February 10th 1862*
- *Russian poet Boris Pasternak born February 10th 1890*
- *Playwright and poet Bertolt Brecht, whose early plays provoked riots, born February 10th 1898*
- *Fleur Adcock born in New Zealand February 10th 1934*

For A Five-Year-Old

A snail is climbing up the window-sill
Into your room, after a night of rain.
You call me in to see, and I explain
That it would be unkind to leave it there:
It might crawl to the floor; we must take care
That no one squashes it. You understand,
And carry it outside, with careful hand,
To eat a daffodil.

I see, then, that a kind of faith prevails:
Your gentleness is moulded still by words
From me, who have trapped mice and shot wild birds,
From me, who drowned your kittens, who betrayed
Your closest relatives, and who purveyed
The harshest kind of truth to many another.
But that is how things are: I am your mother,
And we are kind to snails.

Fleur Adcock
(February 10th 1934 –)

Fleur Adcock comments: "This was written in New Zealand, in 1962, for my son Andrew. At the time it didn't occur to me that he would ever read it and discover that a few years earlier I had forced myself to do what was normal at the time, and sneak down to the river with a couple of newborn kittens in a sack (needless to say, I never did it again). He is now 45, and has long since forgiven me, but since then I've been careful of what I write about children: sooner or later they will find out."

Fleur Adcock was born in New Zealand, but spent the years 1939 to 1947 in England, and returned to live in London in 1963. Her poetry has been collected in *Poems 1960–2000*, published by Bloodaxe Books in 2000.

- *Else Lasker, German Jewish poet and writer, who emigrated to Switzerland in 1933, born February 11th 1869*
- *Poet and novelist Roy Fuller born February 11th 1912*
- *Sylvia Plath committed suicide February 11th 1963, just two weeks after publication of* The Bell Jar

11th February 1963

The worst winter for decades. In the freeze
some things get lost and I'm not even born,
but think until you're many Februaries
deep in thought with me and find London
on that day as held inside a glacier;
a fissure where two postal districts touch,
its people caught mid-floe, at furniture,
the contents of their stomachs, a stopped watch.
At these pressures the distance has collapsed:
the studio clock winds up over Primrose Hill,
or the poet and her sleeping children crossed
the mile to Abbey Road. This milk bottle
might hold what John'll drink for one last take;
that she'll leave out for when the children wake.

Paul Farley
(June 5th 1965 –)

Paul Farley writes: "At some point (I can't remember which came first) I realised that the day the Beatles recorded their first LP was also the day Sylvia Plath took her own life. Two unrelated events, happening a mile or so apart from each other: so what? But it bugged me for ages, and eventually there seems to have been enough fuel for this sonnet."

Paul Farley has published two widely acclaimed collections of poetry with Picador: *The Boy from the Chemist is Here to See You* in 1998, and *The Ice Age* in 2002. He lives in Lancashire.

February 12

- English poet, composer and physician Thomas Campion, born in London February 12th 1567
- Milton formally admitted to Christ's College, Cambridge, February 12th 1625
- Eccentric poet Elkanah Settle died February 12th 1724
- George Meredith, poet and novelist, born February 12th 1828
- New York poet Muriel Rukeyser died February 12th 1980

From Holy Sonnets
VII

At the round earth's imagin'd corners, blow
Your trumpets, angels; and arise, arise
From death, you numberless infinities
Of souls, and to your scattered bodies go:
All whom the flood did, and fire shall, o'erthrow,
All whom war, death, age, agues, tyrannies,
Despair, law, chance hath slain, and you whose eyes
Shall behold God, and never taste death's woe.
But let them sleep, Lord, and me mourn a space,
For, if above all these, my sins abound,
'Tis late to ask abundance of thy grace
When we are there. Here on this lowly ground,
Teach me how to repent; for that's as good
As if thou hadst seal'd my pardon with thy blood.

John Donne
(c. June 1572 – March 31st 1631)

Only four of John Donne's poems were published during his lifetime (two of these he later disavowed), but he became increasingly famous for his brilliant, passionate sermons. He was appointed Dean of St Paul's Church in London in 1621, a position he held with distinction despite his deteriorating health. On this day in 1631 he rose from his deathbed to deliver a final sermon, 'Death's Duel', before the King at Whitehall. After the sermon, Donne returned home and posed for his portrait in a funeral shroud; he died seven weeks later.

- *Tennyson resigned membership of The Apostles debating society on February 13th 1830, being too nervous to speak*
- *Joaquin Miller, American poet of the Old West and dubbed 'Byron of the Rockies', died in California February 13th 1913*
- *Robert Frost and his family returned to the States amidst the threat of impending war on February 13th 1915, taking Edward Thomas' son Mervyn with them*
- *Frances Horovitz born February 13th 1938*

Poem of Absence

to be alone for a month is good
I follow the bright fish of memory
falling deeper into myself
to the endless present
the child's cry is my only clock

yet your singing echoes in corners
who clatters the red tea-pot
or opens the door with a bang
to look at the evening sky?
your typewriter lies silent
it is reproachful
I cannot make it stutter like you

I sit in the woods at dusk
listening for the sound of your singing
there are letters from a thousand miles
you wrote a week ago
like leaves from an autumn tree
they fall on the mat

it was your voice woke me
and the absent touch of your hand

Frances Horovitz
(February 13th 1938 – October 2nd 1983)

Horovitz was born Frances Hooker in London in 1938. In later life she became highly respected as a poetry tutor, working particularly for the Arvon Foundation, and in 1981 the BBC made a film of her work as a poet in schools.

Her second husband, Roger Garfitt, recalls that she "wrote sparely and sparingly," and was "a severe judge of her own work".

February 14

- *Michael Drayton's* To his Valentine *was published February 14th 1606*
- *Oscar Wilde's* The Importance of Being Earnest *stormed the theatre world when it premiered on February 14th 1895*
- *Douglas Stewart, poet, playwright and critic, died in Sydney, Australia, February 14th 1985*

Valentine

My heart has made its mind up
And I'm afraid it's you.
Whatever you've got lined up,
My heart has made its mind up
And if you can't be signed up
This year, next year will do.
My heart has made its mind up
And I'm afraid it's you.

Wendy Cope
(July 21st 1945 –)

Wendy Cope writes: "This little love poem acquired its title when a newspaper commissioned me to write a poem for St Valentine's Day. It is a triolet – an old French form."

Wendy Cope was a London primary school teacher until the publication of her first book, *Making Cocoa for Kingsley Amis*, in 1986. Since then she has been a freelance writer. She lives in Winchester.

• Poet John Philips died February 15th 1708
• The anonymous first edition of Edward Fitzgerald's Rubáiyát of
  Omar Khayyám *was privately printed on February 15th 1859*

February 15

À quoi bon dire

Seventeen years ago you said
  Something that sounded like Good-bye;
  And everybody thinks that you are dead,
    But I.

So I, as I grow stiff and cold
To this and that say Good-bye too;
  And everybody sees that I am old
    But you.

And one fine morning in a sunny lane
Some boy and girl will meet and kiss and swear
  That nobody can love their way again
    While over there
You will have smiled, I shall have tossed your hair.

Charlotte Mew
(November 15th 1869 – March 24th 1928)

Charlotte Mew lived a life beset by poverty and family tragedy: three of her siblings died before the age of five and two later suffered breakdowns and were institutionalised for life while still in their twenties. Their breakdowns coincided with the emergence of the science of eugenics, and Charlotte and her beloved sister Anne, with whom she lived in Bloomsbury for most of her life, both felt morally compelled not to have children.

Charlotte began to write at an early age but her first collection, *The Farmer's Bride,* was not published until she was almost 50. Nevertheless it won her a considerable reputation. She blamed her small output on the trials of domestic life – housework and caring for a demanding mother – but was once heard to remark: "I'm burning up my work. I don't know what else to do with it."

Charlotte Mew went into a nursing home for treatment for neurasthenia on this day in 1928. She was to commit suicide there less than a month later.

February 16

• Russian Symbolist poet Ivanov Vyacheslav Ivanovich born in Moscow February 16th 1866 and died in Rome on the same day in 1949
• Peter Porter, Australian-born British poet and playwright, born February 16th 1929
• Denise Riley, poet and academic, born February 16th 1948
• Poet George MacBeth died in Ireland February 16th 1992

Lyric

Stammering it fights to get
held and to never get held
as whatever motors it swells
to hammer itself out on me

then it can call out high
and rounded as a night
bird's cry falling clean
down out of a black tree.

I take on its rage at the cost
of sleep. If I love it I sink
attracting its hatred. If I
don't love it I steal its music.

Take up a pleat in this awful
process and then fold me flat
inside it so that I don't see
where I was already knotted in.

It is my burden and subject
to listen for sweetness in hope
to hold it in weeping ears though
each hurt each never so much.

Denise Riley
(February 16th 1948 –)

Denise Riley comments: "This 'Lyric' is indeed a reflection on the very act of writing a lyric, and on the hesitancy or the lurching between attraction and repulsion that this task can induce in the writer, so it becomes a bit like a love affair in which the feelings veer violently around."

Denise Riley was born in Carlisle and lives in London. She is Reader in the Department of English & American Studies at the University of East Anglia. She has written a number of books of which the most recent is *The Word of Selves; Solidarity, Identification, Irony* (Stanford University Press, 2000) as well as many collections of poetry, including *Denise Riley: Selected Poems* (Reality Street Editions, 2000).

• James Macpherson, creator of the faux-ancient epic poem
  'Fingal', died February 17th 1796
• German poet Heinrich Heine died February 17th 1856
• Ebenezer Thomas, last of the 19th century Welsh Bards of the
  Eisteddfods, died in Caernarvonshire February 17th 1863
• Andrew "Banjo" Paterson, author of 'Waltzing Matilda', born
  on a New South Wales farm February 17th 1864

Fare Well

When I lie where shades of darkness
Shall no more assail mine eyes,
Nor the rain make lamentation
   When the wind sighs;
How will fare the world whose wonder
Was the very proof of me?
Memory fades, must the remembered
   Perishing be?

Oh, when this my dust surrenders
Hand, foot, lip, to dust again,
May these loved and loving faces
   Please other men!
May the rusting harvest hedgerow
Still the Traveller's Joy entwine,
And as happy children gather
   Posies once mine.

Look thy last on all things lovely,
Every hour. Let no night
Seal thy sense in deathly slumber
   Till to delight
Thou have paid thy utmost blessing;
Since that all things thou wouldst praise
Beauty took from those who loved them
   In other days.

Walter de la Mare
(April 25th 1873 – June 22nd 1956)

Walter de la Mare was born in Charlton, Kent, and was related through his mother's family to the poet Robert Browning. He spent 18 years in the accounting department of the Anglo-American Oil Company and retired aged 35, when a Civil List Pension allowed him to dedicate himself full time to his writing. He wrote stories and poetry for both adults and children and his first successful collection, *The Listeners and Other Poems*, explored his signature themes of death, childhood, dreams and the supernatural.

'Fare Well' first appeared in de la Mare's collection *Motley*. It was written at his home in Netherhampton, probably in February 1916, while he was revising *Songs of Childhood*, or possibly in February of the previous year, when the onset of war and his own close brush with death brought the subject matter into sharp focus. De la Mare recalled that he was walking into the Netherhampton kitchen garden when the poem came to him "in a flash, as it were".

February 18

• *Michelangelo Buonarroti died, aged 89, February 18th 1564*
• *Poet A. R. Ammons born in North Carolina February 18th 1926*
• *Finnish poet Eeva Kilpi born February 18th 1928*

Letter to Anna, Pregnant

When I consider
By the frozen river
How we two shall never
Down some of these days
Meet in loving
Upon the ungrieving
Bank in forgiving
New-made rays

Of April sunlight
When touch is leaf-light
And love is outright
And darkness done,
Then I remember
Times without number
The cold I shouldered
To block your sun.

And I apportion,
By this sad station
Where ice to the ocean
Flows downstream,
All blame attendant
To your correspondent,
Sorrow his tenant,
Drowned that dream.

The hawthorn crouches
In the black wind's clutches
And snags and scratches
The last of light
That is dying over
The winter river
That sails forever
On out of sight.

I'm sorry, darling,
I hope the unfurling
Bud in your sailing
Body may
Beyond shores woeful
Wake you joyful,
Wake you joyful
Some sweet day.

Kit Wright
(June 17th 1944 –)

56

• *Georg Büchner, German author of the poetical drama*
  Woyzeck, died February 19th 1837
• *José Joaquin Olmedo, Ecuadorean poet and political leader, died*
  in Guayaquil February 19th 1847
• *Poet Jeffrey Wainwright born February 19th 1944*
• *Derek Jarman, filmmaker and poet, died February 19th 1994*
• *Pennine poet Brian Merrikin Hill died February 19th 1997*

February 19

O thou whose face hath felt the Winter's wind

'O thou whose face hath felt the Winter's wind,
  Whose eye has seen the snow-clouds hung in mist,
  And the black elm tops, 'mong the freezing stars,
  To thee the spring will be a harvest-time.
O thou, whose only book has been the light
  Of supreme darkness which thou feddest on
  Night after night when Phoebus was away,
  To thee the Spring shall be a triple morn.
O fret not after knowledge – I have none,
  And yet my song comes native with the warmth.
O fret not after knowledge – I have none,
  And yet the Evening listens. He who saddens
At thought of idleness cannot be idle,
And he's awake who thinks himself asleep.'

John Keats
(October 31st 1795 – February 23rd 1821)

Keats enclosed a draft copy of this poem in a letter to his friend John Reynolds on February 19th 1888, having written it that very morning. Reynolds was suffering from rheumatic fever, and Keats sought with his poem "to lift a little time from your Shoulders." In the accompanying letter, Keats explained how the song of a thrush he heard whilst out walking had inspired the poem. It is unique in being Keats' only unrhymed sonnet.

February 20

- *Milton recommended that Andrew Marvell, a fine scholar and translator, become his assistant, February 20th 1653*
- *Charles and Alfred Tennyson matriculated at Trinity College, Cambridge, February 20th 1828*
- *British poet Hugo Williams born in Windsor, Berkshire, February 20th 1942*
- *Dylan Thomas arrived in New York for his first sell-out series of American poetry readings, February 20th 1950*

Joy

Not so much a sting
as a faint burn

not so much a pain
as the memory of pain

the memory of tears
flowing freely down cheeks

in a sort of joy
that there was nothing

worse in the world
than stinging nettle stings

and nothing better
than cool dock leaves.

Hugo Williams
(February 20th 1942 –)

Hugo Williams comments on this poem: "It's a note in parenthesis from a great long ramble about blackberrying, a wholly pleasurable experience to me, perhaps too sweet. This poem sprang up out of the undergrowth much as nettles do among brambles, adding a hint of pain to the pleasures of accumulation and/or eating. I'm not sure it makes sense, but it has spontaneity because of its note-like form and absent subject, helpfully supplied by the title, which I suppose was the poem's inspiration, if any. I find it a good idea to start in the middle of something, a tip I got from my brother Simon, an actor and writer. He told me you have to start acting as soon as you leave the dressing room. If you leave it till the moment you hit the stage, it won't work."

Hugo Williams has earned his living as a journalist and travel writer and has written the 'Freelance' column in the *Times Literary Supplement* since 1988. His latest poetry collection, *Billy's Rain*, the chronicle of a love-affair, won him the T. S. Eliot Prize in 2000. His *Collected Poems* was published in 2002.

- *Poet Thomas Flatman born in London February 21st 1635*
- *Justinus Andreas Christian Kerner, poet and spiritualist writer, died in Weinsberg, Germany, February 21st 1862*
- *Poet W. H. Auden born February 21st 1907. "You can never step in the same Auden twice," wrote the critic Randall Jarrell ('Auden' comes from the word river)*

February 21

Work Without Hope
Lines composed 21st February 1825

All Nature seems at work. Slugs leave their lair—
The bees are stirring—birds are on the wing—
And Winter, slumbering in the open air,
Wears on his smiling face a dream of Spring!
And I, the while, the sole unbusy thing,
Nor honey make, nor pair, nor build, nor sing.

Yet well I ken the banks where amaranths blow,
Have traced the fount whence streams of nectar flow.
Bloom, O ye amaranths! bloom for whom ye may,
For me ye bloom not! Glide, rich streams, away!
With lips unbrightened, wreathless brow, I stroll:
And would you learn the spells that drowse my soul?
Work without Hope draws nectar in a sieve,
And Hope without an object cannot live.

Samuel Taylor Coleridge
(October 21st 1772 – July 25th 1834)

Coleridge drafted this poem on this day in 1825. In his notebook, he referred to writing the poem "on this premature and warm sunny day, antedating Spring", and to it being "in the manner of G. Herbert". George Herbert's poem 'Praise (I)' ends with these lines, which probably inspired Coleridge's poem: 'O raise me then! Poore bees, that work all day, / Sting my delay, / Who have a work, as well as they, / And much, much more.'

In May 1832, Samuel Taylor Coleridge wrote to his nephew Henry Nelson Coleridge noting that, in the Parisian and American editions of his work, the word 'slugs' had been misprinted as 'stags'. Coleridge was much amused by this comic "dignifying" of his slugs, and wrote that it was "so much grander that I grieve, it should be senseless."

February 22

- Dorset poet William Barnes born February 22nd 1801
- Edna St Vincent Millay born in Maine February 22nd 1892
- African-American poet Frances Ellen Watkins Harper died in Baltimore February 22nd 1911
- Henry Reed, poet and translator, born February 22nd 1914
- Ismael Reed, African-American author of poetry, novels and essays, born in Tennessee February 22nd 1938
- Spanish poet Antonio Machado died February 22nd 1939

Is my soul asleep?

Is my soul asleep?
Have those beehives that work
in the night stopped? And the water-
wheel of thought, is it
going around now, cups
empty, carrying only shadows?

No, my soul is not asleep.
It is awake, wide awake.
It neither sleeps nor dreams, but watches,
its eyes wide open
far-off things, and listens
at the shores of the great silence.

Antonio Machado
(July 26th 1875 – February 22nd 1939)

translated by Robert Bly

Antonio Machado was born in Seville and, at the age of eight, moved with his family to Madrid where he attended a school of 'enlightened' education. When his father died in 1893 leaving the family without financial support, Antonio and his brother, Manuel (who later also became a poet), were driven to write and act to make money.

After several spells in France, Machado returned to Madrid, where he remained until the outbreak of the Spanish Civil War. As a supporter of the loyalist cause, he was subsequently forced into exile. With his mother, his brother and his brother's family, Machado joined thousands of refugees on a journey on foot across the Pyrenees in the last days of January 1939. He died a month later in the French village of Collioure.

• *John Keats died in Joseph Severn's arms on February 23rd 1821,*
with the words "I shall die easy: don't be frightened ... thank God
it has come"
• *Ernest Dowson died of alcoholism February 23rd 1900*

February 23

Envoy
Vitae summa brevis spem nos vetat incohare longam[1]

They are not long, the weeping and the laughter,
    Love and desire and hate:
I think they have no portion in us after
      We pass the gate.

They are not long, the days of wine and roses:
    Out of a misty dream
Our path emerges for a while, then closes
      Within a dream.

Ernest Dowson
(August 2nd 1867 – February 23rd 1900)

Ernest Dowson, the archetypal decadent poet and friend of Oscar Wilde and W. B. Yeats, died of tuberculosis on this day in 1900 at the age of 32, after a life marked by family tragedy, poverty, alcoholism and unrequited love. Of his death, Oscar Wilde said: "poor, wounded fellow that he was, a tragic reproduction of all tragic poetry, like a symbol or a scene. I hope bay leaves will be laid on his tomb, and rue, and myrtle too, for he knew what love is."

Included as part of the collection *Verses* (1896), 'Envoy' was placed at the front of the volume, before the dedication. The characteristic themes of death and the brevity of life are undoubtedly informed by the deaths of both his parents the previous year.

1. The shortness of life prevents us from entertaining far-off hopes (Horace, *Odes* 1.4).

February 24

- *Milton married his third wife, Elizabeth Minshull, February 24th 1663*
- *Percy Shelley's* An Address to the Irish People *was published in Dublin February 24th 1812, and aroused the suspicion of the Home Office*
- *George Moore, Irish poet and novelist, born in County Mayo February 24th 1852*

Coming

On longer evenings,
Light, chill and yellow,
Bathes the serene
Foreheads of houses.
A thrush sings,
Laurel-surrounded
In the deep bare garden,
Its fresh-peeled voice
Astonishing the brickwork.
It will be spring soon,
It will be spring soon –
And I, whose childhood
Is a forgotten boredom,
Feel like a child
Who comes on a scene
Of adult reconciling,
And can understand nothing
But the unusual laughter,
And starts to be happy.

Philip Larkin
(August 9th 1922 – December 2nd 1985)

Philip Larkin talked about this poem in a BBC interview in 1964: "The most difficult kind of poem to write is the expression of a sharp uncomplicated experience, the vivid emotion you can't wind yourself into slowly but have to take a single shot at, hit or miss. Some fifteen years ago in February, I heard a bird singing in some garden when I was walking home from work: after tea I tried to describe it, and after supper revised what I had written. That was the poem, and I must say I have always found it successful. It is called 'Coming' – what is coming, I suppose, is spring."

- Poet Vittorio Colonna died in Rome February 25th 1547
- Irish poet Thomas Moore died February 25th 1852
- Robert Hayden, poet and educator who described himself as
  "a romantic forced to be realistic", died February 25th 1980
- A. R. Ammons, acclaimed American Romantic poet, died
  February 25th 2001

25 February 1944

I would like to believe in something,
Something beyond the death that undid you.
I would like to describe the intensity
With which, already overwhelmed,
We longed in those days to be able
To walk together once again
Free beneath the sun.

Primo Levi
(July 31st 1919 – April 11th 1987)

translated by Ruth Feldman and Brian Swann

Vanda Maestro, to whom this poem is cryptically dedicated, was a university friend of Levi's and a fellow Jew. They were arrested together and sent to Fussoli, a holding camp in Northern Italy; it was here that Primo Levi fell in love with her. On February 22nd 1944, the pair were amongst 650 Jews packed onto a train bound for Auschwitz. Observing a synagogue spire from the train window, Levi later noted: "That was the moment I said goodbye to my past for ever." February 25th was the final day of their gruelling journey, when they crossed the border into Poland, and the last night he and Vanda spent together.

February 26

• Christopher Marlowe, dramatist and poet, was baptised in Canterbury February 26th 1564
• French poet and novelist Victor Hugo born February 26th 1802
• John Keats was buried in Rome February 23rd 1821. His tombstone features a lyre "with only half the strings – to show his classical genius cut off by health before its maturity"
• George Barker born in London's East End February 26th 1913

Turn on Your Side and Bear the Day to Me

Turn on your side and bear the day to me
Beloved, sceptre-struck, immured
In the glass wall of sleep. Slowly
Uncloud the borealis of your eye
And show your iceberg secrets, your midnight prizes
To the green-eyed world and to me. Sin
Coils upward into thin air when you awaken
And again morning announces amnesty over
The serpent-kingdomed bed. Your mother
Watched with as dove an eye the unforgivable night
Sigh backward into innocence when you
Set a bright monument in her amorous sea.
Look down, Undine, on the trident that struck
Sons from the rock of vanity. Turn in the world
Sceptre-struck, spellbound, beloved,
Turn in the world and bear the day to me.

George Barker
(February 26th 1913 – October 27th 1991)

Barker decided to be a poet at the age of nine; when he died, aged 78, he was still writing verse. For the duration of his life he dedicated himself to his vocation, allowing nothing to distract him. He relied on the generosity of many people, including other literary figures. Of these, the poet and novelist Elizabeth Smart had perhaps the most far-reaching effect on his life.

Smart became obsessed by Barker before she met him, and shipped both him and his wife over from Japan to the States in order to meet him. In 1944 Smart wrote in her journal that it was exactly four years since the two had met and "it is still messy, if not messier than ever". When Smart suffered from a heart attack, 42 years later, Barker published no elegy at her funeral. Instead he inscribed on a napkin a rebuke in the spirit of her informality: 'O most unreliable of all women of Grace, Could you not wait for one last embrace?'

• *Henry Wadsworth Longfellow born February 27th 1807*
• *Lawrence Durrell, poet and writer, born February 27th 1912*
• *American poet Kenneth Koch born February 27th 1925*
• *Edward Lucie-Smith born in Jamaica February 27th 1933*

February 27

Discipline

Throw away Thy rod,
Throw away Thy wrath;
          O my God,
Take the gentle path.

For my heart's desire
Unto Thine is bent;
          I aspire
To a full consent.

Nor a word or look
I affect to own,
          But by book,
And Thy Book alone.

Though I fail, I weep;
Though I halt in pace,
          Yet I creep
To the throne of grace.

Then let wrath remove,
Love will do the deed;
          For with love
Stony hearts will bleed.

Love is swift of foot;
Love's a man of war,
          And can shoot,
And can hit from far.

Who can scape his bow?
That which wrought on Thee,
          Brought Thee low,
Needs must work on me.

Throw away thy rod:
Though man frailties hath,
          Thou art God;
Throw away Thy wrath.

George Herbert
(April 3rd 1593 – March 1st 1633)

George Herbert, the celebrated poet-priest, and lifelong champion of peace, is commemorated in the Church of England on this day each year.

February 28

- *Blind American poet Virginia Hamilton Adair, who shot to fame when she published her first collection aged 83, born in New York February 28th 1913*
- *Irish poet John Montague born February 28th 1929*
- *Bertolt Brecht fled Germany February 28th 1933*
- *Norman MacCaig awarded an honorary degree at Stirling University February 28th 1981*

Toad

Stop looking like a purse. How could a purse
squeeze under the rickety door and sit,
full of satisfaction, in a man's house?

You clamber towards me on your four corners –
right hand, left foot, left hand, right foot.

I love you for being a toad,
for crawling like a Japanese wrestler,
and for not being frightened.

I put you in my purse hand, not shutting it,
and set you down outside directly under
every star.

A jewel in your head? Toad,
you've put one in mine,
a tiny radiance in a dark place.

Norman MacCaig
(November 14th 1910 – January 23rd 1996)

Norman MacCaig's father was a Lowlander and his mother a Gaelic-speaker from Scalpay in Harris, whose freshness of speech awakened the young MacCaig to the possibilities of language. His first collection of poetry, published in 1943, demonstrated the wilful obscurity characteristic of the New Apocalypse movement with which he was closely aligned, and he later disowned both the movement and his early work. Sorley MacLean, a friend and fellow poet, described his work as a "long haul to lucidity."

MacCaig and his wife were regularly visited by toads at their holiday cottage near Lochinvar; at readings he would re-tell the myth that old toads have precious jewels growing inside their heads. He also wrote a number of much-loved poems about frogs and expressed concern that he might be remembered as 'the frog poet'. "I am a happy man," he confessed, "and most of my poems are about praising things."

• George Seferis (Giorgos Seferiadis) born February 29th 1900 in Smyrna (now Izmir in Turkey). Due to calendar changes, this date is sometimes recorded as March 13th

February 29

Interlude of Joy

That whole morning we were full of joy,
my God, how full of joy.
First, stones leaves and flowers shone
then the sun
a huge sun all thorns and so high in the sky.
A nymph collected our cares and hung them on the trees
a forest of Judas trees.
Young cupids and satyrs played there and sang
and you could see rose-coloured limbs among the black laurels
flesh of little children.
The whole morning long we were full of joy;
the abyss a closed well
tapped by the tender hoof of a young faun.
Do you remember its laugh – how full of joy!
Then clouds rain and the wet earth,
you stopped laughing when you lay down in the hut
and opened your large eyes as you watched
the archangel practising with a fiery sword –
'Inexplicable,' you said, 'inexplicable.
I don't understand people:
no matter how much they play with colours
they all remain pitch-black.'

George Seferis
(February 29th 1900 – September 20th 1971)

translated by Edmund Keeley and Philip Sherrard

George Seferis was a prominent diplomat for most of his life, and ambassador to London from 1957 to 1962, but he is chiefly remembered as one of Greece's finest poets. His first volume of poetry was published in 1931, but he is best known for *Mythistorema* (*Mythical Story*) and for his three *Logbooks* which came out over a 15-year period. As with all his volumes, these display his unique mix of the ancient and the contemporary, in both style and content.

In 1963, the year after he retired from diplomatic service, Seferis was awarded the Nobel Prize for literature, the first Greek to receive the award. In his final years, he publicly resisted the military dictatorship that had come to power in Greece after a coup in 1967, openly condemning the regime in a statement in 1969. Like other writers at the time, he also refused to publish while the so-called 'Colonels' government remained in power, which made *Three Secret Poems* (1966) his final published work. Upon his death in 1970, thousands of people escorted his coffin: to honour him not only as a poet and a diplomat, but also as a defender of freedom in the face of oppression.

March 1

• *Thomas Campion died in London March 1st 1620*
• *George Herbert, poet and priest, died March 1st 1633 in Bemerton, Wiltshire; his death recorded as March 3rd*
• *Robert Lowell born in Boston March 1st 1917*
• *Poet Howard Nemerov born in New York March 1st 1920*
• *Richard Wilbur born in New York March 1st 1921*
• *American poet Tom Clark born in Illinois March 1st 1941*

Because You Asked About the Line Between Prose and Poetry

Sparrows were feeding in a freezing drizzle
That while you watched turned into pieces of snow
Riding a gradient invisible
From silver aslant to random, white, and slow.

There came a moment that you couldn't tell.
And then they clearly flew instead of fell.

Howard Nemerov
(March 1st 1920 – July 5th 1991)

Born in New York, Howard Nemerov served in the Royal Canadian Air Force during the Second World War, and afterwards became a teacher. In addition to his 13 collections of poetry, Nemerov wrote novels, stories and a notable body of criticism. He once said that his ambition was "to see in a thinking way."

• *In response to criticism that his poetry lacked meter, H. G. Wells declared on March 2nd 1883, "Meters are used for gas, not the outpourings of the human heart"*
• *D. H. Lawrence died in Vence, France March 2nd 1930*

Her Anxiety

Earth in beauty dressed
Awaits returning spring.
All true love must die,
Alter at the best
Into some lesser thing.
Prove that I lie.

Such body lovers have,
Such exacting breath,
That they touch or sigh.
Every touch they give,
Love is nearer death.
Prove that I lie.

W. B. Yeats
(June 13th 1865 – January 28th 1939)

In a letter to his friend Olivia Shakespear, on March 2nd 1929, Yeats announced that he was "writing twelve Poems for Music – have done three of them and two other poems – not so much that they may be sung as that I may define their kind of emotion for myself. I want them to be all emotion and all impersonal." 'Her Anxiety' is one such 'Poem for Music'.

March 3

- *Edward Herbert, philosopher and poet, born March 3rd 1583*
- *English MP and poet Edmund Waller born March 3rd 1606*
- *Edward Thomas born in Lambeth, London, March 3rd 1878*
- *Pulitzer prize-winning poet James Merrill born in New York March 3rd 1926*
- *Samuel Schwartzbard, Jewish poet who escaped the Russian pogroms of 1905, died March 3rd 1938*

Words

Out of us all
That make rhymes,
Will you choose
Sometimes—
As the winds use
A crack in a wall
Or a drain,
Their joy or their pain
To whistle through—
Choose me,
You English words?

I know you:
You are light as dreams,
Tough as oak,
Precious as gold,
As poppies and corn,
Or an old cloak:
Sweet as our birds
To the ear,
As the burnet rose
In the heat
Of Midsummer:
Strange as the races
Of dead and unborn:
Strange and sweet
Equally,
And familiar,
To the eye,
As the dearest faces
That a man knows,
And as lost homes are:
But though older far
Than oldest yew, —
As our hills are, old, —

Worn new
Again and again:
Young as our streams
After rain:
And as dear
As the earth which you prove
That we love.

Make me content
With some sweetness
From Wales
Whose nightingales
Have no wings, —
From Wiltshire and Kent
And Herefordshire,
And the villages there, —
From the names, and the things
No less.
Let me sometimes dance
With you,
Or climb
Or stand perchance
In ecstasy,
Fixed and free
In a rhyme,
As poets do.

Edward Thomas
(March 3rd 1878 – April 9th 1917)

Edward Thomas had been a successful prose writer for many years when Robert Frost encouraged him to write poetry. He wrote his first poem in December 1914 and penned 85 of his 144 poems during a creative burst that lasted eight months.

- *Alan Sillitoe, poet and author, born March 4th 1928*
- *Ukranian poet Irina Ratushinskaya born March 4th 1954*
- *William Carlos Williams, American poet, novelist and doctor, died March 4th 1963*
- *Poet and novelist Elizabeth Smart died March 4th 1986*

so much depends

so much depends
upon

a red wheel
barrow

glazed with rain
water

beside the white
chickens

William Carlos Williams
(September 17th 1883 – March 4th 1963)

William Carlos Williams was born in Rutherford, New Jersey, and lived there for the rest of his life, settling with his wife Flora and raising two sons. He repeatedly resisted Pound's invitations to come to Paris, believing it was his responsibility to stay rooted as guardian of all that was "one hundred percent American". Williams' contentment with Rutherford was symptomatic of his belief that a focus on the particular leads to an understanding of the whole; his maxim was "Detail is all." He believed one should think of a "poem as an object, an apple that is red and good to eat ... or better yet a machine for making bolts."

Both doctor and poet, Williams delivered over 3,000 babies in his lifetime, and would jot down poems "in a white heat" between treating patients.

March 5

- *Alun Lewis died on military duty in the Pacific March 5th 1944*
- *Russian poet Anna Akmatova died March 5th 1966, the 13th anniversary of Stalin's death*
- *Irina Ratushinskaya sentenced to seven years' hard labour for the crime of writing 'anti-Soviet' poems, March 5th 1983. During her imprisonment she wrote 300 poems by scratching them onto bars of soap, and washing them away once memorised*

The Sentry

I have begun to die.
For now at last I know
That there is no escape
From Night. Not any dream
Nor breathless images of sleep
Touch my bat's-eyes. I hang
Leathery-arid from the hidden roof
Of Night, and sleeplessly
I watch within Sleep's province.
I have left
The lovely bodies of the boy and girl
Deep in each other's placid arms;
And I have left
The beautiful lanes of sleep
That barefoot lovers follow to this last
Cold shore of thought I guard.
I have begun to die
And the guns' implacable silence
Is my black interim, my youth and age,
In the flower of fury, the folded poppy,
Night.

Alun Lewis
(July 1st 1915 – March 5th 1944)

Alun Lewis, who some regard as the last of the great Romantic poets, was born the son of teachers in Aberdare in South Wales. Despite his pacifist inclinations, he enlisted with the Royal Engineers early in 1940, and in 1941 travelled to the war in India with the South Wales Borders. From there he wrote hundreds of letters to his new wife, Gweno, detailing his daily experiences. Despite his early optimism – Lewis believed he would "meet some tremendous experience" during the war, and added "I would like to survive it" – he died on this day in 1944. His second volume of poems, *Ha! Ha! Among the Trumpets*, was published in 1945.

- *Michelangelo, Italian painter, sculptor, architect and poet, born March 6th 1475*
- *Elizabeth Barrett Moulton Barrett (later Browning), known to her family as 'Ba', born March 6th 1806 in the family's Hertfordshire mansion, Hope End*
- *Joe Sheerin born in Leitrim, Ireland, March 6th 1941*

March 6

Diaries

Tonight I read my first son's
childhood out. A sneak preview

I gather up his toys in armfuls
and put his books
of frog princes and wild geese and
pumpkin brides and dwarfs where they belong

He has crossed the rapid flood
into the sparse terrain where I range

Chest deep in muddy water holding
his innocence aloft like a gun, I draw
my breath in, half hoping he will drown

He shakes himself like a dog on my ground
And now neither of us can go back.

Joe Sheerin
(March 6th 1941 –)

Joe Sheerin comments: "The poem arose from the nostalgic shock which all parents get when they realise that their children have moved into the adult world. I didn't actually read my son's diary, but if I had done, I hope he would forgive me."

Joe Sheerin was born in Ireland and has spent most of his adult life in London. His poetry has appeared in numerous magazines and was included in *Oxford Poets 2000: an anthology* (Carcanet). His most recent collection is *Elves in the Wainscotting*, published by Carcanet in 2002.

March 7

• *Alessandro Manzoni, sacred lyric poet, born March 7th 1785*
• *Thomas Hardy met Emma Lavinia Gifford for the first time on March 7th 1870; they married four years later*
• *Michael Ffinch, poet and writer, born March 7th 1934*
• *Stevie Smith died in Devon March 7th 1971*

Forgive me, forgive me

Forgive me forgive me my heart is my own
And not to be given for any man's frown
Yet would I not keep it for ever alone.

Forgive me forgive me I thought that I loved
My fancy betrayed me my heart was unmoved
My fancy too often has carelessly roved.

Forgive me forgive me for here where I stand
There is no friend beside me no lover at hand
No footstep but mine in my desert of sand.

Stevie Smith
(September 20th 1902 – March 7th 1971)

In the 1960s Smith, in her idiosyncratic librarian's attire, was a popular performer on the poetry circuit. According to Al Alvarez: "In among all that leather and denim, posturing and self-promotion, she could scarcely have been more out of place." And Jeni Couzyn remembered her "standing in all her loneliness as one standing on a great height".

Smith died on this day in 1971, at the height of her fame. She had been awarded the Chomondeley Award for Poetry in 1966 and the Queen's Gold Medal for Poetry in 1969. The *Times* obituary, published two days after her death, described her as "always in some sense a person apart".

• William Roscoe, poet on the slave trade, born in Liverpool *...*
8th 1753. The Butterfly's Ball and the Grasshopper's Feast
is his most lasting poem
• Robert Browning wrote of his much talked of visit to the Queen
in a letter of March 8th 1869: "We took tea together and
pretended to converse for an hour and twenty minutes"
• Erik Linklater, Scottish novelist and poet, born March 8th 1899

Of the Moon

Look how the pale queen of the silent night
Doth cause the ocean to attend upon her,
And he, as long as she is in his sight,
With his full tide is ready her to honour:
But when the silver wagon of the moon
Is mounted up so high he cannot follow,
The sea calls home his crystal waves to wone°,   *dwell*
And with low ebb doth manifest his sorrow.
So you, that are the sovereign of my heart,
Have all my joys attending on your will:
My joys low ebbing when you do depart,
When you return, their tide my heart doth fill.
    So as you come, and as you do depart,
    Joys ebb and flow within my tender heart.

Charles Best
(dated 1602)

This is the one known sonnet by Charles Best, which appeared in Francis Davison's *Poetical Rhapsody* anthology of 1602. There is little other evidence of his existence, beyond his possible authorship of the poem 'The Ghost of Richard III' which appears on a 1614 copy of Shakespeare's play, and has the initials 'C. B.' beneath it.

...wright Richard Savage, indicted for murder,
...lon from the King on March 9th 1728
...Barrett Browning gave birth to her first child, Robert
...owning, on March 9th 1849, her maid having
...ed her to desist from her opium-taking long enough to
...successful pregnancy
...ackville-West born in Kent March 9th 1892

...ıy grave and weep

...grave and weep.
...do not sleep.

...winds that blow.
...nd glints on snow.
...ght on ripened grain.
...de autumn's rain.

W... ...awaken in the morning's hush,
I am the swift uplifting rush
of quiet birds in circled flight.
I am the stars that shine at night.

Do not stand at my grave and cry,
I am not there, I did not die.

Anon

This poem first became widely known when it was reproduced in the *Daily Mail* newspaper in 1989. It had been enclosed with a letter sent by Steven Cummins, a young soldier, to his parents, to be opened only in the event of his death. Cummins died on March 9th that year when a landmine blew up beneath his Land Rover in Londonderry, Northern Ireland. At first it was thought that Cummins himself may have written it, but it has since been attributed to many different authors, most commonly the Native American Hobi tribe or Mary Frye. The original author remains a mystery.

- *Emily Pauline Johnson, a popular poet and entertainer, born on the Six Nations Reserve, Ontario, March 10th 1861; her parents were a Mohawk chief and an Englishwoman from Bristol*
- *Anna Akhmatova's funeral in St Petersburg on March 10th 1966 was attended by thousands of mourners*

There Are Delicacies

there are delicacies in you
   like the hearts of watches
there are wheels that turn
   on the tips of rubies
& tiny intricate locks

i need your help
   to contrive keys
there is so little time
   even for the finest
   of watches

Earle Birney
(May 13th 1904 – September 3rd 1995)

Earle Birney was one of Canada's best poets, and twice the recipient of the Governor's General Award. He remains most famous for his long poem, *David*, about a tragic mountain climbing incident in the Rockies which became standard syllabus material in Canadian schools. He was a compulsive wanderer, reading and teaching in universities all over the world, and single-handedly taking Canadian literature to a wide international audience during the 1960s. He saw his poems as "the best proof I can print of my Humanness, signals out of the loneliness into which each of us are born, and in which we die, affirmations of kinship with all the other wayfarers." He wrote over 20 books, including two novels, and continued to write until a heart attack in 1987 left him with a disabling brain injury.

Wailan Low, Birney's partner for the last 23 years of his life, was a graduate student when they met in 1973, and later a lawyer and Ontario judge. She writes: "March 10th 1973 was the first time he took me to Uxbridge, Ontario, the small village where we eventually bought our house with a large pond and ten acres of forest, which he loved."

March 11

• *Patriotic Spanish poet Manuel José Quintana died in Madrid March 11th 1857*
• *D. J. Enright, editor, novelist and poet, born March 11th 1920*
• *W. H. Auden attended a memorial service for the poet Louise Bogan wearing slippers and carrying all of Bogan's books, March 11th 1970*

Sonnets from the Portuguese
XXI

Beloved, say again and yet again
That thou dost love me—Though the word repeated
Should seem a cuckoo-song, as thou dost treat it,
Remember, never to the hill & plain,
Valley & wood, without her cuckoo-strain,
Comes the sweet Spring in all her green, completed!
Beloved!—I, amid the darkness greeted
By a doubtful spirit = voice, in the doubt's pain
Cry . . speak once more . . thou lovest! Who can fear
Too many stars, though each in heaven should roll . .
Too many flowers, though each should crown the year?—
Say thou dost love me, love me, love me—toll
The silver iterance!—only minding, dear,
To love me also in silence, with thy soul.

Elizabeth Barrett Browning
(March 6th 1806 – June 29th 1861)

By March 11th 1845, Robert Browning was discernibly in love: "I never yet mistook my own feelings, one for another – there! Of what use is talking?" he wrote to Elizabeth Barrett Browning. But he had not yet met the woman with whom he was in love, and the pair would later agree "You can't kiss mind."

- *Gabriele D'Annunzio, Italian poet and political leader, born March 12th 1863*
- *Brazilian symbolist poet Ribero Couto born March 12th 1898*
- *Jack Kerouac, novelist, poet and leading figure of the Beat Generation, and close friend of Allen Ginsberg, born Jean-Louis (Ti Jean) March 12th 1922*

A Supermarket in California

What thoughts I have of you tonight, Walt Whitman, for I walked down the sidestreets under the trees with a headache self-conscious looking at the full moon.
In my hungry fatigue, and shopping for images, I went into the neon fruit supermarket, dreaming of your enumerations!
What peaches and what penumbras! Whole families shopping at night! Aisles full of husbands! Wives in the avocados, babies in the tomatoes! – and you, García Lorca, what were you doing down by the watermelons?

I saw you, Walt Whitman, childless, lonely old grubber, poking among the meats in the refrigerator and eyeing the grocery boys.
I heard you asking questions of each: Who killed the pork chops? What price bananas? Are you my Angel?
I wandered in and out of the brilliant stacks of cans following you, and followed in my imagination by the store detective.
We strode down the open corridors together in our solitary fancy tasting artichokes, possessing every frozen delicacy, and never passing the cashier.

Where are we going, Walt Whitman? The doors close in an hour. Which way does your beard point tonight?
(I touch your book and dream of our odyssey in the supermarket and feel absurd.)
Will we walk all night through solitary streets? The trees add shade to shade, lights out in the houses, we'll both be lonely.
Will we stroll dreaming of the lost America of love past blue automobiles in driveways, home to our silent cottage?
Ah, dear father, graybeard, lonely old courage-teacher, what America did you have when Charon quit poling his ferry and you got out on a smoking bank and stood watching the boat disappear on the black waters of Lethe?

Allen Ginsberg
(June 3rd 1926 – April 5th 1997)

A devotee of Walt Whitman, Ginsberg was indignant that "no attempt's been made to use [his long line form] in the light of early 20th century organisation of new speech-rhythm prosody." This poem was such an attempt. Ginsberg once claimed that he "simply followed [his] angel in the course of compositions" and made the minimum of revisions.

March 13

• *Shelley left Dover and debts for permanent exile in Italy on March 13th 1817*

From The Cloud

I bring fresh showers for the thirsting flowers,
  From the seas and streams;
I bear light shade for the leaves when laid
  In their noon-day dreams.
From my wings are shaken the dews that waken
  The sweet buds every one,
When rocked to rest on their mother's breast,
  As she dances about the Sun.
I wield the flail of the lashing hail,
  And whiten the green plains under,
And then again I dissolve it in rain,
  And laugh as I pass in thunder.

I sift the snow on the mountains below,
  And their great pines groan aghast;
And all the night 'tis my pillow white,
  While I sleep in the arms of the blast.
Sublime on the towers of my skyey bowers,
  Lightning my pilot, sits;
In a cavern under is fettered the thunder,
  It struggles and howls at fits;
Over Earth and Ocean, with gentle motion,
  This pilot is guiding me,
Lured by the love of the genii that move
  In the depths of the purple sea;
Over the rills, and the crags, and the hills,
  Over the lakes and the plains,
Wherever he dream, under mountain or stream,
  The Spirit he loves remains;
And I all the while bask in Heaven's blue smile,
  Whilst he is dissolving in rains.

Percy Bysshe Shelley
(August 4th 1792 – July 8th 1822)

In the summer of 1820, Shelley received the news from England that his two-year-old daughter, Elena, had died. In a spirit of gloom, Shelley wrote to his friends the Gisbornes: "As to us, we are uncertain people who are chased by the spirit of our destiny from purpose to purpose, like clouds by the wind." Shelley wrote 'The Cloud' shortly thereafter, and despatched it to England in time to be included in his *Prometheus Unbound*, published in July of that year.

- *Sir Thomas Malory, English Epic poet and translator, died in Newgate Prison, London, March 14th 1471*
- *Arthur W. E. O'Shaughnessy born March 14th 1844*
- *Poet, critic and founder of The Poetry Bookshop, Harold Monro was born in Brussels March 14th 1879*
- *Poet and author, John Wain, born March 14th 1925*

In my craft or sullen art

In my craft or sullen art
Exercised in the still night
When only the moon rages
And the lovers lie abed
With all their griefs in their arms,
I labour by singing light
Not for ambition or bread
Or the strut and trade of charms
On the ivory stages
But for the common wages
Of their most secret heart.

Not for the proud man apart
From the raging moon I write
On these spindrift pages
Nor for the towering dead
With their nightingales and psalms
But for the lovers, their arms
Round the griefs of the ages,
Who pay no praise or wages
Nor heed my craft or art.

Dylan Thomas
(October 27th 1914 – November 9th 1953)

Thomas began his first major cross-country tour of the US on this day in 1950. He had been contracted to read his own work and the poems of British poets he admired, commenting on both. This he stubbornly refused to do. Thomas had an abject fear of discussing his own work, as well as expounding on the subject of poetry in general. He would flee after a reading before he could be cross-examined, claiming, "I don't mind answering a bit, only I can't."

"I am a painstaking, conscientious, involved and devious craftsman of words," said Thomas, in a rare moment of coherent self-appraisal. His lifelong friend Vernon Watkins remembered Thomas spending "several days on a single line, while the poem was built up phrase by phrase, at glacier like speed."

March 15

• *John Milton appointed Secretary of Foreign Tongues to the Council of State on March 15th 1649, and turned his polemical efforts to the defence of the execution of Charles I*
• *Wilfred Owen evacuated to the Military Hospital at Nesle March 15th 1917*
• *Poet Dick Higgins born in Cambridge March 15th 1938*

I saw his round mouth's crimson

I saw his round mouth's crimson deepen as it fell,
    Like a sun, in his last deep hour;
Watched the magnificent recession of farewell,
    Clouding, half gleam, half glower,
And a last splendour burn the heavens of his cheek.
    And in his eyes
The cold stars lighting, very old and bleak,
    In different skies.

Wilfred Owen
(March 18th 1893 – November 4th 1918)

Wilfred Owen was teaching on the Continent when he visited a hospital for the war wounded and decided to return home and enlist: "I came out in order to help these boys – directly by leading them as well as an officer can; indirectly, by watching their sufferings that I may speak of them as well as a pleader can. I have done the first." He was injured on this day in 1917 and was not fit to return to the front until August 1918.

• Nobel-winning French poet René Sully-Prudhomme born March
  16th 1839
• American poet Percy Mackaye born March 16th 1875
• Peruvian poet César Vallejo born March 16th 1892
• Indian poet A. K. Ramanujan born March 16th 1929
• Harold Monro, whose influential publishing imprint regrettably
  rejected Eliot's 'The Love Song of J. Alfred Prufrock', and the
  work of Edward Thomas, died March 16th 1932

March 16

From In Memoriam A.H.H.
CXV

Now fades the last long streak of snow,
  Now burgeons every maze of quick°   *budding hedgerows*
  About the flowering squares°, and thick   *fields*
By ashen roots the violets blow.

Now rings the woodland loud and long,
  The distance takes a lovelier hue,
  And drown'd in yonder living blue
The lark becomes a sightless song.

Now dance the lights on lawn and lea,
  The flocks are whiter down the vale,
  And milkier every milky sail
On winding stream or distant sea;

Where now the seamew pipes, or dives
  In yonder greening gleam, and fly
  The happy birds, that change their sky
To build and brood; that live their lives

From land to land; and in my breast
  Spring wakens too; and my regret
  Becomes an April violet,
And buds and blossoms like the rest.

Alfred, Lord Tennyson
(August 6th 1809 – October 6th 1892)

The title *In Memoriam A. H. H.* was suggested by Tennyson's (then) future wife Emily Sellwood. Other alternatives considered were *The Way of the Soul* and *Fragments of an Elegy*, the latter being perhaps the most accurate description of the poem's make-up. The structure and (lack of) unity of the poem has been exhaustively debated, although the most telling comment may be Tennyson's own, in which he wrote "the general way of it being written was so queer ... that if there were a blank space I would put in a poem".

Tennyon's second son, Lionel, was born on this day in 1854.

March 17

• St Patrick died in Downpatrick, Ireland, March 17th 461
• Henry Fielding, writing under the name of Capt. Hercules Vinegar, summoned Poet Laureate Colley Cibber to court for the murder of the English language, March 17th 1740
• Poet Ebenezer Elliot born March 17th 1781
• News of Keats' death reached England on March 17th 1821

Postscript

And some time make the time to drive out west
Into County Clare, along the Flaggy Shore,
In September or October, when the wind
And the light are working off each other
So that the ocean on one side is wild
With foam and glitter, and inland among stones
The surface of a slate-grey lake is lit
By the earthed lightning of a flock of swans,
Their feathers roughed and ruffling, white on white,
Their fully grown headstrong-looking heads
Tucked or cresting or busy underwater.
Useless to think you'll park and capture it
More thoroughly. You are neither here nor there,
A hurry through which known and strange things pass
As big soft buffetings come at the car sideways
And catch the heart off guard and blow it open.

Seamus Heaney
(April 13th 1939 –)

Seamus Heaney writes: " 'Postscript' was written quickly a couple of weeks after a drive along the south coast of Galway Bay, along the shore they call "flaggy" – probably because of the flaggy nature of the stones, although the sea wind made you think of invisible flags flapping in the air above you. Four of us, old friends at large for the weekend, were in high spirits, ready for anything, so exposure to the Atlantic bluster brought us to our senses in all kinds of exhilarating ways. The poem arrived like a sudden PS to the actual experience."

Seamus Heaney is the author of more than 16 collections of poetry and prose as well as a play, *The Cure at Troy*, which is a version of Sophocles' *Philoctetes*. He held the chair of Professor of Poetry at Oxford from 1989 to 1994. He now spends part of each year teaching at Harvard University.

- George Herbert wrote on March 18th 1618: "I am now setting foot into Divinity, to lay the platform of my future life"
- Stéphane Mallarmé born March 18th 1842
- Wilfred Owen born in Shropshire March 18th 1893
- Greek poet Odysseus Elytis, winner of the Nobel Prize for literature, died in Athens March 18th 1996

Forget Not Yet

Forget not yet the tried intent
Of such a truth as I have meant,
My great travail so gladly spent
    Forget not yet.

Forget not yet when first began
The weary life ye know since when,
The suit, the service° none tell can,   *actions of a lover*
    Forget not yet.

Forget not yet the great essays,
The cruel wrong, the scornful ways,
The painful patience in denays°,   *refusals*
    Forget not yet.

Forget not yet, forget not this,
How long ago hath been and is
The mind that never meant amiss,
    Forget not yet.

Forget not then thine own approved,
The which so long hath thee so loved,
Whose steadfast faith yet never moved,
    Forget not this.

Thomas Wyatt
(1503 – October 11th 1542)

It was Wyatt who brought the Italian sonnet form and the *terza rima* to English poetry. He was a poetic innovator, using over seventy stanza forms – not always successfully – many of which he invented himself. Wyatt was closely involved with the King; presented to the court by his father at the tender age of 13, he became a prominent courtier and soldier and was even captured by Spanish troops on one expedition. His life was undoubtedly eventful, and surprisingly cosmopolitan. He served at one stage as Marshal of Calais and was later Ambassador to Spain. But he was not consistently in the King's favour. He narrowly escaped execution by confessing to his love for Anne Boleyn in June 1533; she was beheaded for her own part in the relationship in 1536.

Wyatt was knighted on this day in 1535, but was imprisoned the following year after a dispute with the Duke of Suffolk.

March 19

• *A critic hailed Wilde's* Ballad *"the most remarkable poem that has appeared this year", March 19th 1898*
• *T. S. Eliot started work at the Colonial and Foreign Department of Lloyds Bank on March 19th 1917 and remained there for nine years. Ezra Pound called this "a criminal waste"*
• *E. E. Cummings married Elaine Orr March 19th 1924*

Into the Hour

I have come into the hour of a white healing.
Grief's surgery is over and I wear
The scar of my remorse and of my feeling.

I have come into a sudden sunlit hour
When ghosts are scared to corners. I have come
Into the time when grief begins to flower

Into a new love. It had filled my room
Long before I recognised it. Now
I speak its name. Grief finds its good way home.

The apple-blossom's handsome on the bough
And Paradise spreads round. I touch its grass.
I want to celebrate but don't know how.

I need not speak though everyone I pass
Stares at me kindly. I would put my hand
Into their hands. Now I have lost my loss

In some way I may later understand.
I hear the singing of the summer grass.
And love, I find, has no considered end,

Nor is it subject to the wilderness
Which follows death. I am not traitor to
A person or a memory. I trace

Behind that love another which is running
Around, ahead. I need not ask its meaning.

Elizabeth Jennings
(July 18th 1926 – October 26th 2001)

Elizabeth Jennings suffered a breakdown in the early 1960s. The period produced some ill-judged experimental poetry but her collection *Recoveries* (1964), which included the 'Sequence In Hospital', explored the experience with unflinching and characteristic clarity.

• *Publius Ovidius Naso, better known to modern readers as Ovid, born at Sulmo, Italy, March 20th 43 BC*
• *Salomón de la Selva born in Nicaragua March 20th 1893*
• *David Malouf, Australian poet and novelist, born in Brisbane March 20th 1934*
• *Robert Frost's wife, Elinor, died March 20th 1937*

March 20

Waking with Russell

Whatever the difference is, it all began
the day we woke up face-to-face like lovers
and his four-day-old smile dawned on him again,
possessed him, till it would not fall or waver;
and I pitched back not my old hard-pressed grin
but his own smile, or one I'd rediscovered.
Dear son, I was *mezzo del' cammin*
and the true path was as lost to me as ever
when you cut in front and lit it as you ran.
See how the true gift never leaves the giver:
returned and redelivered, it rolled on
until the smile poured through us like a river.
How fine, I thought, this waking amongst men!
I kissed your mouth and pledged myself for ever.

Don Paterson
(October 30th 1963 –)

Don Paterson writes: " 'Waking with Russell' was written for my son when he was a couple of months old. He's a twin, so frankly it was a toss-up whether this poem would be for him or for Jamie. The italicised line is from the first canto of the *Inferno* – we take it that Dante meant that he was half-way through his three-score-years-and-ten; which happened to be the age I was when the boys were born. So you can see this poem is as self-obsessed as any other love poem."

Don Paterson works as a musician, editor and dramatist, and lives in Kirriemuir, Scotland. He is the author of four collections of poetry, and his literary awards include the T. S. Eliot Prize and the Geoffrey Faber Memorial Award. He has also edited a number of anthologies.

March 21

• *Poet Laureate Robert Southey died March 21st 1843*
• *The war poet Geoffrey Dearmer, after whom the prize is named, born March 21st 1893*
• *Philip Larkin began his employment as Librarian at the University of Hull March 21st 1955*

Words, Wide Night

Somewhere on the other side of this wide night
and the distance between us, I am thinking of you.
The room is turning slowly away from the moon.

This is pleasurable. Or shall I cross that out and say
it is sad? In one of the tenses I singing
an impossible song of desire that you cannot hear.

La lala la. See? I close my eyes and imagine
the dark hills I would have to cross
to reach you. For I am in love with you and this

is what it is like or what it is like in words.

Carol Ann Duffy
(December 23rd 1955 –)

Carol Ann Duffy is widely acclaimed as Britain's leading female poet. She was born in Glasgow in 1965, and studied philosophy at Liverpool University. Hailed as a crusading spirit, Duffy is poetry editor of AMBIT magazine and a reviewer for the *Guardian*.

• *Johann Wolfgang von Goethe died March 22nd 1832*
• *Francis William Bourdillon born March 22nd 1852*
• *American poet Billy Collins born March 22nd 1938*

March 22

Forgetfulness

The name of the author is the first to go
followed obediently by the title, the plot,
the heartbreaking conclusion, the entire novel
which suddenly becomes one you have never read, never even heard of.

It is as if, one by one, the memories you used to harbor
decided to retire to the southern hemisphere of the brain,
to a little fishing village where there are no phones.

Long ago you kissed the names of the nine Muses goodbye
and watched the quadratic equation pack its bag,
and even now as you memorize the order of the planets,

something else is slipping away, a state flower perhaps,
the address of an uncle, the capital of Paraguay.

Whatever it is you are struggling to remember
it is not poised on the tip of your tongue,
not even lurking in some obscure corner of your spleen.

It has floated away down a dark mythological river
whose name begins with an *L* as far as you can recall,
well on your own way to oblivion where you will join those
who have even forgotten how to swim and how to ride a bicycle.

No wonder you rise in the middle of the night
to look up the date of a famous battle in a book on war.
No wonder the moon in the window seems to have drifted
out of a love poem that you used to know by heart.

Billy Collins
(March 22nd 1938 –)

Billy Collins has commented: "This seems to be a poem that anyone over 30 has an immediate grasp of, and anyone over 40 or 50 has an intense fondness for ... It begins by describing what one author called 'literary amnesia', which is the realisation that you have forgotten everything you've ever read. It is the kind of feeling that the mind is a small, unfurnished apartment."
Billy Collins was born in New York City in 1941. He is a dog-loving, piano-learning Professor and served a term as US Poet Laureate in 2001.

March 23

• It is thought John Donne composed 'Hymn to God my God, in my sickness' on March 23rd 1631
• John Davidson committed suicide March 23rd 1909 after the failure of much of his later work
• Poet and critic Jeremy Hooker born in Warsash, near Southampton, March 23rd 1941

From The Ancient Mariner
Part IV, lines 272-287

Beyond the shadow of the ship,
I watched the water-snakes:
They moved in tracks of shining white,
And when they reared, the elfish light
Fell off in hoary flakes.

Within the shadow of the ship
I watched their rich attire:
Blue, glossy green, and velvet black,
They coiled and swam; and every track
Was a flash of golden fire.

O happy living things! no tongue
Their beauty might declare:
A spring of love gushed from my heart,
And I blessed them unaware:
Sure my kind saint took pity on me,
And I blessed them unaware.

Samuel Taylor Coleridge
(October 21st 1772 – July 25th 1834)

Wordsworth and Coleridge conceived of 'The Ancient Mariner' jointly, during a walk over Quantoxhead to Watchet in mid-December 1797. Wordsworth had been reading Shelvoche's *Voyages*, which described the presence of albatrosses near Cape Horn, but he swiftly realised the subject matter was more Coleridge's *metier* than his own. A previous collaborative poem, in which Wordsworth and Coleridge determined to write alternate stanzas, collapsed because Wordsworth simply could not keep up with his friend's pace of composition. Coleridge completed the poem on this day in 1780. It first appeared in *Lyrical Ballads*, which included work by both poets, and prompted Hazlitt to write: "It is unquestionably a work of genius - of wild, irregular, overwhelming imagination."

March 24

Northern Lights

We watched the islands from the waterfront
as though they held a clue to what was next.
The wind built up in gusts to match our hearts
and blew the café chairs into the water.

Police in boats fished out the furniture
with poles, making us laugh until the chuckles
rolled through us like the whale's back
rolls through water, like the islands

stretch through the north seas. I have stolen
some of the light which drenches you this midnight
to wish you all the islands in the world
and every one a different kind of peace.

Jo Shapcott
(March 24th 1958 –)

Jo Shapcott writes: "My mother-in-law, a painter, lives in Shetland. Strangely, I wrote the poem long before I had the chance to visit her there because somehow the idea of the landscape and the light played on my imagination."

Jo Shapcott won the Forward Prize for her collection, *My Life Asleep*, in 1999. She was Northern Arts Literary Fellow at the universities of Newcastle and Durham from 1998 to 2000, and the first Visiting Professor of Poetry at Newcastle in 2000-2001 when she gave the inaugural Newcastle/Bloodaxe Poetry Lectures. A collection of selected poems, *Her Book*, was published by Faber in 1999, and *Tender Taxes*, her versions of Rilke's poems in French, in 2001.

March 25

• *Shakespeare amended his will March 25th 1616, a month before his death*
• *Anne Brontë, poet and novelist, born March 25th 1820*
• *Finnish poet Matti Kuusi born March 25th 1914*
• *Poet and playwright John Drinkwater died March 25th 1937*
• *US customs officials confiscated copies of Ginsberg's "obscene" Howl and Other Poems, March 25th 1957*

From Epicoene

Still to be neat, still to be dressed,
As you were going to a feast,
Still to be powdered, still perfumed;
Lady, it is to be presumed,
Though art's hid causes are not found,
All is not sweet, all is not sound.

Give me a look, give me a face
That makes simplicity a grace;
Robes loosely flowing, hair as free—
Such sweet neglect more taketh me
Than all the adulteries of art.
They strike mine eyes, but not my heart.

Ben Jonson
(June 11th 1572 – August 6th 1637)

Epicoene, a misogynist farce, was completed by Ben Jonson in 1609. It targeted arranged marriages and domineering females, and was generally mocking of wedding customs of the time. The character of Epicoene was based on Lady Arabella Stuart, a first cousin of King James, who had been close to marrying a charlatan pretending to be the Prince of Moldavia. Thus lampooned in the play, Lady Stuart was afterwards said by the Venetian ambassador to be "seldom seen outside her rooms and liv[ing] in greater dejection than ever".

Jonson had earlier referred to 'epicoene fury' in a bitter and damning poem to one of his lovers; 'Epitaph to Cecilia Bulstrode' was inspired by Bulstrode's supposed infidelity and lasciviousness, and was so hurtful that she apparently died of "morbid hysteria" a few months after its appearance.

Jonson was far from loyal himself. He is thought to have sired at least two children outside of wedlock during the summer of 1609 (around the time he wrote *Epicoene*). The first of these children, a daughter, was baptised on this day in 1610.

- *A. E. Housman born March 26th 1859. His mother died on his 12th birthday*
- *New England poet Robert Frost born March 26th 1874*
- *Walt Whitman died in New Jersey March 26th 1892*
- *Mrs Oscar Wilde wrote of Wilde's imprisonment: "I think his fate is rather like Humpty Dumpty's: quite as tragic and impossible to put right", March 26th 1897*
- *Beat Generation poet Gregory Corso born March 26th 1930*

From A Shropshire Lad
XL

Into my heart an air that kills
  From yon far country blows:
What are those blue remembered hills,
  What spires, what farms are those?

That is the land of lost content,
  I see it shining plain,
The happy highways where I went
  And cannot come again.

A. E. Housman
(March 26th 1859 – April 30th 1936)

Late in life, Houseman liked to attribute his poetic inspiration to "chiefly ... physical conditions, such as a relaxed sore throat during my most prolific period, the first months of 1895." Whether or not he sought consciously to obfuscate the real source of his inspiration is unclear – he always had an instinct for secrecy – but the greater part of A Shrop*shire Lad* was written at the time of Oscar Wilde's trial for homosexual acts. It is hard not to imagine that his fury, indignation and sorrow at the trial would not have freed his poetic flow, and inspired some of the more violent images in the book. Robert Ross, a friend of Wilde's, learnt a number of the poems by heart and recited them to Wilde when he visited him in jail.

The homosexual references went undetected when *A Shropshire Lad* was published in the aftermath of Wilde's trial. Infused with thwarted longing and nostalgia, the poems are an expression of Housman's unrequited and "disastrous love" for Moses Jackson, whom he had first met at Oxford. Though Jackson married and lived abroad, Housman remained devoted to him throughout his life, speaking in old age of Jackson as "the man who had more influence on my life than anyone else."

March 27

O Ancient Prisons

O peace of ancient prisons, beautiful
    outdated sufferings, the poet's death,
images noble and heroical,
    which find their audience in measured breath –
how far away you are. Who dares to act
    slides into empty void. Fog drizzles down.
Reality is like an urn that's cracked
    and cannot hold its shape; and very soon
its rotten shards will shatter like a storm.
    What is his fate who, while he breathes, will so
speak of what *is* in measure and in form,
    and only thus he teaches how to know?

He would teach more. But all things fall apart.
He sits and gazes, helpless at his heart.

Miklos Radnóti
(May 5th 1909 – c. November 8th 1944)

translated by Frederick Turner and Zsuzsanna Ozsvath

Miklos Radnóti was born to Jewish parents in Budapest. His twin brother and his mother both died at his birth, an issue with which he wrestled and for which he sought resolution through his early poetry. He became one of Hungary's leading poets, but even this fact and his conversion to Catholicism did not spare him the violence of the Jewish pogrom during the Second World War, during which he was repeatedly conscripted into slave labour camps.

As the Nazis evacuated the Balkans, Radnóti was one of a number of prisoners force-marched from a camp in Western Serbia towards Germany. Somewhere between November 6th and the 9th 1944, Radnóti was shot along with 21 others, and buried in a mass grave near Abda in Western Hungary. He was 35 years old.

In June 1946, the grave was reopened, and Radnóti's body identified by a tiny soiled notebook in his back pocket. This contained his last, most acclaimed poems, which came to be published as *Camp Notebook*. His very last poem, written on the back of a bottle label a few days before his death, contained the lines: "I whispered to myself, 'just lie easy now / patience is blossoming into death'." 'O Ancient Prisons', written on this day in 1944, was the first poem Radnóti composed after the German invasion on March 19th 1944.

- *William Wycherley, playwright whose verses Alexander Pope revised, born in Clive near Shrewsbury March 28th 1641*
- *On March 28th 1775, Samuel Johnson wrote of the poet Thomas Gray: "[H]e was dull in company, dull in his closet, dull everywhere. He was dull in a new way, and that made people think him GREAT"*

Poem

Like musical instruments
Abandoned in a field
The parts of your feelings

Are starting to know a quiet
The pure conversion of your
Life into art seems destined

Never to occur
You don't mind
You feel spiritual and alert

As the air must feel
Turning into sky aloft and blue
You feel like

You'll never feel like touching anything or anyone
Again
And then you do

Tom Clark
(March 1st 1941 –)

Tom Clark comments: "This is one of the few poems I've ever written which I'm able to remember by heart. I think that's due in part to the very pronounced closing rhyme (blue/do) which follows up several more 'covert' earlier rhymes (occur/alert, mind/like). Rhymes are a mnemonic wonder, of course.

"To abandon all modesty for a moment, I lately realised that the terms and theme of 'Like musical instruments' are roughly the same ones Keats employed in his 'Ode on a Grecian Urn': how much more transitory, less 'perfect', and more embraceable, 'life' finally seems, when it is compared with 'art'."

Tom Clark studied at the Universities of Michigan, Cambridge and Essex, has worked as an editor and teacher (for the past 20 years at New College of California), He currently lives in Berkeley, California with his wife and partner of the past 35 years, Angelica Heinegg.

March 29

• Charles Wesley, writer of 5,000 hymns (including 'Hark, the Herald Angels sing'), died March 29th 1788
• Welsh priest and poet R. S. Thomas born the son of a sea captain in Cardiff March 29th 1913

Night Sky

What they are saying is
that there is life there, too;
that the universe is the size it is
to enable us to catch up.

They have gone on from the human;
that shining is a reflection
of their intelligence. Godhead
is the colonisation by mind

of untenanted space. It is its own
light, a statement beyond language
of conceptual truth. Every night
is a rinsing myself of the darkness

that is in my veins. I let the stars inject me
with fire, silent as it is far,
but certain in its cauterising
of my despair. I am a slow

traveller, but there is more than time
to arrive. Resting in the intervals
of my breathing, I pick up the signals
relayed to me from a periphery I comprehend.

R. S. Thomas
(March 29th 1913 – September 25th 2000)

R. S. Thomas was a fervent Welsh nationalist and defender of the Welsh language, despite writing all of his poetry in English. He caused controversy in the late 1980s when he seemed to defend the firebombing of English-owned holiday homes, allegedly saying, "I deplore killing, but what is the life of one English person compared to the destruction of a nation?" For the most part, though, he remained out of the public eye, preferring to live quietly in the countryside of North Wales where he felt "more able to be religious and to worship". This sentiment also applied to his poetry; he once said, "I don't write for the public. You make [a poem] for yourself firstly, and then if other people want to join in then there we are."

- *French poet Paul Verlaine born in Metz March 30th 1844*
- *Frances Cornford born March 30th 1886*
- *Julian Grenfell, who wrote 'Into Battle' and was killed at Ypres in 1915, born March 30th 1888*
- *J. V. Cunningham died of heart failure March 30th 1985*

To My Wife

And does the heart grow old? You know
In the indiscriminate green
Of summer or in earliest snow
A landscape is another scene,

Inchoate and anonymous,
And every rock and bush and drift
As our affections alter us
Will alter with the season's shift.

So love by love we come at last,
As through the exclusions of a rhyme,
Or the exactions of a past,
To the simplicity of time,

The antiquity of grace, where yet
We live in terror and delight
With love as quiet as regret
And love like anger in the night.

J. V. Cunningham
(August 23rd 1911 – March 30th 1985)

J. V. Cunningham was raised the son of working-class Catholic Irish parents in Montana in the US. After leaving school, with his family plunged into financial difficulty by the sudden death of his father and intensified by the Great Depression, Cunningham set out in search of work. He drifted though the south-western states of America, suffering frequent bouts of homelessness and starvation before a chance encounter with Yvor Winters, the celebrated poet and critic, led him to study at Stanford University. He remained at university as a teacher and critic until retirement, and taught amongst others, the poet Alan Shapiro. In his first class, the chainsmoking and notoriously mordant poet read the young Shapiro's poem aloud and declared "Nothing more than spilt ink."

Cunningham was educated as a classicist and influenced by the Latin poet Martial. His poetry tends to align itself stylistically with classical verse and has consequently never enjoyed a wide readership, although it won many honours and a number of distinguished devotees. He is best known for his epigrams ('Here lies my wife. Eternal peace / Be to us both with her decease') a form he claimed appealed to him "as a short-breathed man", and which became his signature.

March 31

• *Andrew Marvell born at Winestead in Yorkshire, the son of a clergyman, March 31st 1621*
• *John Donne died at home in London March 31st 1631*
• *Translator and poet Edward Fitzgerald born March 31st 1809*
• *Charlotte Brontë, author of Jane Eyre, died March 31st 1855*
• *Mexican poet and diplomat Octavio Paz born March 31st 1914*

A Hymn to God the Father

Wilt thou forgive that sin where I begun,
    Which is my sin, though it were done before[1]?
Wilt thou forgive that sin through which I run,
    And do run still, though still I do deplore?
        When thou hast done, thou hast not done,
           For I have more.

Wilt thou forgive that sin by which I have won
    Others to sin? and made my sin their door?
Wilt thou forgive that sin which I did shun
    A year or two, but wallowed in a score?
        When thou hast done, thou hast not done,
           For I have more.

I have a sin of fear, that when I have spun
    My last thread, I shall perish on the shore;
Swear by thy self that at my death thy Son
    Shall shine as he shines now and heretofore;
        And, having done that, thou hast done,
           I fear no more.

John Donne
(c. June 1572 – March 31st 1631)

John Donne's biographer, Izaak Walton, relates that Donne set this poem to a solemn tune that was frequenlty sung by the choristers of St Paul's Cathedral. Donne himself confessed to a friend that the hymn "restored to me the same thoughts of joy that possest my Soul in my sickness when I composed it. And, O the power of Church-musick! that Harmony, added to this Hymn has raised the Affections of my heart, and quickened my graces of zeal and gratitude; and I observe, that I always return from paying this publick duty of Prayer and Praise to God, with an inexpressible tranquillity of mind, and a willingness to leave the world."

It is likely that Donne refers to the period of his grave illness in 1623. Donne was 51 when he was taken ill with 'spotted fever' during an epidemic, and almost died. The poem's refrains are informed by two puns, the first and most obvious being that of Donne's own name; the second a pun on his wife's name, Ann More.

1. Through his parents he inherits the original sin of Adam and Eve.

- *John Wilmot, Earl of Rochester, born April 1st 1647*
- *French poet and dramatist Edmond Rostand, author of* Cyrano de Bergerac, *born April 1st 1868*
- *Emily Dickinson's "closest earthly friend", Revd. Charles Wadsworth, died April 1st 1882*
- *Spanish poet Juan Gil-Albert born April 1st 1904*
- *First World War poet Isaac Rosenberg killed April 1st 1918*
- *Poet and painter Frieda Hughes born April 1st 1960*

La Siesta

When I arrive at that secret confine
and they question me, 'What is the Earth?'
I should say a cold place where the dictator overbears
and the oppressed cry long tears
and where, in shadows and gold teeth,
injustice does the rounds
taking up his profits from the men of property
and mankind's permanent tragedy; it is a wasteland.
But again, I should have to say,
when in clear altering situations
the land exhales the somnolence
of not knowing the source of one's fatigue,
while the blue sky pulses like an hallucination
and fruit follows fruit on the white tables
and great windows, set ajar, cool
in the semi-light, we seek out a bower
where we may fall beneath that soft weight.
It is then I should tell them that the Earth
is an original happiness, an inward impulse,
like an unprecedented temptation,
composed both of ardour and renunciation,
a giving up and a giving in, a slow love-potion.

Juan Gil-Albert
(April 1st 1904 – July 4th 1994)

version by John Stammers

Juan Gil-Albert left Spain after the Civil War but returned to live in Valencia. He published a number of books but there has only recently been a revival of interest in his work.

April 2

• Danish poet and author of fairy tales, Hans Christian
  Andersen, born the son of a poor shoemaker April 2nd 1805
• Katharine Tynan died April 2nd 1931
• Anne Waldman, Buddhist poet and devotee of Allen
  Ginsberg, born in New Jersey April 2nd 1945

The Gateway

Now the heart sings with all its thousand voices
To hear this city of cells, my body, sing.
The tree through the stiff clay at long last forces
Its thin strong roots and taps the secret spring.

And the sweet waters without intermission
Climb to the tips of its green tenement;
The breasts have borne the grace of their possession,
The lips have felt the pressure of content.

Here I come home: in this expected country
They know my name and speak it with delight.
I am the dream and you my gates of entry,
The means by which I waken into light.

A. D. Hope
(July 21st 1907 – July 13th 2000)

A(lec) D(erwent) Hope was born in Cooma in New South Wales. After spells at university in Sydney and Oxford, he settled into a life of academia and writing. He wrote his first poem aged eight, and continued to write prodigiously right up until his death at the age of 93. Much of his early work was lost in a house fire in the early 1950s, but the poems that made up his first volume, *The Wandering Islands*, survived to be published in 1955. Ten further collections followed.

Though viewed at times in his career as elitist and even anti-Australian, Hope is now widely regarded as one of Australia's foremost 20th century poets. Like Robert Graves and W. B. Yeats, he believed in the serious, almost sacred, role of the poet, a belief which infuses much of his writing. His major thematic concerns were man's relationship to nature and the interdependence of love and poetry, both of which are evident in 'The Gateway'.

- *George Herbert born in Montgomery Castle April 3rd 1593*
- *Donne preached the first sermon that Charles I heard as new king on April 3rd 1625*
- *Donne buried at St Paul's Cathedral April 3rd 1631*
- *Moses John Jackson, A. E. Housman's muse, who was described as "often lively, but not at all witty", born April 4th 1858*

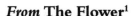

From The Flower[1]

How fresh, O Lord, how sweet and clean
Are Thy returns! even as the flowers in Spring,
    To which, besides their own demean,
The late-past frosts tributes of pleasure bring;
        Grief melts away
        Like snow in May,
As if there were no such cold thing.

    Who would have thought my shrivelled heart
Could have recovered greenness? It was gone
    Quite underground; as flowers depart
To see their mother-root, when they have blown,
        Where they together
        All the hard weather,
Dead to the world, keep house unknown.

    And now in age I bud again,
After so many deaths I live and write;
    I once more smell the dew and rain,
And relish versing: O, my only Light,
        It cannot be
        That I am he
On whom thy tempests fell all night.

George Herbert
(April 3rd 1593 – March 3rd 1633)

Shortly before he died, George Herbert entrusted a manuscript of his poetry, later published as *The Temple*, to Edmond Duncon, with the words:

"Sir, I pray deliver this little book to my brother [Nicholas] Ferrar [of Little Gidding, Oxfordshire], and tell him that he shall find in it a picture of the many spiritual conflicts that have passed betwixt God and my soul, before I could subject mine to the will of Jesus my master; in whose service I have now found perfect freedom; desire him to read it, and then, if he can think it may turn to the advantage of any dejected poor soul, let it be made public; if not let him burn it; for I and it are less than the least of God's mercies."

1. Stanzas 1, 2 & 6 of this 7 stanza poem.

- *Poet, novelist and playwright Oliver Goldsmith, died April 4th 1774. Asked on his deathbed if his mind was at ease he replied, "No, it is not!"*
- *Maya Angelou born Marguerite Johnson in St Louis, Missouri, April 4th 1928*

Come. And Be My Baby

The highway is full of big cars
going nowhere fast
And folks is smoking anything that'll burn
Some people wrap their lives around a cocktail glass
And you sit wondering
where you're going to turn.
I got it.
Come. And be my baby.

Some prophets say the world is gonna end tomorrow
But others say we've got a week or two
The paper is full of every kind of blooming horror
And you sit wondering
What you're gonna do.
I got it.
Come. And be my baby.

Maya Angelou
(April 4th 1928 –)

In 1983, Maya Angelou said in an interview: "From the time I was seven and a half until I was almost 13, I didn't talk. I was persuaded to talk by a woman who knew I loved and memorised poetry. She said, 'Poetry is music written for the human voice. Until you read it (aloud), you will never love it.' That has influenced the way I hear poetry when I'm writing it; I write for the voice, not the eye."

Angelou became mute after she was raped by her mother's boyfriend as a child. She is best known for her autobiographical writings, especially her first book, *I Know Why the Caged Bird Sings* (1970), the title of which was taken from a poem, 'Sympathy', by the black poet Paul Laurence Dunbar (1872-1906). Despite her widespread popularity as a poet, and despite publishing five collections, Angelou's 'sassy' poems received little serious critical attention until 1993, when she read her poem 'On the Pulse of Morning' at the inauguration of President Clinton. Her *Collected Poems* was published in 1994.

- *Algernon Charles Swinburne, alcoholic spendthrift, born April 5th 1837*
- *Oscar Wilde charged with 'indecencies' April 5th 1895*
- *American poet Richard Eberhart born April 5th 1904*
- *Celia Mitchell, wife of Adrian Mitchell, born April 5th 1933*
- *Allen Ginsberg died of liver cancer April 5th 1997*

Celia Celia

When I am sad and weary
When I think all hope has gone
When I walk along High Holborn
I think of you with nothing on

Adrian Mitchell
(October 24th 1932 –)

Adrian Mitchell comments: "This was written while I was working for the *Evening Standard* in 1962. It became extremely popular, finding its way into all sorts of anthologies. It was used in one anthology issued by a florist. They paid me in champagne. But it was also attacked by pirates. Every year the *Guardian* runs pages of Valentines. Readers began to take my poem and adjust its words to suit their own geography:

When I am sad and weary
When I think all hope has gone
When I walk along Billericay High Street (or wherever)
I think of you...

Just like that, with no thought for the exacting prosodical demands entailed in the re-cutting of one of the crown jewels of twentieth century English Literature, with no thought but for their steaming bestial desires...hey ho.

PS This immortal poem has also been slightly adapted and used with permission by The Bluetones in their hit 'Bluetonic'.

PPS Celia and I are happily married and are still together after 40 years, so the poem *worked*."

Adrian Mitchell was educated at Greenways School, Dauntsey's School, and Christ Church, Oxford. He worked as a theatre reviewer and freelance journalist on a wide range of newspapers including the *Sun* (pre-tabloid), the *Sunday Times* and *New Statesman*. He is an immensely popular poet, novelist and playwright for children and adults.

April 6

• *William Wordsworth appointed Poet Laureate April 6th 1843*
• *Edwin Arlington Robinson died of cancer in New York April 6th 1935. His great love, Emily, married his brother, since Robinson believed having a family would impede his writing*
• *W. H. Auden first encountered his lifelong partner, Chester Kallman, whilst doing a US poetry reading April 6th 1939*

The Pilot

From the Past and Unavailing
Out of cloudland we are steering:
After groping, after fearing,
Into starlight we come trailing,
And we find the stars are true.
Still, O comrade, what of you?
You are gone, but we are sailing,
And the old ways are all new.

For the Lost and Unreturning
We have drifted, we have waited;
Uncommanded and unrated,
We have tossed and wandered, yearning
For a charm that comes no more
From the old lights by the shore:
We have shamed ourselves in learning
What you knew so long before.

For the Breed of the Far-going
Who are strangers, and all brothers,
May forget no more than others
Who looked seaward with eyes flowing.
But are brothers to bewail
One who fought so foul a gale?
You have won beyond our knowing,
You are gone, but yet we sail.

Edwin Arlington Robinson
(December 22nd 1869 – April 6th 1935)

Edwin Arlington Robinson was born in Maine and was distantly related through his mother's lineage to the poet Anne Bradstreet. His elder brother, Dean, suffered neuralgia and gradually succumbed to morphine addiction; he died while still young. Edwin witnessed his decline with horror and his early death cast a long shadow over his life. 'The Pilot' is Robinson's tribute to Dean.

Robinson moved to New York where he languished in poverty until assisted, much to his surprise, by President Roosevelt. Impressed by his early work, Roosevelt secured him a job that required him to do nothing but write; "He has given me some of the most powerful loafing that has ever come my way," remarked Robinson. He went on to win three Pulitzer Prizes for his poetry, which is noted for its mastery of traditional forms.

• *William Wordsworth born the second of five children to John and*
Anne Wordsworth at Cockermouth, Cumberland, April 7th 1770

April 7

It is a beauteous evening, calm and free

It is a beauteous evening, calm and free;
The holy time is quiet as a Nun
Breathless with adoration; the broad sun
Is sinking down in its tranquility;
The gentleness of heaven broods o'er the Sea:
Listen! the mighty Being is awake,
And doth with his eternal motion make
A sound like thunder – everlastingly.
Dear Child! dear Girl! that walkest with me here,
If though appear'st untouched by solemn thought,
Thy nature is not therefore less divine:
Thou liest in Abraham's bosom all the year;
And worshipp'st at the Temple's inner shrine,
God being with thee when we know it not.

William Wordsworth
(April 7th 1770 – April 23rd 1850)

William Wordsworth was born in Cumberland on this day in 1770. He and his four siblings attended the local school and had a happy childhood until their mother's death in 1778. Their father died when Wordsworth was 14.

Wordsworth studied at St John's Cambridge, and set out on a walking tour of Europe before his final semester. This episode, during which Wordsworth came into contact with the French Revolution, wrought a powerful influence on the young poet's sensibilities and poetry. Indeed, it was in France that Wordsworth developed the sympathetic interest in the speech and troubles of the "common man" which came to characterise his work.

April 8

• Petrarch was crowned Poet Laureate on the steps of the
Capitoline Hill in Rome April 8th 1341
• Anne Bradstreet set sail for America April 8th 1630

Drinking

The thirsty earth soaks up the rain,
And drinks and gapes for drink again;
The plants suck in the earth, and are
With constant drinking fresh and fair;
The sea itself (which one would think
Should have but little need of drink)
Drinks ten thousand rivers up,
So filled that they o'erflow the cup.
The busy Sun (and one would guess
By's drunken fiery face no less)
Drinks up the sea, and when he's done,
The Moon and Stars drink up the Sun:
They drink and dance by their own light,
They drink and revel all the night:
Nothing in Nature's sober found,
But an eternal health goes round.
Fill up the bowl then, fill it high,
Fill all the glasses there – for why
Should every creature drink but I?
Why, man of morals, tell me why?

Abraham Cowley
(c.1618 – July 28th 1667)

Abraham Cowley was born to a London bookseller in 1618. He wrote his first poem at the age of ten, and his first collection, *Poetical Blossoms*, was published when he was just 15. He progressed from these precocious beginnings to become a popular and established poet, held in universally high esteem. He is best known for his poem 'The Mistress', for his Pindaric Odes, and for his elegies on Richard Crashaw and William Hervey. 'Drinking' is an excerpt from 'Anacreontics', a poem inspired by the convivial and erotic verse of the Greek poet Anacreon. Cowley's collected works were published in 1656.

Cowley was buried in Westminster Abbey next to Chaucer and Spenser, an indication of the high regard in which he was held at the time, and also the degree to which his reputation has waned over the intervening years.

• *Charles Baudelaire born in Paris April 9th 1821*
• *Poet Adela Florence Nicolson Cory (pseudonym 'Laurence Hope')*
  born in Gloucestershire April 9th 1865
• *E(dith) J(oy) Scovell born in Sheffield April 9th 1907*
• *Edward Thomas killed in the battle of Arras April 9th 1917*

April 9

Lights Out

I have come to the borders of sleep,
The unfathomable deep
Forest where all must lose
Their way, however straight,
Or winding, soon or late;
They cannot choose.

Many a road and track
That, since the dawn's first crack,
Up to the forest brink,
Deceived the travellers,
Suddenly now blurs,
And in they sink.

Here love ends,
Despair, ambition ends;
All pleasure and all trouble,
Although most sweet or bitter,
Here ends in sleep that is sweeter
Than tasks most noble.

There is not any book
Or face of dearest look
That I would not turn from now
To go into the unknown
I must enter, and leave, alone,
I know not how.

The tall forest towers;
Its cloudy foliage lowers
Ahead, shelf above shelf;
Its silence I hear and obey
That I may lose my way
And myself.

Edward Thomas
(March 3rd 1878 – April 9th 1917)

Edward Thomas enlisted in the Artists' Rifles in July 1915. A lover of solitude and the English countryside, he sincerely doubted his suitability to the soldier's life. Asked why he would fight, Thomas picked up a handful of soil and said as he crumbled it, "literally for this."

Thomas was killed by an unexploding shell on Easter Monday 1917, the first day of the Battle of Arras. His body showed no outward sign of injury, but his watch was stopped and his pocket diary buckled by the force of the blast.

April 10

• *Coleridge was discharged from the army as 'insane' and returned to Cambridge April 10th 1794*
• *Algernon Charles Swinburne, reformed Bohemian, who lived for some time with Gabriel Rossetti and George Meredith in Cheyne Walk, London, died of influenza April 10th 1909*
• *Poet and painter Adrian Henri born April 10th 1932, the grandson of a Mauritian seaman who settled in Birkenhead*

Sometimes it happens

And sometimes it happens that you are friends and then
You are not friends,
And friendship has passed.
And whole days are lost and among them
A fountain empties itself.

And sometimes it happens that you are loved and then
You are not loved,
And love is past.
And whole days are lost and among them
A fountain empties itself into the grass.

And sometimes you want to speak to her and then
You do not want to speak,
Then the opportunity has passed.
Your dreams flare up, they suddenly vanish.

And also it happens that there is nowhere to go and then
There is somewhere to go,
Then you have bypassed.
And the years flare up and are gone,
Quicker than a minute.

So you have nothing.
You wonder if these things matter and then
As soon as you begin to wonder if these things matter
They cease to matter,
And caring is past.
And a fountain empties itself into the grass.

Brian Patten
(February 7th 1946 –)

Brian Patten has said of the process of writing: "Sometimes it doesn't happen for a long time, then suddenly a line comes. It's like an underground stream which you tap into with a stick until it runs dry."

Brian Patten made his name along with Adrian Henri and Roger McGough as one of the 'Liverpool Poets', who changed the face of poetry in the 1960s. Influenced by the American Beat movement, they placed great importance on live performance of their work, and embraced popular culture as their chief subject matter. The Pop Poetry movement was born, and their first collection, *The Mersey Sound*, soon became one of the best-selling poetry books of the 20th century.

- *Christopher Smart born in Kent April 11th 1722. He later suffered from a form of religious mania that compelled him to continuous public prayer and was confined to an asylum*
- *John Davidson born in Renfrewshire April 11th 1857*
- *Australian poet Bernard O'Dowd born April 11th 1886*
- *Poet and critic Mark Strand born on Prince Edward Island, Canada, April 11th 1934*

On His Mistress Drown'd

Sweet Stream, that dost with equal Pace
Both thyself fly, and thyself chace,
    Forbear awhile to flow,
    And listen to my Woe.
Then go, and tell the Sea that all its Brine
    Is fresh compar'd to mine;
Inform it that the gentler Dame,
Who was the Life of all my Flame,
    In th'Glory of her Bud
    Has pass'd the fatal Flood,
Death by this only Stroke triumphs above
    The greatest Power of Love:
    Alas, alas! I must give o'er,
My sighs will let me add no more.
    Go on, sweet Stream, and henceforth rest
No more than does my troubled Breast;
And if my sad Complaints have made thee stay,
    These Tears, these Tears shall mend thy Way.

Thomas Spratt, Bishop of Rochester
(c.1635 – May 20th 1713)

Thomas Spratt was born the son of a clergyman and educated at Wadham College, Oxford. He took orders after the Restoration, and became chaplain to King Charles II in 1676, as well as curate and lecturer at St Margaret's church in Westminster. As a favourite of John Wilkins, later Bishop of Chester, he was amongst those who met regularly at Wilkins' house to discuss and philosophise – gatherings which eventually led to the foundation of the Royal Society. He became Dean of Westminster in 1683 and oversaw Sir Christopher Wren's restoration of the Abbey. As a member of James II's ecclesiastical commission, Spratt opposed the motion of 1689 declaring the throne vacant, but nonetheless assisted at the coronation of William of Orange and his wife Mary, on this day in 1689.

April 12

• English poet Edward de Vere, 17th Earl of Oxford, born April 12th 1550
• On April 12th 1827, Blake wrote in a letter: "I have been very near the Gates of Death & have returned very weak ... but not in The Imagination which liveth for Ever. In that I am stronger & stronger as the Foolish Body decays"

Alone

From childhood's hour I have not been
As others were – I have not seen
As others saw – I could not bring
My passions from a common spring –
From the same source I have not taken
My sorrow – I could not awaken
My heart to joy at the same tone –
And all I loved – *I* loved alone –
Then – in my childhood – in the dawn
Of a most stormy life – was drawn
From every depth of good and ill
The mystery which binds me still –
From the torrent, or the fountain –
From the red cliff of the mountain –
From the sun that round me rolled
In its autumn tint of gold –
From the lightning in the sky
As it passed me flying by –
From the thunder and the storm –
And the cloud that took the form
(When the rest of Heaven was blue)
Of a demon in my view –

Edgar Allan Poe
(January 19th 1809 – October 7th 1849)

Edgar Allen Poe was orphaned when he was just three years old and was raised (but not adopted) by John Allen, a wealthy tobacco merchant, and his wife, in Virginia. Relations between Poe and his foster father deteriorated rapidly as Poe matured. He was sent to university but withdrawn by Mr Allen after only a year amidst rows over his gambling debts. Poe instead entered West Point cadet school, but could not reconcile his literary ambitions with a military career. His failure to make a decent living and his repeated appeals for money eventually resulted in a complete breakdown in their relations.

Poe sent him a final letter on this day in 1833, imploring "Pity me and save me from destruction." John Allen scribbled on the letter: "His own Talents are of an order that can never prove a comfort for their possessor." Alas, he was proved right: although Poe effectively invented the horror story genre, and was a distinguished critic, editor and poet, he struggled with poverty and alcoholism for most of his short life.

- *John Dryden appointed Poet Laureate April 13th 1668*
- *Olga Rudge, mistress of Ezra Pound, born April 13th 1895*
- *Seamus Heaney born the eldest of nine, April 13th 1939*
- *Meg Bateman born in Edinburgh April 13th 1959*
- *George Mackay Brown, OBE, Scottish poet and storyteller who suffered "Wordsworthian hauntings, Hopkinsesque angsts", died April 13th 1996*

Lightness

It was your lightness that drew me,
the lightness of your talk and your laughter,
the lightness of your cheek in my hands,
your sweet gentle modest lightness;
and it is the lightness of your kiss
that is starving my mouth,
and the lightness of your embrace
that will let me go adrift.

Meg Bateman
(April 13th 1959 –)

translated from the Gaelic by the poet

Meg Bateman comments: "I wrote this bitter-sweet poem in my twenties when I came to realise that the very quality of lightness that I had found attractive in many a young man was the very quality that would make them find me, a brooding poetic type, far too intense. I remember when I wrote it, experiencing a sudden sort of lightness on having understood the situation. This almost made up for losing the young man in question and it gave me the title for my second collection."

Meg Bateman learnt Gaelic as an adult and now teaches at Sabhal Mor Ostaig, the Gaelic College in Skye. She translates some of her own work into English, as well as older Gaelic poetry. Many of her poems deal with the experiences of women, always with great delicacy and frankness. She featured in the seminal *Dream State: The New Scottish Poets;* her second full-length collection of Gaelic poems, *Aotromachd agus dain eile* (*Lightness and other poems*), has facing English translations.

April 14

• Goethe's first play premiered on April 14th 1774
• Leading poet of the Russian Revolution of 1917, Vladimir Mayakovsky became disillusioned under Stalin's reign and, disappointed in love, shot himself on April 14th 1930

Night Thoughts

Stars, you are unfortunate, I pity you,
Beautiful as you are, shining in your glory,
Who guide seafaring men through stress and peril
And have no recompense from gods or mortals,
Love you do not, nor do you know what love is.
Hours that are aeons urgently conducting
Your figures in a dance through the vast heaven,
What journey have you ended in this moment,
Since lingering in the arms of my beloved
I lost all memory of you and midnight.

Johann Wolfgang von Goethe
(August 28th 1749 – March 22nd 1832)

translated by Christopher Middleton

In his lifetime Goethe was, by turns, philosopher, novelist, botanist, anatomist, poet, dramatist and theatre director. For large parts of his life he was also closely involved with the court of Weimar, at one time being both Minister of State and Privy Councillor for the region. However, he became disaffected with the political machinations of court life, and at one stage fled to Italy where he remained for three years, masquerading as a painter under the name Jean Philippe Möller.

'Night Thoughts' ('Die Nacht') was first published in a songbook published by Bernard Breitkopf in 1769, which contained a number of Goethe's early lyrics set to music. Goethe's name appeared nowhere in the book, despite this being the first time his work had been published in any form.

- *William Oldys, poet and bibliographer, died April 15th 1761*
- *Emily Dickinson enclosed four poems in a letter to Thomas Wentworth Higginson on April 15th 1862, asking: "Are you too deeply occupied to say if my Verse is alive?"*
- *Matthew Arnold died in Liverpool April 15th 1888*
- *Emyr Humphreys, Welsh poet, novelist and dramatist, born April 15th 1919*

From Father to Son

There is no limit to the number of times
Your father can come to life, and he is as tender as ever he was
And as poor, his overcoat buttoned to the throat,
His face blue from the wind that always blows in the outer darkness
He comes towards you, hesitant,
Unwilling to intrude and yet driven at the point of love
To this encounter.

You may think
That love is all that is left of him, but when he comes
He comes with all his winters and all his wounds.
He stands shivering in the empty street,
Cold and worn like a tramp at the end of a journey
And yet a shape of unquestioning love that you
Uneasy and hesitant of the cold touch of death
Must embrace.

Then, before you can touch him
He is gone, leaving on your fingers
A little more of his weariness
A little more of his love.

Emyr Humphreys
(April 15th 1919 –)

Emyr Humphreys comments: "My father was wounded and gassed in the first world war. I wrote this poem a while after his death, when I had become a father myself."
Humphreys has written over twenty novels in English and Welsh, as well as four collections of poetry. His *Collected Poems* is published by University of Wales Press (1999).

April 16

• Poet and writer Aphra Behn, Britain's first professional female author and, after Dryden, most prolific dramatist of the Restoration, died April 16th 1689
• Tristan Tzara, French poet and founder of the Dadaist Movement, born in Moinesti, Romania, April 16th 1896
• Novelist and poet Sir Kingsley Amis born in Clapham, South West London, April 16th 1922

Muse

When I kiss you in all the folding places
of your body, you make that noise like a dog
dreaming, dreaming of the long run he makes
in answer to some jolt to his hormones,
running across landfills, running, running
by tips and shorelines from the scent of too much,
but still going with head up and snout
in the air because he loves it all
and has to get away. I have to kiss deeper
and more slowly – your neck, your inner arm,
the neat creases under your toes, the shadow
behind your knee, the white angles of your groin –
until you fall quiet because only then
can I get the damned words to come into my mouth.

Jo Shapcott
(March 24th 1958 –)

Jo Shapcott comments: "This poem is an unrhymed sonnet on that traditional subject, the muse, but with the necessary twist that my muse will always be male."

- *Religious poet Henry Vaughan born in Newton-by-Usk, Powys, c. April 17th 1622*
- *Basil Bunting, who emerged after 15 years of obscurity with his masterpiece, Briggflatts, died April 17th 1985*

April 17

Peace

My soul, there is a country
  Far beyond the stars,
Where stands a wingèd sentry
  All skilful in the wars:
There, above noise and danger,
  Sweet Peace sits crowned with smiles,
And One born in a manger
  Commands the beauteous files.
He is thy gracious friend,
  And – O my soul, awake! –
Did in pure love descend,
  To die here for thy sake.
If thou canst get but thither,
  There grows the flower of Peace,
The Rose that cannot wither,
  Thy fortress, and thy ease.
Leave then thy foolish ranges;
  For none can thee secure,
But ONE who never changes,
  Thy God, thy life, thy cure.

Henry Vaughan
(c. April 17th 1622 – April 23rd 1695)

Henry Vaughan's exact birthdate is unknown, but he was born the elder of twins in Wales, sometime between April 1621 and April 1622. He is assumed to have studied at Jesus College, Oxford, alongside his brother Thomas in the late 1630s, and later to have studied law in London until the outbreak of the civil war in 1642.

Both Vaughans were zealous royalists, but although Henry was imprisoned for a time for his allegiances, certain historians have argued that only Thomas actually bore arms for the king. In 1647 Henry wrote a Latin poem asserting that he had not fought in the war; that "there was a voice in a brother's blood, which could cry to Heaven against the shedder of it."

Thomas Vaughan's wife, Rebecca, died on this day in 1658. A year later, a grieving Thomas wrote: "In ipso Anniversario sive Die solenni Nativitatis suae Aeternae" (meaning that this death day is the commencement of his late wife's eternal life). This Latin phrase has in the past been misinterpreted to mean that April 17th was also Thomas' birthday, and hence also the birthday of his twin brother, Henry; but there is no extant evidence for this.

April 18

• Dick Davis, poet and translator from the Persian, born April 18th 1945

The Silver Swan

The silver swan, who living had no note,
When death approached unlocked her silent throat,
Leaning her breast against the reedy shore,
Thus sung her first and last, and sung no more:
Farewell all joys, O death come close mine eyes,
More geese than swans now live, more fools than wise.

Anon

This poem is the text of the most famous madrigal by Orlando Gibbons, which appeared in his book *The First Set of Madrigals and Motets* in 1612. Though the poem has occasionally been attributed to Gibbons himself, it is more likely that he simply set popular verses of the time to music. One biography of Gibbons suggests that the man responsible for selecting the texts could have been Sir Christopher Hatton, Gibbon's main patron at the time.

Gibbons was baptised on Christmas Day 1583 and became a chorister at King's College, Cambridge at the age of twelve. He was later organist at the Royal Chapel and at Westminster Abbey, and is primarily remembered today for his verse anthems, which are often used in church services. He died in Canterbury on June 5th 1625, while returning from Dover with King Charles I, and is buried in the cathedral there.

- *Byron died of a malarial fever in Greece April 19th 1824. Tennyson described it as a day "when the whole world seemed to be darkened for me"*
- *Poet and First World War naval historian Sir Henry John Newbolt, best remembered for his sea songs, died April 19th 1938*
- *Mexican poet, critic and polymath, Octavio Paz, died in Mexico City April 19th 1998*

More Poems
VII

Stars, I have seen them fall,
    But when they drop and die
No star is lost at all
    From all the star-sown sky.
The toil of all that be
    Helps not the primal fault;
It rains into the sea,
    And still the sea is salt.

A. E. Housman
(March 26th 1859 – April 30th 1936)

On April 19th 1892, Housman applied for the position of Latin Chair at University College. He won the position despite never having held a university post before and having failed his degree at Oxford, in part because his application was supported by a wealth of dazzling recommendations from some of the most eminent scholars of the time. Housman remained eternally grateful to University College for having, as he put it, "picked me out of the gutter – if I may so describe His Majesty's Patent Office." He had worked in the civil service for nine years, but had spent his spare time conducting research at the British Museum, and writing meticulous and exceptionally erudite articles on the Classics. He went on to become Professor of Latin at Trinity College, Cambridge, in 1911.

April 20

• W(illiam) H(enry) Davies born April 20th 1871
• Three times recipient of the Pulitzer Prize, poet Archibald
MacLeish died April 20th 1982

You, Andrew Marvell

And here face down beneath the sun
And here upon earth's noonward height
To feel the always coming on
The always rising of the night:

To feel creep up the curving east
The earthy chill of dusk and slow
Upon those under lands the vast
And ever climbing shadow grow

And strange at Ecbatan the trees
Take leaf by leaf the evening strange
The flooding dark about their knees
The mountains over Persia change

And now at Kermanshah the gate
Dark empty and the withered grass
And through the twilight now the late
Few travelers in the westward pass

And Baghdad darken and the bridge
Across the silent river gone
And through Arabia the edge
Of evening widen and steal on

And deepen on Palmyra's street
The wheel rut in the ruined stone
And Lebanon fade out and Crete
High through the clouds and overblown

And over Sicily the air
Still flashing with the landward gulls
And loom and slowly disappear
The sails above the shadowy hulls

And Spain go under and the shore
Of Africa the gilded sand
And evening vanish and no more
The low pale light across that land

Nor now the long light on the sea:

And here face downward in the sun
To feel how swift how secretly
The shadow of the night comes on . . .

Archibald MacLeish
(May 7th 1892 – April 20th 1982)

118

- *Poet and novelist Charlotte Brontë born in Thornton, Yorkshire, April 21st 1816*
- *Robert Bridges, who spent the years following his marriage in 1884 in domestic seclusion, died April 21st 1930*
- *Langston Hughtes set up and ran the The Harlem Suitcase Theatre (so called because they could fit all their equipment into one suitcase). They first performed on April 21st 1938*

Harlem

What happens to a dream deferred?

Does it dry up
like a raisin in the sun?
Or fester like a sore –
And then run?
Does it stink like rotten meat?
Or crust and sugar over –
Like a syrupy sweet?

Maybe it just sags
like a heavy load.

Or does it explode?

Langston Hughes
(February 1st 1902 – May 22nd 1967)

Born into an abolitionist family in Joplin, Missouri, James Langston Hughes' life and work was instrumental in shaping the Harlem Renaissance of the 1920s. He is best known for his colourful portraits of African American life and was deeply immersed in the world of jazz, an important influence on his writing: "I tried to write poems like the songs they sang on Seventh Street ... [these] had the pulse beat of the people who keep on going."

Langston Hughes has written of this poem: "[It] is marked by conflicting changes, sudden nuances, sharp and impudent interjections, broken rhythms, and passages sometimes in the manner of the jam session, sometimes the popular song, punctuated by the riffs, runs, breaks, and disc-tortions of the music of community in transition."

April 22

• C. H. Sisson, poet and novelist, born April 22nd 1914
• Jeppe Aakjaer, leading exponent of Danish regional literature, died in Denmark April 22nd 1930
• Poet and translator Jean Valentine born April 22nd 1934
• Louise Glück born in New York April 22nd 1943

The Wild Iris

At the end of my suffering
there was a door.

Hear me out: that which you call death
I remember.

Overhead, noises, branches of the pine shifting.
Then nothing. The weak sun
flickered over the dry surface.

It is terrible to survive
as consciousness
buried in the dark earth.

Then it was over: that which you fear, being
a soul and unable
to speak, ending abruptly, the stiff earth
bending a little. And what I took to be
birds darting in low shrubs.

You who do not remember
passage from the other world
I tell you I could speak again: whatever
returns from oblivion returns
to find a voice:

from the center of my life came
a great fountain, deep blue
shadows on azure seawater.

Louise Glück
(April 22nd 1943 –)

Louise Glück writes: " 'The Wild Iris' gave its name to a book written in the summer of 1991: a moment of great fluency at the end of an ordeal of silence that had lasted more than two years. That such silences are common in my experience has not made them easy: each one has seemed terminal, the end of all thought. To write at all after such a period is a gift; the summer in which this poem was written was a period of euphoric relief and gratitude – the garden, which I had so loved, had rescued me."

Louise Glück (pronounced 'Glick'), is the author of seven collections of poetry, and a book of essays. *The Wild Iris*, the book-length sequence for which she won the Pulitzer Prize, explores the mystery of life through the voices of individual flowers.

- *William Shakespeare, tradition has it, born April 23rd[1] 1564, and died April 23rd 1616*
- *Welsh religious poet Henry Vaughan died April 23rd 1695*
- *William Wordsworth died of pleurisy April 23rd 1850; Matthew Arnold solemnly announced: "The last poetic voice is dumb"*
- *Rupert Brooke died April 23rd 1915*

From Antony and Cleopatra
Act V Scene ii

Cleopatra: His legs bestrid the ocean; his rear'd arm
Crested the world. His voice was propertied
As all the tuned spheres, and that to friends;
But when he meant to quail and shake the orb,
He was as rattling thunder. For his bounty,
There was no winter in't, an autumn 'twas
That grew the more by reaping. His delights
Were dolphin-like: they show'd his back above
The element they liv'd in. In his livery
Walk'd crowns and crownets, realms and islands were
As plates dropp'd from his pocket.

William Shakespeare
(April 23rd 1564 – April 23rd 1616)

Cleopatra VII, last of the Egyptian pharaohs, is thought to have committed suicide on August 12th 30 BC. She and Mark Antony had been defeated the year before at the Battle of Actium, and Antony had subsequently killed himself by falling on his sword. Following the failure of negotiations with the Roman emperor Octavian, Cleopatra retired to her room and allowed an asp to bite her, thereby ending her life. Antony and Cleopatra were buried together in accordance with their wishes.

1. While records show that Shakespeare was baptised on April 26th 1564, there is no evidence to support the popular belief that he was actually born – as fifty two years later he was to die – on April 23rd, St George's Day. This is rather based on the assumption that Elizabethan baptisms took place three days after the birth, but it is no more likely that his birth date was Sunday 23rd, than Saturday 22nd April 1564.

April 24

• Robert Herrick was ordained as a priest April 24th 1623
• Poet and writer Robert Penn Warren born in Guthrie, Kentucky, April 24th 1905
• Poet and most noted novelist of Nebraska, Willa Cather died April 24th 1947

From Litany to the Holy Spirit[1]

In the hour of my distress,
When temptations me oppress,
And when I my sins confess,
    Sweet Spirit, comfort me!

When I lie within my bed,
Sick in heart and sick in head,
And with doubts discomforted,
    Sweet Spirit, comfort me!

When the house doth sigh and weep,
And the world is drowned in sleep,
Yet mine eyes the watch do keep,
    Sweet Spirit, comfort me!

When (God knows) I'm tossed about,
Either with despair, or doubt;
Yet before the glass be out,
    Sweet Spirit, comfort me!

When the Judgment is revealed,
And that opened which was sealed,
When to Thee I have appealed;
    Sweet Spirit, comfort me!

Robert Herrick
(August ? 1591 – October 15th 1674)

Robert Herrick was ordained as a priest on this day in 1623, and lived the remainder of this life devoted to the church and his congregation. His manuscripts were widely enjoyed in literary circles and he was hailed by Swinburne as "the greatest songwriter ever born to English race." In 1628 he was nominated to the vicarage of Dean Prior, and spent the next 18 years confined to "dull Devonshire" as he called it, bemoaning his dislocation from the literary and social scene in London, but drawing consolation from his books, especially the Bible and Latin verse, as well as his many household pets and fiercely loyal housekeeper, Prudence.

1. Stanzas 1, 2 , 3, 9 & 12 of this 12 stanza poem.

- *Poet and hymn-writer William Cowper died April 25th 1800*
- *Poet Walter de la Mare born in Kent April 25th 1873*
- *Anna Akhmatova married Nikolay Gumilyov, leader of the Acmeist group of poets, April 25th 1910. Her family regarded the marriage as doomed to failure and refused to attend*
- *James Fenton born in Lincoln April 25th 1949*

The Ideal

This is where I came from.
I passed this way.
This should not be shameful
Or hard to say.

A self is a self.
It is not a screen.
A person should respect
What he has been.

This is my past
Which I shall not discard.
This is the ideal.
This is hard.

James Fenton
(April 25th 1949 –)

James Fenton comments: "I wrote this poem for a friend who had once been in the revolutionary underground in the Philippines, but who was now disillusioned with the communist movement there. Of course, it is stated in such general terms that is has been taken to apply to quite different situations, and I am delighted and moved to find that it means so many different things to different people."

James Fenton received a BA from Magdalen College, Oxford and published his first collection of poems at the age of 23. He won an Eric Gregory Award a year later and used the prize money to travel abroad. As a freelance reporter working in Southeast Asia, he documented periods of momentous political change such as the rise of the Khmer Rouge in Cambodia and the fall of Saigon. He was awarded the Geoffrey Faber Memorial Prize following the publication of *Children in Exile: Poems, 1968-84* and from 1994-1999 served as Professor of Poetry at Oxford University.

April 26

• *George Herbert was installed as rector of the parish of Fuggleston-cum-Bemerton in Wiltshire April 26th 1630*
• *First trial of Oscar Wilde opened April 26th 1895*
• *A valedictory to Rupert Brooke written by Churchill appeared in the Times, April 26th 1915: "[T]his life has closed at the moment when it seemed to have reached its springtime"*

I rose – because He sank

I rose – because He sank –
I thought it would be opposite –
But when his power dropped –
My Soul grew straight.

I cheered my fainting Prince –
I sang firm – even – Chants –
I helped his Film – with Hymn –

And when the Dews drew off
That held his Forehead stiff -
I met him –
Balm to Balm –

I told him Best – must pass
Through this low Arch of Flesh –
No Casque so brave
It spurn the Grave –

I told him Worlds I knew
Where Emperors grew –
Who recollected us
If we were true –

And so with Thews of Hymn –
And Sinew from within –
And ways I knew not that I knew – till then –
I lifted Him –

Emily Dickinson
(December 10th 1830 – May 15th 1886)

Thomas Wentworth Higginson received a second letter from Emily Dickinson on this day in 1862. She thanked him for his "surgery" of her poems, claiming it "was not so painful as I supposed." With characteristic obliquity, Dickinson told Higginson of an unknown "terror" she had suffered since September: "I could tell to none – and so I sing, as the Boy does by the Burying Ground – because I am afraid ... ." But she also gave a full account of her life: "You ask of my Companions Hills [sic] – Sir – and the Sundown – and a Dog – large as myself, that my Father bought me – They are better than Beings because they know – but do not tell – and the noise in the Pool, at Noon – excels my Piano ... I have a Brother and Sister – My Mother does not care for thought – and Father, too busy with his Briefs – to notice what we do – He buys me many books, but begs me not to read them – because he fears they joggle the Mind. They are religious – except me – and address an Eclipse, every morning – whom they call their 'Father'."

- *Milton sold* Paradise Lost *to the publisher Samuel Simmons for £10, April 27th 1667*
- *Ralph Waldo Emerson died April 27th 1882*
- *Cecil Day Lewis born in Ireland April 27th 1904*
- *Edwin Morgan born in Glasgow April 27th 1920*
- *American alcoholic poet Hart Crane committed suicide by jumping from a ship bound for Mexico, April 27th 1932*

In Glasgow

In my smoochy corner
take me on a cloud
I'll wrap you round
and lay you down
in smoky tinfoil
rings and records
sheets of whisky
and the moon all right
old pal all right
the moon all night

Mercy for the rainy
tyres and the violet
thunder that bring you
shambling and shy
from chains of Easterhouse
plains of lights
make your delight
in my nest my spell
my arms and my shell
my barn my bell

I've combed your hair
and washed your feet
and made you turn
like a dark eel
in my white bed
till morning lights
a silent cigarette
throw on your shirt
I lie staring yet
forget forget

Edwin Morgan
(April 27th 1920 –)

'In Glasgow' was published in *From Glasgow to Saturn* in 1973. Edwin Muir served as Glasgow's first Poet Laureate from 1999 to 2002 and was awarded the Queen's Gold Medal for Poetry in 2000.

April 28

• English poet and translator Charles Cotton born at Beresford, Staffordshire, April 28th 1630
• Paul Valéry's masterpiece La Jeune Parque was published April 28th 1917, after a silence of 20 years

Felix Randal

Felix Randal the farrier°, O is he dead then? my duty all ended,   *blacksmith*
Who have watched his mould of man, big-boned and hardy-handsome
Pining, pining, till time when reason rambled in it, and some
Fatal four disorders, fleshed there, all contended?

Sickness broke him. Impatient, he cursed at first, but mended
Being anointed and all; though a heavenlier heart began some
Months earlier, since I had our sweet reprieve and ransom
Tendered to him. Ah well, God rest him all road ever he offended!

This seeing the sick endears them to us, us too it endears.
My tongue had taught thee comfort, touch had quenched thy tears,
Thy tears that touched my heart, child, Felix, poor Felix Randal;

How far from then forethought of, all thy more boisterous years,
When thou at the random grim forge, powerful amidst peers,
Didst fettle for the great grey drayhorse his bright and battering sandal!

Gerard Manley Hopkins
(July 28th 1844 – June 8th 1889)

'Felix Randal' anticipates Hopkins' last sequence, the 'Terrible Sonnets'. It was written on this day in 1880, when Hopkins was working as a priest in the then poor industrial city of Liverpool. After his ordination, the works of Hopkins began to focus on "inscaping the heart", the expression used to render the wide range of responses to God that he observed among those for whom he cared; he would write of the 'heart fine' of a cheery beggar ('A Cheery Beggar', 1879), or the 'heavenlier heart' of Felix Randal.

- *Poet Alison Waley, mistress, muse and eventual wife of the poet Arthur Waley, born April 29th 1901*
- *Greek poet Constantine Cavafy, whose poetry is filled wih sexual longing, born April 29th 1863 and died in Alexandria, Egypt, on this day in 1933*
- *On April 29th 1940, the* Irish Independent *claimed James Joyce had "fouled the nest which was his native city"*

The God Abandons Antony

At midnight, when suddenly you hear
an invisible procession going by
with exquisite music, voices,
don't mourn your luck that's failing now,
work gone wrong, your plans
all proving deceptive – don't mourn them uselessly:
As one long prepared, and full of courage,
say goodbye to her, to Alexandria who is leaving.
Above all, don't fool yourself, don't say
it was a dream, your ears deceived you:
don't degrade yourself with empty hopes like these.
As one long prepared, and full of courage,
as is right for you who were given this kind of city,
go firmly to the window
and listen with deep emotion,
but not with whining, the pleas of a coward;
listen – your final pleasure – to the voices,
to the exquisite music of that strange procession,
and say goodbye to her, to the Alexandria you are losing.

C. P. Cavafy
(April 29th 1863 – April 29th 1933)

translated by Edmund Keeley and Philip Sherrard

Constantine Cavafy was one of the great poets of the 20th century, but was little known until after his death. He worked for thirty years in the Irrigation Service of the Ministry of Public Works, retiring with jubilation in 1922: "I am freed of that despised thing." He lived with his mother up until her death, in seclusion from the literary world, and wrote prolifically. Cavafy published very little, however; he issued occasional pamphlets which he circulated to a select readership of friends and family but his life's work was an increasingly unwieldy folder of poems, all meticulously catalogued and corrected over the years.

Cavafy spent almost his entire life in Alexandria; the city became a central poetic metaphor in his writings, an image of the Sensual City. 'The God Abandons Antony' was written in 1911, the year which marks the birth of his mature poetic voice (he designated the period up to 1911 as 'pre-Cavafy'). The source of the poem is a passage in Plutarch, but Cavafy supplanted Dionysus with Alexandria as the god which the mortal Antony is destined to lose in the hour of defeat.

April 30

• John Crowe Ransom born in Tennessee April 30th 1888
• A. E. Housman, melancholic poet and Latin professor, died April 30th 1936
• Poet and translator Tony Harrison born the son of a baker in Leeds April 30th 1937

The Icing Hand

That they lasted only till the next high tide
bothered me, not him whose labour was to make
sugar lattices demolished when the bride,
with help from her groom's hot hand, first cut the cake.

His icing hand, gritty with sandgrains, guides
my pen when I try shaping memories of him
and his eyes scan with mine those rising tides
neither father nor his son could hope to swim.

His eyes stayed dry while I, the kid, would weep
to watch the castle that had taken us all day
to build and deck decay, one wave-surge sweep
our winkle-stuccoed edifice away.

Remembrance like ice cake crumbs in the throat,
remembrance like windblown Blackpool brine
overfills the poem's shallow moat
and first, ebbing, salts, then, flowing, floods this line.

Tony Harrison
(April 30th 1937 –)

Tony Harrison writes: "This poem both remembers and mourns my father and also celebrates his creativity, his skill at icing wedding cakes and other iced confectionery, and his philosophical attitude to their immediate destruction. My hand that writes the poem about my father's icing hand, is also 'icing' as I grow older and stand on the shore of my death. The main thing is to remember and make poems in the face of the rising tides and not fret that they will be engulfed or swept away."

Tony Harrison writes poetry for the page, the stage and the screen. He has written and directed plays for the National Theatre and films for Channel 4.

- *John Dryden, Poet Laureate and dramatist, died May 1st 1700*
- *E. E. Cummings married his second wife, Anne Barton,*
  May 1st 1929
- *Osip Mandelstam was arrested a second time by the Cheka and*
  sent to a concentration camp, May 1st 1938
- *Paul Celan's body found in the River Seine May 1st 1970*
- *Novelist and poet Sylvia Townsend Warner died May 1st 1978*

since feeling is first

since feeling is first
who pays any attention
to the syntax of things
will never wholly kiss you;

wholly to be a fool
while Spring is in the world

my blood approves,
and kisses are a far better fate
than wisdom
lady i swear by all flowers.   Don't cry
—the best gesture of my brain is less than
your eyelids' flutter which says

we are for each other:then
laugh,leaning back in my arms
for life's not a paragraph

And death i think is no parenthesis

E. E. Cummings
(October 14th 1894 – September 3rd 1962)

Cummings married his second wife, Anne Barton, on this day in 1929. Another beautiful divorcee, Barton was vivacious, party-loving and, at times, cruel. Their strained marriage lasted only two years and its failure had a profound impact on Cummings' personality. Yet, his emotional resilience and ultimate hopefulness is evident in the notes he wrote during his grief: "it suddenly occurs to me that this very experience was the most fortunate of my life: then (& only then) does the curse wonderfully become a blessing, the disappearance an emergence, the agonizing departure an ecstatic arrival".

Cummings' recovery was assisted by Marion Morehouse, an actress and model of immense beauty, whom he met in the summer of 1932. Their friendship blossomed into love and became the basis for a richly fulfilling relationship that lasted the rest of Cummings' life.

May 2

• *Jean Jules Verdenal, to whom Eliot dedicated 'Prufrock', died May 2nd 1915 during the Gallipoli Campaign, having "performed his duties with courage and devotion"*
• *Poet Ruth Fainlight born in New York May 2nd 1931*
• *Claude McKay, Jamaican-born poet, novelist and political activist, who was influential in the Negritude Movement, died destitute in Chicago May 2nd 1948*

You're

Clownlike, happiest on your hands,
Feet to the stars, and moon-skulled,
Gilled like a fish. A common-sense
Thumbs-down on the dodo's mode.
Wrapped up in yourself like a spool,
Trawling your dark as owls do.
Mute as a turnip from the Fourth
Of July to All Fools' Day,
O high-riser, my little loaf.

Vague as fog and looked for like mail.
Farther off than Australia.
Bent-backed Atlas, our traveled prawn.
Snug as a bud and at home
Like a sprat in a pickle jug.
A creel of eels, all ripples.
Jumpy as a Mexican bean.
Right, like a well-done sum.
A clean slate, with your own face on.

Sylvia Plath
(October 27th 1932 – February 11th 1963)

In February 1958 Sylvia Plath wrote in her journal: "After this book-year, after next-Europe-year, a baby-year? Four years of marriage childless is enough for us? Yes, I think I shall have guts by then ... I will write like mad for 2 years – & be writing when Gerald 2nd or Warren 2nd is born, what to call the girl? O dreamer." Her plans were realised: back in England, in February 1960, a heavily pregnant Plath signed a contract with the British publisher Heinemann for the publication of her first book, *The Colossus and Other Poems*. On April 1st Frieda Rebecca Hughes was born, two-and-a-half months short of Plath and Hughes' fourth wedding anniversary.

'You're', one of Plath's most unequivocally positive poems, was written that May.

- *Byron proudly swam the Hellespont on May 3rd 1810, and alluded to the feat in his long poem* Don Juan
- *Thomas Hood, poet and journalist, died May 3rd 1845*
- *(Éleanore) May Sarton born in Belgium May 3rd 1912*
- *After performing the funeral service for a fellow soldier, John McCrae wrote 'In Flanders Fields' May 3rd 1915*
- *Yehuda Amichai born in Germany May 3rd 1924*

Death

It is not death, that sometime in a sigh
This eloquent breath shall take its speechless flight;
That sometime these bright stars, that now reply
In sunlight to the sun, shall set in night;
That this warm conscious flesh shall perish quite,
And all life's ruddy springs forget to flow;
That thoughts shall cease, and the immortal sprite
Be lapp'd in alien clay and laid below;
It is not death to know this – but to know
That pious thoughts, which visit at new graves
In tender pilgrimage, will cease to go
So duly and so oft – and when grass waves
Over the pass'd-away, there may be then
No resurrection in the minds of men.

Thomas Hood
(May 23rd 1799 – May 3rd 1845)

Thomas Hood was born the son of a London bookseller and trained as an engraver before editing and contributing to various well-known periodicals of his time. Despite winning considerable fame and success for his humorous-macabre writings, and grim ballads such as 'The Song of the Shirt' (1843) which compassionately commented on the social ills of his day, Hood repeatedly fell out with his publishers and experienced almost constant financial strain. This was exacerbated by lifelong heart problems. Edgar Allan Poe once said of him: "his peculiar genius was the result of vivid *Fancy* impelled by Hypochondriasis".

Hood was no stranger to death, losing first his father and brother at age 12, then his mother, child and sister, all by the age of 32. From late 1844 he was chronically ill but continued to write from his sickbed. His financial troubles were finally alleviated when his wife was awarded a Civil List pension, but Hood did not live to reap the benfits, dying a few months later.

May 4

• Irish poet, translator and anthologist Thomas Kinsella, born in Dublin May 4th 1928
• Poet and writer, Sir Osbert Sitwell, sister of Edith, died May 4th 1969

The Transmutation

That all should change to ghost and glance and gleam,
And so transmuted stand beyond all change,
And we be poised between the unmoving dream
And the sole moving moment—this is strange

Past all contrivance, word, or image, or sound,
Or silence, to express, that we who fall
Through time's long ruin should weave this phantom ground
And in its ghostly borders gather all.

There incorruptible the child plays still,
The lover waits beside the trysting tree,
The good hour spans its heaven, and the ill,
Rapt in their silent immortality,

As in commemoration of a day
That having been can never pass away.

Edwin Muir
(May 15th 1887 – January 3rd 1959)

In her memoirs, *Belonging*, Edwin Muir's wife Willa (née Anderson) remembers the first time they met: "He led me out for a waltz. The floor was good and our steps matched so well that we floated rather than danced round the hall ... As the evening wore on ... we became more and more wordless. I think we both fell into a trance."

In 1950 Edwin Muir declared 'Transmutation' to be "among the Sonnets I like best".

- On May 5th 1846, Elizabeth Barrett wrote to Browning to say
  "I have been drawn back into life by your means, and for you"
- Gerard Manley Hopkins wrote in his diary, May 5th 1868:
  "Cold. Resolved to be religious"
- Hungarian poet Miklos Radnóti born May 5th 1909

The Sloth

In moving slow he has no Peer.
You ask him something in his Ear,
He thinks about it for a Year;

And then, before he says a Word
There, upside down (unlike a Bird),
He will assume that you have Heard –

A most Ex-as-per-at-ing Lug.
But should you call his manner Smug,
He'll sigh and give his Branch a Hug;

Then off again to Sleep he goes,
Still swaying gently by his Toes,
And you just know he knows he knows.

Theodore Roethke
(May 25th 1908 – August 1st 1963)

Though he is more widely acknowledged for the poetry which emerged from his family life and inner turmoil, Roethke wrote two light-hearted collections for children, *I am! Says the lamb* and *Party at the Zoo*. Both of these volumes were published towards the end of his life in the early 1960s. These included nursery rhymes, limericks and many animal poems, including other classroom favourites such as 'The Donkey', 'The Hippo' and 'The Lizard'.

May 6

• *Rabindranath Tagore born into a large and distinguished Bengali family in Calcutta May 6th 1861*
• *Douglas Stewart, poet, playwright and critic, born in Eltham, New Zealand, May 6th 1913*
• *Randall Jarrell, poet and critic, born May 6th 1914*
• *Poet Erich Fried born in Vienna May 6th 1921*
• *Lord Byron was finally honoured with a plaque in the Poets' Corner of Westminster Abbey May 6th 1969*

From Joy's Loveliest Ocean

From joy's loveliest ocean
    there's a flood springing.
Embark all, and set to –
    to the oar your strength bringing.
        No matter its burden,
        our boat sorrow-laden
        (if death comes, so let it)
           moves through the waves winging.
        From joy's loveliest ocean
        there's a flood springing.

Who cries from behind us
    of doubt or of danger?
Who harps on their fear now,
    where fear is no stranger?
        What curse, or stars' showing
        has frowned on our going?
        Hoist a sail to the wind now
           and we'll move on singing.
        From joy's loveliest ocean
        there's a flood springing.

Rabindranath Tagore
(May 6th 1861 – August 7th 1941)

translated by Joe Winter

This is Song 9 from Tagore's *Gitanjali* (*Song Offerings*), a collection first published in England in 1912, with Tagore's own English translations. In his introduction to this first limited edition, W. B. Yeats wrote: "I have carried the manuscript of these translations about with me for days ... reading it in railway trains, or on top of the omnibuses and in restaurants, and I have often had to close it lest some stranger would see how much it moved me. These lyrics – which are in the original, my Indian friends tell me, full of subtlety and rhythm, of untranslatable delicacies of colour, of metrical invention – display in their thought a world I have dreamed of all my life long." Tagore himself later said that his poems came to him like wild swans "with a rush of sound and a flutter of wings".

• *Robert Browning born in London May 7th 1812*
• *American poet and adviser to the US president during the Second*
  World War, Archibald MacLeish born May 7th 1892
• *Monica Jones, the lecturer who had a long friendship and love*
  affair with Philip Larkin, born May 7th 1922
• *Jenny Joseph, whose poem 'Warning' was voted the nation's*
  favourite, born in Birmingham May 7th 1932

May 7

Never the Time and the Place

Never the time and the place
  And the loved one all together!
This path—how soft to pace!
  This May—what magic weather!
Where is the loved one's face?
In a dream that loved one's face meets mine,
  But the house is narrow, the place is bleak
Where, outside, rain and wind combine
  With a furtive ear, if I strive to speak,
  With hostile eye at my flushing cheek,
With a malice that marks each word, each sign!
O enemy sly and serpentine,
  Uncoil thee from the waking man!
    Do I hold the Past
    Thus firm and fast
    Yet doubt if the Future hold I can?
This path so soft to pace shall lead
Thro' the magic of May to herself indeed!
Or narrow if needs the house must be,
Outside are the storms and strangers: we—
Oh, close, safe, warm sleep I and she,
  —I and she!

Robert Browning
(May 7th 1812 – December 12th 1889)

A comet blazed over England the day Robert Browning was born. It is said that he spoke verse whilst still a very small child, walking around the dining room table, supporting himself with his hands. He resolved to become a poet at 14, a decision supported by his father who financed his first three collections.

For much of his life, Browning's achievements were eclipsed by those of his wife. Elizabeth Barrett Browning was advocated as Wordsworth's successor to the Poet Laureateship, and her verse novel, *Aurora Leigh,* proved a bestseller; his own work, meanwhile, garnered only moderate praise. Although delighted by her success, Browning seemed at points close to abandoning his own writing altogether, much to Barrett Browning's chagrin. He was, in fact, more productive after her death, when he wrote two highly acclaimed collections and seemed to recover some of his earlier popularity.

Browning composed this poem in May 1882, just after his 70th birthday. Elizabeth Barrett Browning had died in 1861.

May 8

• Edmund Wilson, poet, author and critic, born in New Jersey
  May 8th 1895
• American Zen primitivist poet, and Pulitzer Prize-winner,
  Gary Snyder born May 8th 1930

Badly-Chosen Lover

Criminal, you took a great piece of my life,
And you took it under false pretences,
That piece of time
– In the clear muscles of my brain
I have the lens and jug of it!
Books, thoughts, meals, days, and houses,
Half Europe, spent like a coarse banknote,
You took it – leaving mud and cabbage stumps.

And, Criminal, I damn you for it (very softly).
My spirit broke her fast on you. And, Turk,
You fed her with the breath of your neck
– In my brain's clear retina
I have the stolen love-behaviour.
Your heart, greedy and tepid, brothel-meat,
Gulped it, like a flunkey with erotica.
And very softly, Criminal, I *damn* you for it.

Rosemary Tonks
(1932 –)

Rosemary Tonks is something of an enigma. She first published a children's book at the age of 16, after being expelled from boarding school. Married at 19, she and her husband went to live in Karachi where she began to write poetry in earnest. In the 1960s she published three novels and two poetry collections, Notes on Cafés and Bedrooms and Illiad of Broken Sentences, which were characterised by their lavish use of exclamation and their urban surreality. "My subject is city life," she wrote, "with its sofas, hotel corridors, cinemas, underworlds, cardboard suitcases, self-willed buses, banknotes, soapy bathrooms, newspaper-filled parks; and its anguish, its enraged excitement, its great lonely joys."
Since her conversion to evangelical Christianity in the early 1970s, Tonks has all but disappeared.

- *Poet, priest and peace activist Daniel Berrigan, born in Minnesota May 9th 1921*
- *Pulitzer Prize-winning poet Charles Simic born in war-torn Belgrade May 9th 1938*
- *Jorie Graham born in New York May 9th 1951*

From The Rape of Lucrece
Lines 135–154

Those that much covet are with gain so fond
For what they have not, that which they possess
They scatter and unloose it from their bond,
And so, by hoping more, they have but less;
Or, gaining more, the profit of excess
     Is but to surfeit, and such griefs sustain
     That they prove bankrupt in this poor-rich gain.

The aim of all is but to nurse the life
With honour, wealth, and ease in waning age;
And in this aim there is such thwarting strife
That one for all, or all for one we gage:
As life for honour in fell battle's rage;
     Honour for wealth; and oft that wealth doth cost
     The death of all, and all together lost.

So that in venturing ill we leave to be
The things we are for that which we expect;
And this ambitious foul infirmity,
In having much, torments us with defect
Of that we have; so then we do neglect
     The thing we have, and, all for want of wit,
     Make something nothing by augmenting it.

William Shakespeare
(April 23rd 1564 – April 23rd 1616)

The Rape of Lucrece was entered into the Stationers' Register on this day in 1594. It was dedicated to Henry Wriothesly, the Earl of Southampton, with the following words: "The love I dedicate to your lordship is without end; whereof this pamphlet, without beginning, is but a superfluous moiety. The warrant I have of your honourable disposition, not the worth of my untutored lines, makes it assured of acceptance. What I have done is yours; what I have to do is yours; being part in all I have, devoted yours. Were my worth greater, my duty would show greater; meantime, as it is, it is bound to your lordship, to whom I wish long life, still lengthened by all happiness."

• German Expressionist Fritz Unruh, dramatist, poet and novelist, born in Koblenz May 10th 1885
• American Imagist poet Amy Lowell died May 10th 1925
• African-American jazz poet Jayne Cortez born in Arizona May 10th 1936
• Alison Waley, children's writer and poet, died May 10th 2001

From A Shropshire Lad
II

Loveliest of trees, the cherry now
Is hung with bloom along the bough,
And stands about the woodland ride
Wearing white for Eastertide.

Now, of my threescore years and ten,
Twenty will not come again,
And take from seventy springs a score,
It only leaves me fifty more.

And since to look at things in bloom
Fifty springs are little room,
About the woodlands I will go
To see the cherry hung with snow.

A. E. Housman
(March 26th 1859 – April 30th 1936)

Housman's diaries have never been published, but his brother Lawrence has given some insight into the main preoccupations of his 1888-1890 diary. This, he claims, covers two areas of interest, namely "the variety of the seasons – mainly spring and autumn – the weather, and the dates at which flowers came into bloom"; and his tireless and unrequited love for Moses Jackson.

• *Jean Jules Verdenal born in the French Pyrenees May 11th 1890*
• *Edmund Wilson wrote to Dos Passos, May 11th 1933: "I heard*
  T. S. Eliot read his poems the other night ... He is an actor and
  really put on a better show than Shaw!'"

May 11

From The Love Song of J. Alfred Prufrock

Let us go then, you and I,
When the evening is spread out against the sky
Like a patient etherised upon a table;
Let us go, through certain half-deserted streets,
The muttering retreats
Of restless nights in one-night cheap hotels
And sawdust restaurants with oyster-shells:
Streets that follow like a tedious argument
Of insidious intent
To lead you to an overwhelming question . . .
Oh, do not ask, 'What is it?'
Let us go and make our visit.
.....

And indeed there will be time
To wonder, 'Do I dare?' and, 'Do I dare?'
Time to turn back and descend the stair,
With a bald spot in the middle of my hair—
[They will say: 'How his hair is growing thin!']
My morning coat, my collar mounting firmly to the chin,
My necktie rich and modest, but asserted by a simple pin—
[They will say: 'But how his arms and legs are thin!']
Do I dare
Disturb the universe?
In a minute there is time
For decisions and revisions which a minute will reverse.
.....

No! I am not Prince Hamlet, nor was meant to be;
Am an attendant lord, one that will do
To swell a progress, start a scene or two,
Advise the prince; no doubt, an easy tool,
Deferential, glad to be of use,
Politic, cautious, and meticulous;
Full of high sentence, but a bit obtuse;
At times, indeed, almost ridiculous—
Almost, at times, the Fool.

T. S. Eliot
(September 26th 1888 – January 4th 1965)

Eliot met Jean Jules Verdenal, to whom 'Prufrock' is dedicated, in Paris in 1910. They became close friends, but did not meet again after Eliot's return to America. Verdenal died in the Dardanelles "while dressing a wounded man on the field of battle" in 1915, a few days short of his 25th birthday.

May 12

• *Nonsense poet Edward Lear born May 12th 1812*
• *Dante Gabriel Rossetti born May 12th 1828*
• *T. S. Eliot's* Poems *first published May 12th 1919*
• *Poet Laureate John Masefield died May 12th 1967*
• *Poet and founder of Objectivist Poetics, Louis Zukofsky,
  died in Port Jefferson, New York, May 12th 1978*

Sudden Light

I have been here before,
    But when or how I cannot tell:
I know the grass beyond the door,
    The sweet keen smell,
The sighing sound, the lights around the shore.

You have been mine before, –
    How long ago I may not know:
But just when at that swallow's soar
    Your neck turned so,
Some veil did fall, – I knew it all of yore.

Has this been thus before?
    And shall not thus time's eddying flight
Still with our lives our love restore
    In death's despite,
And day and night yield one delight once more?

Dante Gabriel Rossetti
(May 12th 1828 – April 9th 1882)

Painter, designer, writer and translator, Dante Gabriel Rossetti was, according to John Ruskin, the most important and original artistic force in Britain in the second half of the 19th century. He was a leading member of the Pre-Raphaelite Brotherhood along with William Morris and Edward Burne-Jones whom he met at Oxford.
'Sudden Light' deals with one of his most deeply held beliefs: that true lovers occupy an eternal space which defines their relationship, a fact which is registered by "déjà vu experiences".

- *Poet and writer Earle Birney born in Canada May 13th 1904*
- *Osip Mandelstam arrested by Cheka because of a satirical anti-Stalin poem May 13th 1934*
- *Poet A. S. J. Tessimond died May 13th 1962*
- *Scottish poet Kathleen Jamie born May 13th 1962*
- *A memorial service was held in Westminster Abbey for the late Poet Laureate Ted Hughes, May 13th 1999*

Skeins o Geese

Skeins o geese write a word
across the sky. A word
struck lik a gong
afore I wis born.
The sky moves like cattle, lowin.

I'm as empty as stane, as fields
ploo'd but not sown, naked
an blin as a stane. Blin
tae the word, blin
tae a' soon but geese ca'ing.

Wire twists lik archaic script
roon a gate. The barbs
sign tae the wind as though
it was deef. The word whustles
ower high for ma senses. Awa.

No lik the past which lies
strewn aroun. Nor sudden death.
No like a lover we'll ken
an connect wi forever.
The hem of its goin drags across the sky.

Whit dae birds write on the dusk?
A word niver spoken or read.
The skeins turn hame,
on the wind's dumb moan, a soun,
maybe human, bereft.

Kathleen Jamie
(May 13th 1962 –)

Kathleen Jamie writes: " 'Skeins o Geese' was written at a difficult time in my life. I've always loved the sight, and sound, of the migrating geese. The poem was written first in standard English, and it took me a while to understand that was what was wrong with it. The wild geese didn't suit 'proper' language. This was my first use of any sort of Scots."

Jamie was born in Renfrewshire in Scotland. She received an Eric Gregory award when she was just 18 and has since published four collections of poetry, including the highly acclaimed *The Queen of Sheba* (1994) and *Jizzen* (1999). Her selected poems, *Mr and Mrs Scotland are Dead: Poems 1980–1994*, was published by Bloodaxe Books in 2002. She lives in Fife and teaches creative writing at St Andrews University.

May 14

- *Tennyson's two-volume* Poems *published May 14th 1842*
- *Canadian lyric poet Robert Finch born in Freeport, New York, May 14th 1900*
- *After meeting T. S. Eliot, Lytton Strachey described the poet as "rather ill and rather American ... But by no means to be sniffed at", May 14th 1919*
- *Poet and outspoken critic of American poetry Karl Shapiro died May 14th 2000*

Thankyou Note

for the unbidden swish of morning curtains
you opened wide – letting sleep-baiting shafts
of sunlight enter to lie down by my side;
for adagio afternoons when you did the punting
(my toiling eyes researched the shifting miles of sky);
for back-garden evenings when you chopped the wood
and I, incomparably, did the grunting;
(a man too good for this world of snarling
is no good for his wife – truth's the safest lie);

for applauding my poetry, O most perceptive spouse;
for the improbable and lunatic, my darling;
for amorous amnesties after rancorous rows
like the sweet-nothing whisperings of a leafy park
after the blatant noise of a city street
(exit booming cannons, enter peaceful ploughs);
for kindnesses the blind side of my night-moods;
for lamps you brought in to devour the dark.

Dannie Abse
(September 22nd 1923 –)

Dannie Abse writes: "The years have proved that the best and most decisive thing I have ever done was to choose Joan Mercer (as she was known then) to be my wife. So it's hardly surprising that on the evening road I would write a thankyou note addressed to her. I do hope the poem is less soppy than the above confession."

Abse is a doctor and poet. He has written 15 books of poetry and his latest work is his autobiography, *Goodbye, Twentieth Century*.

- *Emily Dickinson died of nephritis May 15th 1886*
- *Scottish poet Edwin Muir born in Deerness May 15th 1887*
- *Alexis Kagame, Rwandan poet and Roman Catholic Priest, born May 15th 1912*
- *On May 15th 1944, Anna Akhmatova returned to Moscow from exile in Uzbekistan, delighted to be home and engaged to be married*

Exultation is the going

Exultation is the going
Of an inland soul to sea,
Past the houses – past the headlands –
Into deep Eternity –

Bred as we, among the mountains,
Can the sailor understand
The divine intoxication
Of the first league out from land?

Emily Dickinson
(December 10th 1830 – May 15th 1886)

Austin Dickinson, Emily's brother, wrote of her death in his diary: "The day was awful. She ceased to breathe that terrible breathing just before the whistles sounded for six."

May 16

- *François Marie Arouet (Voltaire) imprisoned for the first time in the Bastille for writing subversive satire, May 16th 1717*
- *Edgar Allan Poe married his 13-year-old tubercular cousin, Virginia Clemm, May 16th 1836*
- *Adrienne Rich born in Baltimore May 16th 1929*
- *James Agee, American poet, novelist, and influential film critic of the 1930s and '40s, died in New York May 16th 1955*

Song

You're wondering if I'm lonely:
OK then, yes, I'm lonely
as a plane rides lonely and level
on its radio beam, aiming
across the Rockies
for the blue-strung aisles
of an airfield on the ocean.

You want to ask, am I lonely?
Well, of course, lonely
as a woman driving across country
day after day, leaving behind
mile after mile
little towns she might have stopped
and lived and died in, lonely

If I'm lonely
it must be the loneliness
of waking first, of breathing
dawn's first cold breath on the city
of being the one awake
in a house wrapped in sleep

If I'm lonely
it's with the rowboat ice-fast on the shore
in the last red light of the year
that knows what it is, that knows it's neither
ice nor mud nor winter light
but wood, with a gift for burning

Adrienne Rich
(May 16th 1929 –)

In her introduction to the anthology, *Best American Poetry* (1996), Rich writes that she wants "poems good enough to eat, to crunch between the teeth, to feel their juices bursting under the tongue, unmicrowavable poems". Of her own poetry she has said: "It always surprises me when people write of my work as if I had taken up the cudgels for the 'underprivileged' or the 'oppressed', as a kind of missionary work. I write from absolute inner necessity ..."

Why Brownlee left

Why Brownlee left, and where he went,
Is a mystery even now.
For if a man should have been content
It was him; two acres of barley,
One of potatoes, four bullocks,
A milker, a slated farmhouse.
He was last seen going out to plough
On a March morning, bright and early.

By noon Brownlee was famous;
They had found all abandoned, with
The last rig unbroken, his pair of black
Horses, like man and wife,
Shifting their weight from foot to
Foot, and gazing into the future.

Paul Muldoon
(June 20th 1951 –)

Paul Muldoon comments: "This poem began with a musing on the name on a bathroom door in the office building in which I worked in Belfast. The maker of the door was a company known as Brownlee. I started thinking about the etymology of the word. It summoned up a ploughed field, and I could see in it a plough, two horses, but no ploughman."

Paul Muldoon was born in Country Armagh, Northern Ireland, in 1951. He graduated from Queen's University Belfast, where Seamus Heaney was his tutor, and his debut collection, *New Weather*, was published by Faber to considerable acclaim when he was just 21. His latest collection is *Moy Sand and Gravel*. Muldoon moved to the United States in 1987 and is currently Howard Clark Professor of Humanities at Princeton University, where he lives with his wife and two children.

May 18

• Persian poet, mathematician and astronomer Omar Khayyám, born in Naishapur May 18th 1048
• A warrant was issued for the arrest of Christopher Marlowe, accused of atheism, May 18th 1593
• Novelist and poet George Meredith died May 18th 1909

From The Rubáiyát of Omar Khayyám of Naishapur[1]

Here with a Loaf of Bread beneath the Bough,
A Flask of Wine, a Book of Verse—and Thou
   Beside me singing in the Wilderness—
And Wilderness is Paradise enow.

"How sweet is mortal Sovranty!"—think some:
Others—"How blest the Paradise to come!"
   Ah, take the Cash in hand and waive the Rest;
Oh, the brave Music of a *distant* Drum!

Look to the Rose that blows about us—"Lo,
Laughing," she says, "into the World I blow:
   At once the silken Tassel of my Purse
Tear, and its Treasure on the Garden throw."

The Worldly Hope men set their Hearts upon
Turns Ashes—or it prospers; and anon,
   Like Snow upon the Desert's dusty Face
Lighting a little Hour or two—is gone.

Edward Fitzgerald
(March 31st 1809 – June 14th 1883)

Edward Fitzgerald was introduced to Omar Khayyám's poetry by his friend Edward Cowell in May 1857, and set about translating 75 of the quatrains that summer. The first edition of his version of the Rubáiyát was published in March 1859.

Cowell and Fitzgerald always disagreed about the sensuality of the poetry. While Cowell, a linguist, argued that "By Drunkenness is meant Divine Love", Fitzgerald was insistent that Omar, as an "Epicurean", was "too honest of Heart as well as of Head for this": that the worldly pleasures in the poetry were literal and not at all allegorical. By the time Fitzgerald told Cowell, "I take old Omar rather more as my property than yours. ... You see all his beauty, but you don't feel with him the way I do," and started to sign his letters 'Edward FitzOmar', Cowell began to regret ever having introduced his friend to *The Rubáiyát*.

1. Stanzas 11-14 of this 75 stanza poem.

- *Thomas Wyatt, imprisoned in the Tower of London along with five other suspected lovers of Anne Boleyn, watched her execution on May 19th 1536. He was later released and rusticated*
- *Milton (a staunch anti-royalist) went into hiding, fearing for his life, as Charles I entered London, May 19th 1660*
- *Ogden Nash died May 19th 1971*
- *Sir John Betjeman died May 19th 1984*
- *Andrew Motion was appointed 19th Poet Laureate May 19th 1999*

To Whom It May Concern

This poem about ice cream
has nothing to do with government,
with riot, with any political scheme.

It is a poem about ice cream. You see?
About how you might stroll into a shop
and ask: *One Strawberry Split. One Mivvi.*

What did I tell you? No one will die.
No licking tongues will melt like candle wax.
This is a poem about ice cream. Do not cry.

Andrew Motion
(October 26th 1952 –)

Andrew Motion writes: "I wrote 'To Whom It May Concern' late one night a few years ago, without much clue about what I was trying to say. When I look at it now, I see it as an untypical poem for me to have written – in the sense that it is as much (or more) about how poetry works, as it is an example of a poem in action. Specifically, it wants to alert readers to the symbolic value of everyday things, and to register the ways in which big horrors can be suggested by small next-to-nothings."

Andrew Motion is a poet, critic, novelist and acclaimed biographer of Philip Larkin and Keats. Since 1995 he has been Professor of Creative Writing at the University of East Anglia and he is also a Fellow of the Royal Society of Literature. Motion succeeded Ted Hughes to the Laureateship in 1999, a post he will hold for ten years.

May 20

• English poet Thomas Spratt died May 20th 1713
• John Clare died in an asylum May 20th 1864
• W. H. Auden became an American citizen May 20th 1946
• Michèle Roberts born of a French mother and English father May
    20th 1949
• Poet and electroplater Alison Brackenbury born May 20th 1953

Lacrimae rerum

Another leak
in the lavatory roof
drip drip down the lightbulb.
I pissed in the dark, raindrops
smacking my shoulder-blades.

This morning I woke
to fresh wet birdsong
under a cloud of quilt
last night's hot sweetness
still fizzing between my legs.

I was fooled into swallowing spring
jumping up to make tea
and rinse dishes, whistle
a liquid kitchen oratorio.

It's your birthday next week.
This time next year
I think you'll be gone
quietly as this water
slipping over my hands.

After your funeral
we'll return
to your parched house.
We'll try to hold our mother up
like this exhausted roof.

I carry your dying
inside me
as real as milk

as I'll carry on
getting the roof fixed
making love
weeping into the washing-up.

Michèle Roberts
(May 20th 1949 –)

Poet, reviewer and author of ten highly-praised novels, Michèle Roberts has said: "My theory is that inspiration is born of loss. So that if there's an empty space inside you, something can come and fill it."

- *Alexander Pope, whom Lord Byron once described as the "most faultless of Poets, and almost of men", born May 21st 1688*
- *"Scribe-evangelist" poet Christopher Smart died May 21st 1771*
- *Poet Laureate Thomas Warton died in Oxford May 21st 1790*
- *American poet Robert Creeley born May 21st 1926*

The Rain

All night the sound had
come back again,
and again falls
this quiet, persistent rain.

What am I to myself
that must be remembered,
insisted upon,
so often? Is it

that never the ease,
even the hardness,
of rain falling
will have for me

something other than this,
something not so insistent –
am I to be locked in this
final uneasiness.

Love, if you love me,
lie next to me.
Be for me, like rain,
the getting out

of the tiredness, the fatuousness, the semi-
lust of intentional indifference.
Be wet
with a decent happiness.

Robert Creeley
(May 21st 1926 –)

Robert Creeley writes: "I recall we were living then (1959-1961) in a small village in Guatemala, where I was teaching the young children of two coffee plantation owners, together with two of our daughters. The roof of our cement block house was corrugated iron. When it rained in great, heavy bursts, as it often did, the sound was thunderous and also curiously reassuring. So the poem becomes melded with that experience, prompted by it, even permitted by it."

Creeley taught at Black Mountain College in the 1950s and now teaches at Brown University. His art has no impulse to enclose itself in the literary solely, or to move apart from the common terms of the given world. Coming of age in the years of the Second World War, he feels his world has been one insistently involved with the unrelieved consequence of being literally human – the cultish 'existentialism' of his youth grown universal.

May 22

- *Victor Hugo died in Paris May 22nd 1885*
- *Lady Gregory, Irish poet, playwright, and object of Yeats' desire, died May 22 1932*
- *German-Jewish emigré Ernst Toller hanged himself May 22nd 1939*
- *Langston Hughes died in New York May 22nd 1967*
- *Poet Laureate C. Day-Lewis died May 22nd 1972*

I, Too

I, too, sing America.

I am the darker brother.
They send me to eat in the kitchen
When company comes,
But I laugh,
And eat well,
And grow strong.

Tomorrow,
I'll be at the table
When company comes.
Nobody'll dare
Say to me,
"Eat in the kitchen,"
Then.

Besides,
They'll see how beautiful I am
And be ashamed –

I, too, am America.

Langston Hughes
(February 1st 1902 – May 22nd 1967)

Hughes spent much of his life travelling. On one occasion, hoping to return to America from Genoa, both his passport and wallet were stolen. In dismay, he watched as one white sailer after another found passages out while he was left behind. This incident was the inspiration for 'I, Too' (also known as 'Epilogue'), which represents a conscious departure from Walt Whitman's celebrated chant.

Whitman remained for Hughes an important figure, preoccupied as he was with the crucial relationship between American vernacular speech and traditional poetic practices, as well as between the nation's democratic ideals and the mysteries of poetic inspiration. Upon leaving for Africa, Hughes discarded all his books except for *Leaves of Grass*: "I had no intention of throwing that one away", he said.

Hughes' death was caused by prolonged heart and kidney trouble. He never married, nor had any children.

- Guiseppe Parini, Italian prose writer and poet remembered for a series of Horation odes, born in Bosisio, near Milan, May 23nd 1729
- Poet Thomas Hood born in London May 23rd 1799
- Dante Gabriel Rossetti married Lizzie Siddal at St Clement's Church, Hastings, May 23rd 1860

Politics

**In our time the destiny of man presents
its meanings in political terms –
Thomas Mann**

How can I, that girl standing there,
My attention fix
on Roman or on Russian
Or on Spanish politics?
Yet here's a travelled man that knows
What he talks about,
And there's a politician
That has read and thought,
And maybe what they say is true
Of war and war's alarms,
But O that I were young again
And held her in my arms!

*W. B. Yeats
(June 13th 1865 – January 28th 1939)*

Yeats composed this poem on this day in 1938, after a heated debate at Penns in the Rocks. Stalin and Mussolini were in power and the Spanish Civil war was still raging. Many readers have noted that there is no reference to German politics in the poem, despite it being written shortly before the outbreak of the Second World War. Yeats was, of course, perfectly capable of turning his full attention to politics. Pablo Neruda, who organised a writers' conference in Madrid when the city was besieged by the Falangists in 1937, recollected in his memoirs that Yeats, by then too old to travel to the bomb-blasted city, nonetheless "rallied to the defence of the Spanish Republic".

The girl in the poem is Edith Shackleton Head, with whom Yeats had a relationship from April 1937 till his death in 1939.

May 24

• *A young Rimbaud appealed to a reviewer, May 24th 1870: "I feel there is something in me ... that wishes to rise ... Hold out your hand to me"*
• *Joseph Brodsky born in Leningrad May 24th 1940*
• *Michael Donaghy born May 24th 1954*
• *Poet, critic and novelist John Wain, died May 24th 1994*
• *Dorothy Nimmo died May 24th 2001*

The Present

For the present there is just one moon,
though every level pond gives back another.

But the bright disc shining in the black lagoon,
perceived by astrophysicist and lover,

is milliseconds old. And even that light's
seven minutes older than its source.

And the stars we think we see on moonless nights
are long extinguished. And, of course,

this very moment, as you read this line,
is literally gone before you know it.

Forget the here-and-now. We have no time
but this device of wantonness and wit.

Make me this present then: your hand in mine,
And we'll live out our lives in it.

Michael Donaghy
(May 24th 1954 –)

Michael Donaghy writes: "I wrote this post-Einsteinian sonnet partly as a play on the old 'carpe diem' theme. I have a very precise memory of the circumstance of its composition. I was in Rosslare. I'd just missed the ferry and had to wait around for several hours during which time I composed this poem on the back of my ticket. Upon my return I presented it to my partner. 20 years on we're still together, though it seems like no time at all has passed."

Donaghy was born in the Bronx, New York, and moved to Britain in 1985. His most recent collection, *Conjure*, won the Forward Prize; previous collections have won the Whitbread Prize for Poetry and the Geoffrey Faber Memorial Prize. He teaches at City University and Birkbeck College, and is a Fellow of the Royal Society of Literature and the Royal Society for the Arts.

- English poet Elijah Fenton who collaborated with Alexander Pope in a translation of The Odyssey, born in Shelton, Staffordshire, May 25th 1683
- Ralph Waldo Emerson born in Boston May 25th 1803
- Theodore Roethke born in Michigan May 25th 1908
- Raymond Carver born May 25th 1938

From What the Doctor Said

he said are you a religious man do you kneel down
in forest groves and let yourself ask for help
when you come to a waterfall
mist blowing against your face and arms
do you stop and ask for understanding at those moments
I said not yet but I intend to start today

Raymond Carver
(May 25th 1938 – August 2nd 1988)

Raymond Carver was married at 19 and had fathered two children by 20; his early married life was spent drifting in and out of poorly paid jobs. His first book of short stories took 12 years to write, compared to the three months it took him to complete *Cathedral*, largely because Carver had by then adopted "full-time drinking as a serious pursuit". At 39, alcohol had shattered his career, his marriage, and his health; he was hospitalised for acute alcoholism four times between 1976 and 1977.

Carver finally gave up drinking in 1977: "I've had two lives. My second began on June 2nd 1977 when I quit drinking," he said. Carver did not write for almost a year, but felt too grateful for his new life to care much. He met the poet Tess Gallagher and thus began an intensely productive and happy relationship: Carver began to write poetry and Gallagher to write prose. In their ten years together the pair produced 25 books between them, and frequently collaborated on projects up until Carver's early death from lung cancer in 1988.

- On May 26th 1845, Elizabeth Barrett Browning wrote from Florence: "At Pisa we say 'How beautiful' – here we say nothing – it is enough if we can breathe"
- Rilke wrote the first of 100 poems to his beloved Lou Andreas-Salomé May 26th 1897; at her request, he never published them
- Simon Armitage born in Marsden, Yorkshire, May 26th 1963

Kid

Batman, big shot, when you gave the order
to grow up, then let me loose to wander
leeward, freely through the wild blue yonder
as you liked to say, or ditched me, rather,
in the gutter . . . well, I turned the corner.
Now I've scotched that 'he was like a father
to me' rumour, sacked it, blown the cover
on that 'he was like an elder brother'
story, let the cat out on that caper
with the married woman, how you took her
downtown on expenses in the motor.
Holy robin-redbreast-nest-egg-shocker!
Holy roll-me-over-in-the-clover,
I'm not playing ball boy any longer
Batman, now I've doffed that off-the-shoulder
Sherwood-Forest-green and scarlet number
for a pair of jeans and crew-neck jumper;
now I'm taller, harder, stronger, older.
Batman, it makes a marvellous picture:
you without a shadow, stewing over
chicken giblets in the pressure cooker,
next to nothing in the walk-in larder,
punching the palm of your hand all winter,
you baby, now I'm the real boy wonder.

Simon Armitage
(May 26th 1963 –)

Simon Armitage comments: "It gave me great pleasure taking a big, swanky character like Batman and placing him in a little terraced house in West Yorkshire. See how *he* liked it. I suppose the poem is about power dynamics: father/son, employer/employee, funny-guy/straight man, etc. Bravado fuelled by bitterness is the tone of voice I was hoping to catch."

Simon Armitage was born in 1963 in West Yorkshire. He has won numerous prizes for his nine collections of poetry, and is the author of the novel *Little Green Man* and the best-selling prose memoir *All Points North*. He is also a playwright, anthologist and song-lyricist, and has written extensively for television, film and radio. He teaches at the Metropolitan University of Manchester.

• *Suffragette Julia Ward Howe, best known for 'The Battle Hymn of the Republic' (1861) sung to the tune of 'John Brown's Body', born in New York May 27th 1819*

May 27

Ode on Melancholy

No, no, go not to Lethe, neither twist
    Wolf's-bane, tight-rooted, for its poisonous wine:
Nor suffer thy pale forehead to be kissed
    By nightshade, ruby grape of Proserpine;
Make not your rosary of yew-berries,
    Nor let the beetle, nor the death-moth be
      Your mournful Psyche, nor the downy owl
A partner in your sorrow's mysteries;
    For shade to shade will come too drowsily,
      And drown the wakeful anguish of the soul.

But when the melancholy fit shall fall
    Sudden from heaven like a weeping cloud,
That fosters the droop-headed flowers all,
    And hides the green hill in an April shroud;
Then glut thy sorrow on a morning rose,
    Or on the rainbow of the salt sand-wave,
      Or on the wealth of globèd peonies;
Or if thy mistress some rich anger shows,
    Emprison her soft hand, and let her rave,
      And feed deep, deep upon her peerless eyes.

She dwells with Beauty – Beauty that must die;
    And Joy, whose hand is ever at his lips
Bidding adieu; and aching Pleasure nigh,
    Turning to poison while the bee-mouth sips:
Ay, in the very temple of Delight
    Veiled Melancholy has her sovran shrine,
      Though seen of none save him whose strenuous tongue
Can burst Joy's grape against his palate fine;
His soul shall taste the sadness of her might,
      And be among her cloudy trophies hung.

John Keats
(October 31st 1795 – February 23rd 1821)

This poem was written, along with all of Keats' other odes, ('Psyche', 'Grecian Urn', 'Nightingale' and 'Indolence'), in a remarkable burst of creativity in May 1819. His principal source for the poem was Robert Burton's *Anatomy of Melancholy*, a misogynistic book which Keats first read in 1818. The book attacked marriage, and put forward the idea of 'love-madness' as a disease, a concept which Keats took seriously. Indeed, while torn between wanting to be with Fanny Brawne, and wanting to remain free from the "adamantine ... bond of marriage" (Burton's words), Keats at one point stopped eating meat to lessen the "physical torment" of his desire – another of Burton's recommendations.

May 28

- Thomas Moore, Irish poet friend of Byron, born May 28th 1779
- Anne Brontë, whose poems expressed her religious concerns, died in Scarborough May 28th 1849
- South African poet, novelist and dramatist Daniel François Malherbe, born in Cape Colony May 28th 1881

The Glass

To love you in shadow as in the light
is light itself. In subterranean night
you sow the fields with fireflies of delight.

Lanarkshire holds you, under its grim grass.
But I hold what you were, like a bright glass
I carry brimming through the darkening pass.

Edwin Morgan
(April 27th 1920 –)

Edwin Morgan writes: " 'The Glass' is about a much loved person who died in 1978 and was buried on a cold bleak day in a Lanarkshire cemetery. The poem was written about twenty years later and was published in *Virtual and Other Realities* (Carcanet, 1997). Although many poems are immediate, the persistence of memory can be extremely vivid and fruitful; a dead person can be both virtual and real."

Edwin Morgan took his degree at Glasgow University, though his studies were interrupted when he joined the Royal Army Medical Corps in 1940. After graduation he taught at Glasgow University from 1947 until his retirement in 1980. Much of his poetry is grounded in the city, and is characterised by a distinctive openness, inventiveness and an irrepressible energy. He is also a skilled translator from an impressively wide range of languages. Morgan has translated a number of plays into Scots, including his prize-winning version of Racine's *Phèdre*, and has written his own drama, a trilogy about the life of Christ.

- *Dramatist and poet Lope de Vega set out to join the Spanish Armada May 29th 1588*
- *Gilbert Keith Chesterton born in Campden Hill, Kensington, May 29th 1874*
- *Dramatist and poet W. S. Gilbert died while attempting to save a drowning woman, May 29th 1911*
- *Spanish poet Juan Ramón Jiménez died May 29th 1958*

The Donkey

When fishes flew and forests walked
   And figs grew upon thorn,
Some moment when the moon was blood
   Then surely I was born.

With monstrous head and sickening cry
   And ears like errant wings,
The devil's walking parody
   On all four-footed things.

The tattered outlaw of the earth,
   Of ancient crooked will;
Starve, scourge, deride me: I am dumb,
   I keep my secret still.

Fools! For I also had my hour;
   One far fierce hour and sweet:
There was a shout before my ears,
   And palms before my feet.

G. K. Chesterton
(May 29th 1874 – June 14th 1936)

Chesterton was five when his brother was born and was heard to remark, "now I shall always have an audience". He began studying Fine Art at University College London in October 1893, and was fortunate enough to have A. E. Housman as his Latin teacher, and a further personal audience. His first volume of poetry, *The Wild Knight*, emerged a few years later and included 'The Donkey'. Rudyard Kipling, having been sent the book by a friend, responded with the words: "I agree with you that there is any amount of promise in the work – and I think marriage will teach him a good deal too. It will be curious to see how he'll develop in a few years."

May 30

• Christopher Marlowe died May 30th 1593
• Alexander Pope died May 30th 1744[1]
• Alfred Austin, Poet Laureate, born May 30th 1834
• Boris Leonidovich Pasternak, poet, novelist and translator, died May 30th 1960

Ode on Solitude

Happy the man whose wish and care
    A few paternal acres bound,
Content to breathe his native air,
        In his own ground.

Whose herds with milk, whose fields with bread,
    Whose flocks supply him with attire,
Whose trees in summer yield him shade,
        In winter fire.

Blest, who can unconcernedly find
    Hours, days, and years slide soft away,
In health of body, peace of mind,
        Quiet by day.

Sound sleep by night; study and ease,
    Together mixed; sweet recreation;
And innocence, which most does please
        With meditation.

Thus let me live, unseen, unknown;
    Thus unlamented let me die;
Steal from the world, and not a stone
        Tell where I lie.

Alexander Pope
(May 21st 1688 – May 30th 1744)

In 1709 Alexander Pope sent a copy of this poem to Henry Cromwell – "a distant cousin of the Protector, a gay man about town, and something of a pedant" – and said it was written before he was 12 years old. At about that age Pope had been struck by a devastating illness, probably tuberculosis of the spine, leaving him deformed and debilitated. He never grew beyond 1.37m and was subject to violent headaches, which perhaps explains his reputation for irritability and hypersensitivity.

1. Pope was buried at Twickenham Parish Church, beside his mother. In 1761, his friend William Warburton erected a monument on the north wall of the church with the inscription: "to one who would not be buried in Westminster Abbey".

- *Walt Whitman born in West Hills, near Huntington, Long Island, May 31st 1819*
- *French poet St-John Perse born on a coral island off Guadeloupe May 31st 1887*
- *Australian poet Judith Wright born May 31st 1915*

When I Heard the Learn'd Astronomer

When I heard the learn'd astronomer,
When the proofs, the figures, were ranged in columns before me,
When I was shown the charts and diagrams, to add, divide,
    and measure them,
When I sitting heard the astronomer where he lectured with
    much applause in the lecture-room,
How soon unaccountable I became tired and sick,
Till rising and gliding out I wander'd off by myself,
In the mystical moist night-air, and from time to time,
Look'd up in perfect silence at the stars.

Walt Whitman
(May 31st 1819 – March 26th 1892)

Though this poem explicitly criticises science for detracting from simple natural beauty, Whitman was one of the first poets to wholly embrace science in his poetry. He was conversant with the basics of contemporary science, in the fields of astronomy, geology, physics, chemistry and biology, and there are manifold references to specific scientific theories and phenomena in his poetry. An avid reader of popular scientific books and journals, Whitman once wrote: "Hurrah for positive science! Long live exact demonstration!"

In one anonymous self-review, Whitman described 'the poet' as one of "pure American breed, of reckless health, his body perfect, free from taint from top to toe, free forever from headaches and dyspepsia, full-blooded, six feet high, a good feeder, never once using medicine, drinking water only – a swimmer in the river or by the sea-shore."

June 1

• *Publication of Tennyson's* In Memoriam *June 1st 1850*
• *Canadian lyric poet William Wilfred Campbell born June 1st 1861*
• *John Masefield born in Ledbury June 1st 1878*
• *John Drinkwater, poet and playwright, born June 1st 1882*

From In Memoriam A. H. H.
V

I sometimes hold it half a sin
  To put in words the grief I feel:
  For words, like Nature, half reveal
And half conceal the Soul within.

But, for the unquiet heart and brain,
  A use in measured language lies;
  The sad mechanic exercise,
Like dull narcotics, numbing pain.

In words, like weeds, I'll wrap me o'er,
  Like coarsest clothes against the cold;
  But that large grief which these enfold
Is given in outline and no more.

Alfred, Lord Tennyson
(August 6th 1809 – October 6th 1892)

Tennyson's friend Arthur Hallam was engaged to his sister Emily when he died suddenly in Vienna; the death affected both siblings greatly. Tennyson was too upset to attend the funeral and never forgot his closest friend. When Tennyson's wife gave birth to a son, in August 1852, 19 years after the tragic event, they had no hesitation in naming him Hallam.

Though this poem takes Arthur Hallam's funeral as its starting point, and Tennyson's sister Cecilia's marriage as its end, *In Memoriam A. H. H.* is not just a biographical poem. As Tennyson himself wrote to his friend James Knowles: "It is rather the cry of the whole human race than mine. In the poem, altogether private grief swells out into thought of, and hope for, the whole world".

In Memoriam A. H. H. was first published on this day in 1850.

- Thomas Hardy born June 2nd 1840 in Higher Bockhampton, Dorset. He was thought to be a stillbirth until the midwife noticed signs of life
- John Lehmann, poet, writer and publisher, born in Buckinghamshire June 2nd 1907

The Trees

The trees are coming into leaf
Like something almost being said;
The recent buds relax and spread,
Their greenness is a kind of grief.

Is it that they are born again
And we grow old? No, they die too.
Their yearly trick of looking new
Is written down in rings of grain.

Yet still the unresting castles thresh
In fullgrown thickness every May.
Last year is dead, they seem to say,
Begin afresh, afresh, afresh.

Philip Larkin
(August 9th 1922 – December 2nd 1985)

In his manuscript notebook Philip Larkin wrote beneath this poem "Bloody awful tripe." In a piece of autobiographical writing of the 1940s, Larkin concluded: "literary failure is the most shaming and disappointing of failures," adding "I admit sex runs pretty close." Larkin wrote 'The Trees' on this day in 1967.

June 3

• Allen Ginsberg, author of 'Howl', born June 3rd 1926
• Turkish poet Nâzim Hikmet died in Moscow June 3rd 1963
• Poet and social inventor Nicholas Albery died June 3rd 2001

The Truth the Dead Know

For my mother, born March 1902, died March 1959,
and my father, born February 1900, died June 1959

Gone, I say and walk from church,
refusing the stiff procession to the grave,
letting the dead ride alone in the hearse.
It is June. I am tired of being brave.

We drive to the Cape. I cultivate
myself where the sun gutters from the sky,
where the sea swings in like an iron gate
and we touch. In another country people die.

My darling, the wind falls in like stones
from the whitehearted water and when we touch
we enter touch entirely. No one's alone.
Men kill for this, or for as much.

And what of the dead? They lie without shoes
in their stone boats. They are more like stone
than the sea would be if it stopped. They refuse
to be blessed, throat, eye and knucklebone.

Anne Sexton
(November 9th 1928 – October 4th 1974)

Anne Sexton was the third daughter born to Ralph and Mary Gray Staples Harvey in Newton, Massachusetts. Her father was a successful wool salesman and her mother the well-educated only child of adoring parents. Mary was dismissive of Sexton's earliest poetic efforts, and discouraged her from writing for many years. After their deaths, Sexton said of them: "If you tapped my father he fell apart like a jigsaw puzzle. But my mother was solid and that's what I want to be." They died in quick succession, her father dying on this day in 1959.

A year before she committed suicide, Sexton said that "of all my old poems, 'The Truth the Dead Know' and the last two stanzas of 'The Touch' have the most meaning for me to this day".

- On June 4th 1677, the Earl of Rochester was falsely suspected
  of stabbing a cook at a tavern in the Mall where he was dining
- Catherine Wordsworth died June 4th 1812

June 4

To Catherine Wordsworth 1808–1812

Surprised by joy – impatient as the Wind
I turned to share the transport – Oh! with whom
But Thee, deep buried in the silent tomb,
That spot which no vicissitude can find?
Love, faithful love, recalled thee to my mind –
But how could I forget thee? Through what power,
Even for the least division of an hour,
Have I been so beguiled as to be blind,
To my most grievous loss! – That thought's return
Was the worst pang that sorrow ever bore,
Save one, one only, when I stood forlorn,
Knowing my heart's best treasure was no more;
That neither present time, nor years unborn
Could to my sight that heavenly face restore.

William Wordsworth
(April 7th 1770 – April 23rd 1850)

William Wordsworth wrote that this sonnet, published in 1915, "was in fact suggested by my daughter Catherine long after her death". Catherine was his fourth child by his wife, Mary. Despite suffering partial paralysis following an early brain seizure, Catherine was a lively and cheerful child, "the arrantest Mischief that ever lived", according to her mother.

In early June 1812, while William was in London and Mary on her way to visit relatives in Hereford, the Wordsworth children were in the care of their aunts at the family home in Grasmere. Catherine suffered a convulsion in the night and died the following morning. One aunt, who could not bear to look at her Catherine's dead body herself, wrote that "she is beautiful they say as an angel". In her parents' absence, Catherine was buried in Grasmere churchyard on June 8th.

June 5

- *Federico García Lorca born in Granada June 5th 1898*
- *Stephen Crane, author and poet, died June 5th 1900*
- *Irish poet, painter and novelist Christy Brown, born June 5th 1932*

In the Desert
III

In the desert
I saw a creature, naked, bestial,
Who, squatting upon the ground,
Held his heart in his hands,
And ate of it.
I said, 'Is it good, friend?'
'It is bitter – bitter,' he answered;
'But I like it
Because it is bitter,
And because it is my heart.'

Stephen Crane
(November 1st 1871 – June 5th 1900)

Stephen Crane is best known for his novel of the Civil War, *The Red Badge of Courage*, which shot him to fame when it was published in the autumn of 1895. Crane was just 23 and an impoverished newspaper reporter living in New York when he emerged as one of the most innovative American writers of the 1890s. That May he also published a controversial collection of poems, *The Black Riders and Other Lines*, which confounded many critics with its unusual typeface: Crane used capital letters throughout and exceptionally wide margins.

Little is known of the details of Crane's life. He himself admitted: "I cannot help vanishing and disappearing and dissolving. It is my foremost trait." As a war correspondent he covered the Greco-Turkish war before settling in England, where he befriended the writers H. G. Wells, Henry James, and Joseph Conrad and ricocheted between poverty and wild partying. In his last tubercular years, he wrote furiously in an attempt to fend off mounting debts, but died aged 29 in a sanatorium in the Black Forest in Germany.

• Pierre Corneille, author of 'Le Cid', born June 6th 1606
• Russian poet Alexander Pushkin born June 6th 1799
• Maxine Kumin, Pulitzer Prize-winning poet, novelist and
  children's author, born in Philadelphia June 6th 1925

June 6

After Love

Afterwards, the compromise.
Bodies resume their boundaries.

These legs, for instance, mine.
Your arms take you back in.

Spoons of our fingers, lips
admit their ownership.

The bedding yawns, a door
blows aimlessly ajar

and overhead, a plane
singsongs, coming down.

Nothing is changed, except
there was a moment when

the wolf, the mongering wolf
who stands outside the self

lay lightly down, and slept.

Maxine Kumin
(June 6th 1925 –)

Maxine Kumin attended the famous writing group chaired by Robert Lowell which also included
Anne Sexton, Sylvia Plath and C. K. Williams. She describes her own work as "the exploration
of the world around me. I write out of my own experience. For me, my life is a metaphor for my
work."
Her life nearly ended in 1998 when she suffered a hangman's fracture of the neck in a horse-riding
accident. Her account of her recovery is titled *Inside the Halo* (2000).

• *German lyric poet Friedrich Hölderlin died June 7th 1843*
• *Poet Pete Morgan born in Lancashire June 7th 1939*
• *Dorothy Parker, short story writer and poet, died June 7th 1967*

My Enemies Have Sweet Voices

I was in a bar called Paradise
the fiddler from the band
           asked me, 'Why do you stand
here crying?'
           I answered him, 'Musician,
this may come as a surprise –
I was trying to split the difference
when it split before my eyes.'

    My enemies have sweet voices
    their tones are soft and kind
    when I hear my heart rejoices
    and I do not seem to mind

I was playing brag in Bedlam
the doctor wouldn't deal
           asking, 'Why does he kneel
down weeping?'
           I answered him, 'Physician,
I think you would have cried
I was falling back on failure
when the failure stepped aside.'

    My enemies have sweet voices
    their tones are soft and kind
    when I hear my heart rejoices
    and I do not seem to mind

I was blind side to the gutter
when Merlin happened by
           asking, 'Why do you lie
there bleeding?'
           I answered him, 'Magician,
as a matter of a fact
I was jumping to conclusions
when one of them jumped back.'

    My enemies have sweet voices
    their tones are soft and kind
    when I hear my heart rejoices
    and I do not seem to mind

Pete Morgan
(June 7th 1939 –)

Pete Morgan comments: " 'My Enemies Have Sweet Voices' was written after reading the story of how opposing troops had briefly gathered to sing Christmas carols during the First World War. As soon as the celebration was over they returned to their trenches to carry on killing each other. In my case the 'enemies' referred to were more intellectual temptations than physical opponents."

• Gerard Manley Hopkins, Jesuit priest and poet, died of typhoid
fever in Dublin June 8th 1889, with the words "I am so
happy, I am so happy"
• Welsh poet Gillian Clarke born in Cardiff June 8th 1937

Carrion Comfort

Not, I'll not, carrion comfort, Despair, not feast on thee;
Not untwist – slack they may be – these last strands of man
In me ór, most weary, cry *I can no more*. I can;
Can something, hope, wish day come, not choose not to be.
But ah, but O thou terrible, why wouldst thou rude on me
Thy wring-world right foot rock? lay a lionlimb against me? scan
With darksome devouring eyes my bruisèd bones? and fan,
O in turns of tempest, me heaped there; me frantic to avoid thee and flee?

  Why? That my chaff might fly; my grain lie, sheer and clear.
Nay in all that toil, that coil, since (seems) I kissed the rod,
Hand rather, my heart lo! lapped strength, stole joy, would laugh, chéer.
Cheer whom though? the hero whose heaven-handling flung me, fóot tród
Me? or me that fought him? O which one? is it each one? That night, that year
Of now done darkness I wretch lay wrestling with (my God!) my God.

Gerard Manley Hopkins
(July 28th 1844 – June 8th 1889)

'Carrion Comfort' was probably written in 1885, and may be the poem which Hopkins described
as being "written in blood" in a letter to his friend and literary executor Robert Bridges in May
of that year. It is regarded as the first of Hopkins' series of so-called 'terrible sonnets', an epithet
which refers to the inner despair and turmoil which gave rise to them.

June 9

• *John Gillespie Magee Jr, pilot and poet, born in Shanghai June 9th 1922*
• *Keith Douglas killed in action near St Pierre, Normandy, on June 9th 1944, three days after the start of the D-Day invasion*
• *Miguel Angel Asturias, Guatemalan poet and winner of the 1967 Nobel Prize for literature, died in Madrid June 9th 1974*

Simplify me when I'm dead

Remember me when I am dead
and simplify me when I'm dead.

As the processes of earth
strip off the colour and the skin
take the brown hair and blue eye

and leave me simpler than at birth,
when hairless I came howling in
as the moon entered the cold sky.

Of my skeleton perhaps
so stripped, a learned man will say
'He was of such a type and intelligence,' no more.

Thus when in a year collapse
particular memories, you may
deduce, from the long pain I bore

the opinions I held, who was my foe
and what I left, even my appearance
but incidents will be no guide.

Time's wrong-way telescope will show
a minute man ten years hence
and by distance simplified.

Through that lens see if I seem
substance or nothing: of the world
deserving mention or charitable oblivion

not by momentary spleen
or love into decision hurled,
leisurely arrive at an opinion.

Remember me when I am dead
and simplify me when I'm dead.

Keith Douglas
(January 24th 1920 – June 9th 1944)

Wounded by a land mine in 1943, Keith Douglas wrote from his hospital bed in Palestine in defence of his poetry: "I see no reason to be either musical or sonorous about things at present ... I suppose I reflect the cynicism ... with which I view the world."

• Luis de Camoes, Portugal's great national poet and author of
  the epic poem, Os Lusiadas, died in Lisbon June 10th 1580
• Michael Wigglesworth, renowned pastor and poet of the time,
  died in Massachusetts June 10th 1705
• American poet Nina Bogin born June 10th 1952

The Stillborn

The stillborn have no claim
on this world. They are quiet
and distant, taking care of themselves,
perfect as seashells,
as starfish navigating point by point
along the shallows,
as the smallest seahorses
grazing in the sands.

They have nothing in common with death.
No, it's as if a path
had been traced for them across a clean beach
with footprints ready for them to fall into step,
to walk into the dazzling wind of their lives.
And when they turned back,
remained crustacean,
slowly the footprints unmade themselves,
each grain of sand, one after the other,
tumbled back into the sea...

Nina Bogin
(June 10th 1952 –)

Nina Bogin writes: "This poem is dedicated to my stillborn son, who initiated us to the mysteries of life and death."
Nina Bogin was raised on Long Island and has been living in France for many years. She has published two collections of poems, In the North (Graywolf Press, 1989) and The Winter Orchards (Anvil, 2001). She lives with her husband and two daughters in eastern France.

June 11

- *Poet and dramatist Ben Jonson, author of* Volpone *and* Bartholomew Fair, *born in Westminster June 11th 1572*
- *Poet W. E. Henley, of 'Invictus' fame, died June 11th 1903*
- *Poet Kate Clanchy born in Glasgow June 11th 1965*

Slattern

I leave myself about, slatternly,
bits of me, and times I liked:
I let them go on lying where
they fall, crumple, if they will,
I know fine how to make them walk
and breathe again. Sometimes at night,
or on the train, I dream I'm dancing,
or lying in someone's arms who says
he loves my eyes in French, and again
and again I am walking up your road,
that first time, bidden and wanted,
the blossom on the trees, light,
light and buoyant. *Pull yourself
together*, they say, quite rightly,
but she is stubborn, that girl,
that hopeful one, still walking.

Kate Clanchy
(June 11th 1965 –)

Kate Clanchy writes: "The 11th of June is my birthday. This was the first poem I ever wrote – another kind of birthday. It was very easy to write and I have altered it very little since – a sort of bribe from the powers that be. It was only later that I found that writing is actually very hard." Kate Clanchy was born in Glasgow and educated in Edinburgh and Oxford. She was a schoolteacher in London's East End for several years before returning to Oxford as a teacher and freelance writer. She has written two award-winning poetry collections, *Slattern* (1996) and *Samarkand* (1999).

- *Anne Bradstreet reached Salem with her family June 12th 1630*
- *Thomas Gray completed the 'Elegy Written in a Country Churchyard' at Stoke Poges and sent it to his friend Walpole, June 12th 1750*
- *William Collins died in Chichester, Sussex, June 10th 1759. His* Persian Eclogues *were composed when he was just 17*

To my Dear and Loving Husband

If ever two were one, then surely we.
If ever man were loved by wife, then thee;
If ever wife was happy in a man,
Compare with me, ye women, if you can.
I prize thy love more than whole mines of gold
Or all the riches that the East doth hold.
My love is such that rivers cannot quench,
Nor ought but love from thee, give recompense.
Thy love is such I can no way repay,
The heavens reward thee manifold, I pray.
Then while we live, in love let's so persevere
That when we live no more, we may live ever.

Anne Bradstreet
(c. 1612 – September 16th 1672)

Anne Bradstreet, then Anne Dudley, married her husband Simon Bradstreet in 1628. Bradstreet was 16 at the time, and had just recovered from a near-fatal case of smallpox. Two years later, she, her husband and her parents set sail for America as Puritans hoping to start afresh in the New World. They arrived at Salem, Massachusetts, on this day in 1630 and proceeded to raise eight children.

As a Puritan, Bradstreet believed in the family as a unit of government – the state was divided into families rather than districts or regions – and she thus had a view of marriage that was as practical as it was romantic.

Interestingly, she was distantly related, via the ancient aristocratic Sutton-Dudley family, to the Elizabethan poet Philip Sidney, who had a much more courtly, exalted view of love and marriage.

June 13

- *Tennyson married Emily Sellwood on June 13th 1850*
- *W. B. Yeats born in Sandymount June 13th 1865*
- *Portuguese poet Fernando Pessoa born in Lisbon June 13th 1888*
- *American poet Mark Van Doren born in Illinois June 13th 1894*

Calypso

Driver drive faster and make a good run
Down the Springfield Line under the shining sun.

Fly like an aeroplane, don't pull up short
Till you brake for Grand Central Station, New York.

For there in the middle of that waiting-hall
Should be standing the one that I love best of all.

If he's not there to meet me when I get to town,
I'll stand on the side-walk with tears rolling down.

For he is the one that I love to look on,
The acme of kindness and perfection.

He presses my hand and he says he loves me,
Which I find an admirable peculiarity.

The woods are bright green on both sides of the line;
The trees have their loves though they're different from mine.

But the poor fat old banker in the sun-parlour car
Has no one to love him except his cigar.

If I were the Head of the Church or the State,
I'd powder my nose and just tell them to wait.

For love's more important and powerful than
Even a priest or a politician.

> *W. H. Auden*
> *(February 21st 1907 – September 29th 1973)*

Auden wrote this poem in May 1939, just four months after he left England to live in America. Already, the influence of his new country of residence can be seen in the poem, which includes American phrases (and spellings) like 'waiting-hall', 'side-walk' and 'parlour car' (rather than waiting-room, pavement and parlour carriage).

Auden's departure from England, as a result of the Second World War, was a controversial one, so much so that his residence in the US was the subject of a question in the House of Commons on this day in 1940.

- *As Browning accepted an honorary degree from Oxford University on June 14th 1882, students lowered a night cap onto his head from the gallery*
- *Scholar and poet Edward Fitzgerald died June 14th 1883*
- *Poet Kathleen Raine born June 14th 1908*
- *G. K. Chesterton died June 14th 1936*
- *Italian poet Salvatore Quasimodo died June 14th 1968*

Gold Leaves

Lo! I am come to autumn,
    When all the leaves are gold;
Grey hairs and autumn leaves cry out
    The year and I are old.

In youth I sought the prince of men,
    Captain in cosmic wars,
Our Titan, even the weeds would show
    Defiant, to the stars.

But now a great thing in the street
    Seems any human nod,
Where shift in strange democracy
    The million masks of God.

In youth I sought the golden flower
    Hidden in wood or wold,
But I am come to autumn,
    When all the leaves are gold.

G. K. Chesterton
(May 29th 1874 – June 14th 1936)

Chesterton's death on this day in 1936 was followed a fortnight later by a memorial requiem mass at Westminster Cathedral which was attended by over 2000 people. At the service a telegram from Pope Pius XI was read out, which expressed his deep grief at Chesterton's death and offered sympathy to the people of England.

The papal message was controversial, since in it Chesterton had been called a 'defender of the faith', a title held exclusively by the King. The newspapers expressed their royal allegiance by refusing to print the message.

June 15

• *Dante Alighieri became Prior of Florence June 15th 1300*
• *Thomas Campbell, poet and writer of war-songs, died in Boulogne June 15th 1844*
• *Poet Amy Clampitt born in Iowa June 15th 1920*
• *Auden married Thomas Mann's daughter, Erika, to provide her with a British passport, June 15th 1935. Auden said of the vicar, "He would have married me to a shovel"*

Sonnets from the Portuguese
XV

Accuse me not, beseech thee, that I wear
Too calm and sad a face in front of thine,
For we two look two ways, and cannot shine
With the same sunlight on our brow & hair.
Thou lookest, sweet, on me, without a care,
As on a bee shut in a crystalline . .
For sorrow hath shut me safe in love's divine,
And to spread wing & fly in the outer air
Were most impossible failure, if I strove
To fail so—But I look on thee . . on thee . .
Beholding besides love, the end of love,
Hearing oblivion beyond memory . . .
As one who sits and gazes, from above,
Over the rivers to the bitter sea.

Elizabeth Barrett Browning
(March 6th 1806 – June 29th 1861)

One morning in the summer of 1849, not long after the death of Browning's mother, Elizabeth Barrett Browning slipped a sheaf of papers into her husband's pocket as he stood gazing out of the window: this was the sequence of 44 poems that came to be called *Sonnets from the Portuguese* – some of the most ardent love poems in the English language.

"Yes, that was a strange heavy crown, that wreath of Sonnets, put on me one morning unawares, three years after it had been twined ... " recalled Browning. The last of the sonnets was written two days before their wedding on September 12th.

Originally called 'Sonnets Translated from the Bosnian' to disguise the highly personal nature of the poems, Robert Browning suggested the final title as an oblique reference to his pet name for his wife: 'my Portuguese'. Barrett Browning intended that only her husband should read the poems, but they were published at his insistence in 1850.

The Lilacs and the Roses

O months of blossoming, months of transfigurations,
May without a cloud and June stabbed to the heart,
I shall not ever forget the lilacs or the roses
Nor those the Spring has kept folded away apart.

I shall not ever forget the tragic sleight-of-hand,
The cavalcade, the cries, the crowd, the sun,
The lorries loaded with love, the Belgian gifts,
The road humming with bees, the atmosphere that spun,
The feckless triumphing before the battle,
The scarlet blood the scarlet kiss bespoke
And those about to die bolt upright in the turrets
Smothered in lilac by a drunken folk.

I shall not ever forget the flower-gardens of France –
Illuminated scrolls from eras more than spent –
Nor forget the trouble of dusk, the sphinx-like silence,
The roses all along the way we went;
Flowers that gave the lie to the soldiers passing
On wings of fear, a fear importunate as a breeze,
And gave the lie to the lunatic push-bikes and the ironic
Guns and the sorry rig of the refugees.

But what I do not know is why this whirl
Of memories always comes to the same point and drops
At Sainte-Marthe . . . a general . . . a black pattern . . .
A Norman villa where the forest stops;
All is quiet here, the enemy rests in the night
And Paris has surrendered, so we have just heard –
I shall never forget the lilacs nor the roses
Nor those two loves whose loss we have incurred:

Bouquets of the first day, lilacs, Flanders lilacs,
Soft cheeks of shadow rouged by death – and you,
Bouquets of the Retreat, delicate roses, tinted
Like far-off conflagrations: roses of Anjou.

Louis Aragon
(October 3rd 1897 – December 24th 1982)

translated by Louis MacNeice

Aragon, who abandoned literary surrealism for Marxism, was an active member of the intellectual Resistance during the Nazi occupation of France, and wrote the intensely patriotic poems collected in *Le Crève-coeur*. The above poem was widely circulated in underground movements but was not published until 1941.

June 17

- Poet and editor Allen Curnow born in Timaru, New Zealand, June 17th 1911
- Poet Gwendolyn Brooks born in Topeka June 17th 1917
- Christopher Benson, who wrote 'Land of Hope and Glory', died June 17th 1925
- Poet and writer Kit Wright born June 17th 1944
- Poet and novelist John Cowper Powys died June 17th 1963

Campionesque for Anna

When I lay down where I had lain with you
Some many nights, beloved, of the days
Lit by your sun, I dreamed all touch untrue,
Error my star and darkness all my ways
Till where I lay, I lay again with you.

Till where I go, I go again with you
Through all the days, beloved, and the nights
By your sweet self illumined, I can do
Not one good thing: not till your beauty lights
Me where I go, and go again with you.

Kit Wright
(June 17th 1944 –)

Kit Wright began writing poetry at the age of six and later won a scholarship to Oxford. He published his first collection in 1974 and since then has written a number of prize-winning collections for adults, as well as two immensely popular poetry books for children. His latest book is *Hoping It Might Be So: Poems 1974-2000* (Leviathan, 2000).

- *Ambrose Phillips, known as the 'Namby Pamby' poet for his adulatory verses ('Dimpley damsel, sweetly smiling'), died in London June 18th 1749*
- *A. E. Housman met Thomas Hardy for the first time June 18th 1899*
- *Poet Geoffrey Hill born in Bromsgrove June 18th 1932*

From An Essay on Criticism: Part 2

Of all the causes which conspire to blind
Man's erring judgment, and misguide the mind,
What the weak head with strongest bias rules,
Is pride, the never-failing vice of fools.
Whatever Nature has in worth denied,
She gives in large recruits of needful pride;
For as in bodies, thus in souls, we find
What wants in blood and spirits, swelled with wind:
Pride, where wit fails, steps in to our defence,
And fills up all the mighty void of sense.
If once right reason drives that cloud away,
Truth breaks upon us with resistless day.
Trust not yourself: but your defects to know,
Make use of every friend—and every foe.
    A little learning is a dangerous thing;
Drink deep, or taste not the Pierian[1] spring.
There shallow draughts intoxicate the brain,
And drinking largely sobers us again.

Alexander Pope
(May 21st 1688 – May 30th 1744)

Alexander Pope wrote 'Essay on Criticism' when he was 23, and it is his earliest didactic poem. On this day in 1711, Pope wrote a letter to his great friend, John Caryll, Baron of Durford, in which he defended the poem 'Essay on Criticism' from its detractors in the Catholic church. They had picked out the following two lines as being particularly worthy of condemnation: 'This wit, like Faith, by each man is applied / To one small sect, and all are damned beside.'

In the letter to Caryll, Pope gave a detailed grammatical explanation of why these particular lines were *not* damning of the Church, and went on to rebuke his critics with the words, "I fear these gentlemen understand grammar as little as they do criticism, and perhaps out of good nature to the monks are willing to take from them the censure of ignorance and to have it to themselves."

1. A spring on Mount Olympus, sacred to the Muses.

June 19

• James VI, minor poet and King of Scots, who became known
  as the "wisest fool in Christendom", born June 19th 1566
• John Wilmot, Earl of Rochester, was released from the Tower
  of London June 19th 1665. A plague raged for the three
  weeks of his imprisonment

Love and Life, A Song

All my past life is mine no more;
   The flying hours are gone;
Like transitory dreams given o'er
Whose images are kept in store
   By memory alone.

Whatever is to come, is not;
   How can it then be mine?
The present moment's all my lot,
And that, as fast as it is got,
   Phyllis, is wholly thine.

Then talk not of inconstancy,
   False hearts, and broken vows;
If I, by miracle, can be
This live-long minute true to thee,
   'Tis all that heaven allows.

John Wilmot, Earl of Rochester
(April 1st 1647 – July 26th 1680)

It would have been a miracle indeed had the infamously dissolute rake, the Earl of Rochester, been true to his mistress. His attempts to secure Elizabeth Malet – sole heiress to a huge fortune – as a wife, resulted in a thwarted abduction, for which Rochester spent three weeks in prison. In his petitions to the King he pleaded 'Inadvertancy', as well as the usual 'Ignorance in ye law and Passion'. He was released on this day in 1665.

Undeterred, Rochester succeeded in securing the union in January 1667; the wedding took place without the knowledge or consent of Malet's guardians. Rochester bedded her immediately "to make sure work of it" but lost interest in her soon after. Malet, for her part, tried to impress Rochester with her own verses but it was not long before he was involved with the actress Elizabeth Barry, and countless others besides.

• Edward Thomas married Helen Noble at Fulham Registry
  Office, June 20th 1899; Helen was expecting their first child
• Irish poet Paul Muldoon born in Portadown, County
  Armagh, June 20th 1951
• Vikram Seth, poet and author, born June 20th 1952

June 20

And You, Helen

And you, Helen, what should I give you?
So many things I would give you
Had I an infinite great store
Offered me and I stood before
To choose. I would give you youth,
All kinds of loveliness and truth,
A clear eye as good as mine,
Lands, waters, flowers, wine,
As many children as your heart
Might wish for, a far better art
Than mine can be, all you have lost
Upon the travelling waters tossed,
Or given to me. If I could choose
Freely in that great treasure-house
Anything from any shelf,
I would give you back yourself,
And power to discriminate
What you want and want it not too late,
Many fair days free from care
And heart to enjoy both foul and fair,
And myself, too, if I could find
Where it lay hidden and it proved kind.

Edward Thomas
(March 3rd 1878 – April 9th 1917)

Edward Thomas met Helen Noble, the daughter of his early mentor, James Ashcroft Noble, when they were still teenagers. They found they shared a passion for poetry, and Thomas soon introduced Helen to the pleasures of the countryside. At just 19, Thomas had already had a diary of his nature walks published. In 1897 he won a scholarship to Lincoln College, Oxford, and married Helen two years later; their first child was born six months before his finals.

From the first, Helen Thomas was attracted to Edward's 'melancholic beauty', but she learnt only later the agonies of spirit which tormented him throughout his life. Helen, for her part, remained steadfast and loving. He wrote in a letter to her: "Nobody but you would ever be likely to respond as I wished. I don't like to think anybody but I could respond to you. If you turned to anybody else I should come to an end immediately."

June 21

- Louis MacNeice married Mariette June 21st 1929 at Carfax in Oxford. Mariette, mistaken for the Princess Royal who was visiting Oxford that day, was met at the Registry Office by cheering crowds
- Poet, playwright and performer, John Agard born in British Guiana (now Guyana) June 21st 1949
- African-American poet, novelist, and playwright of more than 35 plays, Owen Dodson died June 21st 1983

From A Midsummer Night's Dream
Act V Scene i

Theseus: The lunatic, the lover, and the poet
Are of imagination all compact:
One sees more devils than vast hell can hold;
That is the madman: the lover, all as frantic,
Sees Helen's beauty in a brow of Egypt:
The poet's eye, in a fine frenzy rolling,
Doth glance from heaven to earth, from earth to heaven;
And as imagination bodies forth
The forms of things unknown, the poet's pen
Turns them to shapes, and gives to airy nothing
A local habitation and a name.
Such tricks hath strong imagination,
That if it would but apprehend some joy,
It comprehends some bringer of that joy:
Or, in the night, imagining some fear,
How easy is a bush suppos'd a bear!

William Shakespeare
(April 23rd 1564 – April 23rd 1616)

The longest day of the year is June 21st, although Midsummer's Day is often celebrated on the 23rd or 24th of the month. It has been an important date since ancient times (when stone monuments were aligned to the sunrise on the day), and became an important day in the Christian calendar as the birthday of St John the Baptist.

There are many superstitions associated with the magical time of Midsummer, some of which found their way into Shakespeare's play. Midsummer's Eve was the time when fairies were thought to be at their most powerful, while washing with Midsummer dew was thought to increase beauty and youthful looks. More curiously, collecting the seeds from a fern leaf on Midsummer's Eve, having approached it backwards without looking, allegedly endows the seeds with the power to make you invisible.

• American war poet Alan Seeger born in New York City
  June 22nd 1888
• Amy Lowell gave an 'Imagist' dinner party on June 22nd
  1913. One guest, Ford Madox Ford, claimed he had no idea
  what the word meant and suspected no one else did either
• Poet and novelist Walter De La Mare died in Twickenham
  June 22nd 1956[1]

The Song of Shadows

Sweep thy faint strings, Musician,
  With thy long lean hand;
Downward the starry tapers burn,
  Sinks soft the waning sand;
The old hound whimpers couched in sleep,
  The embers smoulder low;
Across the walls the shadows
  Come, and go.

Sweep softly thy strings, Musician,
  The minutes mount to hours;
Frost on the windless casement weaves
  A labyrinth of flowers;
Ghosts linger in the darkening air,
  Hearken at the open door;
Music hath called them, dreaming,
  Home once more.

Walter de la Mare
(April 25th 1873 – June 22nd 1956)

At the age of ten, Walter de la Mare won a place at St Paul's Cathedral Choristers' School, and in later life he would continue to sing in private with friends. He also enjoyed listening to the haunting Bach aria, 'Have mercy, Lord, on me', which is sung to a weeping violin obligato, played loudly on the gramophone: "I love it ... It seems to me to be a flawless revelation of the human heart and spirit."

In the 1920s and '30s the English composer Cecil Armstrong Gibbs set some of de la Mare's poems to music; 'Song of Shadows' was one of them. The two men were to become close friends, and upon de la Mare's death Gibbs wrote the passionate 'Threnody for Walter de la Mare' for string quartet and string orchestra.

1. De la Mare died peacefully at home. On his death-bed, he is reported to have said to the pretty nurse taking care of him: "It's a long time since we met – you must have come out of a dream." After his funeral, his ashes were interred in the crypt of St Paul's.

June 23

- Poet Anna Akhmatova born in Odessa, the daughter of a naval officer, June 23rd 1889
- Poet and critic Anthony Thwaite born June 23rd 1930
- E. E. Cummings first met his great love, Marion Morehouse, June 23rd 1932

You will hear thunder and remember me

You will hear thunder and remember me,
And think: she wanted storms. The rim
Of the sky will be the colour of hard crimson,
And your heart, as it was then, will be on fire.

That day in Moscow, it will all come true,
When, for the last time, I take my leave,
And hasten to the heights that I have longed for,
Leaving my shadow still to be with you.

Anna Akhmatova
(June 23rd 1889 – March 5th 1966)

For much of her life, Akhmatova endured censorship and persecution under Stalin's regime, including the repeated imprisonment of her son, Lev. Her writing is characterised by tremendous subtlety, while the frequent ellipses testify to the impossibility of confronting the horror of Stalinist Russia directly. Not until the year of her death when she was visiting Paris, by then a dignified portly lady in her 70s, did Akhmatova finally speak about the suffering she had endured: "Fate did not leave anything out for me," she said, "Everything anyone could possibly experience fell on my lot."

Akhmatova married three times and was always surrounded by admirers, especially young poets who looked to her for validation and a symbolic 'handing down of the lyre'. She died in a convalescent home in Moscow, leaving behind a huge body of work.

• Edward de Vere, proposed as the true author of Shakespeare's
plays, died in Hackney June 24th 1604
• Cambridge poet J. H. Prynne born June 24th 1936

June 24

Variation on a Theme by Rilke
(The book of Hours, Book 1, Poem 1, Stanza 1)

A certain day became a presence to me;
there it was, confronting me – a sky, air, light:
a being. And before it started to descend
from the height of noon, it leaned over
and struck my shoulder as if with
the flat of a sword, granting me
honor and a task. The day's blow
rang out, metallic or it was I, a bell awakened,
and what I heard was my whole self
saying and singing what it knew: *I can.*

Denise Levertov
(October 24th 1923 – December 20th 1997)

Denise Levertov's 1987 collection, *Breathing the Water*, contains her acclaimed variations on Rilke's
The Book of Hours, including the one above. Rilke was a substantial influence on Levertov from
her earliest days as a poet (one of her essays is called simply 'Rilke as Mentor'), particularly his view
of poetry as a vocation requiring intensity of attention and imagination. Like Rilke, Levertov gave
herself wholly to her art with what was described by her editor as "a singular and pure
commitment". She was politically active, campaigning on issues such as Vietnam, the environment
and nuclear weapons, and she addressed these with characteristic passion in her poetry of the 1960s
and '70s. Her final book of poems, *This Great Unknowing: Last Poems*, was published posthumously
in 1999.

June 25

• Baudelaire's Les Fleurs du Mal *published June 25th 1857. Both he and his publisher were prosecuted for offending public morals*
• *Poet, critic, short-story writer and activist Judith Wright died June 25th 2000*

Woman to Man

The eyeless labourer in the night,
the selfless, shapeless seed I hold,
builds for its resurrection day –
silent and swift and deep from sight
foresees the unimagined light.

This is no child with a child's face;
this has no name to name it by:
yet you and I have known it well.
This is our hunter and our chase,
the third who lay in our embrace.

This is the strength that your arm knows,
the arc of flesh that is my breast,
the precise crystals of our eyes.
This is the blood's wild tree that grows
the intricate and folded rose.

This is the maker and the made;
this is the question and reply;
the blind head butting at the dark,
the blaze of light along the blade.
Oh hold me, for I am afraid.

Judith Wright
(May 31st 1915 – June 25th 2000)

Judith Wright was born into a wealthy pastoral family in New South Wales and began writing at the age of six. Sent to boarding school, her sole consolation and "only thing I had to treasure was poetry and the knowledge that I was going to be a poet." She saw her mission in poetry to recover the land and the country imaginatively; to reconcile man with his environment. For it was Wright's belief that "the true function of art and culture is to interpret us to ourselves, and to relate us to the country and the society in which we live."

Although she was a prolific writer who in her lifetime produced over 50 books, she stopped writing poetry after the death of her husband, and turned to social protest with formidable vigour. She was an uncompromising conservationist and political activist who was greatly troubled by the decline of Australia's landscape, as well as the fate of its Aboriginal people.

• T. S. Eliot married Vivien Haigh-Wood at Hampstead
Registry Office, June 26th 1915. Eliot registered himself as
of 'no occupation'. Later he wrote: "To her the marriage
brought no happiness ... to me it brought the state of mind out
of which came The Waste Land"
• Poet and novelist Ford Madox Ford died June 26th 1939

Ode on a Grecian Urn

Thou still unravished bride of quietness,
  Thou foster-child of silence and slow time,
Sylvan historian, who canst thus express
  A flowery tale more sweetly than our rhyme:
What leaf-fringed legend haunts about thy shape
  Of deities or mortals, or of both,
    In Tempe or the dales of Arcady?
  What men or gods are these? What maidens loth?
What mad pursuit? What struggle to escape?
  What pipes and timbrels? What wild ecstasy?

Heard melodies are sweet, but those unheard
  Are sweeter; therefore, ye soft pipes, play on;
Not to the sensual ear, but, more endeared,
  Pipe to the spirit ditties of no tone:
Fair youth, beneath the trees, thou canst not leave
  Thy song, nor ever can those trees be bare;
    Bold Lover, never, never canst thou kiss,
Though winning near the goal – yet, do not grieve:
  She cannot fade, though thou hast not thy bliss,
  For ever wilt thou love, and she be fair!

Ah, happy, happy boughs! that cannot shed
  Your leaves, nor ever bid the Spring adieu;
And, happy melodist, unwearièd
  For ever piping songs for ever new;
More happy love! more happy, happy love!
  For ever warm and still to be enjoyed,
    For ever panting and for ever young –
All breathing human passion far above,
  That leaves a heart high-sorrowful and cloyed,
    A burning forehead, and a parching tongue.

Who are these coming to the sacrifice?
  To what green altar, O mysterious priest,
Lead'st thou that heifer lowing at the skies,
  And all her silken flanks with garlands dressed?
What little town by river or sea shore,
  Or mountain-built with peaceful citadel,

[Continued]

Is emptied of this folk, this pious morn?
And, little town, thy streets for evermore
  Will silent be; and not a soul to tell
    Why thou art desolate, can e'er return.

O Attic shape! Fair attitude! with brede
Of marble men and maidens overwrought,
  With forest branches and the trodden weed;
    Thou, silent form, dost tease us out of thought
As doth eternity: Cold Pastoral!
  When old age shall this generation waste,
    Thou shalt remain, in midst of other woe
Than ours, a friend to man, to whom thou say'st,
  'Beauty is truth, truth beauty, – that is all
    Ye know on earth, and all ye need to know.'

John Keats
(October 31st 1795 – February 23rd 1821)

In March 1819, Keats wrote in a journal letter to his brother George: "Neither Poetry, nor Ambition, nor Love have any alertness of countenance as they pass by me: they seem rather like three figures on a Greek vase – a Man and two women – whom no one but myself could distinguish in their disguisement. This is the only happiness; and is a rare instance of advantage in the body overpowering the Mind."

Keats composed this ode somewhere between late April and mid-May of 1819, possibly at Wentworth Place, the Hampstead home of his friend Charles Brown. Keats would often compose his poetry as he walked in the gardens at early dawn.

Keats was inspired to write the 'Ode on A Grecian Urn' by his friend Robert Haydon, who encouraged him to use the urn as a symbol of the way in which the perfection of Greek art reflected the society that produced it. The poem was included in *Lamia, Isabella, The Eve of St Agnes, and other Poems*, published on this day in 1820.

- Paul Lawrence Dunbar, the first black writer in the US to support himself through his writing, born June 27th 1872
- Francis (Frank) O'Hara born in Grafton, Massachusetts, June 27th 1926
- Lucille Clifton ("I am Lucille, which stands for light"), African-American poet, born June 27th 1936

To the Harbormaster

I wanted to be sure to reach you;
though my ship was on the way it got caught
in some moorings. I am always tying up
and then deciding to depart. In storms and
at sunset, with the metallic coils of the tide
around my fathomless arms, I am unable
to understand the forms of my vanity
or I am hard alee with my Polish rudder[1]
in my hand and the sun sinking. To
you I offer my hull and the tattered cordage
of my will. The terrible channels where
the wind drives me against the brown lips
of the reeds are not all behind me. Yet
I trust the sanity of my vessel; and
if it sinks, it may well be in answer
to the reasoning of the eternal voices,
the waves which have kept me from reaching you.

Frank O'Hara
(June 27th 1926 – July 25th 1966)

Frank O'Hara originally intended to be a composer or concert pianist but at Harvard, where he met the poet John Ashbery, O'Hara soon gave up music for poetry. After graduation he headed for booming 1950s New York, and promptly found a job working at the front desk of the Museum of Modern Art. O'Hara worked there throughout his short life and went on to become a respected curator and a highly perceptive art critic. As an influential member of the New York School, O'Hara was closely involved with artists such as Jackson Pollock and Larry Rivers, whose work proved inspirational to his poetry. Their collaborations resulted in 'poem-paintings' – paintings with word texts. A hard-drinking, jazz-loving, all-night reveller and quintessential member of the New York art and social scene, his poetry may be seen as a continuous celebration of the city and the people he loved.

1. 'Polish rudder' is thought to be a comic reference to *The Polish Rider* by Rembrandt.

June 28

- *Robert Louis Stevenson left San Francisco on his first voyage to the South Seas June 28th 1888*
- *G. K. Chesterton married Frances Blogg, who inspired many of the poems in* The Wild Knight, *June 28th 1901*
- *Alfred Noyes, poet and novelist, died June 28th 1958*
- *Poet and novelist Sophie Hannah born June 28th 1971*

Leaving and Leaving You

When I leave your postcode and your commuting station,
When I leave undone the things that we planned to do
You may feel you have been left by association
But there is leaving and there is leaving you.

When I leave your town and the club that you belong to,
When I leave without much warning or much regret
Remember, there's doing wrong and there's doing wrong to
You, which I'll never do and I haven't yet,

And when I have gone, remember that in weighing
Everything up, from love to a cheaper rent,
You were all the reasons I thought of staying
And you were none of the reasons why I went

And although I leave your sight and I leave your setting
And our separation is soon to be a fact,
Though you stand beside what I'm leaving and forgetting,
I'm not leaving you, not if motive makes the act.

Sophie Hannah
(June 28th 1971 –)

Sophie Hannah comments: "I wrote the poem when I was about to move from Manchester, where I'd lived all my life, to Cambridge. There was a particular person I was leaving behind, and I didn't want that person to take my desertion as a sign that I no longer cared about them. More generally, the poem is about the dilemma of whether emotional ties are or should be enough to keep you in a place when there are other powerful reasons for moving on."

Sophie Hannah was born in Manchester and now lives in Yorkshire. She has published four collections of poetry, all with Carcanet Press. Her latest collection is *First of the Last Chances*. She has also written three novels, *The Superpower of Love* (Arrow 2002) being the most recent.

- *The Globe theatre burnt to the ground, apparently caused by a cannon spark during a performance of* All is True (Henry VIII), *June 29th 1613*
- *Elizabeth Barrett Browning died in her husband's arms in their Florence home, June 29th 1861*
- *Poet James K. Baxter born in New Zealand June 29th 1926*

Sonnets from the Portuguese
VI

Go from me. Yet I feel that I shall stand
Henceforward in thy shadow nevermore
Alone upon the threshold of my door
Of individual life, I shall command
The uses of my soul, nor lift my hand
Serenely in the sunshine as before,
Without the sense of that which I forbore, . . .
Thy touch upon the palm—The widest land
Doom takes to part us, leaves thy heart in mine
With pulses that beat double. What I do
And what I dream include thee, as the wine
Must taste of its own grapes. And when I sue
God for myself, He hears that name of thine,
And sees within my eyes, the tears of two—

Elizabeth Barrett Browning
(March 6th 1806 – June 29th 1861)

Elizabeth Barrett Browning died on this day in 1861. Her father's death in 1857 had severely diminished her enthusiasm for life, as well as her already frail health. Edward Moulton Barrett had disowned Elizabeth as soon as he learnt of her secret marriage to Robert Browning (as he later disowned her sister Henrietta when she too married without his consent). But Barrett Browning never relinquished hope of a reconciliation: she sent him hundreds of letters begging his forgiveness, all of which were returned unopened, and made frequent visits to the family home on her return to England in the hope of a chance encounter. Mr Barrett, however, remained intransigent. His death, after 11 years estrangement, saw Barrett Browning increasingly dependent on spiritualism and obsessed with contacting his spirit. Neither her son, Pen, nor her husband, nor her passion for politics or poetry could fully engage her any longer.

At her death, Elizabeth Barrett Browning threw her arms around her husband; "Then came what my heart will keep till I see her again and longer –," wrote Browning, "the most perfect experience of her love to me with my whole knowledge of her."

June 30

• English poet and dramatist John Gay born June 30th 1685
• Czeslaw Milosz, winner of the 1980 Nobel Prize for
  literature, born in Szetejnie, Lithuania, June 30th 1911

Encounter

We were riding through frozen fields in a wagon at dawn.
A red wing rose in the darkness.

And suddenly a hare ran across the road.
One of us pointed to it with his hand.

That was long ago. Today neither of them is alive,
Not the hare, nor the man who made the gesture.

O my love, where are they, where are they going
The flash of a hand, streak of movement, rustle of pebbles.
I ask not out of sorrow, but in wonder.

Czeslaw Milosz
(June 30th 1911 –)

translated by Czeslaw Milosz and Lillian Vallee

In 1940 Czeslaw Milosz escaped from Soviet-occupied Wilno (Vilnius in Lithuania today) to Nazi-occupied Warsaw, where he joined the socialist resistance. Throughout the war, Milosz was involved in clandestine publishing and reading of poetry, and has been quoted as saying that "when an entire community is struck by misfortune … poetry becomes as essential as bread".

After the war, Milosz worked as a diplomat for the new Polish government before becoming an exile in Paris and, later, in America. He continued to write poetry (in Polish only) for the next 20 years, while working as an academic in various American universities. In 1980, after he had been awarded the Nobel Prize for literature, his books were published in Poland for the first time since 1945. The following year, he paid a visit to his homeland for the first time in over 30 years.

Of this poem, written in 1937, Milosz has said simply: "That's a moment. A hare really did run across the road. The point there was to catch something that had actually happened. At one moment, one second. Odd that I should feel the need."

• *Elizabeth Barrett Browning's funeral held in Florence July
1st 1861. Robert Browning left Italy with his son at the end
of the month and never returned*
• *Poet Alun Lewis born in Wales July 1st 1915*
• *Yeats proposed to Maud Gonne again July 1st 1916*

July 1

Raiders' Dawn

Softly the civilized
Centuries fall,
Paper on paper,
Peter on Paul.

And lovers waking
From the night –
Eternity's masters,
Slaves of Time –
Recognize only
The drifting white
Fall of small faces
In pits of lime.

Blue necklace left
On a charred chair
Tells that Beauty
Was startled there.

*Alun Lewis
(July 1st 1915 – March 5th 1944)*

On this day in 1940, his 25th birthday, Alun Lewis wrote a letter to his wife Gweno (whom he described as "A singing rib within my dreaming side") from his army camp, and enclosed copies of several new poems, including 'Raiders' Dawn'. In that letter, Lewis wrote: "I'm not a pacifist anymore. I'll be sorry to my dying day, but I won't shirk it. It's a new world to me, this world where war has entered the dream world of poetry. It's taken me a long time to admit its necessity. Now I hope to act up to my convictions." A note on 'Raider's Dawn' in his diary described the lovers as "the seed of humanity" that would survive the war, life being "normally and perpetually a miracle".

Lewis died in 1944, while on duty in Burma. He was just 28.

July 2

- *Richard Henry Stoddard, American poet, critic and editor, born in Hingham, Massachusetts, July 2nd 1825*
- *Wislawa Szymborska born July 2nd 1923*
- *Russian novelist and poet Vladimir Nabokov died July 2nd 1977*

Homecoming

He was back. Said nothing.
But it was clear something had upset him.
He lay down his suit.
Hid his head under the blanket.
Drew up his knees.
He's about forty, but not at this moment.
He exists – but only as much as in his mother's belly
behind seven skins, in protective darkness.
Tomorrow he is lecturing on homeostasis
in metagalactic space travel.
But now he's curled up and fallen asleep.

Wislawa Szymborska
(July 2nd 1923 –)

translated by Adam Czerniawski

Wislawa Szymborska was born in Kornik in Western Poland. Since 1931 she has lived in Krakow, where she studied literature and sociology at the Jagiellonian University after the war.

Szymborska has published 16 collections of poetry and her work has been translated into many languages. In 1996 she was awarded the Nobel Prize for literature. In her acceptance speech she said that "in the language of poetry ... nothing is usual or normal ... not a single existence, not anyone's existence in this world."

• William Henry Davies, tramp poet who printed his first collection, The Soul's Destroyer, from the money he earned from begging, born in Newport, Wales, July 3rd 1871
• Adrienne Rich refused the National Medal for the Arts from the White House on July 3rd 1997, "because the very meaning of art, as I understand it, is incompatible with the cynical politics of [the Clinton] administration"

In Those Years

In those years, people will say, we lost track
of the meaning of *we*, of *you*
we found ourselves
reduced to *I*
and the whole thing became
silly, ironic, terrible:
we were trying to live a personal life
and yes, that was the only life
we could bear witness to

But the great dark birds of history screamed and plunged
into our personal weather
They were headed somewhere else but their beaks and pinions drove
along the shore, through the rags of fog
where we stood, saying *I*

Adrienne Rich
(May 16th 1929 –)

Adrienne Rich's early verse was praised by Auden, but she stopped writing when she married in 1953 and had three sons before she was 30. She later analysed the tensions she felt at this time: "to be a female human being trying to fulfil traditional female functions in a traditional way is in direct conflict with the subversive function of the imagination." She left her husband in 1970, and by 1974 she had won the National Book Award for her collection, *Diving into the Wreck*. She rejected the award as an individual, but accepted it "in the name of all women".

Now a lesbian feminist, she is one of America's most political writers. She wrote this poem in 1991 about the 1960s' 'the personal is political' movement in feminism, of which she has said: "That statement was necessary because in other political movements of that decade the power relation of men to women ... had been dismissed – often contemptuously – as the sphere of the personal life ... And in the crossover between personal and political, we were also pushing at the limits of experience reflected in literature, certainly in poetry."

July 4

• On July 4th 1845, Henry David Thoreau moved to his cabin by Walden Pond to "live deliberately, to front only the essential facts of life, and ... learn what it had to teach"
• American poet Alan Seeger killed in action July 4th 1916
• Polish poet Antoni Slonimski died in Warsaw July 4th 1976
• American poet Ted Berrigan died July 4th 1983
• Spanish poet Juan Gil-Albert died July 4th 1994

The Peace of Wild Things

When despair grows in me
and I wake in the middle of the night at the least sound
in fear of what my life and my children's lives may be,
I go and lie down where the wood drake
rests in his beauty on the water, and the great heron feeds.
I come into the peace of wild things
who do not tax their lives with forethought
of grief. I come into the presence of still water.
And I feel above me the day-blind stars
waiting for their light. For a time
I rest in the grace of the world, and am free.

Wendell Berry
(August 5th 1934 –)

Wendell Berry's childhood desire to be a farmer was finally fulfilled on July 4th 1965, when he moved back to the family farmhouse in Lane's Landing, Kentucky; he now farms full time with the help of his wife and children. Berry has been called an agrarian regionalist: he defends farming as a way of life and espouses self-reliance and environmental responsibility. His 1970 essay 'Think Little' anticipated E. F. Schumacher's book *Small is Beautiful*, published three years later, in calling for Americans to consume less, produce more, and be less wasteful.

- *Jean Cocteau, French poet, film director and novelist,*
  a wealthy Parisian family July 5th 1889
- *After many years absence, Nikos Kazantzakis returned to ι.*
  native Crete on July 5th 1924 and began work on his epic
  poem The Odyssey: A Modern Sequel
- *Alun Lewis married Gweno Ellis July 5th 1941*
- *Howard Nemerov died July 5th 1991*

From Prayer Before Birth

I am not yet born; O hear me.
Let not the bloodsucking bat or the rat or the stoat or the
   club-footed ghoul come near me.

I am not yet born, console me.
I fear that the human race may with tall walls wall me,
   with strong drugs dope me, with wise lies lure me,
     on black racks rack me, in blood-baths roll me.

I am not yet born; provide me
With water to dandle me, grass to grow for me, trees to talk
   to me, sky to sing to me, birds and a white light
     in the back of my mind to guide me.

I am not yet born; forgive me
For the sins that in me the world shall commit, my words
   when they speak me, my thoughts when they think me,
     my treason engendered by traitors beyond me,
       my life when they murder by means of my
         hands, my death when they live me.

I am not yet born; rehearse me
In the parts I must play and the cues I must take when
   old men lecture me, bureaucrats hector me, mountains
     frown at me, lovers laugh at me, the white
       waves call me to folly and the desert calls
         me to doom and the beggar refuses
           my gift and my children curse me.

I am not yet born; O hear me,
Let not the man who is beast or who thinks he is God
   come near me.

Louis MacNeice
(September 12th 1907 – September 3rd 1963)

This poem first appeared in MacNeice's 1944 collection, *Springboard*, and could be read autobio-
graphically as a father's reaction to bringing a child into a world at war. MacNeice's daughter, Brigid
Corinna, was born on this day in 1943.

• Siegfried Sassoon sent his pacifist Statement to his command-
  ing officer on July 6th 1917, declaring "I am fully aware of
  what I am letting myself in for"
• Elizabeth Smart first met George Barker July 6th 1940
• American poet Kenneth Koch, who was associated with the
  New York School of poets, died July 6th 2002

From Song of Myself (in *Leaves of Grass*)

I have said that the soul is not more than the body,
And I have said that the body is not more than the soul,
And nothing, not God, is greater to one than one's self is,
And whoever walks a furlong without sympathy walks to
  his own funeral drest in his shroud,
And I or you pocketless of a dime may purchase the pick of
  the earth,
And to glance with an eye or show a bean in its pod
  confounds the learning of all times,
And there is no trade or employment but the young man
  following it may become a hero,
And there is no object so soft but it makes a hub for the
  wheel'd universe,
And I say to any man or woman, Let your soul stand cool
  and composed before a million universes.

Walt Whitman
(May 31st 1819 – March 26th 1892)

Walt Whitman was still a part-time builder when *Leaves of Grass* was published on this day in 1855.
Arguably the most original poetry yet written in America, the book had a curiously inauspicious
start. The album-sized book bore neither a publisher's nor an author's name, but boasted a portrait
of Walt Whitman in a workman's shirt, sporting a look of "mild defiance"; the twelve untitled
poems were probably typeset by Whitman himself. His brother, George, was entirely dismissive
of the book, and only a handful were sold throughout the country.

But *Leaves of Grass* soon came to the attention of its most important reader, Ralph Waldo Emerson.
In late July, the eminent poet wrote to "greet [Whitman] at the beginning of a great career",
proclaiming *Leaves of Grass* "the most extraordinary piece of wit and wisdom that America has yet
contributed". Whitman promptly had the letter printed in a national newspaper (and in the next
edition of *Leaves of Grass*), incensing Emerson and invoking charges of shameless self-publicity
from his critics. Whitman himself wrote three anonymous reviews of the collection, and in one
hailed it "the most genius of triumphs".

- *Robert Burns wrote to a friend on July 7th 1796: "You actually would not know me if you saw me – Pale, emaciated & so feeble ... my spirits fled! fled!"*
- *Saint Bernadette entered the Mother House of the Congregation of the Sisters of Charity of Nevers July 7th 1866*
- *Russian poet and playwright Vladimir Mayakovsky born in Georgia July 7th 1893*

Nevers

Passions never spoken,
never broken but preserved,
never layered under marriages
or burnt to dust by fast affairs
are saints to us,

the sacred ones,
bodily enshrined
to lie in state like Bernadette
at Nevers of the mind;
amazing, garlanded and fair.

Older, at the inkling
of an accent or a smile,
we travel there.

Colette Bryce
(March 6th 1970 –)

Colette Bryce writes: "I wrote this after suffering from what I thought was unrequited love for a year – and would have settled for a fast affair at the time. That love turned out to be requited after all and we got together not long after. I still haven't been to Nevers in France, but I've been to Nevers of the mind a few times."

Colette Bryce was born in Derry, Northern Ireland. Her first collection, *The Heel of Bernadette*, was published by Picador in 2000.

July 8

- *Percy Bysshe Shelley died July 8th 1822*
- *Poet and novelist Richard Aldington born July 8th 1892*
- *Oscar Wilde began* Ballad of Reading Gaol *July 8th 1897*

One word is too often profaned

One word is too often profaned
  For me to profane it,
One feeling too falsely disdained
  For thee to disdain it;
One hope is too like despair
  For prudence to smother,
And pity from thee more dear
  Than that from another.

I can give not what men call love;
  But wilt thou accept not
The worship the heart lifts above
  And the Heavens reject not,–
The desire of the moth for the star,
  Of the night for the morrow,
The devotion to something afar
  From the sphere of our sorrow?

Percy Bysshe Shelley
(August 4th 1792 – July 8th 1822)

When the bodies of Shelley and his two friends washed up on shore eight days after their boat sank, Shelley was identified by a volume of Keats' poetry in his pocket, the pages turned over at 'The Eve of Saint Agnes'. On cremation of his body, it is said that his heart refused to burn and was taken from the flames at Byron's insistence and later given to Mary Shelley. It was found among her possessions at her death. In England, Shelley was hardly mourned; one obituary even declared triumphantly: "Shelley, the writer of some infidel poetry, has been drowned; *now* he knows whether there is a God or no."

His ashes were eventually interred in the protestant cemetery in Rome, where Keats was buried in 1820. In his preface to *Adonais* (1821), Shelley wrote: "The cemetery is an open space among the ruins, covered in winter with violets and daisies. It might make one in love with death, to think that one should be buried in so sweet a place."

• On July 9th 1735, 25-year-old Samuel Johnson married
Elizabeth Jervis Porter, a wealthy widow 20 years his senior who
considered him "the most sensible man I ever saw in my life"
• Blind poet John Heath-Stubbs born in London July 9th 1918

Some Trees

These are amazing: each
Joining a neighbour, as though speech
Were a still performance.
Arranging by chance

To meet as far this morning
From the world as agreeing
With it, you and I
Are suddenly what the trees try

To tell us we are:
That their merely being there
Means something; that soon
We may touch, love, explain.

And glad not to have invented
Such comeliness, we are surrounded:
A silence already filled with noises,
A canvas on which emerges

A chorus of smiles, a winter morning.
Placed in a puzzling light, and moving,
Our days put on such reticence
These accents seem their own defence.

John Ashbery
(July 28th 1927 –)

With his friends Kenneth Koch and Frank O'Hara, John Ashbery formed the nucleus of a group of artists who came to be known as The New York School. They met at Harvard in the 1950s and proceeded to shock and delight America with their innovative poetry that revelled in the absurd. Influenced by the music of John Cage and by the process-focused paintings of Abstract Expressionism, Ashbery's poetry has been described as being like abstract paintings in words. He aims, he says, "to record a kind of generalized transcript of what's really going on in our minds all day long."

Ashbery is the author of 20 books. His 1975 collection, *Self-Portrait in a Convex Mirror*, won the Pulitzer Prize, the National Book Award, and the National Book Critics Circle Award and the title poem has been hailed as one of the finest long poems in contemporary poetry. He presently divides his time between New York City and Hudson, New York, and teaches at Bard College.

July 10

- *In a celebrated speech at the election of Lord Mayor of Dublin, July 10th 1790, Philpot Curran proclaimed: "The condition upon which God hath given liberty to man is eternal vigilance"*
- *Poet and novelist Marcel Proust born in Paris July 10th 1871*
- *Paul Verlaine bought a gun on a two-day drinking binge, and shot Rimbaud twice in the arm to punish him for leaving, July 10th 1873*

The Deserter

If sadly thinking,
With spirits sinking,
Could more than drinking
  My cares compose,
A cure for sorrow
From sighs I'd borrow,
And hope tomorrow
  Would end my woes.
But as in wailing
There's not availing,
And Death unfailing
  Will strike the blow,
Then for that reason,
And for a season,
Let us be merry
  Before we go.
To joy a stranger,
A way-worn ranger,
In every danger
  My course I've run;
Now hope all ending
And Death befriending,
His last aid lending,
  My cares are done:
No more a rover,
Or hapless lover,
My griefs are over,
  My grass runs low;
Then for that reason,
And for a season,
Let us be merry
  Before we go!

John Philpot Curran
(July 24th 1750 – October 14th 1817)

An Irish politician and judge, John Philpot Curran was the most popular advocate of his day, admired for his erudite yet passionate speeches. On meeting him, Lord Byron wrote to a friend that Curran had "fifty faces and twice as many voices when he mimics – I never met his equal ... were I a woman and a virgin, that is the man I would make my Scamander – he is quite fascinating".

- *Thomas Hardy articled to John Hicks, Dorchester architect, July 11th 1856*
- *Edith Sitwell, remembering Virgina Woolf in a letter to a friend on July 11th 1955, wrote: "I ... thought nothing of her writing. I considered her a beautiful little knitter"*
- *Jane Griffiths, poet, born in Exeter July 11th 1970*
- *Poet Vicki Feaver married Alasdair Young July 11th 1998*

Coat

Sometimes I have wanted
to throw you off
like a heavy coat.

Sometimes I have said
you would not let me
breathe or move.

But now that I am free
to choose light clothes
or none at all

I feel the cold
and all the time I think
how warm it used to be.

Vicki Feaver
(November 14th 1943 –)

Vicki Feaver comments: " 'The Coat' was one of the first complete poems I wrote. It reflected my experience and feelings at the time. I was in my mid-30s and married with four young children. The heavy coat (I'd recently bought an old fur coat on a second-hand stall in Brixton market) was an image for a love that had often seemed stifling and constricting. But when it was withdrawn I desperately missed it.

"I am almost ashamed now of the poem's simplicity but I suppose it does reflect what I still think of as the impossible balancing act of love: to hold and to be held but not so tightly the life is squeezed out of you."

Vicki Feaver has published two collections of poetry: *Close Relatives* (Secker, 1981) and *The Handless Maiden* (Cape, 1994). A selection of her work is also included in *Penguin Modern Poets, Vol. 2*. She has five grandchildren and lives on the edge of the Pentlands with her psychiatrist husband, owls and buzzards.

• Philosopher, poet and naturalist Henry David Thoreau, born
  the son of a pencil manufacturer, July 12th 1817
• Chilean poet Pablo Neruda born Neftalí Ricardo Reyes
  Basoalto, July 12th 1904
• Robin Robertson born in Scone, Perthshire, July 12th 1955
• American poet Delmore Schwartz died July 12th 1966

Roundel

Now welcome, Somer, with thy sonne softe,
That hast this wintres wedres° overshake°,   *storms; shaken off*
And driven away the longe nyghtes blake!

Saynt Valentyn, that art ful hy on-lofte°,   *above*
Thus syngen smale foules° for thy sake: *fowls (birds)*
Now welcome, Somer, with thy sonne softe,
That hast this wintres wedres overshake.

Wel han° they cause for to gladen ofte,   *have*
Sith ech of hem recovered hath hys make°.   *mate*
Ful blissful mowe they synge when they wake:
Now welcome, Somer, with they sonne softe,
That hast this wintres wedres overshake,
And driven away the longe nyghtes blake!

Geoffrey Chaucer
(c.1340 – October 25th 1400)

This roundel is from *The Parliament of Fowls*, a 699 line poem which Chaucer wrote in the early
1380s, possibly in honour of the marriage of Richard II and Anne of Bohemia. In the poem, three
eagles contest the love of a female, a dispute which the goddess Nature asks the other birds to settle.
The case is left unresolved, and the other birds choose their mates (it being St Valentine's day) and
sing the above poem in honour of Nature.
On this day in 1389, Chaucer was made Chief Clerk of the King's Works by Richard II. His areas
of responsibilities included the upkeep and repair of governmental buildings in London. At the
time he was writing his *Canterbury Tales*, which he had begun two years earlier.

• *John Clare born in Northants July 13th 1793. His twin sister Bessy died in infancy*
• *Wole Soyinka, the first African to win the Nobel Prize for literature (1986), born in Western Nigeria July 13th 1934*
• *Indian poet, translator and folklorist A. K. Ramanujan, died July 13th 1993*

A Hindu to His Body

Dear pursuing presence,
dear body: you brought me
curled in womb and memory.

Gave me fingers to clutch
at grace, at malice; and ruffle
someone else's hair; to fold a man's
shadow back on his world;
to hold in the dark of the eye
through a winter and a fear
the poise, the shape of a breast;
a pear's silence, in the calyx
and the noise of a childish fist.

You brought me: do not leave me
behind. When you leave all else,
my garrulous face, my unkissed
alien mind, when you muffle
and put away my pulse

to rise in the sap of trees
let me go with you and feel the weight
of honey-hives in my branching
and the burlap weave of weaver-birds
in my hair.

A. K. Ramanujan
(March 16th 1929 – July 13th 1993)

A. K. Ramanujan's widow, Molly Daniels-Ramanujan, writes: "On the day A. K. Ramanujan died, poet Alane Rollings went to stand under the flag flying half-mast in the quadrangle of the University of Chicago. She saw that a student had taped a copy of the poem, 'A Hindu to His Body' to the flagpole. At that instant, three minds were one: two poets and an ideal reader."

Ramanujan was in his lifetime one of the finest Indian poets writing in English. He was also a considerable scholar, and an authority on folklore and anthropology. Ramanujan lived in Chicago for the last thirty years of his life, and was Professor of Linguistics at the University of Chicago, yet he remained rooted in Hindu culture and preoccupied with Indian literature. He is best known for his pioneering translations of ancient Tamil poetry, which altered perceptions of the Indian literary map in the West.

July 14

• Anne Sexton's beloved 'Nana', Anna Ladd Dingley, died July 14th 1954. Sexton's play Mercy Street centred on their relationship
• Celebrated Czech poet and immunologist Miroslav Holub died July 14th 1998

The Door

Go and open the door.
  Maybe outside there's
a tree, or a wood,
a garden,
or a magic city.

Go and open the door.
  Maybe a dog's rummaging.
  Maybe you'll see a face,
or an eye,
or the picture
       of a picture.

Go and open the door.
  If there's a fog
it will clear.

Go and open the door.
  Even if there's only
the darkness ticking,
even if there's only
the hollow wind,
even if
    nothing
       is there,
go and open the door.

At least
there'll be
a draught.

Miroslav Holub
(September 23rd 1923 – July 14th 1998)

translated by Ian Milner and George Theiner

Miroslav Holub is the best-known Czech poet of the 20th century. After working as a labourer during the Second World War, he studied medicine and received his PhD in 1954, the same year his first book of poems was published. In the following 15 years he released almost a book a year, while simultaneously building what was to be a distinguished career as an immunologist. Following the Soviet invasion of 1968, the government's Stalinist cultural policy declared Holub officially a 'non-person', and his poems were banned in the Czech Republic (then Czechoslovakia) until 1982. He continued to work as a writer and scientist up until his death in 1998.

• *Jean Cocteau's first poem, 'Les Facades', was published in a Parisian journal July 15th 1908, when he was just 18*
• *Nâzim Hikmet was released from prison July 15th 1951*

July 15

Maybe I

Maybe I
    long before
        that day
    shall sway
    early one morning at the bridgehead
        where I shall thrust my shadow on the asphalt way.

Maybe I
    long after
        that day
– on my shaven cheek my stubble turning grey –
        shall remain alive.

And I
    long after
        that day
        (if I've been able to survive)
shall lean on the side walls of the city squares
    on the evening of a holiday
        and play
the violin to the old-timers
    who survived like myself the last fight.

All around us are the glittering sidewalks
        of a marvellous night
and the steps
    of brave new human beings
        singing brave new songs.

Nâzim Hikmet
(November 20th 1902 – June 3rd 1963)

translated by Richard McKane, Ruth Christie and Talât Sait Halman

Nâzim Hikmet was the foremost Turkish poet of the 20th century. He was repeatedly arrested during the 1930s on charges of political activity and "spreading communist propaganda". Then, in 1938, he was charged with inciting revolt in the armed forces and, "with a decision resembling the conviction of Dreyfus" was sentenced to a total of 28 years imprisonment. In his poem 'Autobiography', Hikmet writes 'some people know all about plants some about fish / I know about separation.'

Hikmet continued to write in prison, and his sequence of verse letters to his wife, Piraye, are a moving testament to his spiritual resilience. He was eventually released on this day in 1951 following an international campaign, and settled in Moscow.

July 16

- *Mary Evans, author of the poetry collections* I Am a Black Woman *and* Nightstar, *born in Ohio July 16th 1932*
- *English poet Hilaire Belloc died July 16th 1953*
- *Dorothy Parker's ashes were mailed to her lawyer on July 16th 1973 and kept in a filing cabinet for 15 years*
- *May Sarton, poet and novelist, died July 16th 1995*

The Secret

I loved thee, though I told thee not,
    Right earlily and long,
Thou wert my joy in every spot,
    My theme in every song.

And when I saw a stranger face
    Where beauty held the claim,
I gave it like a secret grace
    The being of thy name.

And all the charms of face or voice
    Which I in others see
Are but the recollected choice
    Of what I felt for thee.

John Clare
(July 13th 1793 – May 20th 1864)

It is, in fact, no secret whom John Clare loved 'right earlily and long'; her name was Mary Joyce, and the two first met in 1800 when he was seven and she was three. They went to the same school in Glinton, near Peterborough, in a church vestry. It is there that Clare recorded his love for Mary by carving 'J. C. 1808 Mary' in the wood. Their friendship seems to have ended around 1815, and Clare probably saw her for the final time in the 1820s. She died on this day in 1838.

All of the poems about Mary are thought to have been written much later in Clare's life, and this led to him idealising her as a perfect muse. As he wrote in his autobiographical *Sketches*, "she was a beautiful girl & as the dream never awoke into reality her beauty was always fresh in my memory".

• G. M. Hopkins converted to Catholicism on July 17th 1886
• H. D. met her life-long partner, Bryher, July 17th 1918
• Pre-eminent post-war critic and poet Donald Davie born in
  Barnsley, Yorkshire, July 17th 1922
• AE (George William Russell), once considered an equal to Yeats,
  died in Bournemouth July 17th 1935

July 17

Time Passing, Beloved

Time passing, and the memories of love
Coming back to me, carissima, no more mockingly
Than ever before; time passing, unslackening,
Unhastening, steadily; and no more
Bitterly, beloved, the memories of love
Coming into the shore.

How will it end? Time passing and our passages of love
As ever, beloved, blind
As ever before; time binding, unbinding
About us; and yet to remember
Never less chastening, nor the flame of love
Less like an ember.

What will become of us? Time
Passing, beloved, and we in a sealed
Assurance unassailed
By memory. How can it end,
This siege of a shore that no misgivings have steeled,
No doubts defend?

Donald Davie
(July 17th 1922 – September 18th 1995)

After serving in the Royal Navy in World War II, Donald Davie settled into a life of literature and academia, studying at Cambridge before teaching at universities in Dublin, Essex, California and Tennessee. He is renowned for his many critical works, including books on Hardy, Pound and Whitman, for translating Pasternak and Mandelstam, and also for his interest in the purity of English language and syntax.

• *Italian poet and author Marino Moretti born July 18th 1885*
• *Elizabeth Jennings born in Boston, Lincolnshire, July 18th 1926*
• *Yevgeny Yevtushenko born in Zima, Siberia, July 18th 1933*
• *Weldon Kees' abandoned car was found on the approach to the Golden Gate Bridge in San Francisco on July 18th 1955*

You Are Great in Love

You are great in love.
                You are bold.
My every step is timid.
I'll do nothing bad to you,
but can hardly do you any good.
It seems you are
            leading me
off the beaten path through a forest.
Now we're up to our waist in wildflowers.
I don't even know
            what flowers they are.
Past experience is of no help here.
I don't know
          what to do or how.
You're tired.
          You ask to be carried in my arms.
Already you're in my arms.
"Do you see
         how blue the sky is?
Do you hear
         what birds are in the forest?
Well, what are you waiting for?
            Well?
              Carry me then!"
And where shall I carry you? . . .

Yevgeny Yevtushenko
(July 18th 1932 –)

translated by Albert C. Todd

Yevgeny Yevetushenko was born and raised in Siberia near Lake Baikal, before moving to Moscow at the age of 11. His poetry was some of the first to overtly criticise Stalin, and he has been politically active throughout his life, even serving in the first freely elected parliament of the USSR from 1988 to 1991. He was Russia's most popular poet of the 1960s, often attracting thousands to his readings, and has written over 40 books of poetry. He divides his time between his homeland and the US, and travelled widely in what he calls "the biggest country of all, the one called Humanity."

- *Italian lyric poet Petrarch died July 19th 1374*
- *Dorchester dialect poet and scholar William Barnes married Julia Miles July 19th 1827*
- *A. S. J. Tessimond born July 19th 1902*
- *Edward Thomas enlisted in the Artists' Rifles, July 19th 1915 – "the natural culmination of a long series of moods and thoughts"*

Black Monday Lovesong

In love's dances, in love's dances,
One retreats and one advances.
One grows warmer and one colder,
One more hesitant, one bolder.
One gives what the other needed
Once, or will need, now unheeded.
One is clenched, compact, ingrowing
While the other's melting, flowing.
One is smiling and concealing
While the other's asking, kneeling.
One is arguing or sleeping
While the other's weeping, weeping.

And the question finds no answer
And the tune misleads the dancer
And the lost look finds no other
And the lost hand finds no brother
And the word is left unspoken
Till the theme and thread are broken.

When shall these divisions alter?
Echo's answer seems to falter:
'Oh the unperplexed, unvexed time
Next time . . . one day . . . one day . . . next time!'

A. S. J. Tessimond
(July 19th 1902 – May 13th 1962)

Arthur Seymour John Tessimond was perhaps the quintessential British bachelor, with a self-confessed penchant for kippers, marmalade, Pimms No.1 and Gentleman's relish. He was "tolerably well known" as a poet but fell swiftly into obscurity following his death.

Tessimond worked as a copywriter until the outbreak of the Second World War. He believed he would be "intensely miserable" in service, if not "useless and even dangerous to others" and went into hiding to avoid enlisting. After many months on the breadline, he finally submitted to a medical and was deemed unfit anyway.

Tessimond suffered from manic depression for much of his life and was treated with frequent bouts of electric-shock therapy, which may well have precipitated his early death.

- *Petrarch born into an exiled Florentine family in Arezzo July 20th 1304*
- *Oscar Wilde finished his masterpiece,* The Ballad of Reading Gaol, *July 20th 1897*
- *Paul Valéry died July 20th 1945*

The Footsteps

Your steps, born of my silence here,
Process with slow, religious tread,
Dumbly and icily, to where
I lie awake, on watch, in bed.

Pure person, shade of deity,
Your steps, held back, are doubly sweet.
God! – all the gifts I could foresee
Are coming now on those bare feet!

If you advance your lips to make
A peace with hunger, and to press
The inhabitant of my thoughts to take
The thoughtful nourishment of a kiss,

Don't hurry with their tender dew,
Sweetness complete and incomplete;
For I have lived to wait for you:
My heart was your approaching feet.

Paul Valéry
(October 30th 1871 – July 20th 1945)

translated by Alistair Elliot

Paul Valéry's first poem was published in 1889; this had a profound effect on him: "My name in print induced an impression similar to that experienced in dreams where you are deeply mortified to discover yourself stark naked in an elegant drawing-room."

After a failed love affair with a woman ten years his senior in 1891, and a consequent emotional crisis, Valéry renounced human passions and stopped writing poetry. He moved to Paris and spent the next 20 years studying mathematics, philosophy and language. In 1912 Gide finally cajoled him into collecting and revising his earlier poems. Valéry's second published collection, *Charmes*, which included 'Les Pas' ('The Footsteps'), appeared in 1922.

He had written many of the *Charmes* poems during the summer of 1920, which he spent in the beautiful countryside near Avranches in Normandy. Every morning he would leave his room before dawn to walk barefoot on the cold grass. As soon as the sun began to rise he would head back to his room to write. He retained this habit of writing early in the morning throughout his life, even during the Second World War and the occupation of Paris.

- *Burns died on July 21st 1796; his body was conveyed to the burial ground as his wife Jean gave birth to their son*
- *Poet Hart Crane born in Ohio July 21st 1899*
- *Australian poet A. D. Hope born July 21st 1907*
- *American poet Tess Gallagher born July 21st 1943*
- *Wendy Cope born in Kent July 21st 1945*

Being Boring

'May you live in interesting times.' Chinese curse

If you ask me 'What's new?', I have nothing to say
Except that the garden is growing.
I had a slight cold but it's better today.
I'm content with the way things are going.
Yes, he is the same as he usually is,
Still eating and sleeping and snoring.
I get on with my work. He gets on with his.
I know this is all very boring.

There was drama enough in my turbulent past:
Tears and passion - I've used up a tankful.
No news is good news, and long may it last,
If nothing much happens, I'm thankful.
A happier cabbage you never did see,
My vegetable spirits are soaring.
If you're after excitement, steer well clear of me.
I want to go on being boring.

I don't go to parties. Well, what are they for,
If you don't need to find a new lover?
You drink and you listen and drink a bit more
And you take the next day to recover.
Someone to stay home with was all my desire
And, now that I've found a safe mooring,
I've just one ambition in life: I aspire
To go on and on being boring.

Wendy Cope
(July 21st 1945 –)

Wendy Cope writes: "I hadn't written a poem for a while, and I thought to myself, 'I'm too boring to write poems these days.' Then I sat down and wrote this. It goes down well with adult audiences but I rarely read it in schools because I imagine that adolescents would find it shocking."

July 22

• *Alfred Percival Graves, a leader of the Irish literary renaissance, father of Robert Graves, born July 22nd 1846*
• *James Whitcomb Riley, known as the 'Hoosier poet', whose homely style made him one of America's best-loved poets, died July 22nd 1916. 35, 000 mourners paid their respects*
• *Poet and writer Carl Sandburg, famous for his* Chicago Poems, *died in North Carolina July 22nd 1967*

The Moon Sails Out

When the moon sails out
the church bells die away
and the paths overgrown
with brush appear.

When the moon sails out
the waters cover the earth
and the heart feels it is
a little island in the infinite.

No one eats oranges
under the full moon[1].
The right things are fruits
green and chilled.

When the moon sails out
with a hundred faces all the same,
the coins made of silver
break out in sobs in the pocket.

Federico García Lorca
(June 5th 1898 – August 19th 1936)

translated by Robert Bly

Federico García Lorca was born the elder son of a wealthy landowner in Fuente Vaqueros, a small Andalucian farming town, and spent his adolescence in Granada. He would later say: "[Granada] formed me and made me what I am: a poet from birth and unable to help it."

From 1909 to 1925 Lorca would spend the long hot summers at Asquerosa, a tiny village in the middle of the Granadan plain. In August 1921 he wrote in a letter to a friend: "A few days ago a purple-green moon came out over the bluish mist of the Sierra Nevada and in front of my door a woman sang a *berceuse* that was like a golden streamer entangling the whole countryside. Especially at twilight one lives in the fullest fantasy, a half erased dream ... There are times when everything evaporates and we're left in a desert of pearl gray, of rose and dead silver ... At night our very flesh hurts from so many bright stars and we get drunk on wind and water." 'The Moon Sails Out' is thought to have been written in July 1921.

1. A reference to an old Spanish superstition. In his 1855 *Handbook for Spain*, Richard Ford writes: "The natives are not very fanciful about eating [Seville oranges]: they do not think them good before March, and poison if eaten after sunset."

- Coventry Patmore born in Woodford, Essex, July 23rd 1823
- Henry David Thoreau was arrested on July 23rd 1845 for failing to pay his taxes in protest at slavery and the US invasion of Mexico
- George Barker wrote rapturously of his new love for Elizabeth Smart, "Oh My Canadian", July 23rd 1940

Birth of a Child in Wartime

Slapdash into the bloody pan
Is thrown the longed-for son of man.
Between the gossiping cups of tea
God attains mortality.

In the cathedral calm and cold
Kneel the erroneous-memoried old.
But in the womb's cathedral calm
The walls collapse in a birth psalm.

The blood sings from the soiled hand
The apprentice cleans at the washstand
Undismayed by omission,
For everything, everything is won.

The proof blazes in impudence
Above the miopics of science,
Swaggering in love inviolate
Over the uninitiate.

And over all the angels dart
Like squadrons in a war apart
Dropping parachutes of bliss
On everything that is.

Elizabeth Smart
(December 27th 1913– March 4th 1986)

At parties Canadian writer Elizabeth Smart would ask "Do you know George Barker, because I'd like to meet and marry him." She had come across a collection of his whilst browsing in a London bookshop and fell in love with him through his poems. The story of their meeting and passionate affair was immortalised in her classic debut novel *By Grand Central Station I Sat Down and Wept.* In March 1942, Smart, five months pregnant and with her young daughter by Barker in tow, braved a transatlantic wartime crossing in the hope that Barker would follow; three convoy ships were sunk and their own boat torpedoed. Back in England she supported herself by working as an advertising copywriter and had two more children by Barker. Their relationship persisted despite his later marriage to another woman. In 1966 she escaped London for a quieter life in Suffolk where she resumed her writing, later returning to prominence in 1977 with the semi-autobiographical *The Assumption of the Rogues and the Rascals.*

Smart's son, Christopher Barker, was born in England on this day in 1942.

July 24

• Robert Graves born July 24th 1895. His successful novels, such as I Claudius, financed his first love, poetry: "Prose books are the show dogs I breed to support my cat"
• D. H. Lawrence wrote of Thomas Hardy on July 24th 1928: "What a commonplace genius he has; or a genius for the commonplace"

One Hard Look

Small gnats that fly
In hot July
And lodge in sleeping ears,
Can rouse therein
A trumpet's din
With Day of Judgement fears.

Small mice at night
Can wake more fright
Than lions at midday;
A straw will crack
The camel's back –
There is no easier way.

One smile relieves
A heart that grieves
Though deadly sad it be,
And one hard look
Can close the book
That lovers love to see.

Robert Graves
(July 24th 1895 – December 7th 1985)

This poem was included in Graves' 1920 collection, *Country Sentiment,* so-called because he considered war poetry to be "played-out commercially": "Country sentiment is the most acceptable dope now," he said. The "acceptable" volume did not sell well, however, and received mixed reviews.

Graves wrote 'One Hard Look' in the months following his ill-fated marriage to Nancy Nicholson, which was for Graves a period of profound disillusionment.

- *Samuel Taylor Coleridge died July 25th 1834*
- *An ailing Walter de la Mare wrote on July 25th 1954: "My days are getting shorter. But there is more and more magic. Everything is increasingly wonderful"*
- *American poet Frank O'Hara died July 25th 1966. His tombstone bears the inscription "Grace to be born & live as variously as possible"*

Avenue A

We hardly ever see the moon any more
                                        so no wonder
    it's so beautiful when we look up suddenly
and there it is gliding broken-faced over the bridges
brilliantly coursing, soft, and a cool wind fans
            your hair over your forehead and your memories
                of Red Grooms'[1] locomotive landscape
I want some bourbon/you want some oranges/I love the leather
            jacket Norman gave me
                                and the corduroy coat David
        gave you, it is more mysterious than spring, the El Greco
heavens breaking open and then reassembling like lions
                                in a vast tragic veldt
        that is far from our selves and our temporally united
passions in the cathedral of Januaries

        everything is too comprehensible
these are my delicate and caressing poems
I suppose there will be more of those others to come, as in the past
                        so many!
but for now the moon is revealing itself like a pearl
                    to my equally naked heart

                                        Frank O'Hara
                            (June 27th 1926 – July 25th 1966)

Frank O'Hara is best known for his realistic "I do this, I do that" poems, which chronicle his life as a busy art critic, curator and poet on the move in New York. Written during the intervals at ballets, at parties, on the backs of menus, or during his lunchtime strolls, and filled with everyday objects, and friends, O'Hara's poems captured the present moment like no poet before him: "What is happening to me ... goes into my poems ... my experiences ... are just there in whatever form I can find them," he said. He was struck by a dune buggy on a dark Fire Island beach and died of his injuries on this day in 1966, at the age of 40.

His poetry was largely neglected by critics during his lifetime. After his death, the vast body of his poems, many of them sent in letters to friends, were gathered together and published in *Collected Poems*.

1. Red Grooms is the name of a well-known pop-artist of the time.

July 26

• *John Wilmot, Earl of Rochester, died aged 33 July 26th 1680*
• *Spanish poet Antonio Machado born July 26th 1875*
• *Pound indicted for treason for his fascist wartime broadcasts, July 26th 1943. Archibald MacLeish suggested treason was "too serious a crime and too dignified for a man who has made such an incredible ass of himself"*

The Garret

Come, let us pity those who are better off than we are.
Come, my friend, and remember
     that the rich have butlers and no friends,
And we have friends and no butlers.
Come, let us pity the married and the unmarried.

Dawn enters with little feet
     like a gilded Pavlova,
And I am near my desire.
Nor has life in it aught better
Than this hour of clear coolness,
     the hour of waking together.

Ezra Pound
(October 30th 1885 – November 1st 1972)

A patron to such great modern writers as T. S. Eliot, James Joyce, W. B. Yeats, Robert Frost and William Carlos Williams, Pound is best known for his epic masterpiece *The Cantos*. On their publication in 1933, Ernest Hemingway wrote the following testimonial: "Any poet born in this century or in the last ten years of the preceding century who can honestly say that he has not been influenced by the work of Ezra Pound deserves to be pitied rather than rebuked … The best of Pound's writing – and it is in *The Cantos* – will last as long as there is any literature."

Pound also became infamous for his twice-weekly pro-Fascist broadcasts on Italian radio during the Second World War. He made 125 broadcasts from Rome between December 1941 and July 1943, of wildly varying content and tone. On this day in 1943 he was indicted for treason by the United States government. He was hospitalised for mental illness while controversy raged as to whether he should be tried as a traitor. He remained in care from 1946 to 1948. Declared incompetent to stand trial, Pound was released on this day in 1958 and returned to Italy. Once on Italian turf, he gave a fascist salute for the attendant photographers and resumed his old life.

• *Poet and journalist Thomas Campbell born in Glasgow July 27th 1777*
• *(Joseph-Pierre) Hilaire Belloc born in France July 27th 1870*

First Love

I ne'er was struck before that hour
    With love so sudden and so sweet
Her face it bloomed like a sweet flower
    And stole my heart away complete
My face turned pale a deadly pale
    My legs refused to walk away
And when she looked what could I ail
My life and all seemed turned to clay

And then my blood rushed to my face
    And took my eyesight quite away
The trees and bushes round the place
    Seemed midnight at noon day
I could not see a single thing
    Words from my eyes did start
They spoke as chords do from the string
    And blood burnt round my heart

Are flowers the winter's choice
    Is love's bed always snow
She seemed to hear my silent voice
    Not love's appeals to know
I never saw so sweet a face
    As that I stood before
My heart has left its dwelling place
    And can return no more –

John Clare
(July 13th 1793 – May 20th 1864)

John Clare's first love was his childhood friend Mary Joyce. As Clare's mental health deteriorated in the last 20 years of his life, he began to believe that he had married Mary, although this was not the case. This led him not only to address letters to Mary as his wife, but also to become worried that he was committing bigamy with his actual wife, Martha.

In a letter to Mary dated July 27th 1841, shortly before he was taken away to Northampton asylum, Clare wrote: "my hopes are not entirely hopeless while even the memory of Mary lives so near me", before signing it: "Your affectionate Husband, John Clare". Unfortunately, Mary Joyce had died in July three years earlier, unmarried and unaware of the poetry that she inspired.

• *Percy Bysshe Shelley, already married to Harriet Westbrook, eloped to France with Mary Wollstonecraft, July 28th 1814*
• *Gerard Manley Hopkins born in London July 28th 1844*
• *John Ashbery born in Rochester, New York, July 28th 1927*
• *Poet and social inventor Nicholas Albery born July 28th 1948*

w A Poem By Heart

To know a poem
    by heart
    is to know
in the biblical sense

    making love
ore than an intercourse of bodies —
to enter the mind of the poet
    is an intercourse of souls

        to know a poem
            by heart
        is to slow down
        to the heart's time

        to recite a poem
        from the heart
        is to *be* the poet
    to pay homage to intensity
        to enter eternity
    to find solace for sorrows
        spurs for endeavour
        serotonin for blues
        endorphins for bliss

    learning a poem every day
        is the stations of the cross
    a throng of sub-personalities
        a throb of sympathy
            for every mood

        a poem at your side
    through the valley and the shadows
        in the day, in the night
    a polymorphic, polygamous, orgiastic
        communion of poetry

Nicholas Albery
(July 28th 1948 – June 3rd 2001)

Nicholas Albery's widow, Josefine Speyer, recalls: "Nicholas wrote this poem during one of our Saturday walks and recited it at the Poetry Challenge the following Sunday by way of introduction."

Nicholas Albery was editor of the original volume of *Poem for the Day*.

• U(rsula) A(skham) Fanthorpe, the first woman ever to be
nominated for the post of Oxford Professor of Poetry, born in
London July 29th 1929

An Old-Fashioned Song

No more walks in the wood:
The trees have all been cut
Down, and where once they stood
Not even a wagon rut
Appears along the path
Low brush is taking over.

No more walks in the wood;
This is the aftermath
Of afternoons in the clover
Fields where we once made love
Then wandered home together
Where the trees arched above,
Where the branches made our own weather
When branches were the sky.
Now they are gone for good,
And you, for ill, and I
Am only a passer-by.

We and the trees and the way
Back from the fields of play
Lasted as long as we could.
No more walks in the wood.

John Hollander
(October 28th 1929 –)

John Hollander's first collection of poems, *A Crackling of Thorns*, was brought to wider attention
in 1958 after being included by W. H. Auden in the Yale Series of Younger Poets. Since then,
Hollander has published over 20 further collections, including *Tesserae,* from which this poem
comes, and his *Selected Poems*, which were released simultaneously in 1993. He is also well-known
as a literary critic and editor, and has been a professor and lecturer at many of America's most
prestigious universities.

• *Thomas Gray died July 30th 1771*
• *Siegfried Sassoon's wilful defiance of miltary action was raised in the House of Commons, July 30th 1917*

The Sword of Surprise

Sunder me from my bones, O sword of God,
Till they stand stark and strange as do the trees;
That I whose heart goes up with the soaring woods
May marvel as much at these.

Sunder me from my blood that in the dark
I hear that red ancestral river run,
Like branching buried floods that find the sea
But never see the sun.

Give me miraculous eyes to see my eyes,
Those rolling mirrors made alive in me,
Terrible crystal more incredible
Than all the things they see.

Sunder me from my soul, that I may see
The sins like streaming wounds, the life's brave beat;
Till I shall save myself, as I would save
A stranger in the street.

G. K. Chesterton
(May 29th 1874 – June 14th 1936)

G. K. Chesterton was received into the Catholic Church on this day in 1922, completing his conversion from Anglicanism. His wife Frances was said to have spent the entire day in tears, since she and her husband were now separated by their respective faiths (she remained an Anglican).

• *Burns' first collection*, Poems Chiefly in the Scottish Dialect, *was printed July 31st 1786*
• *Primo Levi, chemist, author, poet and Holocaust survivor, born in Turin July 31st 1919*
• *French aviator and poet Antoine de Saint-Exupéry took his final flight July 31st 1944*

At Lord's

It is little I repair to the matches of the Southron folk,
    Though my own red roses there may blow;
It is little I repair to the matches of the Southron folk,
    Though the red roses crest the caps, I know.
For the field is full of shades as I near the shadowy coast,
And a ghostly batsman plays to the bowling of a ghost,
And I look through my tears on a soundless-clapping host
    As the run-stealers flicker to and fro,
        To and fro:-
O my Hornby and my Barlow long ago!

Francis Thompson
(December 18th 1859 – November 13th 1907)

'At Lord's' celebrates the cricketing prowess of the Lancashire players Albert Hornby and Dick Barlow. Hornby, known as 'Monkey' due to his slight stature, was an exceptional sportsman across the board: as well as a forceful opening bat for Lancashire for over 30 years, he became an international rugby player and skilled horseman, and was the first man to captain England teams at both cricket and rugby football.

Dick Barlow was a superb bowler and played for Lancashire for 20 years. Near the end of his life he said: "I don't think any cricketer has enjoyed his cricketing career better than I have done, and if I had my time to come over again I should certainly be what I have been all my life – a professional cricketer." Barlow died on this day in 1919.

Born in Lancashire, Francis Thompson was a life-long devotee of the Lancashire cricket team.

August 1

- The "most ingenious ... and unfortunate" poet Richard Savage, died in a debtor's jail August 1st 1743. He was buried at the expense of the jailer
- F. R. Scott, Canadian poet and scholar, born in Quebec August 1st 1899
- Theodore Roethke died of a heart attack whilst swimming August 1st 1963

From The Shape of the Fire
4

Morning-fair, follow me further back
Into that minnowy world of weeds and ditches,
When the herons floated high over the white houses,
And the little crabs slipped into silvery craters.
When the sun for me glinted the sides of a sand grain.
And my intent stretched over the buds at their first trembling.

That air and shine: and the flicker's loud summer call:
The bearded boards in the stream and the all of apples;
The glad hen on the hill; and the trellis humming.
Death was not. I lived in a simple drowse:
Hands and hair moved through a dream of wakening blossoms.
Rain sweetened the cave and dove still called;
The flowers leaned on themselves, the flowers in hollows;
And love, love sang toward.

Theodore Roethke
(May 25th 1908 – August 1st 1963)

'The Shape of the Fire' is one of four long poems which form the book *The Lost Son and Other Poems,* widely regarded as Roethke's finest achievement. Primarily autobiographical, the poems widen in scope to deal with other myths and journeys from different ages and writers. Several of the poems, including 'The Shape of the Fire', were written shortly after Roethke's second spell in a mental hospital, in the winter of 1945 to 1946, where he underwent shock treatment.

Upon his death, Roethke left behind 277 notebooks containing rough drafts, memos, complete poems, diary entries and quotations. One of these contained the single sentence, "A poem that is the shape of the psyche itself; in times of great stress, that's what I tried to write."

• Ernest Dowson, poet of the Decadent school, born in Lee,
  Kent, August 2nd 1867
• American poet Stephen Berg born August 2nd 1934
• Wallace Stevens died August 2nd 1955
• Raymond Carver died August 2nd 1988

August 2

Exchanges

All that I had I brought,
  Little enough I know;
A poor rhyme roughly wrought,
  A rose to match thy snow:
All that I had I brought.

Little enough I sought:
  But a word compassionate,
A passing glance, or thought,
  For me outside the gate:
Little enough I sought.

Little enough I found:
  All that you had, perchance!
With the dead leaves on the ground,
  I dance the devil's dance.
All that you had I found.

Ernest Dowson
(August 2nd 1867 – February 23rd 1900)

In 1889, Ernest Dowson first met 11-year-old Adelaide Foltinowicz, the daughter of a Soho restaurant owner. She was to become a symbol of love and innocence in his verse and leave him "idolatrous for the rest of [his] days". Dowson courted her for two years, and even proposed, but was rejected in favour of a waiter whom she eventually married at 19. A friend described how thereafter "Dowson could never recover his fragile hope on life and love".

Dowson was born in Kent, and educated at Oxford, though he left without taking a degree. In the 1890s he joined the Rhymers' club and contributed poems to the periodicals *The Yellow Book* and *The Savoy*. Following the death of both his parents, he wandered aimlessly between England, France and Ireland. He was a friend of Yeats, who described him as "timid, silent and a little melancholy".

August 3

- Burns married his sweetheart Jean Armour August 3rd 1788
- Rupert Brooke, whom Yeats proclaimed "the handsomest young man in England", born at Rugby School August 3rd 1887
- Siegfried Sassoon enlisted with the Sussex Yeomanry August 3rd 1914

The Dead

These hearts were woven of human joys and cares,
    Washed marvellously with sorrow, swift to mirth.
The years had given them kindness. Dawn was theirs,
   And sunset, and the colours of the earth.
These had seen movement, and heard music; known
    Slumber and waking; loved; gone proudly friended;
Felt the quick stir of wonder; sat alone;
    Touched flowers and furs and cheeks. All this is ended.

There are waters blown by changing winds to laughter
And lit by the rich skies, all day. And after,
    Frost, with a gesture, stays the waves that dance
And wandering loveliness. He leaves a white
    Unbroken glory, a gathered radiance,
A width, a shining peace, under the night.

Rupert Brooke
(August 3rd 1887 – April 23rd 1915)

Rupert Brooke was born to a master at Rugby School, and his wife, on this day in 1887. He was the second of three brothers: his elder brother, Dick, died in 1907, and his younger, Alfred, was killed in action at Loos in June 1915. Rupert himself died of acute blood poisoning – contracted from an infected insect bite on his lip – whilst on the Greek island of Skyros the same year.

On August 3rd 1913, during a year's world tour to recuperate from a nervous breakdown suffered the previous year, Brooke wrote from Lake George in Canada: "I'm 26 years old – and I've done so little. I'm very much ashamed. By God, I am going to make things hum though – but that's all so far away. I'm lying quite naked on a beach of golden sand ... cooking and eating a meal naked is the most solemnly primitive thing one can do."

He was back in England by early June 1914, and enlisted in the navy in September. About his five-sonnet sequence entitled '1914', he said: "God, they're in the rough, these five camp-children – 4 [the above poem] and 5 are good enough, and there are phrases in the rest."

- *Shelley born in Field Place, near Horsham, August 4th 1792*
- *John Morley described Swinburne in a review as "libidinous laureate of a pack of satyrs", August 4th 1866*
- *Hans Christian Andersen died August 4th 1873*
- *American poet and novelist Conrad Aiken born August 4th 1889*
- *Black American poet Robert Hayden born Asa Bundy (later renamed by his foster parents) August 4th 1913*

August 1914

What in our lives is burnt
In the fire of this?
The heart's dear granary?
The much we shall miss?

Three lives hath one life –
Iron, honey, gold.
The gold, the honey gone –
Left is the hard and cold.

Iron are our lives
Molten right through our youth.
A burnt space through ripe fields,
A fair mouth's broken tooth.

Isaac Rosenberg
(November 25th 1890 – April 1st 1918)

Poet and painter Isaac Rosenberg was visiting his sister and her new husband in South Africa when war broke out on this day in 1914. He returned to England the following May, and enlisted later that year, just before conscription came into force – not for patriotic reasons but because he thought the separation allowance would help his mother.

Rosenberg hated the army, "the most detestable invention on this earth", and was a hopeless soldier. However, he determined "that this war, with all its powers for devastation, shall not master my poeting ... I will not leave a corner of my consciousness covered up, but saturate myself with the strange and extraordinary new condition of this life, and it will all refine itself into poetry later on."

Rosenberg was killed in a dawn raid on April 1st 1918.

August 5

- Poet Anne Finch died August 5th 1720 after a lifetime of depression
- On August 5th 1918, Woolf wrote of Christina Rossetti: "[S]he starved into austere emaciation, a very fine original gift"
- Wendell Berry, "prophet of rural America", born August 5th 1934
- Edgar A. Guest, whose daily poems were syndicated to over 300 newspapers in the US, died in Detroit August 5th 1959

Flying Crooked

The butterfly, a cabbage-white,
(His honest idiocy of flight)
Will never now, it is too late,
Master the art of flying straight,
Yet has – who knows so well as I? –
A just sense of how not to fly:
He lurches here and here by guess
And God and hope and hopelessness.
Even the aerobatic swift
Has not his flying-crooked gift.

Robert Graves
(July 24th 1895 – December 7th 1985)

Robert Graves discussed this poem in an unposted letter of 1933; he lamented that scientists "fail to understand that the cabbage-white's seemingly erratic flight provides a metaphor for all original and constructive thought".

Graves fought in the First World War and sustained terrible injuries at the Somme in July 1916. Shortly after writing to Sassoon, in a depressed mood, that he was "at last looking out for a cushy wound ... I want to go home", he was pierced through the chest and groin by shrapnel. He was written off by the battalion doctor as having "no chance". News of his death was sent to his parents and was printed in the *Times'* casualty list.

On August 5th the *Times* made good their mistake, announcing that Graves had in fact survived. He later claimed "the joke contributed greatly to my recovery. The people with whom I had been on the worst terms during my life wrote the most enthusiastic condolences to my parents."

• "O rare Ben Jonson" died August 6th 1637
• Alfred, Lord Tennyson born in Somersby, Lincolnshire,
  August 6th 1809
• Irish poet Richard Murphy born August 5th 1927
• Diane di Prima, Beat poet, born August 6th 1934

August 6

If I were loved, as I desire to be

If I were loved, as I desire to be,
What is there in this great sphere of earth,
And range of evil between death and birth,
That I should fear,—if I were loved by thee?
All the inner, all the outer world of pain
Clear love would pierce and cleave, if thou wert mine,
As I have heard that, somewhere in the main,
Fresh-water springs come up through bitter brine.
'Twere joy, not fear, clasped hand in hand with thee,
To wait for death—mute—careless of all ills,
Apart upon a mountain, though the surge
Of some new deluge from a thousand hills
Flung leagues of roaring foam into the gorge
Below us, as far on as eye could see.

Alfred, Lord Tennyson
(August 6th 1809 – October 6th 1892)

Tennyson was delighted when in 1830 his best friend, Arthur Hallam, and his sister, Emily, fell in love. It was only a few months later that Tennyson himself met his future wife, Emily Sellwood.

Their wedding, some 20 years later, took place in great secrecy, largely because both Tennyson and Emily were embarrassed after an exceptionally long and strained courtship: Tennyson was not deemed financially secure enough to marry, Emily doubted his religious steadfastness, and his brother's marriage to Emily's sister had proved disastrous. Although fraught – the wedding dress and cake arrived too late for the wedding – Tennyson nonetheless thought it "the nicest wedding [he] had ever been at" and later recollected: "The peace of God came into my life before the altar where I wedded her."

227

August 7

• William Blake wrote to his biographer, the poet William
  Hayley, August 7th 1804: "Money flies from me. Profit
  never ventures upon my threshold"
• Rabindranath Tagore died in Calcutta August 7th 1941

Life's honouring-deeds we start and do not do –

Life's honouring-deeds we start and do not do –
I know, I know that these are counted too.
   The flowers that do not come to flower
   but drop to earth and lose their power,
the rivers that run dry in desert, never to renew,
I know, I know that these are counted too.

Today's intentions that are not seen through,
I know, I know that these are not untrue.
   All my deeds so long delayed,
   all the tunes I have not played
sound out on your *bina's* strings, all performed by you.
I know, I know that these are counted too.

Rabindranath Tagore
(May 6th 1861– August 7th 1941)

translated by Joe Winter

Rabindranath Tagore won the Nobel Prize for literature in 1913. He was knighted in 1915, but surrendered his knighthood four years later following the Amritsar massacre, when British troops killed over 400 Indian demonstrators protesting against colonial laws.

• *Sara Teasdale, who wrote lyrical poetry on the theme of idealised love and beauty, born in St Louis, Missouri, August 8th 1884*
• *Wilfred Owen wrote to his mother from Craiglockhart hospital on August 8th 1917: "At present I am a sick man in hospital at night; a poet for quarter of an hour after breakfast"*

Proportion

It is not growing like a tree
In bulk, doth make man better be,
Or standing long an oak, three hundred year,
To fall a log at last, dry, bald, and sear:
A lily of a day
Is fairer far in May,
Although it fall and die that night;
It was the plant, and flower of light.
In small proportions we just beauties see,
And in short measures life may perfect be.

Ben Jonson
(c. June 11th 1572 – August 6th 1637)

This poem is an excerpt from Jonson's ode to 'The Immortal Memory and Friendship of that Noble Pair, Sir Lucius Cary and Sir H. Morison'. Cary, Viscount of Falkland, was a generous patron of several writers, including Jonson. He supported the Royalist cause in the Civil War, and was killed at the battle of Newbury in 1643. The ode was written for Cary in 1629, when Morison, his friend and brother-in-law, died at the age of 20.

Jonson lived into his sixties. On this day in 1637, two days after his death, he was buried upright in the north aisle of the nave in Westminster Abbey.

August 9

• Blackfriars theatre in London was leased for 21 years by Shakespeare and his colleagues, August 9th 1608
• English poet John Dryden born August 9th 1631
• Social innovator and poet Michael Young born August 9th 1915
• Philip Larkin born in Coventry August 9th 1922

Solar

Suspended lion face
Spilling at the centre
Of an unfurnished sky
How still you stand,
And how unaided
Single stalkless flower
You pour unrecompensed.

The eye sees you
Simplified by distance
Into an origin,
Your petalled head of flames
Continuously exploding.
Heat is the echo of your
Gold.

Coined there among
Lonely horizontals
You exist openly.
Our needs hourly
Climb and return like angels.
Unclosing like a hand,
You give for ever.

Philip Larkin
(August 9th 1922 – December 2nd 1985)

This was the first poem Larkin wrote after completing *The Whitsun Weddings*, and its devotional nature is strikingly out of character; there is little else like it in the body of his work. Seamus Heaney has said of 'Solar': "The poem is most unexpected and daring, close to the pulse of primitive poetry ... The poet is bold to stand uncovered in the main of light, far from the hatless one who took off his cycle-clips in awkward reverence" [a reference to Larkin's poem 'Church Going'].

• Laurence Binyon, whose poem 'For the Fallen' adorns war
  memorials throughout Britain, born in Lancaster August 10th 1869
• Sylvia Plath's first published poem appeared in the Boston Herald
  August 10th 1941, when Plath was just eight years old

August 10

The Flea

Mark but this flea, and mark in this,
How little that which thou deniest me is;
Me it sucked first, and now sucks thee,
And in this flea our two bloods mingled be[1];
Thou know'st that this cannot be said
A sin, or shame, or loss of maidenhead,
    Yet this enjoys before it woo,
    And pampered swells with one blood made of two,
    And this, alas, is more than we would do.

Oh stay, three lives in one flea spare,
Where we almost, nay more than married are.
This flea is you and I, and this
Our marriage bed and marriage temple is;
Though parents grudge, and you, we are met,
And cloistered in these living walls of jet.
    Though use° make you apt to kill me,   *habit*
    Let not to that, self-murder added be,
    And sacrilege, three sins in killing three.

Cruel and sudden, hast thou since
Purpled thy nail in blood of innocence[2]?
In what could this flea guilty be,
Except in that drop which it sucked from thee?
Yet thou triumph'st, and say'st that thou
Find'st not thy self nor me the weaker now;
    'Tis true; then learn how false fears be:
    Just so much honour, when thou yield'st to me,
    Will waste, as this flea's death took life from thee.

John Donne
(c. June 1572 – March 31st 1631)

Donne wrote to his wife's brother on this day in 1614, "We had not one another at so cheap a rate as that we should ever be so weary of one another." He was referring to his ill-fated secret marriage in 1601 to Ann More, niece of his employer's wife. Ann's father, Sir George, was furious; Donne lost his job and prospects; and the couple fell into ignominy and poverty. A reconciliation was not effected between Donne and his father-in-law until 1609, when Ann's dowry was finally paid. By that time the couple already had two children, with another on the way.

1. It was believed that conception consisted of the mingling of the man and the woman's blood.
2. Like Herod, she has slaughtered the innocents and is now clothed in imperial purple.

August 11

• Henry James Pye, the much-derided Poet Laureate, died in
  Pinner, Middlesex, August 11th 1813
• Hugh MacDiarmid born in Langholm August 11th 1892
• Poet and critic Louise Bogan born in Maine August 11th 1897

Dusk

The sun sets
in a wall that holds the sky.

You'll not
be here long, maybe.

The window
filled with reflections
turns on its pivot;

beyond its edge
the air goes on cold and deep;
your hand feels it,
or mine, or both;
it's the same air for ever.

Now reach across the dark.

Now touch the mountain.

Roy Fisher
(June 11th 1930 –)

Roy Fisher writes: "A room in North Wales, overlooking a deserted beach with mountains rising beyond it."

Roy Fisher was born in Handsworth, Birmingham, and took degrees at Birmingham University. He went on to teach American literature at Keele University, Staffordshire, and later became a freelance writer and jazz musician. He has published numerous collections of poetry, the most recent being *The Dow Low Drop: New and Selected Poems* (Bloodaxe Books, 1996).

• Poet Laureate Robert Southey born August 12th 1774
• William Blake died in London August 12th 1827
• On August 12th 1915, Ezra Pound wrote to John Quinn: "A
  young chap named Eliot has gone back to America for a bit. I
  have more or less discovered him"
• Poet Donald Justice born in Miami August 12th 1925
• Irish poet Medbh McGuckian born in Belfast August 12th 1950

August 12

Ah! Sunflower

Ah! sunflower, weary of time,
Who countest the steps of the sun,
Seeking after that sweet golden clime
Where the traveller's journey is done;

Where the youth pined away with desire,
And the pale virgin shrouded in snow
Arise from their graves, and aspire
Where my sunflower wishes to go.

William Blake
(November 28th 1757 – August 12th 1827)

This is one of a trio of poems which together constitute song 43 of Blake's *Songs of Experience*, along with 'My Pretty Rose Tree' and 'The Lilly'. The accompanying drawing shows a girl lying wistfully beneath a tree, a dejected-looking boy sat beside her.

Blake was born to a hosier and his wife in London and spent almost his entire life in the city he loved. He first saw a vision of God at the age of four and intermittently communicated with religious figures throughout his life. His parents encouraged both his mysticism and his artistic aspirations and he was apprenticed to an engraver at the age of 14. His craftsmanship was exercised with utmost delicacy in his *Songs of Innocence* and *Songs of Experience*; his wife, Catherine, assisted him in hand-painting and binding the books which they sold for a few shillings each.

• *Otto Manninen, Finnish writer, poet and translator, born August 13th 1872*

Grief

I tell you, hopeless grief is passionless;
That only men incredulous of despair
Half-taught in anguish, through the midnight air
Beat upward to God's throne in loud access
Of shrieking and reproach. Full desertness,
In souls as countries, lieth silent-bare
Under the blanching, vertical eye-glare
Of the absolute Heavens. Deep-hearted man, express
Grief for thy Dead in silence like to death—
Most like a monumental statue set
In everlasting watch and moveless woe
Till itself crumble to the dust beneath.
Touch it; the marble eyelids are not wet:
If it could weep, it could arise and go.

Elizabeth Barrett Browning
(March 6th 1806 – June 29th 1861)

On July 11th 1840, Elizabeth Barrett Browning parted with "a pettish word" from her eldest brother, Edward Moulton, as he left the house to go sailing with friends in Torbay. He was never heard of again, and his body was washed to shore on August 4th. Between July and October Elizabeth was in deep mourning for her 'Bro', and she would not read nor write. Later she wrote that she felt "bound ... in chains, heavy and cold enough to be iron – and which have indeed entered into the soul". Her father wrote: "I confess ... it is wonder to me that she lives, for her love for him we mourn was truly great."

Her poetry from this period is filled with images of death and angels, and from this time on she wore only black. Finally, in January 1841, she accepted her friend's offer of a spaniel pup to help her in her grief: the famous 'Flush' of her poem of the same name.

Everything Changes

Everything changes. You can make
A fresh start with your final breath.
But what has happened has happened. And the water
You once poured into the wine cannot be
Drained off again.

What has happened has happened. The water
You once poured into the wine cannot be
Drained off again, but
Everything changes. You can make
A fresh start with your final breath.

Bertolt Brecht
(February 10th 1898 – August 14th 1956)

translated by John Willett

Though better known as a playwright, Bertolt Brecht was also an accomplished poet. As a young boy in Bavaria, he wrote patriotic poems praising the Kaiser. Later, he expressed his increasing disillusionment with the government in a satirical pacifist poem, 'Legend of the Dead Soldier', which caused him to be blacklisted by the Nazis. Brecht's friends – including Karl Korsch, a leader of the German Communist party in the 1920s, and various members of the Dadaist group – were influential in developing his own vehemently anti-bourgeois attitudes.

Brecht was driven into exile in 1933, and lived for some time in Scandinavia and Denmark before settling in the States, where he worked, rather unsuccessfully, in Hollywood. In Germany, Brecht's books were burnt and his citizenship annulled. He returned to Berlin only in 1949, where he set up the Berliner Ensemble as a vehicle for his experimental theatre. He was awarded the Stalin Peace Prize in 1955.

August 15

• Donne's wife, Ann, died after giving birth to their eleventh child, August 15th 1617
• Walter Scott, novelist and poet, born in Edinburgh August 15th 1771

An Hour With Thee

An hour with thee! When earliest day
  Dapples with gold the eastern gray,
Oh, what can frame my mind to bear
  The toil and turmoil, cark and care,
New griefs, which coming hours unfold,
And sad remembrance of the old?
    One hour with thee.

One hour with thee! When burning June
  Waves his red flag at pitch of noon;
What shall repay the faithful swain,
  His labour on the sultry plain;
And, more than cave or sheltering bough,
Cool feverish blood and throbbing brow?
    One hour with thee.

One hour with thee! When sun is set,
  Oh, what can teach me to forget
The thankless labours of the day;
  The hopes, the wishes, flung away;
The increasing wants, and lessening gains,
The master's pride, who scorns my pains?
    One hour with thee.

Sir Walter Scott
(August 15th 1771 – September 21st 1832)

Walter Scott's father was called Walter Scott, as was his great-grandfather who was, in turn, the second son of another Walter Scott who was himself a grandson of ... Walter Scott. *The* Walter Scott was known as 'Wattie' in his early years, and looked set to follow his father into law before changing direction in favour of writing. His greatest success was the verse novel *The Lady in the Lake*, and he was at the height of his fame in the early 1800s. He declined the offer of the laureateship in 1813, so Robert Southey took up the post instead.

'An Hour with Thee' may well be about his wife Charlotte, who Scott married on Christmas Day in 1797. They were together until her death in 1826.

236

• Andrew Marvell died August 16th (or 18th) 1678
• Thomas Wentworth Higginson wrote on August 16th 1870
  of his visit to see Emily Dickinson: "I never was with anyone
  who drained my nerve power so"
• Charles Bukowski born in Andernach in Germany August
  16th 1920

startled into life like fire

in grievous deity my cat
walks around
he walks around and around
with
electric tail and
push–button
eyes

he is
alive and
plush and
final as a plum tree

neither of us understands
cathedrals or
the man outside
watering his
lawn

if I were all the man
that he is
cat—
if there were men
like this
the world could
begin

he leaps up on the couch
and walks through
porticoes of my
admiration.

Charles Bukowski
(August 16th 1920 – March 9th 1994)

Charles Bukowski, known as a writer, mailman, and self-confessed 'barfly', was also a great animal-
lover. In later life, he surrounded himself with stray cats at his house in San Pedro, near Los Angeles.

August 17

• Wilfrid Scawen Blunt, English writer and poet, born
  August 17th 1843
• Ted Hughes born in Mytholmroyd, Yorkshire, August 17th 1930
• Charlotte Perkins Gilman, poet and short story writer, committed
  suicide August 17th 1935

Full Moon and Little Frieda

A cool small evening shrunk to a dog bark and the clank of a bucket –

And you listening.
A spider's web, tense for the dew's touch.
A pail lifted, still and brimming – mirror
To tempt a first star to a tremor.

Cows are going home in the lane there, looping the hedges with their
                                                warm wreaths of breath –
A dark river of blood, many boulders,
Balancing unspilled milk.

'Moon!' you cry suddenly, 'Moon! Moon!'

The moon has stepped back like an artist gazing amazed at a work

That points at him amazed.

                                        Ted Hughes
                        (August 17th 1930 – October 28th 1998)

In 1961, Ted Hughes moved with his young family to North Devon, where he was to remain until his death in 1998. Hughes' poetry is characterised by its sensitivity to place and the natural world, informed by his lifelong passion for the countryside.

Frieda Hughes, just two years old when Hughes wrote this poem, is now herself a poet and artist. Her latest collection is *Stonepicker* (Bloodaxe Books, 2001).

• *Andrew Marvell died August 18th (or 16th) 1678*
• *William Blake married Catherine Boucher August 18th 1782*
• *Wilfred Owen summoned the courage to appoach "the great man"*
  Siegfried Sassoon at Craiglockhart hospital on August 18th 1917
• *Geoffrey Dearmer, the last of the Great War poets who fought at*
  Gallipoli and the Somme, died August 18th 1996, aged 103

August 18

I will make you brooches and toys

I will make you brooches and toys for your delight
Of bird-song at morning and star-shine at night.
I will make a palace fit for you and me
Of green days in forests and blue days at sea.

I will make my kitchen, and you shall keep your room,
Where white flows the river and bright blows the broom,
And you shall wash your linen and keep your body white
In rainfall at morning and dewfall at night.

And this shall be for music when no one else is near,
The fine song for singing, the rare song to hear!
That only I remember, that only you admire,
Of the broad road that stretches and the roadside fire.

Robert Louis Stevenson
(November 13th 1850 – December 3rd 1894)

Robert Louis Stevenson, who wrote such classic tales as *Treasure Island, Kidnapped!* and *Dr Jekyll and Mr Hyde*, also published a few books of poetry, including *A Child's Garden of Verses* and *Songs of Travel*. This poem was first published the year after his death, as part of his collected works.

Stevenson lived the last few years of his life in Samoa, where the climate gave him relief from the symptoms of his lifelong illness (thought to be tuberculosis or bronchiectasis). From there, he wrote to his friend Sidney Colvin, in 1891, about the people around him, including his wife Fanny, and "Ratke, a German cook, good – and Germanly bad; he don't make *my* kitchen". The latter is a reference to the first line of the second stanza in the poem above.

Stevenson met Fanny Osborne, a married American woman ten years his senior, whilst on a writers' retreat in France in 1878. By the time she returned to the US the following year, Stevenson was deeply in love with her. He left Scotland to be with her, and arrived ill and penniless in New York on this day in 1879. They were married in 1880.

• Ogden Nash, ancestor of General Nash who gave his name to Nashville, born in Rye, New York, August 19th 1902
• Federico García Lorca killed by Franco sympathisers on about August 19th 1936
• Jack Kerouac took off for Mexico in July 1955 and by August 19th had "knocked off 150 bloody poetic masterpieces ... each one of uniform length and wailing"

Portrait of the Artist as a Prematurely Old Man

It is common knowledge to every schoolboy and even every Bachelor of Arts,
That all sin is divided into two parts.
One kind of sin is called a sin of commission, and that is very important,
And it is what you are doing when you are doing something you ortant,
And the other kind of sin is just the opposite and is called a sin of
  omission and is equally bad in the eyes of all right-thinking people,
  from Billy Sunday to Buddha,
And it consists of not having done something you shuddha.
I might as well give you my opinion of these two kinds of sin as long as,
  in a way, against each other we are pitting them,
And that is, don't bother your head about the sins of commission because
  however sinful, they must at least be fun or else you wouldn't be
  committing them.
It is the sin of omission, the second kind of sin,
That lays eggs under your skin.
The way you get really painfully bitten
Is by the insurance you haven't taken out and the checks you haven't
  added up the stubs of and the appointments you haven't kept and
  the bills you haven't paid and the letters you haven't written.
Also, about sins of omission there is one particularly painful lack of beauty,
Namely, it isn't as though it had been a riotous red-letter day or night
  every time you neglected to do your duty;
You didn't get a wicked forbidden thrill
Every time you let a policy lapse or forget to pay a bill;
You didn't slap the lads in the tavern on the back and loudly cry Whee,
Let's all fail to write just one more letter before we go home, and this
  round of unwritten letters is on me.
No, you never get any fun
Out of the things you haven't done,
But they are the things that I do not like to be amid,
Because the suitable things you didn't do give you a lot more trouble
  than the unsuitable things you did.
The moral is that it is probably better not to sin at all, but if some kind
  of sin you must be pursuing,
Well, remember to do it by doing rather than by not doing.

Ogden Nash
(August 19th 1902 – May 19th 1971)

- *Poet and playwright Sir Charles Sedley died August 20th 1701*
- *Saul Tchernichowsky, poet, born in Crimea August 20th 1875*
- *Edgar A. Guest, who became US 'poet of the people' for his deeply sentimental verse, born in England August 20th 1881*
- *Nobel Prize-winning poet Salvatore Quasimodo ('Everyone stands alone on the heart of the earth / Transfixed by a sun-ray: And it is suddenly night') born in Modica, Italy, August 20th 1901*

When the heart

When the heart
is cut or cracked or broken
Do not clutch it
Let the wound lie open

Let the wind
From the good old sea blow in
To bathe the wound with salt
And let it sting

Let a stray dog lick it
Let a bird lean in the hole and sing
A simple song like a tiny bell
And let it ring

Michael Leunig
(1945 –)

Michael Leunig is an Australian cartoonist who was born in East Melbourne in 1945. Having emerged as a satirical talent in the 1960s, Leunig has since become widely known in Australia and beyond as a poignant and insightful chronicler of society. Indeed, his devotees think of him as much a philosopher and poet as a cartoonist. He is a regular contributor to his local paper, the *Melbourne Age*, and has published thirteen books since 1974, the most recent being *The Curly Pyjama Letters* (Penguin, 2001).

August 21

- *Religious poet Richard Crashaw died August 21st 1649*
- *Christopher Robin Milne, immortalised by his father in the Winnie the Pooh series ("One day I will write verses about him and see how he likes it"), born August 21st 1920*
- *Poet X. J. Kennedy born Joseph Charles Kennedy in Dover, New Jersey, August 21st 1929*

Dark August

So much rain, so much life like the swollen sky
of this black August. My sister, the sun,
broods in her yellow room and won't come out.

Everything goes to hell; the mountains fume
like a kettle, rivers overrun; still,
she will not rise and turn off the rain.

She's in her room, fondling old things,
my poems, turning her album. Even if thunder falls
like a crash of plates from the sky,

she does not come out.
Don't you know I love you but am hopeless
at fixing the rain? But I am learning slowly

to love the dark days, the steaming hills,
the air with gossiping mosquitoes,
and to sip the medicine of bitterness,

so that when you emerge, my sister,
parting the beads of the rain,
with your forehead of flowers and eyes of forgiveness,

all will not be as it was, but it will be true
(you see they will not let me love
as I want), because, my sister, then

I would have learnt to love black days like bright ones,
the black rain, the white hills, when once
I loved only my happiness and you.

Derek Walcott
(January 23rd 1930 –)

When he appeared on Desert Island Discs, Walcott chose cigarettes as his luxury, Joyce's *Ulysses* as his one book, and a mix of music that included Bob Marley, Paul Simon and several calypso artists. Walcott and Simon are friends, and they famously collaborated on the (not altogether successful) 1997 musical, *The Capeman*.

• *Dorothy Parker born in West End, New Jersey, August 22nd 1893. On her 70th birthday, in 1963, she declared, "If I had any decency I'd be dead. Most of my friends are"*

August 22

Comment

Oh, life is a glorious cycle of song,
A medley of extemporanea;
And love is a thing that can never go wrong;
And I am Marie of Roumania.

Dorothy Parker
(August 22nd 1893 – June 7th 1967)

Dorothy Parker began her flamboyant career writing captions for *Vogue*. She swiftly became a respected journalist, critic and reviewer, employed for many years as a 'Constant Reader' for the *New Yorker*. Parker was an intrinsic member of the esteemed Round Table literary circle who met regularly in the Algonquin Hotel in Manhattan during the 1920s. It was later described by Parker as "just a bunch of people making jokes and telling each other how good they were."

Much like the failed relationships Parker depicted in her poetry and short stories, Parker's own love life was disastrous. She married Edwin Pond Parker in 1917 but they divorced in 1928, and her subsequent marriage to a film actor, Alan Campbell, also failed.

Parker once declared, "I don't care what is written about me so long as it isn't true."

• Free-verse poet, critic and editor W. E. Henley, born in
Gloucester August 23rd 1849
• American poet and professor J. V. Cunningham born in
Cumberland, Maryland, August 23rd 1911

A Lyric Afterwards

There was a taut dryness all that summer
and you sat each day in the hot garden
until those uniformed comedians
filled the street with their big white ambulance,
fetching you and bringing you back to me.

Far from the sea of ourselves we waited
and prayed for the tight blue silence to give.
In your absence I climbed to a square room
where there were dried flowers, folders of sonnets
and crossword puzzles: call them musical

snuffboxes or mannered anachronisms,
they were all too uselessly intricate,
caskets of the dead spirit. Their bitter
constraints and formal pleasures were a style
of being perfect in despair; they spoke

with the vicious trapped crying of a wren.
But that is changed now, and when I see you
walking by the river, a step from me,
there is this great kindness everywhere:
now in the grace of the world and always.

Tom Paulin
(January 25th 1949 –)

Tom Paulin comments: "I wrote this poem in 1977, after my wife Giti was badly injured in a road accident in the North of Ireland."

Paulin was born in Leeds but grew up in Belfast. He was educated at Hull University and Oxford, where he is presently the G. M. Young Lecturer in English at Hertford College. He won the Somerset Maugham Award for *A State of Justice* in 1977, the Geoffrey Faber Memorial Prize for *The Strange Museum* in 1980, and received a NESTA award in 2000. His latest book is *The Invasion Handbook*, the first installment of an epic poem about the Second World War. He is a regular panellist on the BBC show *Late Review*.

- *The flirtatious poet-priest Robert Herrick born in London August 24th 1591*
- *Thomas Chatterton, who claimed his poems were written by a 15th century monk, committed suicide August 30th 1770*
- *Jorge Luis Borges born in Buenos Aires August 24th 1899*
- *Poet Charles Causley born in Cornwall August 24th 1917*

I Am the Great Sun
(From a Normandy crucifix of 1632)

I am the great sun, but you do not see me,
  I am your husband, but you turn away.
I am the captive, but you do not free me,
  I am the captain you will not obey.

I am the truth, but you will not believe me,
  I am the city where you will not stay,
I am your wife, your child, but you will leave me,
  I am that God to whom you will not pray.

I am your counsel, but you do not hear me,
  I am the lover whom you will betray,
I am the victor, but you do not cheer me,
  I am the holy dove whom you will slay.

I am your life, but if you will not name me,
Seal up your soul with tears, and never blame me.

Charles Causley
(August 24th 1917 –)

Charles Causley wanted to be a writer from an early age, and began his first novel when he was nine, but he left school at 15 and worked as a clerk for seven years. He then joined the navy in 1940 and served in the Second World War. It was his war experiences that gave him the subject matter he had been lacking, and his first two poetry collections consist mostly of war poems.

It was his third collection, *Union Street* (1957), which included 'I Am the Great Sun', that secured his reputation as a major poet. He has continued to write prolifically since then, and is particularly admired for his children's poetry. Though unfashionable with literary critics, Causley has remained one of the most popular poets writing in English. Ted Hughes said of him that he was "among all known poets, the only one who could be called a man of the people, in the old, best sense".

August 25

• Poet and playwright Thomas Dekker died August 25th 1632
• Burns began his third and most arduous (600 mile) tour of Scotland to collect Scottish songs and folklore, August 25th 1787
• Russian poet Nikolai Gumilov, Anna Akhmatova's first husband, shot for alleged complicity in an anti-Bolshevik conspiracy, August 25th 1921
• Poet Charles Wright born in Tennessee August 25th 1935

Praise in Summer

Obscurely yet most surely called to praise,
As sometimes summer calls us all, I said
The hills are heavens full of branching ways
Where star-nosed moles fly overhead the dead;
I said the trees are mines in air, I said
See how the sparrow burrows in the sky!
And then I wondered why this mad *instead*
Perverts our praise to uncreation, why
Such savor's in this wrenching things awry.
Does sense so stale that it must needs derange
The world to know it? To a praiseful eye
Should it not be enough of fresh and strange
That trees grow green, and moles can course in clay,
And sparrows sweep the ceiling of our day?

Richard Wilbur
(March 1st 1921 –)

Richard Wilbur comments: "Aristotle once said, 'The making of metaphor is the peculiar gift of the poet, the mark of poetic genius.' This early poem of mine – a Spenserian sonnet, by the way – begins as an impatient attack on metaphor, but by the close has capitulated and become helplessly metaphorical. That's as it should be, because the likening of things, the implication that all things are connatural, is of poetry's essence."

Richard Wilbur served in the Second World War, and saw action in Italy, France and Germany. He returned from the war to assemble his first collection of poems *The Beautiful Changes and Other Poems* (which included 'Praise in Summer'); it was published when Wilbur was just 26. Many critics were mystified by the apparent optimism of Wilbur's poetry, and he has been criticised for failing to write a poetry that bears witness to suffering. Nonetheless, this and his subsequent books were widely praised, and established Wilbur as one of the most important poets writing in America.

• Guillaume Apollinaire, poet and playwright, born in Rome to an aristocratic Polish adventuress, and (it is thought) an Italian army officer August 26th 1880

The Mirabeau Bridge

Under the Mirabeau Bridge the Seine
Flows and our love
Must I be reminded again
How joy came always after pain

Night comes the hour is rung
The days go I remain

Hands within hands we stand face to face
While underneath
The bridge of our arms passes
The loose wave of our gazing which is endless

Night comes the hour is rung
The days go I remain

Love slips away like this water flowing
Love slips away
How slow life is in its going
And hope is so violent a thing

Night comes the hour is rung
The days go I remain

The days pass the weeks pass and are gone
Neither time that is gone
Nor love ever returns again
Under the Mirabeau Bridge flows the Seine

Night comes the hour is rung
The days go I remain

Guillaume Apollinaire
(August 26th 1880 – November 9th 1918)

translated by W. S. Merwin

Christened Guglielmo de Kostrowitzky, Apollinaire changed his name following a visit to the Apollinariskirche at Remagen in the Rhineland when he was 21. He later befriended Picasso and Max Jacob in Paris, and became closely involved with contemporaneous art movements, coining the term 'sur-réalisme'. His first book of poems, *Le Bestiaire*, was published in 1911; the same year he was wrongfully arrested (and released) on suspicion of stealing the Mona Lisa. He enlisted in 1914 and served in the infantry until a head injury and trepanation forced him out of service.

'Le Pont Mirabeau', first published in 1912, is believed to be about the painter Marie Laurencin, with whom Apollinaire had a four-year relationship.

August 27

- *Milton's books were burned in London following his attacks on Charles II, August 27th 1660*
- *Scottish poet James Thompson died August 27th 1748*
- *Exiled poet and novelist Cesare Pavese, who said, "Mine would be a biography to be written with a scalpel", committed suicide in Turin August 27th 1950*

The Linen Industry

Pulling up flax after the blue flowers have fallen
And laying our handfuls in the peaty water
To rot those grasses to the bone, or building stooks
That recall the skirts of an invisible dancer,

We become a part of the linen industry
And following its processes to the grubby town
Where fields are compacted into window-boxes
And there is little room among the big machines.

But even in our attic under the skylight
We make love on a bleach green, the whole meadow
Draped with material turning white in the sun
As though snow reluctant to melt were our attire.

What's passion but a battering of stubborn stalks,
Then a gentle combing out of fibres like hair
And a weaving of these into christening robes,
Into garments for a marriage or funeral?

Since it's like a bereavement once the labour's done
To find ourselves last workers in a dying trade,
Let flax be our matchmaker, our undertaker,
The provider of sheets for whatever the bed –

And be shy of your breasts in the presence of death,
Say that you look more beautiful in linen
Wearing white petticoats, the bow of your bodice
A butterfly attending the embroidered flowers.

Michael Longley
(July 27th 1939 –)

Michael Longley has said of his work: "I live for those moments when language itself takes over the enterprise, and insight races ahead of knowledge."

Michael Longley read Classics at Trinity College, Dublin and then taught in schools in England and Ireland. His collection *The Weather in Japan* (2000) won the T. S. Eliot prize and the Hawthornden prize, and he was awarded the Queen's Gold Medal for Poetry in 2001. He and his wife, the critic Edna Longley, live and work in Belfast.

Younger

A hundred lives ago, with someone like you,
up among the stucco wedding cakes of Campden Hill,
before the absolute estoppel
of split up and the long-range meteorology
of becoming old friends,
before swagger became stagger,
before my first look in the mirror of Dorian Grey,
I stood in front of the big studio window
and thought I could really see
the hyper-bright air, the warm days roll in,
the anticyclone isobars
drawn languidly across the southern hemisphere of my life.

Sometimes I see the open window,
in the variegated light that can occur in a room,
in cloud shapes observable after rain,
or when I talk with you of what you will come to do.

John Stammers
(August 28th 1954 –)

John Stammers writes: "This poem arose from an occasion when I unexpectedly arrived at a place I had once lived. It felt like that part in *Brideshead Revisited* where Rider happens across the house again. It's to do with how you can only live your life forwards."

Stammers' first collection, *Panoramic Lounge-Bar* (Picador), won the Forward prize for Best First Collection 2001.

August 29

• Thom Gunn born in Gravesend, Kent, August 29th 1929
• Robert Frost departed for a goodwill tour of the USSR, sponsored by the US state department, on August 29th 1962, aged 88

Touch

You are already
asleep. I lower
myself in next to
you, my skin slightly
numb with the restraint
of habits, the patina of
self, the black frost
of outsideness, so that even
unclothed it is
a resilient chilly
hardness, a superficially
malleable, dead
rubbery texture.

You are a mound
of bedclothes, where the cat
in sleep braces
its paws against your
calf through the blankets,
and kneads each paw in turn.

Meanwhile and slowly
I feel a is it
my own warmth surfacing or
the ferment of your whole
body that in darkness beneath
the cover is stealing
bit by bit to break
down that chill.

You turn and
hold me tightly, do
you know who
I am or am I
your mother or
the nearest human being to
hold on to in a
dreamed pogrom.

What I, now loosened,
sink into is an old
big place, it is
there already, for
you are already
there, and the cat
got there before you, yet
it is hard to locate.
What is more, the place is
not found but seeps
from our touch in
continuous creation, dark
enclosing cocoon round
ourselves alone, dark
wide realm where we
walk with everyone.

Thom Gunn
(August 29th 1929 –)

Gunn fell in love with an American man while at Cambridge University and followed him to the US. It is this relationship which informs his first unmetred verse poem, 'Touch', the title poem of his 1967 collection, which saw Gunn writing with greater risk and freedom.

Fatal interview XLVII

Well, I have lost you, and lost you fairly,
In my own way and with my full consent.
Say what you will, Kings in a tumbrel rarely
Went to their deaths more proud than this one went.
Some nights of apprehension and hot weeping
I will confess: but that's permitted me;
Day dried my eyes; I was not one for keeping
Rubbed in a cage a wing that would be free.
If I had loved you less or played you slyly
I might have held you for a summer more,
But at the cost of words I value highly,
And no such summer as the one before.
Should I outlive this anguish – and men do –
I shall have only good to say of you.

Edna St Vincent Millay
(February 22nd 1882 – October 19th 1950)

Fatal Interview, a sequence of 52 Shakespearian sonnets, was first published in 1931, and sold 50,000 copies within three months. Millay wrote the sequence after meeting a young graduate, George Dillon, at a reading in 1928. Millay was 36, while Dillon was just 22. He recalled their fateful meeting with the words, "For my part I was permanently won." Millay's sonnets play with the myth of Selene and Endymion: Selene was the eternally beautiful goddess of the Moon who begged Zeus to grant the handsome mortal Endymion eternal life. In the myth, Endymion chooses to sleep forever, remaining deathless and ageless, while Selene visits him nightly, eventually bearing him a total of 50 daughters.

Millay and Dillon lived together in Paris during the winter and spring of 1932, although Millay was still married to Eugen Jan Boissevain. Boissevain remained devoted to Millay, managing her literary career and other public engagments up until his death on this day in 1949.

The sequence title, *Fatal Interview*, is taken from a line in Donne's 'Elegie XVI: On His Mistris': "By our first and fatal interview, / By all desires which thereof did ensue ..."

August 31

• John Bunyan died of a fever two months short of his 60th
  birthday, August 31st 1688
• French Symbolist poet Charles Baudelaire died in Paris, aged
  46, on August 31st 1867. It is believed he died of syphilis
• Poet Charles Reznikoff born in Brooklyn August 31st 1894
• Russian poet Marina Tsvetayeva hanged herself in a fit of
  grief and despair, August 31st 1941
• Alice Oswald born August 31st 1966

Sea Sonnet

A field, a sea–flower, three stones, a stile.
Not one thing close to another
throughout air. The cliff's uplifted lawns.
You and I walk light as wicker in virtual contact.

Prepositions lie exposed. All along
the swimmer is deeper than the water.
I have looked under the wave,
I saw your body floating on the darkness.

But time and water cannot touch.
Not once. Only a blob far out,
your singularity and the sea's
inalienable currents flow at angles . . .

and if I love you this is incidental
as on the sand one blue towel, one white towel.

Alice Oswald
(August 31st 1966 –)

Alice Oswald comments on this poem: "It's about the extraordinary North Cornish coast, where all single things – even man and wife – feel far away from each other."

Oswald trained as a Classicist and gardener. Her first collection, *The Thing in the Gap-Stone Stile*, won the Forward Prize in 1996. Her second collection, *Dart*, which won the 2002 T. S. Eliot Prize, is a long many-voiced poem which follows the course of the river Dart in Devon. It is the culmination of two years spent interviewing people who live and work along the river. Oswald is married with two children and lives in Devon.

• Australian poet Bernard O'Dowd died September 1st 1953
• Writer and poet Siegfried Sassoon died at home in Wiltshire
  September 1st 1967, one week short of his 81st birthday

Invocation

Come down from heaven to meet me when my breath
Chokes, and through drumming shafts of stifling death
I stumble toward escape, to find the door
Opening on morn where I may breathe once more
Clear cock-crow airs across some valley dim
With whispering trees. While dawn along the rim
Of night's horizon flows in lakes of fire,
Come down from heaven's bright hill, my song's desire.

Belov'd and faithful, teach my soul to wake
In glades deep-ranked with flowers that gleam and shake
And flock your paths with wonder. In your gaze
Show me the vanquished vigil of my days.
Mute in that golden silence hung with green,
Come down from heaven and bring me in your eyes
Remembrance of all beauty that has been,
And stillness from the pools of Paradise.

Siegfried Sassoon
(September 8th 1886 – September 1st 1967)

Sassoon made a resolution at the end of 1917 to "write happy poems". He wrote 'Invocation' in early December 1917 whilst on leave, in the relatively peaceful period following his release from Craiglockhart hospital and before his return to the Front. Later he was to call 'Invocation' and 'Thrushes' the only "pure poetry" in his anti-war collection *Counter Attack*.

September 2

• Eugene Field, best known for his children's poetry, born in St Louis September 2nd 1850
• A letter to the still anonymous translator of The Rubáiyát (Edward Fitzgerald) read: "I never did – till this day – read anything so glorious", September 2nd 1863
• Poet, critic and writer Laura Riding, died September 2nd 1991

To Marguerite

Yes: in the sea of life enisl'd,
With echoing straits between us thrown,
Dotting the shoreless watery wild,
We mortal millions live *alone*.
The islands feel the enclasping flow,
And then their endless bounds they know.

But when the moon their hollows lights
And they are swept by balms of spring,
And in their glens, on starry nights,
The nightingales divinely sing;
And lovely notes, from shore to shore,
Across the sounds and channels pour;

Oh then a longing like despair
Is to their farthest caverns sent;
For surely once, they feel, we were
Parts of a single continent.
Now round us spreads the watery plain —
Oh might our marges meet again!

Who order'd, that their longing's fire
Should be, as soon as kindled, cool'd?
Who renders vain their deep desire? —
A God, a God their severance ruled;
And bade betwixt their shores to be
The unplumb'd, salt, estranging sea.

Matthew Arnold
(December 24th 1822 – April 15th 1888)

In September 1848, Matthew Arnold travelled to Switzerland, where it is thought he met the woman who inspired the series of 'Marguerite' poems. The true identity of 'Marguerite' has evaded scholars and researchers for years, but most are convinced that she at least existed. In a letter Arnold wrote from Switzerland to his friend A. H. Clough, Arnold wrote of his intent to "linger one day at the Hotel Bellevue for the sake of the blue eyes of one of its inmates"; other poems about 'Marguerite' refer to the blueness of her eyes.

In 1849, Arnold returned to Switzerland for a reunion with his love. This failed, and he wrote 'To Marguerite' and several other poems in the winter of that year.

• E. E. Cummings died September 3rd 1962
• Louis MacNeice died of pneumonia September 3rd 1963

September 3

The Sunlight on the Garden

The sunlight on the garden
Hardens and grows cold,
We cannot cage the minute
Within its nets of gold,
When all is told
We cannot beg for pardon.

Our freedom as free lances
Advances towards its end;
The earth compels, upon it
Sonnets and birds descend;
And soon, my friend,
We shall have no time for dances.

The sky was good for flying
Defying the church bells
And every evil iron
Siren and what it tells:
The earth compels,
We are dying, Egypt, dying[1]

And not expecting pardon,
Hardened in heart anew,
But glad to have sat under
Thunder and rain with you,
And grateful too
For sunlight on the garden.

Louis MacNeice
(September 12th 1907 – September 3rd 1963)

This poem was written in November 1936, shortly after Louis MacNeice's divorce from Mary Beazley had been finalised. He had just moved into a garden flat in Keats Grove in Hampstead, so called because Keats lived and wrote close by from 1818 to 1820.

Beazley and MacNeice were married for six and a half years, and MacNeice continued to refer to her, even after the divorce, as "the best dancer in Oxford". There was a distinct lack of acrimony between the two, despite the failure of the marriage and despite MacNeice having written intriguingly in his autobiography of the divorce going through "after an eleventh-hour flutter with detectives".

1. From Antony's speech in *Antony and Cleopatra*, Act 4.15.41: "I am dying, Egypt, dying".

September 4

• American poet Phoebe Cary born in Mount Healthy, near Cincinnati, Ohio, September 4th 1824
• Anna Akhmatova expelled from the Writers' Union September 4th 1946

Let any, who will, still bask in the south

You are with me once more, Autumn my friend! — Annensky

Let any, who will, still bask in the south
On the paradisal sand,
It's northerly here—and this year of the north
Autumn will be my friend.

I'll live, in a dream, in a stranger's house
Where perhaps I have died,
Where the mirrors keep something mysterious
To themselves in the evening light.

I shall walk between black fir-trees,
Where the wind is at one with the heath,
And a dull splinter of the moon will glint
Like an old knife with jagged teeth.

Our last, blissful unmeeting I shall bring
To sustain me here—
The cold, pure, light flame of conquering
What I was destined for.

Anna Akhmatova
(June 23rd 1889 – March 5th 1966)

translated by D. M. Thomas

Anna Akhmatova's fourth collection, *From Six Books*, was published in 1940 but was withdrawn almost immediately on Stalin's orders. The outbreak of war prompted a relaxation of the controls on her publication, but this freedom ended in August 1946. When Akhmatova attended a meeting at the Union of Soviet Writers on August 15th she was studiously avoided; later, buying fish at the market on her way home, she met her friend and fellow writer, Zoshchenko, in deep despair. Only when she unwrapped the newspaper from her fish did Akhmatova read about the Central Committee resolution to expel herself and Zoshchenko from the Writers' Union.

Andre Zhandanov, Secretary of the Committee, had branded Akhmatova "half-nun, half-harlot", asking: "What positive contribution can Akhmatova's poetry make to our young people? It can do nothing but harm." She was officially expelled the following month. Her ration book was removed and she was left dependent upon the support of friends and the little money she was able to earn through translating. Her own poetry was not published again for over a decade, and even then it was heavily censored.

• *After the theft of her beloved dog Flush, Elizabeth Barrett Browning went personally to negotiate a ransom with the dog-robbers, September 5th 1846*
• *American poet Jorie Graham born September 5th 1951*

September 5

Considering the Snail

The snail pushes through a green
night, for the grass is heavy
with water and meets over
the bright path he makes, where rain
has darkened the earth's dark. He
moves in a wood of desire,

pale antlers barely stirring
as he hunts. I cannot tell
what power is at work, drenched there
with purpose, knowing nothing.
What is a snail's fury? All
I think is that if later

I parted the blades above
the tunnel and saw the thin
trail of broken white across
litter, I would never have
imagined the slow passion
to that deliberate progress.

Thom Gunn
(August 29th 1929 –)

Thom Gunn was born in Gravesend, Kent, but moved with his family to London when he was eight. He developed a passion for books from his mother, who died when he was a teenager. He was "mad about Keats and Marlowe" and has said of his early ambition: "When I was 17 I wanted to be a poet and I started learning poetry from *The Oxford Book of Poetry* because I thought it would help my sense of rhythm."

Gunn's first collection, *Fighting Terms*, was published to considerable acclaim following his graduation from Trinity College, Cambridge; he was perhaps the first poet to speak out in the period of 'angry young men'. Gunn has since published over 30 books, among them *The Man With Night Sweats*, a moving memorial to friends and acquaintances who fell victim to AIDS; and, more recently, *Boss Cupid* (2000). Gunn travelled to the US on a writing fellowship in 1954 and has since settled in San Francisco.

September 6

• Galway Kinnell's son, Fergus, born September 6th 1966

After Making Love We Hear Footsteps

For I can snore like a bullhorn
or play loud music
or sit up talking with any reasonably sober Irishman
and Fergus will only sink deeper
into his dreamless sleep, which goes by all in one flash,
but let there be that heavy breathing
or a stifled come-cry anywhere in the house
and he will wrench himself awake
and make for it on the run—as now, we lie together,
after making love, quiet, touching along the length of our bodies,
familiar touch of the long-married,
and he appears—in his baseball pajamas, it happens,
the neck opening so small he has to screw them on —
and flops down between us and hugs us and snuggles himself to sleep,
his face gleaming with satisfaction at being this very child.

In the half darkness we look at each other
and smile
and touch arms across this little, startlingly muscled body —
this one whom habit of memory propels to the ground of his making,
sleeper only the mortal sounds can sing awake,
this blessing love gives again into our arms.

Galway Kinnell
(February 1st 1927 –)

Galway Kinnell writes: "Awakened, most probably, by a certain mild commotion coming from the parental bedroom, Fergus, aged six, got out of bed and made his way to our bedside just as we had settled into post-coital bliss, and said, "Are you loving and snuggling? May I join?" As the poem recounts, he climbed into bed with us and soon fell asleep. His lovely questions and the courtliness of his phrasing came back to me the next morning, and I wrote this poem with his words at their centre.

"Years later, when I happened to read through the published poem, I suddenly saw that those words, so pleasant when spoken, looked quite cute on the page, causing the whole poem to sound a bit like a sentimental anecdote from an adoring parent. In the next edition of *Mortal Acts, Mortal Words*, the book in which the poem had appeared, I deleted the sweet words, but reluctantly, because without them this poem would never have been written."

- Critic, novelist, poet and acclaimed eccentric, Dame Edith Sitwell was born in Scarborough September 7th 1887
- French detectives arrested Guillaume Appolllinaire in the case of the stolen Mona Lisa, September 7th 1911. He implicated Picasso, who was questioned and released
- Louise Bennett, folk poet, born in Jamaica September 7th 1919
- Poet Frederic E. Weatherly died September 7th 1929

Spring and Fall

to a young child

Márgarét, áre you gríeving
Over Goldengrove unleaving?
Leáves líke the things of man, you
With your fresh thoughts care for, can you?
Áh! ás the heart grows older
It will come to such sights colder
By and by, nor spare a sigh
Though worlds of wanwood leafmeal lie;
And yet you will weep and know why.
Now no matter, child, the name:
Sórrows's spríngs áre the same.
Nor mouth had, no nor mind, expressed
What heart heard of, ghost guessed:
It ís the blight man was born for,
It is Margaret you mourn for.

Gerard Manley Hopkins
(July 28th 1844 – June 8th 1889)

'Spring and Fall' was written by Gerard Manley Hopkins on this day in 1880 at Rose Hill, a country house in Lydiate, north of Liverpool. Hopkins started writing a letter to his friend and fellow poet Robert Bridges on September 5th. He included 'Spring and Fall', writing: "I enclose a little piece composed since I began this letter, not founded on real incident." That there was no such person as 'Margaret' has led some readers to conclude that the poem shows the poet mourning for himself in the midst of a bout of depression. Certainly it is true that he liked to escape the strains and stresses of city life for the solitude and quiet of Rose Hill, a place where he could compose his poetry in peace.

September 8

- *Italian poet Ludovico Ariosto born September 8th 1474*
- *Frédéric Mistral, Provençal writer and poet, winner of the 1904 Nobel Prize for literature, born September 8th 1830*
- *Siegfried Sassoon born September 8th 1886*

The Power and the Glory

Let there be life, said God. And what He wrought
Went past in myriad marching lives, and brought
This hour, this quiet room, and my small thought
Holding invisible vastness in its hands.

Let there be God, say I. And what I've done
Goes onward like the splendour of the sun
And rises up in rapture and is one
With the white power of conscience that commands.

Let life be God . . . What wail of fiend or wraith
Dare mock my glorious angel where he stands
To fill my dark with fire, my heart with faith?

Siegfried Sassoon
(September 8th 1886 – September 1st 1967)

Of Jewish descent, Sassoon converted to Roman Catholicism shortly after his birthday in 1957. Much of his poetry thereafter assumed a religious theme, but it remains overshadowed by the popularity of his early war poetry.

Skald's Death

I have known all the storms that roll.
I have been a singer after the fashion
Of my people – a poet of passion.
All that is past.
Quiet has come into my soul.
Life's tempest is done.
I lie at last
A bird cliff under the midnight sun.

Hugh MacDiarmid
(August 11th 1892 – September 9th 1978)

Hugh MacDiarmid was born Christopher Murray Grieve in 1892 in Langholm, Dumfriesshire. He took up his literary pseudonym 30 years later. He was a passionate advocate of Scottish independence, and was one of the founders of the Scottish Nationalist movement in 1928. He called himself "a Communist, a Scottish separatist, and [a] republican", but was also fiercely individual in his particular point of view, something which led to him being expelled by both the Scottish Nationalist and Communist parties.

In an effort to give Scotland its own literary language, he devised what became known as 'Synthetic Scots' in which to write his poetry. Through his verse, his autobiography (*Lucky Poet*) and his other writings, MacDiarmid fought for Scottish independence throughout his life – something he felt born to do. One of the foremost poets of the 20th century, he also found time to be a politician, a polemicist, a journalist, a campaigner and a prolific letter-writer.

September 10

• Ugo Foscolo, Italian poet and patriot in exile, died destitute in Turnham Green, London, September 10th 1827
• American imagist poet Hilda Doolittle (H. D.) born in Bethlehem, Pennsylvania, September 10th 1886
• Mary Oliver, American poet ('I want to say all my life / I was a bride married to amazement'), born September 10th 1935
• American poet Amy Clampitt died September 10th 1994

Wild Geese

You do not have to be good.
You do not have to walk on your knees
for a hundred miles through the desert, repenting.
You only have to let the soft animal of your body
    love what it loves.
Tell me about despair, yours, and I will tell you mine.
Meanwhile the world goes on.
Meanwhile the sun and the clear pebbles of the rain
are moving across the landscapes,
over the prairies and the deep trees,
the mountains and the rivers.
Meanwhile the wild geese, high in the clean blue air,
are heading home again.
Whoever you are, no matter how lonely,
the world offers itself to your imagination,
calls to you like the wild geese, harsh and exciting —
over and over announcing your place
in the family of things.

Mary Oliver
(September 10th 1935 –)

Mary Oliver was born in Cleveland, Ohio, and attended the prestigious Vassar College for women. She won the Pulitzer Prize in 1984 for her collection *American Primitive*.

• *Scottish poet James Thompson born September 11th 1700*
• *Poet and novelist D. H. Lawrence born September 11th 1885*
• *English-born Canadian poet, Robert W. Service, died at his home in Lancieux, France, September 11th 1958*

Fall
after Rilke

The leaves are falling, falling from trees
in dying gardens far above us; as if their slow
free-fall was the sky declining.

And tonight, this heavy earth is falling away
from all the other stars, drawing into silence.

We are all falling now. My hand, my heart,
stall and drift in darkness, see-sawing down.

And we still believe there is one who sifts and holds
the leaves, the lives, of all those softly falling.

Robin Robertson
(July 12th 1955 –)

Robin Robertson writes: "This free version of Rilke's early poem 'Herbst' ('Autumn') concludes my second book, *Slow Air*: a collection much concerned with the vertigos of grief and age. I was in France, checking the proofs of the book, when the towers fell, then found myself – the following month – reading the poem to an audience at New York University.

"It was only when I went to check the exact date of the German original, that I found that Rilke wrote the poem soon after arriving in Paris in 1902, on September 11th."

Robin Robertson was born in Scotland. His first book, *A Painted Field* (1997), won the three major British literary awards available to a first collection – including the Forward Prize – and his second, *Slow Air*, was published in 2002. He lives in London.

September 12

• Elizabeth Barrett and Robert Browning married secretly on
  September 12th 1846, with Elizabeth's maid as witness
• Louis MacNeice born in Belfast September 12th 1907
• Robert Lowell died in New York September 12th 1977
• Eugenio Montale, Italian poet and critic, and winner of the
  1975 Nobel Prize, died in Milan September 12th 1981

Will Not Come Back
after Becquer

Dark swallows will doubtless come back killing
the injudicious nightflies with a clack of the beak;
but these that stopped full flight to see your beauty
and my good fortune . . . as if they knew our names—
they'll not come back. The thick lemony honeysuckle,
climbing from the earthroot to your window,
will open more beautiful blossoms to the evening;
but these . . . like dewdrops, trembling, shining, falling,
the tears of day—they'll not come back . . .
Some other love will sound his fireword for you
and wake your heart, perhaps, from its cool sleep;
but silent, absorbed, and on his knees,
as men adore God at the altar, as I love you—
don't blind yourself, you'll not be loved like that.

Robert Lowell
(March 1st 1917 – September 12th 1977)

Robert Trail Spence Lowell IV was born into a distinguished family whose members included the
poets James Russell Lowell and Amy Lowell. He is considered one of the greatest American poets
of the second half of the 20th century. Lowell courted controversy throughout his life: as a
conscientious objector he was imprisoned in 1943, having declared his views in a much publicised
letter to President Roosevelt; he later demonstrated his disapprobation of the Vietnam war by
refusing an invitation to the White House. Lowell's ground-breaking collection, *The Dolphin*,
which besides revelations of his madness and alcoholism, included excerpts from his wife's troubled
letters, proved Lowell to be one of the most determined advocates of the 'Confessional' school.
Many felt he had gone too far.

In 1949, Lowell, only recently divorced from the novelist Jean Stafford and probably in love with
Elizabeth Bishop, met novelist and essayist Elizabeth Hardwick, whom he married. He divorced
her 23 years later and married Lady Caroline Blackwood the same day. He died of a heart attack
in the back of a New York City cab on this day in 1977, returning to Hardwick at their old
apartment.

• F. T. Prince, of whom John Ashbery said, "So much is clear: [He] is all his own man, he is like no one else, he is a major poet", born in South Africa September 13th 1912

From Invitation

(1)

If my fat
was too much for me
I would have told you
I would have lost a stone
or two

I would have gone jogging
even when it was fogging
I would have weighed in
sitting the bathroom scale
with my tail tucked in

I would have dieted
more care than a diabetic

But as it is
I'm feeling fine
feel no need
to change my lines
when I move I'm target light

Come up and see me sometime

Grace Nichols
(January 18th 1950 –)

Grace Nichols was born in Georgetown, Guyana, and worked as a teacher and journalist. She emigrated to England with her partner, the poet John Agard, in 1977. Her first collection, *I Is a Long-memoried Woman*, which chronicles the history of the African diaspora, won the Commonwealth Poetry Prize and was the basis for an award-winning film. Her highly-acclaimed collection, *The Fat Black Woman's Poems*, from which 'Invitation' is taken, was published on this day in 1984.

September 14

• Italian poet Dante Alighieri, "the Chief imagination of Christendom", died in Ravenna September 14th 1321
• At 49, poet, critic and novelist John Gardner died in a motorcycle crash near Susquehanna, Pennsylvania, September 14th 1982

The Silken Tent

She is as in a field a silken tent
At midday when a sunny summer breeze
Has dried the dew and all its ropes relent,
So that in guys it gently sways at ease,
And its supporting central cedar pole,
That is its pinnacle to heavenward
And signifies the sureness of the soul,
Seems to owe naught to any single cord,
But strictly held by none, is loosely bound
By countless silken ties of love and thought
To everything on earth the compass round,
And only by one's going slightly taut
In the capriciousness of summer air
Is of the slightest bondage made aware.

Robert Frost
(March 26th 1874 – January 29th 1963)

In September 1938, as Frost was struggling to shake off the debilitating depression and long periods of illness he had suffered since the death of his wife in 1937, he met and fell in love with Kay Morrison. Although Morrison was married to a fellow academic, Frost proposed almost immediately. Morrison refused, but she became his secretary, manager, muse and lover for the next 25 years of his life – a "devoted, astringent, and affectionate amanuensis". When *The Witness Tree*, Frost's seventh collection, was published in April 1942, it was dedicated to Morrison. Frost admitted in a letter that "but for her there would have been no seventh book ... The dedication is no ordinary acknowledgement". 'The Silken Tent', written in September 1938, is one of a nucleus of love poems to Morrison that appeared in the collection. The book won him his fourth Pulitzer Prize.

The poem is representative of Frost's belief that the ties of marriage and community are productive ones. "What is a man but all his connections", he once said. "He's just a tiny invisible knot so that he can't discern it himself: the knot where all his connections meet." In his notebook he had scribbled: "Connections and community – the basis of love – and the product."

- *Courtier and poet Sir Thomas Overbury was poisoned whilst imprisoned in the Tower of London September 15th 1613*
- *Claude McKay, prominent member of the Harlem Renaissance, born in Jamaica September 15th 1889*
- *Rainer Maria Rilke began his employment with Rodin September 15th 1902*

The Panther
In the Jardin des Plantes, Paris

His vision, from the constantly passing bars,
has grown so weary that it cannot hold
anything else. It seems to him there are
a thousand bars; and behind the bars, no world.

As he paces in cramped circles, over and over,
the movement of his powerful soft strides
is like a ritual dance around a centre
in which a mighty will stands paralysed.

Only at times, the curtain of the pupils
lifts, quietly—. An image enters in,
rushes down through the tensed, arrested muscles,
plunges into the heart and is gone.

Rainer Maria Rilke
(December 4th 1875 – December 29th 1926)

translated by Stephen Mitchell

Rilke's attempts to set up home with his new wife, the sculptor Klara Westhoff, and their young daughter, were not a success. He was frustrated by domesticity and resentful of the impediment to his writing. Commissioned to write a monograph on the Warpswede artists, including the French sculptor Rodin, Rilke escaped to Paris to observe him at work.

Rilke became Rodin's private secretary on this day in 1902. Though he spoke only halting French, Rodin spent many hours talking with him each day; Rodin's absolute dedication to his art and his unflagging observation of the minutiae of life exerted a powerful influence on the poet. When he complained that he had not written for some time, Rodin famously encouraged the poet to go to the Jardins des Plantes to observe the animals. Legend has it that Rilke spent nine hours staring into the panther's cage before writing his poem. It remains a paradigm of the 'object poem' which attempts to describe physical objects with utmost clarity and thereby capture the 'silence of their concentrated reality'.

September 16

• Anne Bradstreet died September 16th 1672
• On September 16th 1788, Burns claimed his wife had "the handsomest figure ... and the kindest heart in the country"
• Poet Alfred Noyes born in Wolverhampton September 16th 1880
• Imagist poet T. E. Hulme born September 16th 1883

As imperceptibly as Grief

As imperceptibly as Grief
The Summer lapsed away –
Too imperceptible at last,
To seem like Perfidy –
A Quietness distilled
As Twilight long begun
Or Nature spending with herself
Sequestered Afternoon –
The Dusk drew earlier in –
The Morning foreign shone –
A courteous, yet harrowing Grace,
As Guest, that would be gone –
And thus, without a Wing
Or service of a Keel
Our Summer made her light escape
Into the Beautiful.

Emily Dickinson
(December 10th 1830 – May 15th 1886)

Emily Dickinson's accelerated retreat from society in the 1860s coincided with her increased creative output. During this time she maintained a vigorous correspondence with a wide circle of friends, many of whom she never actually met. Amongst these was the writer Helen Hunt Jackson who wrote to Emily in exasperation: "[Y]ou are a great poet – and it is wrong to the day you live in, that you will not sing aloud."

• Francisco Gomez de Quevedo born September 17th 1580
• In Florence, Italy, English poet Walter Savage Landour died September 17th 1864
• William Carlos Williams born September 17th 1883
• Popular author of whimsical quatrains, Gelett Burgess died in California September 17th 1951. He is credited with adding several new words to the English language, including 'blurb'

September 17

Love Constant Beyond Death

The final shadow that will close my eyes
will in its darkness take me from white day
and instantly untie the soul from lies
and flattery of death, and find its way,
and yet my soul won't leave its memory
of love there on the shore where it has burned:
my flame can swim cold water and has learned
to lose respect for laws' severity.
My soul, whom a God made his prison of,
my veins, which a liquid humor fed to fire,
my marrows, which have gloriously flamed,
will leave their body, never their desire;
they will be ash but ash in feeling framed;
they will be dust but will be dust in love.

Francisco Gomez de Quevedo
(September 17th 1580 – September 8th 1645)

translated by Willis Barnstone

Francisco Gomez de Quevedo first had his poems published in 1605, when he was just 17. By the time he was 23, he was an acclaimed poet and wit, and could speak several languages, including Greek, Latin, Hebrew, French, Italian and English. Despite his burgeoning reputation, he chose politics over poetry and became a close advisor of the Duke of Osuna, who later became viceroy of Sicily and Naples. When the Duke fell from favour on the ascension of Philip IV, Quevedo was placed under house arrest. He never held political office again, instead concentrating on increasingly satirical verse and prose. It was a satirical poem that led to his arrest and imprisonment in 1639. He was released four years later, and continued writing until his death in 1645.

September 18

• Poet, essayist and lexicographer Samuel Johnson, born September 18th 1709
• English poet Mathew Prior died September 18th 1721
• Keats set sail from Gravesend September 18th 1820
• Scottish poet George Macdonald died September 18th 1905
• Irish poet Michael Hartnett born September 18th 1941
• Australian poet Amy Witting died September 18th 2001

In the Dead Afternoon's Gold More

In the dead afternoon's gold more –
The no-place gold dust of late day
Which is sauntering past my door
And will not stay –

In the silence, still touched with gold,
Of the woods' green ending, I see
The memory. You were fair of old
And are in me . . .

Though you're not there, your memory is
And, you not anyone, your look.
I shake as you come like a breeze
And I mourn some good . . .

I've lost you. Never had you. The hour
Soothes my anguish so as to leave,
In my remembering being, the power
To feel love,

Though loving be a thing to fear,
A delusory and vain haunting,
And the night of this vague desire
Have no morning.

Fernando Pessoa
(June 13th 1888 – November 30th 1935)

translated by Jonathan Griffin

Fernando Pessoa was unique in writing under at least 19 names. Of these, one of the most frequently used was 'F. P.': he regarded himself as much a creation as the other characters. "No artist should have only one personality," he explained, claiming that the heteronyms "express ideas I do not accept and feelings I have not felt." Pessoa gave each heteronym a full biography, complete with date of birth, education, physical appearance and beliefs, and even included such incidental detail as "slightly stooping ... wears a monocle". He declared himself essentially a dramatist, and recalled his desire, from early childhood, to surround himself with fictitious characters.

Though he used his heteronyms to contradict himself repeatedly, he also seems to have become confused about which 'identity' penned each poem. Manuscript drafts reveal that Pessoa frequently changed his mind about the precise authorship of a poem and that poems continued to be written posthumously, long after a particular heteronym's 'death.' Curiously, 'pessoa' means 'person' or 'persona' in Portuguese.

- *The newly-married Brownings left for the continent to escape the wrath of Elizabeth's father, September 19th 1846*
- *When 19-year-old feminist novelist and poet Rebecca West reviewed* Marriage *by 45-year-old H. G. Wells, calling him "The old maid among novelists", Wells asked to meet her, instigating a ten-year love affair, September 19th 1912*
- *Alison Croggon born September 19th 1962*

September 19

Seduction Poem

I want the slew of muscle, a less
cerebral meeting place; no word
but your male shout, the shirred
unpublic face and honest skin
crying to me, yes,
the mouthless, eyeless tenderness
crying to be let in.

Unbutton all your weight, like a bird
flying the night's starred nakedness:
put down your grammatical tongue, undress
your correct and social skin:
come white and absurd
all your language one word
crying to be let in.

Alison Croggon
(September 19th 1962 –)

Alison Croggon comments: " 'Seduction Poem' was written when I was about 20. I had a huge crush on my literature lecturer, but nothing happened except the poem."

Croggon writes poetry, prose, criticism and texts for theatre. Her books of poetry include *This is the Stone* (Penguin Books Australia), *The Blue Gate* (Black Pepper Press), *Mnemosyne* (Wild Honey Press) and *Attempts at Being* (Salt Publishing). Amongst other awards she has received the Anne Elder and Dame Mary Gilmore prizes, and her theatre texts have been produced by companies across Australia. She edits the webzine *Masthead* and her first novel for young adults, *The Gift*, was released in Australia by Penguin in 2002.

September 20

- *Chidiock Tichborne executed in London September 20th 1586*
- *Shakespeare was called "an upstart crow" for his audacity in competing with established playwrights. The criticism was lodged with the Stationers' Register September 20th 1592*
- *Margaret Florence 'Stevie' Smith born September 20th 1902*
- *A group of English poets led by Edward Marsh and Rupert Brooke founded* Georgian Poetry *September 20th 1912*

Elegy for Himself
Written in the Tower before his execution

My prime of youth is but a frost of cares;
　My feast of joy is but a dish of pain;
My crop of corn is but a field of tares°;　　　　weeds
　And all my good is but vain hope of gain:
The day is past, and yet I saw no sun;
And now I live, and now my life is done.

My tale was heard, and yet it was not told;
　My fruit is fall'n, and yet my leaves are green;
My youth is spent, and yet I am not old;
　I saw the world, and yet I was not seen:
My thread is cut¹, and yet it is not spun;
And now I live, and now my life is done.

I sought my death, and found it in my womb;
　I looked for life, and saw it was a shade;
I trod the earth, and knew it was my tomb;
　And now I die, and now I was but made;
My glass is full, and now my glass is run;
And now I live, and now my life is done.

Chidiock Tichborne
(c. 1558 – September 20th 1586)

It is believed that Chidiock Tichborne was born into an ardently Catholic family in Southampton. Both he and his father were champions of the Roman Catholic Church and were investigated over the possession and use of "popish relics" in 1583. Chidiock joined a group of conspirators and was one of six who pledged to murder the Queen and restore the kingdom to Rome. But their plans were discovered and Chidiock's co-conspirators fled. Chidiock, immobilised by a leg injury, remained in London where he was eventually arrested and taken to the Tower. He was tried, and pleaded guilty, and was executed on this day in 1586, at the age of 28. Historical rumour has it that he was "disembowelled before life was extinct", and that when news of his horrific death reached the Queen, she "forbade the recurrence" of the practice.

Chidiock sent this poem in a letter to his wife, Agnes, the day before his execution. The poem became famous immediately after his death.

1. A reference to the oldest of the three classical Greek Fates, Atropos, who cut the thread of Lachesis' life with her shears.

- *Roman poet Virgil died September 21st 19 BC*
- *Scottish novelist and poet Sir Walter Scott died at Abbotsford September 21st 1832*
- *Leonard Cohen born in Montreal September 21st 1934*
- *Irish poet Theo Dorgan born September 21st 1953*

If It Be Your Will

If it be your will
that I speak no more,
and my voice be still
as it was before;
I will speak no more,
I shall abide until
I am spoken for,
if it be your will.

If it be your will
that a voice be true,
from this broken hill
I will sing to you.
From this broken hill
all your praises they shall ring
if it be your will
to let me sing.

If it be your will
if there is a choice,
let the rivers fill,
let the hills rejoice.
Let your mercy spill
on all these burning hearts in hell,
if it be your will
to make us well.

And draw us near
and bind us tight,
all your children here
in their rags of light;
in our rags of light,
all dressed to kill;
and end this night,
if it be your will.

Leonard Cohen
(September 21st 1934 –)

Leonard Cohen is best known as a singer-songwriter; 'If It Be Your Will' is a song from his 1984 album, *Various Positions*. A Jew who practises Zen Buddhism, Cohen's interest in Judaism was reawakened in the 1980s and he began using Hebrew prayer in his songs. This song was inspired by the opening lines of the Kol Nidre service on Yom Kippur eve, which begins 'May it therefore be Your will, Lord our God, and God of our Fathers, to forgive us all our sins ...'

September 22

• *Alice Meynell, essayist and poet, born September 22nd 1847*
• *T. S. Eliot first met Ezra Pound, with an introduction from Conrad Aiken, September 22nd 1914*
• *Dannie Abse, Welsh poet and critic, born September 22nd 1923*
• *Yehuda Amichai, Israeli poet, died September 22nd 2000*

Near the Wall of a House

Near the wall of a house painted
to look like stone,
I saw visions of God.

A sleepless night that gives others a headache
gave me flowers
opening beautifully inside my brain.

And he who was lost like a dog
will be found like a human being
and brought back home again.

Love is not the last room: there are others
after it, the whole length of the corridor
that has no end.

Yehuda Amichai
(May 3rd 1924 – September 22nd 2000)

translated by Chana Bloch

Yehuda Amichai was born Yehuda Pfeuffer to Orthodox parents in Würzberg, Germany. The family moved to Jerusalem when Amichai was 11 and, as a teenager, he fought in the British army's Jewish Brigade in the Second World War, and later in the 1948 War of Independence.

That year, shortly after adopting his new surname (which means 'My nation lives!') he went to university to study literature. On graduating, he released his first collection of poetry, *Achshav u'beyamim ha'acherim* (*Now and in other days*), which revealed his unique style, incorporating autobiography, colloquial vocabulary and religion.

Amichai went on to publish many more collections, and plays, essays and children's books, and became Israel's unofficial Poet Laureate. He was introduced to America and Britain in the 1970s by Ted Hughes, and his poetry has since been translated into over 30 languages. In 1982, he was awarded the Israel Prize, his country's highest award for cultural achievement.

• Novelist and poet Mary Coleridge born September 23rd 1861
• Andrew Greig born in Scotland September 23rd 1951
• Chilean poet Pablo Neruda died of leukaemia in Santiago
  September 23rd 1973

September 23

Oh Earth, Wait for Me

Return me, oh sun,
to my wild destiny,
rain of the ancient wood,
bring me back the aroma and the swords
that fall from the sky,
the solitary peace of pasture and rock,
the damp at the river-margins,
the smell of the larch-tree,
the wind alive like a heart
beating in the crowded restlessness
of towering araucaria.

Earth, give me back your pure gifts,
the towers of silence which rose
from the solemnity of their roots.
I want to go back to being what I have not been,
and learn to go back from such deeps
that amongst all natural things
I could live or not live; it does not matter
to be one stone more, the dark stone,
the pure stone which the river bears away.

Pablo Neruda
(July 12th 1904 – September 23rd 1973)

translated by Alaistair Reid

Pablo Neruda won third prize in a poetry competition in 1919, and adopted his pseudonym soon after (the 'Neruda' part coming from a Czech writer of the time) to avoid conflict with his disapproving family. In 1923 he sold all of his possessions to finance the publication of his first book, *Crepusculario (Twilight)*. The following year, he published *Veinte poemas de amor y una cancion desesperada (Twenty Love Poems and a Song of Despair)* which made him famous, and cemented his devotion to poetry for life.

A diplomat for much of his adult life, Neruda was politically active in the Communist party, which led to him being expelled from the Chilean Senate in the 1940s. Whilst in exile, he wrote his masterpiece *Canto General*, which brought him worldwide acclaim. On returning to Chile in 1952, Neruda resumed his diplomatic and political career, and in 1969 he was presidential candidate for the Communist party, before stepping aside to allow Salvatore Allende to unite the left. In October 1971, to add to his numerous peace prizes, Neruda was awarded the Nobel Prize for literature. He died two years later, a fortnight after his friend Allende was killed in the military coup led by General Pinochet.

September 24

• Horace Walpole, man of letters and poet, born in London
  September 24th 1717
• Poet, novelist, philosopher and playwright Miguel de
  Unamuno born in Bilboa, Spain, September 24th 1864
• Leo Marks, cryptographer and poet, born in London
  September 24th 1920

A Drinking Song

Wine comes in at the mouth
And love comes in at the eye;
That's all we shall know for truth
Before we grow old and die.
I lift the glass to my mouth,
I look at you, and I sigh.

W. B. Yeats
(June 13th 1865 – January 28th 1939)

Yeats fell hopelessly in love with Maud Gonne the day he first caught sight of her in January 1889.
"I had never thought to see in a living woman so great a beauty," he recalled, "It belonged to
famous pictures, to poetry, to some legendary past." Thus began what he later called "the troubling
of my life". Yeats proposed to Maud Gonne regularly over the years but was always refused. He
later became infatuated with Gonne's daughter, Iseult, but his proposal to her, just a week after
his final proposal to Maud, also resulted in a rebuttal. In desperation, Yeats travelled down to Sussex
on this day in 1917 to propose to the 25-year-old George Hyde Lees. They married the following
month, only telling family members a few days before the wedding. Despite the inauspicious start
– Yeats was miserable at the wedding and wrote lovesick letters to Iseult during their honeymoon
– Hyde Lees swiftly won Yeats' interest with her surprising facility for 'automatic writing' and
clairvoyance.

- *Robert Herrick began a ten-year goldsmith apprenticeship in Cheapside September 25th 1607 and signed an agreement vowing not to "commit fornication nor contract matrimony ... without license of his said master"*
- *Samuel Butler died in poverty September 25th 1680*
- *Poet Felicia Dorothea Hemans born September 25th 1793*
- *R. S. Thomas, Welsh poet-priest, died September 25th 2000*

The Moor

It was like a church to me.
I entered it on soft foot,
Breath held like a cap in the hand.
It was quiet.
What God was there made himself felt,
Not listened to, in clean colours
That brought a moistening of the eye,
In movement of the wind over grass.

There were no prayers said. But stillness
Of the heart's passions – that was praise
Enough; and the mind's cession
Of its kingdom. I walked on,
Simple and poor, while the air crumbled
And broke on me generously as bread.

R. S. Thomas
(March 29th 1913 – September 25th 2000)

R. S. Thomas' first book of poetry, *The Stones of the Field*, was published in 1946, by which time he had been an ordained priest for ten years. Thomas went on to publish more than 20 volumes of poetry in his lifetime, and is now widely regarded as one of the most important poets of the post-war era. The main themes of his poetry mirror his passions: religion, the countryside, and Welsh history and language. In 1996 he was nominated for the Nobel Prize for literature.

In 1997 'The Moor' was used as the basis and inspiration for a duet for unaccompanied soprano and mezzo-soprano by the Welsh composer Hilary Tann.

September 26

- T. S. Eliot born in St Louis September 26th 1888
- Marina Tsvetayeva born September 26th 1892
- Poet and critic Harriet Monroe died September 26th 1936
- W. H. Davies, tramp poet, died September 26th 1940

I know the truth – give up all other truths!

I know the truth – give up all other truths!
No need for people anywhere on earth to struggle.
Look – it is evening, look, it is nearly night:
what do you speak of, poets, lovers, generals?

The wind is level now, the earth is wet with dew,
the storm of stars in the sky will turn to quiet.
And soon all of us will sleep under the earth, we
who never let each other sleep above it.

Marina Tsvetayeva
(September 26th 1892 – August 31st 1941)

translated by Elaine Feinstein

As a young woman, Tsvetayeva witnessed the appalling hardship and suffering endured by her people during the October revolution and documented it all. She herself, left to bring up her children alone in Moscow while her husband Sergei Efron fought with the White Guards, was often hungry and survived as best she could. One of her notes in the book which came to be published as *Earthly Traits* reads: " 'I won't leave you.' Only God can say such a thing – or a peasant with milk in Moscow during the winter of 1918."

She and her husband lost everything in the revolution, including their youngest daughter, who died of malnutrition in an orphanage. Life thereafter was not any easier: the couple moved to Czechoslovakia and then to Paris, but were integrated in neither city, partly due to Efron's associations with the Soviet secret police. At the start of the Second World War, Tsvetayeva returned reluctantly to Moscow, writing in her memoirs: "Now I will go: like a dog." Her daughter and husband were arrested by the secret police the month after she arrived and loneliness, poverty and despair eventually drove her to suicide.

- *After two bottles of port, Tennyson wept as he read* Maud *to the Brownings and Dante Gabriel Rossetti, September 27th 1855*
- *Poet and critic Sir William Empson born in Howden, Yorkshire, September 27th 1906*
- *H(ilda) D(oolittle) died September 27th 1961*
- *English poet and novelist Roy Fuller died September 27th 1991*

Stars Wheel in Purple

Stars wheel in purple, yours is not so rare
as Hesperus, nor yet so great a star
as bright Aldeboran or Sirius,
nor yet the stained and brilliant one of War;

stars turn in purple, glorious to the sight;
yours is not gracious as the Pleiads are
nor as Orion's sapphires, luminous;

yet disenchanted, cold, imperious face,
when all the others blighted, reel and fall,
your star, steel-set, keeps lone and frigid tryst
to freighted ships, baffled in wind and blast.

H. D.
(September 10th 1886 – September 27th 1961)

H. D.'s father was a respected Professor of Astronomy and her mother a music and art teacher. At the University of Pennsylvania, her friends included William Carlos Williams and Ezra Pound. She had a turbulent affair with Pound in 1905; they became engaged and then disengaged at least twice. She travelled to Europe in 1911, intending to stay only the summer, but spent the rest of her life abroad. In London, H. D., Pound and Richard Aldington, whom H. D. later married, formed the Imagist movement. Sending H. D.'s poems in to his friend Harriet Monroe at Poetry magazine, Pound famously signed her poems "H. D., Imagiste". She swiftly became identified as a leading figure of the movement.

Pronounced bisexual by her analyst, Freud, H. D.'s relationships were fraught with the tensions of heterosexual and lesbian attractions. She finally found contentment with Bryher (born Annie Winifred Ellerman), whom she met in Cornwall in 1918. The two were devoted companions until H. D.'s death in 1961.

28

- *Francis Turner Palgrave, poet and anthologist, born September 28th 1824*
- *Poet and novelist Herman Melville died September 28th 1891*
- *Poet Stephen Spender born in London September 28th 1909*
- *Soldier-poet T. E. Hulme killed in Nieuport, Belgium, September 28th 1917*
- *Ivor Gurney declared insane September 28th 1922 and admitted to a private asylum*

Death

1

as on the edge of something
For which there is no precise name . . .
An insistent drowsiness,
A self-evasion . . .

2

And I am standing on the threshold of something
That befalls everyone, but at different cost . . .
On this ship there is a cabin for me
And wind in my sails—and the terrible moment
Of taking leave of my native land.

Anna Akhmatova
(June 23rd 1889 – March 5th 1966)

translated by Judith Hemschemeyer

On this day in 1941, as war broke out, Anna Akhmatova was reluctantly evacuated to Tashkent in Central Asia along with a number of other esteemed Russian artists and writers. She remained there for the duration of the war. She wrote 'Death' after a severe bout of typhus in 1942, which almost killed her.

- *Miguel de Cervantes Saavedra, Spanish novelist and poet, born circa September 29th 1547*
- *Vojka Djikic born in Northern Bosnia September 29th 1932*
- *W. H. Auden died in Vienna after a reading of his work, September 29th 1973*

A Guest May Come

Hold on tight to me
And we'll find the way home
There the fire's still burning
And in the corners
Books lie open
That ought to be read
And the garden's there to dig
The roses to prune
Thus it was said
When we mend the roof
And paint the red door red
A guest may come

Vojka Djikic
(September 29th 1932 –)

translated by Chris Agee

Vojka Djikic was born in Mrkonji'c Grad, northern Bosnia, and studied literature at Belgrade University. She was poetry editor for Sarajevo Radio and TV from 1973 to the outbreak of the war, and also edited the journal *The Third Programme* produced by Sarajevo Radio. *Joie de vivre*, stoicism and an apprehension of historical calamity are fused in a poetry of brevity and atmosphere. Recent volumes of poetry include *Ash Wednesday* and *Another Country*, and she is a professional translator of French and Algerian literature. She now edits *Sarajevo Notebook*, a new Balkan journal of contemporary writing and continues to live in Sarajevo, where she remained throughout the 1992 to 1996 siege.

September 30

• Sir Fulke Greville, poet and courtier, murdered by his servant
Haywood, who thought he had been omitted from his master's
will, September 30th 1628
• W. S. Merwin born in New York September 30th 1927

For the Anniversary of My Death

Every year without knowing it I have passed the day
When the last fires will wave to me
And the silence will set out
Tireless traveller
Like the beam of a lightless star

Then I will no longer
Find myself in life as in a strange garment
Surprised at the earth
And the love of one woman
And the shamelessness of men
As today writing after three days of rain
Hearing the wren sing and the falling cease
And bowing not knowing to what

W. S. Merwin
(September 30th 1927 –)

W. S. Merwin was born in New York and raised in Union City. He is also an inspired translator
(he has written over 20 books of translations), a peace activist and an environmentalist – a champion
of the Hawaiian rainforest near his home. His father was a Presbyterian minister, and his early
poems were hymns. His desire to be a poet arose out of anguish at the state of the world, and he
was encouraged in his efforts by the poet John Berryman.

282

- *Shakespeare was listed as a defaulter for non-payment of taxes in his parish in Bishopsgate, October 1st 1598*
- *Keats entered Guy's Hospital as a student October 1st 1815*
- *Tennyson learnt of Hallam's death on October 1st 1833 and began composing* In Memoriam A. H. H. *that winter*
- *Louis Untermeyer, anthologist, editor and poet, born in New York October 1st 1885*

October 1

Bright star! would I were steadfast as thou art

Bright star! would I were steadfast as thou art—
    Not in lone splendour hung aloft the night
And watching, with eternal lids apart,
    Like nature's patient, sleepless Eremite,
The moving waters at their priestlike task
    Of pure ablution round earth's human shores,
Or gazing on the new soft fallen mask
    Of snow upon the mountains and the moors—
No—yet still steadfast, still unchangeable,
    Pillowed upon my fair love's ripening breast,
To feel for ever its soft fall and swell,
    Awake for ever in a sweet unrest,
Still, still to hear her tender-taken breath,
And so live ever—or else swoon to death.

John Keats
(October 31st 1795 – February 23rd 1821)

Keats knew he was dying when he wrote his final letters to his beloved Fanny Brawne. Beside himself with anguish and grief he wrote: "They talk of my going to Italy. It's certain I shall never recover if I am to be so long separate from you." But he also railed against what he perceived to be Fanny's unfaithfulness.

On this day in 1820, the ship on which Keats and his companion Joseph Severn were to travel to Italy docked briefly at Lulworth Cove, off the Dorset coast. Here Keats transcribed on a blank page of Shakespeare's *Poems* the revised version of 'Bright Star' for Fanny. Stars, whose fires corresponded with his own ardour (from the Latin 'ardere'– 'to burn') were an endless preoccupation for Keats, and symptomatic of his sense of kinship with the transcendent world.

October 2

• *Wallace Stevens born in Pennsylvania October 2nd 1879*
• *South African poet and journalist Roy Campbell, who fought for Franco in the Spanish Civil War, born October 2nd 1901*
• *Frances Horovitz died in Herefordshire October 2nd 1983*

The Emperor of Ice-Cream

Call the roller of big cigars,
The muscular one, and bid him whip
In kitchen cups concupiscent curds.
Let the wenches dawdle in such dress
As they are used to wear, and let the boys
Bring flowers in last month's newspapers.
Let be be finale of seem.
The only emperor is the emperor of ice-cream.

Take from the dresser of deal,
Lacking the three glass knobs, that sheet
On which she embroidered fantails once
And spread it so as to cover her face.
If her horny feet protrude, they come
To show how cold she is, and dumb.
Let the lamp affix its beam.
The only emperor is the emperor of ice-cream.

Wallace Stevens
(October 2nd 1879 – August 2nd 1955)

Wallace Stevens wrote of this poem: "I think I should select from my poems as my favourite 'The Emperor of Ice-Cream'. This wears a deliberately commonplace costume, and yet seems to me to contain something of the essential gaudiness of poetry; that is the reason why I like it. I do not remember the circumstances under which this poem was written, unless this means the state of mind from which it came. I dislike niggling, and like letting myself go. Poems of this sort are the pleasantest on which to look back, because they seem to remain fresher than others. This represented what was in my mind at the moment, with the least possible manipulation."

- St Francis of Assisi died October 3rd 1226, though his official remembrance day is October 4th
- Poet and courtier Sir Fulke Greville born in Beauchamp Court, Warwickshire, October 3rd 1554
- William Morris, poet and printer, born October 3rd 1896
- Surrealist poet Louis Aragon, fighter against the Nationalists in the Spanish Civil War and member of the French Resistance in the Second World War, born in Paris October 3rd 1897

Saint Francis and the Sow

The bud
stands for all things,
even for those things that don't flower,
for everything flowers, from within, of self-blesssing;
though sometimes it is necessary
to reteach a thing its loveliness,
to put a hand on its brow
of the flower
and retell it in words and in touch
it is lovely
until it flowers again from within, of self-blessing;
as Saint Francis
put his hand on the creased forehead
of the sow, and told her in words and in touch
blessings of earth on the sow, and the sow
began remembering all down her thick length,
from the earthen snout all the way
through the fodder and slops to the spiritual curl of the tail,
from the hard spininess spiked out from the spine
down through the great broken heart
to the sheer blue milken dreaminess spurting and shuddering
from the fourteen teats into the fourteen mouths sucking and
     blowing beneath them:
the long, perfect loveliness of sow.

Galway Kinnell
(February 1st 1927 –)

Galway Kinnell comments: "How to rouse a student from a temporary slough of despond is a problem that from time to time, as a teacher of aspiring poets, I am called upon to try to solve. Profound loss of all self-confidence is not the perfect state for the production of poetry. Probably it's not good for the production of almost anything. 'St Francis and the Sow' came to me while I was trying to think how I could bestir one particularly gifted student from his funk."

October 4

• Coleridge married Sara Fricker October 4th 1795
• Wordsworth married Mary Hutchinson October 4th 1802
• Tennyson received a telegram from the Queen on his deathbed October 4th 1892
• Anne Sexton, who once said, "I could perform just before I die, I think", committed suicide October 4th 1974

Her Kind

I have gone out, a possessed witch,
haunting the black air, braver at night;
dreaming evil, I have done my hitch
over the plain houses, light by light:
lonely thing, twelve-fingered, out of mind.
A woman like that is not a woman, quite.
I have been her kind.

I have found the warm caves in the woods,
filled them with skillets, carvings, shelves,
closets, silks, innumerable goods;
fixed the suppers for the worms and the elves:
whining, rearranging the disaligned.
A woman like that is misunderstood.
I have been her kind.

I have ridden in your cart, driver,
waved my nude arms at villages going by,
learning the last bright routes, survivor
where your flames still bite my thigh
and my ribs crack where your wheels wind.
A woman like that is not ashamed to die.
I have been her kind.

Anne Sexton
(November 9th 1928 – October 4th 1974)

Anne Sexton claimed that it was "the bad witch" in her who wrote poetry – "By God, I don't think I'm the one who writes the poems! They don't centre in my house" – and she chose the picture for the cover of her first book carefully, commenting that she "didn't want it to look suburban, wanted just to be a face, a person whose life you couldn't define."

'Her Kind' is from Sexton's collection *To Bedlam and Part Way Back*. In July 1959, whilst looking for a keynote poem for the first section of the book, Sexton revisited an old, previously unpublished poem, 'Night Voice on a Broomstick'. One week and 19 pages of drafts later 'Her Kind' was born. From this point on, 'Her Kind' became her signature poem, the one with which Sexton began all her alcohol-fuelled poetry readings.

- On October 5th 1869, Dante Gabriel Rossetti exhumed the manuscript of his poems buried with his wife in 1862
- Australian poet Christopher Brennan died October 5th 1932
- Poet Jonathan Steffen born October 5th 1958
- Seamus Heaney awarded the Nobel Prize for literature, "for an authorship filled with lyrical beauty and ethical depth", October 5th 1995

Glanmore Sonnets
VIII

Thunderlight on the split logs: big raindrops
At body heat and lush with omen
Spattering dark on the hatchet iron.
This morning when a magpie with jerky steps
Inspected a horse asleep beside the wood
I thought of dew on armour and carrion.
What would I meet, blood-boltered, on the road?
How deep into the woodpile sat the toad?
What welters through this dark hush on the crops?
Do you remember that *pension* in Les Landes
Where the old one rocked and rocked and rocked
A mongol in her lap, to little songs?
Come to me quick, I am upstairs shaking.
My all of you birchwood in lightning.

Seamus Heaney
(April 13th 1939 –)

In his Nobel Prize acceptance speech, Seamus Heaney described poetry as "the power to persuade that vulnerable part of our consciousness of its rightness in spite of the evidence of wrongness all around it, the power to remind us that we are hunters and gatherers of values, that our very solitudes and distresses are creditable".

October 6

- *New Zealand poet Mary Ursula Bethell born in England October 6th 1874*
- *Alfred, Lord Tennyson died at Aldworth October 6th 1892*
- *American poet Elizabeth Bishop died October 6th 1979. At her request her tombstone reads 'Awful, but cheerful'*

Break, Break, Break

Break, break, break
  On thy cold gray stones, O Sea!
And I would that my tongue could utter
  The thoughts that arise in me.

O, well for the fisherman's boy,
  That he shouts with his sister at play!
O, well for the sailor lad,
  That he sings in his boat on the bay!

And the stately ships go on
  To their haven under the hill,
But O for the touch of a vanished hand
  And the sound of a voice that is still!

Break, break, break
  At the foot of thy crags, O Sea!
But the tender grace of a day that is dead
  Will never come back to me.

Alfred, Lord Tennyson
(August 6th 1809 – October 6th 1892)

In his memoir Tennyson wrote that this poem was "made in a Lincolnshire lane at five o'clock in the morning between blossoming hedges", probably in 1842.

Tennyson's biographer, Peter Levi, relates an incident when Tennyson was living in London's Upper Wimpole street in 1871. He had invited a few of his well-connected neighbours over for a small concert, during which a performer sang 'Break, Break, Break'. When he had finished, the audience waited breathlessly for the Poet's verdict: Tennyson covered his face with his handkerchief. The audience showed their respect by doing likewise.

• *Edgar Allan Poe died in Baltimore October 7th 1849*
• *James Whitcombe Riley, the Indiana-born 'Hoosier poet' who wrote 'Little Orfant Annie', was born October 7th 1849*
• *Dialect poet William Barnes died October 7th 1886*
• *Black Muslim poet Amiri Baraka born as Everett LeRoi Jones in Newark October 7th 1934*

October 7

With you first shown to me

With you first shown to me,
With you first known to me,
My life-time loom'd, in hope, a length of joy:
  Your voice so sweetly spoke,
  Your mind so meetly spoke,
My hopes were all of bliss without alloy,
As I, for your abode, sought out, with pride,
This house with vines o'er-ranging all its side.

  I thought of years to come,
  All free of tears to come,
When I might call you mine, and mine alone,
  With steps to fall for me,
  And day cares all for me,
And hands for ever nigh to help my own;
And then thank'd Him who had not cast my time
Too early or too late for your sweet prime.

  Then bright was dawn, o'er dew,
  And day withdrawn, o'er dew,
And mid-day glow'd on flow'rs along the ledge,
  And wall in sight, afar,
  Were shining white, afar,
And brightly shone the stream beside the sedge.
But still, the fairest light of those clear days
Seem'd that which fell along your flow'ry ways.

William Barnes
(February 22nd 1801 – October 7th 1886)

William Barnes was born the son of a Dorset farmer. He had little formal education, but was an exceptional scholar and polymath, and had mastered 60 languages by the time of his death. He established an influential school in Dorchester where he developed his own progressive teaching methods, and became a mentor to the young Thomas Hardy.

At the age of 18 he saw an elegant young woman named Julia Miles alight from a bus and fell instantly in love. The couple were devoted, and her death at the age of 47 prompted the first of many elegies to her. For the rest of his life he closed each day's diary entry with the Italian form of her name: 'Guilia'. He was a passionate philologist and is best known for his dialect poems, which he wrote to give "local people a poetry of his own". He was ordained in 1848 and spent the last 25 years of his life as Rector of Winterborne Came outside Dorchester.

October 8

• William Blake began his studies at the Royal Academy aged
  21, October 8th 1779
• American poet Philip Booth born October 8th 1935

First Lesson

Lie back, daughter, let your head
be tipped back in the cup of my hand.
Gently, and I will hold you. Spread
your arms wide, lie out on the stream
and look high at the gulls. A dead-
man's float is face down. You will dive
and swim soon enough where this tidewater
ebbs to the sea. Daughter, believe
me, when you tire on the long thrash
to your island, lie up, and survive.
As you float now, where I held you
and let go, remember when fear
cramps your heart what I told you:
lie gently and wide to the light-year
stars, lie back, and the sea will hold you.

Philip Booth
(October 8th 1925 –)

Born in Hanover, New Hampshire, Booth's poetry deals mainly with the landscape of New England, particularly the coast of Maine, and the life of its inhabitants. He was taught by Robert Frost at Dartmouth College.

- *Poet and playwright Ambrose Philips baptised in Shrewsbury October 9th 1674*
- *Keats avowed in a letter to his friend, J. Hessy, "I would sooner fail than not be among the greatest", October 9th 1818*
- *Polish poet and dramatist Tadeusz Rozewicz born in Radomsko, Poland, October 9th 1921*

Busy with Many Jobs

Busy with very urgent jobs
I forgot
one also has
to die

irresponsible
I kept neglecting that duty
or performed it
perfunctorily

as from tomorrow
things will be different

I'll start dying meticulously
wisely optimistically
without wasting time

Tadeusz Rozewicz
(October 9th 1921 –)

translated by Adam Czerniawski

Tadeusz Rozewicz was a member of the Polish resistance during the Second World War. His brother – to whom he dedicated his collection of short stories, *Our Elder Brother* – was shot by the Gestapo. His first book of poems was published clandestinely in 1944, having been printed on a makeshift press.

Rozewicz constantly questions the role and importance of poetry in his work, writing in one essay that he was afraid of the task of being a poet, but that he was "always ready to sacrifice every amusement for it, every free moment, every day and every night". This directness and honesty, which characterises much of his poetry, has made him one of the most highly regarded poets of Eastern Europe of the past half-century.

October 10

• An under-age Earl of Rochester took his seat in the House of
  Lords October 10th 1667, to the protestations of the Lords
• Charles Madge born October 10th 1912
• Poet David Gascoyne born in Harrow October 10th 1916
• Mexican polymath Octavio Paz announced as winner of the
  Nobel Prize for literature October 10th 1990

From Letter of Testimony
Coda

Perhaps to love is to learn
to walk through this world.
To learn to be silent
like the oak and the linden of the fable.
To learn to see.
Your glance scattered seeds.
It planted a tree.
       I talk
because you shake its leaves.

Octavio Paz
(March 31st 1914 – April 19th 1998)

translated by Eliot Weinberger

As a young writer Octavio Paz was encouraged by Pablo Neruda, and published his first book of
poetry, *Luna silvestre* (*Forest Moon*) when he was 19. Many volumes of poetry, criticism and essays
followed over the years, including his famous long poem *Piedra de Sol* (*Sun Stone*, 1957), and the
influential study of Mexico *El laberinto de la soledad* (*The Labyrinth of Solitude*, 1950). Like Neruda,
Paz served his country as a diplomat for many years, before resigning in 1968 in protest at the brutal
treatment of some student demonstrators. For the next thirty years, he devoted himself to writing
and editing, and became recognised as a major worldwide literary figure. His reputation was assured
by the time he became the first Mexican to receive the Nobel Prize for literature on this day in
1990.

• *Sir Thomas Wyatt died October 11th 1542*
• *Jean Cocteau, French poet, writer and director, died in France October 11th 1963. Cocteau believed that "The worst tragedy for a poet is to be admired through being misunderstood"*

I do not Speak

I do not ask for mercy for understanding for peace
And in these heavy days I do not ask for release
I do not ask that suffering shall cease.

I do not pray to God to let me die
To give an ear attentive to my cry
To pause in his marching and not hurry by.

I do not ask for anything I do not speak
I do not question and I do not seek
I used to in the days when I was weak.

Now I am strong and lapped in sorrow
As in a coat of magic mail and borrow
From Time today and care not for tomorrow.

Stevie Smith
(September 20th 1902 – March 7th 1971)

Stevie Smith was baptised on this day in 1902, during a period of illness. As an adult she was often openly critical of the Church of England and maintained an ambivalent relationship with God, once remarking: "I'm a back-slider as a non-believer."

In an interview with fellow poet John Horder in 1963, Smith said that humans invented God out of a fear of loneliness. She believed, however, that loneliness is an essential part of the human condition; that we must accept it, and must learn to draw inspiration from it.

October 12

• Tennyson buried in Westminster Abbey October 12th 1892
• Eugenio Montale, Italian poet whose debut collection, Ossi di Seppia, established him as a major talent, born in Genoa October 12th 1896
• Canadian poet Dorothy Livesay born October 12th 1909
• Poet and translator Robert Fitzgerald born in New York October 12th 1920

Acquainted with the Night

I have been one acquainted with the night.
I have walked out in rain—and back in rain.
I have outwalked the furthest city light.

I have looked down the saddest city lane.
I have passed by the watchman on his beat
And dropped my eyes, unwilling to explain.

I have stood still and stopped the sound of feet
When far away an interrupted cry
Came over houses from another street,

But not to call me back or say good-by;
And further still at an unearthly height
One luminary clock against the sky

Proclaimed the time was neither wrong nor right.
I have been one acquainted with the night.

Robert Frost
(March 26th 1874 – January 29th 1963)

In 1921, Robert Frost's growing reputation as an American poet led him to be invited to be the first artist-in-residence at an American university. He took up the Fellowship in Creative Arts at the University of Michigan, Ann Arbor, in October 1921; it was here that he wrote 'Acquainted with the Night'.

Frost's poetry is usually centred on the rural, but this urban poem is nonetheless typical of his work, with its characteristic atmosphere of quiet, dark solitude. He claimed the poem was "written for the tune"; a terza-rima sonnet, it reveals Frost's affinity with Dante in the circularity of its structure and its foreboding tone.

- Scottish poet Allan Ramsay born October 13th 1686
- Poet and critic W. J. Turner born October 13th 1889
- Scottish poet Charles Hamilton Sorley killed in battle in the
  First World War October 13th 1915
- Selima Hill born October 13th 1945
- Allen Ginsberg delivered the famous first recital of 'Howl' at
  the Six Gallery in San Francisco October 13th 1955

October 13

Nuage Argente

Nuage Argente –
the name of the house
you betrayed us in,
sucking each other to bits
like two chunks of chopped fish
made fat from feeding on the blood and tears
of other people's partners
and your own.
What a noise
you must be making
behind the curtains
in the little room.
You sometimes soak the sheets.
You sometimes lie.
You 'can't believe you did this'.
Nor can I.
Every day I'll dip you in my syrup.
I'll dip you in and force you to be lovable
and roll you around
in trays of hundreds and thousands.
The lowest of the low my mother called them,
men who messed with other people's wives.
Today's today.
It will not come again.
Somewhere in your heart
there must be tenderness.
If you've got one.
Which they say you have.
You know how farmers
run their hands through grain
to coax large animals to come to them?
I'm running my words
through buckets of prayers like that
to coax something out of the dark
to come and save us.

> *Selima Hill*
> *(October 13th 1945 –)*

Selima Hill comments: "I think I was trying to find a way out of anger and towards a place of tenderness and hope – and aware that there is a sort of taboo against tenderness in what we write today."

October 14

• *John Philpot Curran died October 14th 1817*
• *May Wedderburn Canaan, poet of the First World War, born a twin October 14th 1893*
• *E. E. Cummings born in Massachusetts October 14th 1894*
• *American critic, poet and children's writer Randall Jarrell, died after being hit by a car, October 14th 1965*

the little horse is newlY

the little horse is newlY

Born)he knows nothing,and feels
everything;all around whom is

perfectly a strange
ness(Of sun
light and of fragrance and of

Singing)is ev
erywhere(a welcom
ing dream:is amazing)
a worlD.and in

this world lies:smoothbeautifuL
ly folded;a(brea
thing and a gro

Wing)silence,who;
is:somE

oNe.

E. E. Cummings
(October 14th 1894 – September 3rd 1962)

When Cummings' *Collected Poems* was published in 1938, it was more charitably received than any of his previous "booksofpoems". One of the most striking aspects of the book was the intensely personal nature of the preface: "you and i are not snobs. We can never be born enough. We are human beings;for whom birth is a supremely welcome mystery,the mystery of growing:the mystery which happens only and whenever we are faithful to ourselves. you and i wear the dangerous looseness of doom and find it becoming. Life,for eternal us,is now;and now is much too busy being a little more than everything to seem anything catastrophic included."

• Roman poet Virgil born in Andes, near Mantua, October
  15th 70BC
• Robert Herrick, poet and priest, died October 15th 1674
• Scottish poet William Soutar died October 15th 1943
• Scottish poet Iain Crichton Smith died October 15th 1998

October 15

Listen

Listen, I have flown through darkness towards joy,
I have put the mossy stones away from me,
and the thorns, the thistles, the brambles.
I have swum upward like a fish

through the black wet earth, the ancient roots
which insanely fight with each other
in a grave which creates a treasure house
of light upward-springing leaves.

Such joy, such joy! Such airy drama
the clouds compose in the heavens,
such interchange of comedies,
disguises, rhymes, denouements.

I had not believed that the stony heads
would change to actors and actresses,
and that the grooved armour of statues
would rise and walk away

into a resurrection of villages,
townspeople, citizens, dead exiles,
who sing with the salt in their mouths,
winged nightingales of brine.

Iain Crichton Smith
(January 1st 1928 – October 15th 1998)

Iain Crichton Smith was a fiercely passionate and political poet, as well as one blessed with great understanding and humility. His upbringing on the island of Lewis, which was still very much under the influence of the powerful and authoritarian Free Church, provoked him to open his eyes, ears and mind to the world, and to reject dogma wherever he found it. As a result, though some of his poetry has a regional focus (notably the long poem 'Shall Gaelic Die?'), it also has a global perspective and reach. Crichton Smith's favourite writers were Auden, Kierkegaard, Robert Lowell and Dostoevsky, a quartet which reflects his international outlook.

October 16

• Georg Büchner, German poet, playwright and revolutionary, born October 16th 1813
• Oscar Wilde born in Dublin October 16th 1854
• Auden left America and retired to Oxford October 16th 1972
• Anne Ridler, OBE, died in Oxford October 16th 2001

If I Could Tell You

Time will say nothing but I told you so,
Time only knows the price we have to pay;
If I could tell you I would let you know.

If we should weep when clowns put on their show,
If we should stumble when musicians play,
Time will say nothing but I told you so.

There are no fortunes to be told, although,
Because I love you more than I can say,
If I could tell you I would let you know.

The winds must come from somewhere when they blow,
There must be reasons why the leaves decay;
Time will say nothing but I told you so.

Perhaps the roses really want to grow,
The vision seriously intends to stay;
If I could tell you I would let you know.

Suppose the lions all get up and go,
And all the brooks and soldiers run away;
Will Time say nothing but I told you so?
If I could tell you I would let you know.

W. H. Auden
(February 21st 1907 – September 29th 1973)

In October 1940, Auden resumed the religious belief he had held during his childhood, pronouncing himself an "Anglo-Catholic though not too spiky". He later maintained that, had he not been a poet, he would like to have been an Anglican bishop.

Auden did not relinquish hope that his lifelong partner, Chester Kallman, would follow him into the church. He privately identified 'If I Could Tell You' (previously titled 'Villanelle') and 'Leap Before You Look' as among those poems addressed to or concerned with Kallman, and reflecting his hope of communicating to him the implications of his conversion.

W. H. Auden delivered a sermon at Westminster Abbey on this day in 1966.

- *Sir Philip Sidney died October 17th 1586*
- *US feminist poet Julia Ward Howe died October 17th 1910*
- *Poet and novelist George MacKay Brown born in Stromness, Orkney, where he lived until his death, October 17th 1921*
- *Les Murray, renowned Australian poet, born in Nabiac, New South Wales, October 17th 1938*
- *'Language poet' S. J. Perelman died October 17th 1979*

Leave Me, O Love

Leave me, O Love which reachest but to dust,
And thou my mind aspire to higher things;
Grow rich in that which never taketh rust;
Whatever fades but fading pleasure brings.

Draw in thy beams, and humble all thy might
To that sweet yoke where lasting freedoms be;
Which breaks the clouds and opens forth the light,
That doth both shine and give us sight to see.

O take fast hold; let that light be thy guide
In this small course which birth draws out to death,
And think how evil becometh him to slide,
Who seeketh heaven, and comes of heavenly breath.
    Then farewell world; thy uttermost I see;
    Eternal Love, maintain thy life in me.

Sir Philip Sidney
(November 30th 1554 – October 17th 1586)

Philip Sidney, the Elizabethan courtier and poet, is best known for his sonnet sequence 'Astrophil and Stella' which deals with a poet's love for his muse. The names of the two lovers mean 'star-lover' and 'star' respectively, although Astro-*phil* also points to the poet being closely related to *Philip* Sidney himself. Similarly, it is suspected that the model for Stella was Lady Penelope Devereux, whom Sidney had hoped to marry in 1576. She eventually married Lord Rich in 1581, and there are several punning uses of the word 'rich' in Sidney's sequence, which was written in the months following the pair's marriage.

Sidney was knighted in 1582, and married Frances Walsingham on September 21st 1583. He planned to accompany Sir Francis Drake and Sir Walter Raleigh on a trip to the West Indies in 1585, but was sent to the Netherlands instead. There he was killed in battle, aged 31. Sidney never saw his first and only daughter, Elizabeth, who was born while he was away fighting in the Dutch campaign.

October 18

• Poet and novelist Thomas Love Peacock, who wrote
  caricatures of the Romantic poets, born October 18th 1785
• William Blake's wife Catherine died October 18th 1831
• H. D. married the novelist and poet Richard Aldington in
  Kensington October 18th 1913

Entirely

If we could get the hang of it entirely
    It would take too long;
All we know is the splash of words in passing
    And falling twigs of song,
And when we try to eavesdrop on the great
    Presences it is rarely
That by a stroke of luck we can appropriate
    Even a phrase entirely.

If we could find our happiness entirely
    In somebody else's arms
We should not fear the spears of the spring nor the city's
    Yammering fire alarms
But, as it is, the spears each year go through
    Our flesh and almost hourly
Bell or siren banishes the blue
    Eyes of Love entirely.

And if the world were black or white entirely
    And all the charts were plain
Instead of a mad weir of tigerish waters,
    A prism of delight and pain,
We might be surer where we wished to go
    Or again we might be merely
Bored but in the brute reality there is no
    Road that is right entirely.

Louis MacNeice
(September 12th 1907 – September 3rd 1963)

Louis MacNeice, W. H. Auden and Stephen Spender recited poems together on BBC radio on this day in 1938.

MacNeice worked as a staff writer and producer for the BBC from 1941 to 1963, and many of his own plays were first performed on the radio during those years. While on location with a BBC team, in August 1963, MacNeice went down a mineshaft to check the sound effects. He caught a chill which was diagnosed as pneumonia too late to save him. He died in early September, shortly before the publication of what was to be his final book, *The Burning Perch*.

- *Leigh Hunt, poet and editor of the* Examiner, *who enjoyed a volatile relationship with Keats, born October 19th 1784*
- *Edna St Vincent Millay died at Steepletop, her 700-acre farm at Austerlitz, New York, having stayed up all night smoking and reading* The Illiad, *October 19th 1950*

Sonnet

What my lips have kissed, and where, and why,
I have forgotten, and what arms have lain
Under my head till morning; but the rain
Is full of ghosts tonight, that tap and sigh
Upon the glass and listen for reply,
And in my heart there stirs a quiet pain
For unremembered lads that not again
Will turn to me at midnight with a cry.
Thus in the winter stands the lonely tree,
Nor knows what birds have vanished one by one,
Yet knows its boughs more silent than before:
I cannot say what loves have come and gone,
I only know that summer sang in me
A little while, that in me sings no more.

Edna St Vincent Millay
(February 22nd 1892 – October 19th 1950)

Millay first came to the attention of Arthur Ficke when he read one of her first poems in an anthology in which his work also featured. Ficke, a (married) poet and Army officer corresponded regularly with Millay for six years before the couple finally met in 1918. It was love at first sight: "You were the first man I ever kissed without thinking that I should be sorry about it afterwards," she wrote.

At that time Millay was living in New York City and had many suitors, but she did not wish to marry any of the Greenwich Village "lads", as she called them. She wrote to Ficke, in October 1920: "I love you, too, my dear, and shall always, just as I did the first moment I saw you. You are part of Loveliness to me ... You will never grow old to me, or die, or be lost in any way."

Ficke soon divorced his wife for another woman, but Millay took the news well and the two remained friends, and, later, neighbours, until Ficke's death in 1945.

October 20

• Precocious boy-poet of French Symbolism, Arthur Rimbaud was born in Charleville October 20th 1854
• Yeats married Georgie Hyde Lees on October 20th 1917. Ezra Pound was best man
• Robert Pinsky born in New Jersey October 20th 1940

Lair

Inexhaustible, delicate, as if
Without source or medium, daylight
Undoes the mind; the infinite,

Empty actual is too bright,
Scattering to where the road
Whispers, through a mile of woods . . .

Later, how quiet the house is:
Dusk-like and refined,
The sweet Phoebe-note

Piercing from the trees;
The calm globe of the morning,
Things to read or to write

Ranged on a table; the brain
A dark, stubborn current that breathes
Blood, a deaf wadding,

The hands feeding it paper
And sensations of wood or metal
On its own terms. Trying to read

I persist a while, finish the recognition
By my breath of a dead giant's breath—
Stayed by the space of a rhythm,

Witnessing the blue gulf of the air.

Robert Pinsky
(October 20th 1940 –)

Robert Pinsky writes: "Reading my early poem 'Lair' now, I recognize two elements that seem still to guide all my work in poetry. One is breath: 'the recognition / By my breath of a dead giant's breath- / Stayed by the space of a rhythm'. Vocality remains the animating centre of my work: to write – or, rather, to compose – with my voice, for the reader's voice.

"Secondly, 'Lair' reminds me of the paradox of including the surrounding frame within the poem – sometimes, including the moment of composition: here, what it feels like to be in my room, alone, attempting to make or perceive lines in the bright, unlined, azure gulf of the actual."

Robert Pinsky is the author of six collections of poetry as well as books of criticism and translation; his most recent collection is *Jersey Rain*. He was US Poet Laureate for three terms, and founded the highly successful Favorite Poem Project. He currently teaches at Boston University.

- *Samuel Taylor Coleridge born in Devon October 21st 1772*
- *Patrick Kavanagh born in Inniskeen October 21st 1904*
- *Writer and poet Maureen Duffy born October 21st 1933*
- *Poet Ai (the Japanese word for 'love') born of a Japanese father and a Choctaw Indian mother, October 21st 1947*
- *Jack Kerouac died of alcoholism in Florida October 21st 1969*

From Thoughts about the Person from Porlock

Coleridge received the Person from Porlock
And ever after called him a curse,
Then why did he hurry to let him in?
He could have hid in the house.

It was not right of Coleridge in fact it was wrong
(But often we all do wrong)
As the truth is I think he was already stuck
With Kubla Khan.

He was weeping and wailing: I am finished, finished,
I shall never write another word of it,
When along comes the Person from Porlock
And takes the blame for it.

It was not right, it was wrong,
But often we all do wrong.

★

May we inquire the name of the Person from Porlock?
Why, Porson, didn't you know?
He lived at the bottom of Porlock Hill
So had a long way to go,

He wasn't much in the social sense
Though his grandmother was a Warlock,
One of the Rutlandshire ones I fancy
And nothing to do with Porlock,

And he lived at the bottom of the hill as I said
And had a cat named Flo,
And had a cat named Flo.

I long for the Person from Porlock
To bring my thoughts to an end,
I am becoming impatient to see him
I think of him as a friend,

[Continued]

Often I look out of the window
Often I run to the gate
I think, He will come this evening,
I think it is rather late.

I am hungry to be interrupted
For ever and ever amen
O Person from Porlock come quickly
And bring my thoughts to an end.

Stevie Smith
(September 20th 1902 – March 7th 1971)

'The Person from Porlock' mocks the famous truncation of Coleridge's poem, 'Kubla Khan'. In Coleridge's preface to the poem, he described how the poem resulted from a vision experienced during a profound sleep. On awakening, he "appeared to have a distinct recollection of the whole", but as he began to transcribe the lines, however, a "person on business from Porlock" interrupted him, and he was never able to recover the full poem.

Stevie Smith is certainly not alone in contesting the veracity of Coleridge's 'person from Porlock'; it has been described variously as "a Coleridgean hoax, albeit a harmless one", and simply "one of his apologies for uncompleted work" – as though Coleridge were a naughty schoolboy casting about wildly for excuses.

- *The poet Lord Alfred Douglas ('Bosie'), with whom Oscar Wilde was infatuated, born October 22nd 1870*
- *W. H. Auden's* Look, Stranger! *was published on October 22nd 1936. He described it as sounding "like the work of a vegetarian lady novelist"*
- *James K. Baxter died October 22nd 1972*
- *Novelist and poet Kingsley Amis died October 22nd 1995*

The Buried Stream

Tonight our cat, Tahi, who lately lost
One eyebrow, yowls in the bush with another cat;

Our glass Tibetan ghost-trap has caught no ghost
Yet, but jangles suspended in the alcove that

We varnished and enlarged. Unwisely I have read
Sartre on Imagination – very dry, very French,

An old hound with noises in his head
Who dreams the hunt is on, yet fears the stench

Of action – he teaches us that human choice
Is rarely true or kind. My children are asleep.

Something clatters in the kitchen. I hear the voice
Of the buried stream that flows deep, deep,

Through caves I cannot enter, whose watery rope
Tugs my divining rod with the habit some call hope.

James K. Baxter
(June 29th 1926 – October 22nd 1972)

Baxter began to write verse at the age of seven and later recollected that "a sense of grief... attached itself to my early life [and] has been with me as long as I can remember." His writing is distinguished by a pervasive melancholy and an almost mystical appreciation of the New Zealand landscape.

His struggle with alcoholism began while still a student; he dropped out of university and worked in an abattoir and as a postman before training as a primary school teacher. He later converted to Catholicism. In the 1960s Baxter became a passionate advocate of social change based on the spiritual values of the Catholic church and Maori culture, and founded communities that offered a sanctuary to the poor and marginalised. He himself renounced all possessions and took a vow of poverty. He was in his own words "a Christian guru, a barefooted and bearded eccentric, a bad smell in the noses of many good citizens." In a dream he heard himself summoned to Jerusalem – a small Maori settlement on the Wanganui River – and left with only a change of clothes and a Bible. He died there at the age of 46, having written over 30 books of poetry.

- *Robert Bridges born in Walmer October 23rd 1844*
- *Douglas Dunn born in Renfrewshire October 23rd 1942*
- *Soviet poet Boris Pasternak, whose only novel, Dr Zhivago, was smuggled out of the USSR and first published in Italy, awarded the Nobel Prize for literature October 23rd 1958*
- *Gavin Ewart died October 23rd 1995*

Prayer for Belfast

Night, be starry-sensed for her,
Your bitter frost be fleece to her.
Comb the vale, slow mist, for her.
Lough, be a muscle, tensed for her.

And coals, the only fire in her,
And rain, the only news of her.
Small hills, keep sisters' eyes on her.
Be reticent, desire for her.

Go, stories, leave the breath in her,
The last word to be said by her,
And leave no heart for dead in her.
Steer this ship of dread from her.

No husband lift a hand to her,
No daughter shut the blind on her.
May sails be sewn, seeds grown, for her.
May every kiss be kind to her.

Carol Rumens
(December 10th 1944 –)

Carol Rumens comments: "I wrote this poem after the bombing of the Shankhill Road fish-shop on October 23rd 1995. It is a love poem to Belfast. I also see it as a metaphorical warning against the possessiveness of love. I am asking that the warring ideologies should set Belfast free, but I am also asking myself to let go of a person I love, or think I love, who is resistant. The last line refers, of course, to Judas' betraying kiss."

Born in London, Carol Rumens was based in Belfast during the 1990s. There she was Poet-in-Residence and, later, a creative writing tutor at Queen's University. She has also edited the *Irish News Poetry Club,* has published extensively, and has translated work by the Russian poets Pushkin and Yevgeny Rein. *Hex* (Bloodaxe Books, 2002) is her latest collection.

- On October 24th 1818, Keats wrote to his family: "I feel more and more ... that I do not live in this world alone but in a thousand worlds"
- Denise Levertov born October 24th 1923
- Poet, translator and novelist Elaine Feinstein, born in Bootle October 24th 1930
- Adrian Mitchell born in London October 24th 1932
- Susan Wicks born October 24th 1947

Joy

The authorities do not permit us
to take pictures: this dance is ephemeral
as sex or April dogwoods, the pink-skirted
ripple of her body, her emaciated
trunk gleaming, the snapped wishbone
of her thigh sparking light. The pink wit
of her flexed foot stirs us unaccountably
to laughter. This is the dancer's way, this meeting
of tangent bodies, this cool coffee
at café tables, the momentary pink stasis
of words, the fading blossom
drifted from chestnuts. This must be spring,
her limbs' own joy, as his arms lift her,
carry her on his shoulders
into darkness. We may not take pictures.
We look and look, drinking
the small death of each step, each contact
of flesh on sliding flesh, the precise circles
of what we crave, the gasps that express us.

Susan Wicks
(October 24th 1947 –)

Susan Wicks comments: "This poem was inspired by a pas de deux given by two dancers from the Washington Ballet in Lynchburg, Virginia. I owe its existence, and that of another poem, 'Rain Dance', to both that evening of ballet and to the Irish poet, Macdara Woods, who had written me a generous, morale-boosting note the evening before. That moment of freedom and possibility doesn't come very often."

Susan Wicks has published three collections of poetry, two novels and a short memoir, *Driving My Father*, all with Faber. Her poetry collections include *Singing Underwater* (1992) and *The Clever Daughter* (1996). She is Director of Creative Writing at the University of Kent at Canterbury. A new collection, *Night Toad: New Selected Poems*, was published by Bloodaxe Books in autumn 2003.

October 25

• *Geoffrey Chaucer died October 25th 1400. He was the first poet to be honoured by burial in Westminster Abbey*
• *John Berryman born John Smith in Oklahoma October 25th 1914*
• *Sydney Goodsir Smith, poet, playwright and critic, born in New Zealand October 25th 1915*

From Ode to the West Wind
V

Make me thy lyre, even as the forest is:
What if my leaves are falling like its own!
The tumult of thy mighty harmonies

Will take from both a deep, autumnal tone,
Sweet though in sadness. Be thou, Spirit fierce,
My Spirit! Be thou me, impetuous one!

Drive my dead thoughts over the universe
Like withered leaves to quicken a new birth!
And, by incantation of this verse,

Scatter, as from an unextinguished hearth
Ashes and sparks, my words among mankind!
Be through my lips to unawakened earth

The trumpet of a prophecy! O, Wind,
If Winter comes, can Spring be far behind?

Percy Bysshe Shelley
(August 4th 1792 – July 8th 1822)

Shelley went for a long solitary walk along the banks of the river Arno in Florence on this day in 1819 and observed a violent storm brewing, the wind coming hard from the west. By the time he reached home, Shelley had his poem. "This poem was conceived and chiefly written in a wood that skirts the Arno ... when that tempestuous wind, whose temperature is at once mild and animating, was collecting the vapours which pour down the autumnal rains ..."

• Baroness Carolina Nairne, Jacobite songwriter ('Charlie is my darling'), died October 26th 1845
• Andrew Motion born in London October 26th 1952
• Elizabeth Jennings died in Oxford October 26th 2001

October 26

Light

To touch was an accord
Between life and life;
Later we said the word
And felt arrival of love
And enemies moving off.

A little apart we are,
(Still aware, still aware)
Light changes and shifts.
O slowly the light lifts
To show one star
And the darkness we were.

Elizabeth Jennings
(July 18th 1926 – October 26th 2001)

Elizabeth Jennings believed writing poetry was "like mystical experience, a gratuitous gift" and confessed that she wrote "in order to know, to discover, to get things clear". She wrote quickly, with little revision, and produced over 20 collections.

The outbreak of the Second World War coincided with Jennings' first serious foray into both poetry and religion, which she stated as "a real and important part of my life". Indeed, Jennings was the only Roman Catholic member of the Oxford group which came to be known as The Movement, and which included amongst others Kingsley Amis and Philip Larkin. She later worked as a librarian at Oxford City library and as a publisher's reader.

Jennings never married but was a much-loved member of the Oxford scene; a passionate connoisseur of ice-cream, she was frequently to be found at Oxford's Häagen-Dazs parlour and was such a dedicated film-goer that her local cinema granted her a free pass for life.

October 27

- *Poet George Barker died October 27th 1913*
- *Dylan Thomas born in Swansea October 27th 1914*
- *Poet Sylvia Plath born in Boston October 27th 1932*
- *After winning the Nobel Prize, Boris Pasternak was expelled from the Union of Soviet Writers on October 27th 1958*

Morning Song

Love set you going like a fat gold watch.
The midwife slapped your footsoles, and your bald cry
Took its place among the elements.

Our voices echo, magnifying your arrival. New statue.
In a drafty museum, your nakedness
Shadows our safety. We stand round blankly as walls.

I'm no more your mother
Than the cloud that distils a mirror to reflect its own slow
Effacement at the wind's hand.

All night your moth-breath
Flickers among the flat pink roses. I wake to listen:
A far sea moves in my ear.

One cry, and I stumble from bed, cow-heavy and floral
In my Victorian nightgown.
Your mouth opens clean as a cat's. The window square

Whitens and swallows its dull stars. And now you try
Your handful of notes;
The clear vowels rise like balloons.

Sylvia Plath
(October 27th 1932 – February 11th 1963)

In January 1961 Plath learned that she was pregnant again. She had found temporary employment with the *Bookseller*, and was involved in the editing of the children's section, a job which further inspired her to seek out children's names. So Plath was devastated when she miscarried in early February. The event occasioned the pained, tender poem 'Parliament Hill Fields' in which Plath observes 'Your absence is inconspicuous; / Nobody can tell what I lack'. That February inspired six more poems, including 'Barren Women' and, perhaps surprisingly, 'Morning Song', which Plath elected to be the opening poem of *Ariel*, published posthumously in 1964.

- *Ella Wheeler Wilcox, whose* Poems of Passion *courted controversy, died October 28th 1919*
- *Poet Ian Hamilton Finlay born October 28th 1925*
- *American poet John Hollander born October 28th 1929*
- *Ted Hughes, Poet Laureate since 1984, died October 28th 1998, just months after releasing* Birthday Letters

Song

O lady, when the tipped cup of the moon blessed you
You became soft fire with a cloud's grace;
The difficult stars swam for eyes in your face;
You stood, and your shadow was my place:
You turned, your shadow turned to ice
    O my lady.

O lady, when the sea caressed you
you were a marble of foam, but dumb.
When will the stone open its tomb?
When will the waves give over their foam?
You will not die, nor come home,
    O my lady.

O lady, when the wind kissed you
You made him music for you were a shaped shell.
I follow the waters and the wind still
Since my heart heard it and all to pieces fell
Which your lovers stole, meaning ill,
    O my lady.

O lady, consider when I shall have lost you
The moon's full hands, scattering waste,
The sea's hands, dark from the world's breast,
The world's decay where the wind's hands have passed,
And my head, worn out with love, at rest
In my hands, and my hands full of dust,
    O my lady.

Ted Hughes
(August 17th 1930 – October 28th 1998)

Ted Hughes won an Open Exhibition to read English at Pembroke College, Cambridge, in 1948, but his studies were postponed while he completed his mandatory two years of National Service. He served as an RAF wireless mechanic on an isolated three-man station in East Yorkshire, where he claimed there was "nothing to do but reread Shakespeare and watch the grass grow".

Hughes read voraciously in preparation for Cambridge, and continued to write. 'Song' is the earliest poem that he kept and was written whilst out on night duty at the beginning of his service, when he was just 19.

October 29

• Sir Walter Raleigh was executed October 29th 1618. He is reported to have said "This is sharp medicine, but it is a sure cure for all diseases"
• Polish poet Zbigniew Herbert born in Lvov October 29th 1924

The Author's Epitaph, Made By Himself

Even such is time, which takes in trust
Our youth, our joys, and all we have,
And pays us but with age and dust,
Who in the dark and silent grave
When we have wandered all our ways
Shuts up the story of our days,
And from which earth, and grave, and dust
The Lord shall raise me up, I trust.

Sir Walter Raleigh
(c. 1552 – October 29th 1618)

Imprisoned for 12 years on charges of treason, Sir Walter Raleigh was liberated in 1616, on the promise of securing fortunes for the King on his travels. But his first expedition ended in disaster and he was executed on his return. As was common practice, his head was embalmed and presented to his wife. Legend has it she carried it with her everywhere for the last 29 years of her life.

During the 17th century it was believed that Raleigh composed this poem the night before his death, and it was said to have been found in the flyleaf of his Bible, in the Abbey Gatehouse at Westminster. The poem is in fact a version of the last stanza of Raleigh's love poem 'Nature, That Washed Her Hands in Milk'.

• *French poet and writer Paul Valéry born in a small Mediterra-*
nean sea-side town near Montpellier, October 30th 1871
• *Ezra Pound, the father of modernist literature, whose ground-*
breaking translations from the Chinese and epic, The Cantos,
secured his literary reputation, born October 30th 1885
• *Don Paterson born in Dundee October 30th 1963*

October 30

The Wreck

But what lovers we were, what lovers,
even when it was all over –

the deadweight, bull-black wines we swung
towards each other rang and rang

like bells of blood, our own great hearts.
We slung the drunk boat out of port

and watched our unreal sober life
unmoor, a continent of grief;

the candlelight strange on our faces
like the tiny silent blazes

and coruscations of its wars.
We blew them out and took the stairs

into the night for the night's work,
stripped off in the timbered dark,

gently hooked each other on
like aqualungs, and thundered down

to mine our lovely secret wreck.
We surfaced later, breathless, back

to back, and made our way alone
up the mined beach of the dawn.

Don Paterson
(October 30th 1963 –)

Don Paterson comments: " 'The Wreck' is about as late in the day as a love poem gets before it turns into something else, I think. I suppose it's about how couples often stay on the train several stops past their destination. I don't think love is ever the same length as a relationship; it always falls short, or exceeds it. The latter state of affairs is easily the unhappiest."

October 31

• Earl of Rochester appointed a Deputy Lieutenant of Somerset
October 31st 1672
• John Keats born in London October 31st 1795

When I have fears that I may cease to be

When I have fears that I may cease to be
   Before my pen has gleaned my teeming brain,
Before high-pilèd books, in charactery°,   *written symbols*
   Hold like rich garners the full-ripened grain;
When I behold, upon the night's starred face,
   Huge cloudy symbols of a high romance,
And think that I may never live to trace
   Their shadows, with the magic hand of chance;
And when I feel, fair creature of an hour!
   That I shall never look upon thee more,
Never have relish in the faery° power,   *magical*
   Of unreflecting love! – then on the shore
Of the wide world I stand alone, and think
Till love and fame to nothingness do sink.

John Keats
(October 31st 1795 – February 23rd 1821)

Keats was keenly aware of his own fame during his lifetime. He told his brother George that writing the 4,000-line poem *Endymion* was intended to bring him "[B]ut a dozen paces towards the Temple of Fame" as much as it was to exercise and challenge his poetic imagination.

After witnessing the death of his other brother to tuberculosis, he wrote: "I have scarce a doubt of immortality of some nature or other – neither had Tom."

Report on Experience

I have been young, and now am not too old;
And I have seen the righteous forsaken,
His health, his honour and his quality taken.
    This is not what we were formerly told.

I have seen a green country, useful to the race,
Knocked silly with guns and mines, its villages vanished,
Even the last rat and last kestrel banished –
    God bless us all, this was peculiar grace.

I knew Seraphina; Nature gave her hue,
Glance, sympathy, note, like one from Eden.
I saw her smile warp, heard her lyric deaden;
    She turned to harlotry; – this I took to be new.

Say what you will, our God sees how they run.
These disillusions are His curious proving
That He loves humanity and will go on loving;
    Over there are faith, life, virtue in the sun.

Edmund Blunden
(November 1st 1896 – January 20th 1974)

Edmund Blunden fought at both the Somme and at Ypres and was awarded the Military Cross. His memoir, *Undertones of War* (1928), remains one of the great chronicles of the First World War. He was elected Oxford Professor of Poetry in 1966, succeeding fellow war poet Robert Graves. He wrote prolifically and died having published over 1,000 poems and 3,000 articles and reviews. His gravestone bears the inscription, "I live still to love still things quiet and unconcerned."

'Report on Experience' appeared in Blunden's second collection *Near and Far*, published in September 1929. He was not pleased with the poem at the time of composition, and wrote to a friend to say it was "unpremeditated" and "almost thrown away".

November 2

• Greek Nobel prize-winning poet Odysseus Elytis born
  November 2nd 1911
• T. S. Eliot became a British subject November 2nd 1927
• Émile Cammaerts, an anglicised Belgian poet and professor,
  died November 2nd 1953

My November Guest

My Sorrow, when she's here with me,
　　Thinks these dark days of autumn rain
Are beautiful as days can be;
She loves the bare, the withered tree;
　　She walks the sodden pasture lane.

Her pleasure will not let me stay.
　　She talks and I am fain to list:
She's glad the birds are gone away,
She's glad her simple worsted gray
　　Is silver now with clinging mist.

The desolate, deserted trees,
　　The faded earth, the heavy sky,
The beauties she so truly sees,
She thinks I have no eye for these,
　　And vexes me for reason why.

Not yesterday I learned to know
　　The love of bare November days
Before the coming of the snow,
But it were vain to tell her so,
　　And they are better for her praise.

Robert Frost
(March 26th 1874 – January 29th 1963)

During his time in England, Frost befriended the poet Edward Thomas. They shared a passion for the countryside and frequently went on long 'botanizing' walks, as Frost liked to call them. Thomas often deliberated over which path to take, or later regretted not taking the other, prompting Frost to say, "No matter which road you take, you'll always sigh, and wish you'd taken another." This of course was the inspiration for Frost's most famous poem, 'The Road Not Taken'. Frost was devastated at Thomas's death and wrote: "[He] was the only brother I ever had ... I hadn't a plan for the future that didn't include him."

'My November Guest' was published in Frost's first collection *A Boy's Own Will*, which Yeats pronounced "the best poetry written in America for a long time."

- *After witnessing the agonies of 90 serious casualties of war, the Austrian poet Georg Trakl took a cocaine overdose and died November 3rd 1914*
- *Oodgeroo of the Noonuccal, the first Aboriginal to have a book published, born Kath Walker November 3rd 1920*

Evening

The sky puts on the darkening blue coat
held for it by a row of ancient trees;
you watch: and the lands grow distant in your sight,
one journeying to heaven, one that falls;

and leave you, not at home in either one,
not quite so still and dark as the darkened houses,
not calling to eternity with the passion
of what becomes a star each night, and rises;

and leave you (inexpressibly to unravel)
your life, with its immensity and fear,
so that, now bounded, now immeasurable,
it is alternately stone in you and star.

Rainer Maria Rilke
(December 4th 1875 – December 29th 1926)

translated by Stephen Mitchell

On this day in 1899, Rilke wrote in his diary: "The greatest portion of fleetingness, frailty, and instability is a consequence of the not-having-been of so many people. It is not enough to have been born in order to be. One must splice oneself into some great circuit; but one must also insulate oneself, in order not to mischannel, not to use up, not to lose the current that one carries."

November 4

- *Wilfred Owen killed in action November 4th 1918*
- *Poet Patricia Beer born in Exmouth November 4th 1924*
- *After a final drinking binge on November 4th 1953, Dylan Thomas announced: "I've had 18 straight whiskies. I think that's the record." He slipped into a coma the following day*

Rainbow

When you see
de rainbow
you know
God know
wha he doing –
one big smile
across the sky –
I tell you
God got style
the man got style

When you see
raincloud pass
and de rainbow
make a show
I tell you
is God doing
limbo
the man doing
limbo

But sometimes
you know
when I see
de rainbow
so full of glow
and curving
like she bearing child
I does want to know
if God
ain't a woman

If that is so
the woman got style
man she got style

John Agard
(June 21st 1949 –)

John Agard writes: "This poem grew into a sequence called *Limbo Dancer in Dark Glasses*, about a mytho-poetic character of ambivalent gender."

John Agard was born in Guyana and came to Britain with his partner, the poet Grace Nichols, on this day in 1977. He has written poetry for children and adults, and his latest collection, *Weblines*, was published by Bloodaxe Books in 2002.

- *American poet Ella Wheeler Wilcox born November 5th 1856*
- *Poet James Elroy Flecker born November 5th 1884*
- *Art critic, novelist and poet John Berger, born in London November 5th 1926*
- *Sylvia Plath's father, Otto Plath, died November 5th 1940. The eight-year-old vowed "I'll never speak to God again"*

From In Memoriam A. H. H.

CXXIII

There rolls the deep where grew the tree.
  O earth, what changes hast thou seen!
  There where the long street roars hath been
The stillness of the central sea.

The hills are shadows, and they flow
  From form to form, and nothing stands;
  They melt like mist, the solid lands,
Like clouds they shape themselves and go.

But in my spirit will I dwell,
  And dream my dream, and hold it true;
  For tho' my lips may breathe adieu,
I cannot think the thing farewell.

> *Alfred, Lord Tennyson*
> *(August 6th 1809 – October 6th 1892)*

The year 1850 was a pivotal one in Tennyson's life: he was married, completed *In Memoriam A. H. H.* to widespread acclaim, and, on this day, was offered the Poet Laureateship. Tennyson maintained that he had no expectation of the Laureateship, but this seems doubtful: he dreamt he was visited by the Prince and the Queen the very morning the letter of invitation arrived. Besides, it would have been virtually impossible to ignore the flurry of media speculation as to who would succeed Wordsworth (the *Times* proposed the post should be dissolved, believing there to be no poet of equal merit), especially since of those in the running – Leigh Hunt, Elizabeth Browning, Sheridan Knowles and Henry Taylor – Tennyson was the odds-on favourite.

Tennyson also claimed diffidence about his acceptance of the Laureateship, saying he "wrote two letters, one accepting and one declining, and threw them then on the table, and settled to decide which I would send after my dinner and bottle of port." He was concerned that the annual wage of £100 was insufficient but was finally persuaded by a friend's reminder that he would always be offered the liver-wing of fowl when he dined out.

November 6

* Louis Aragon and Elsa Triolet met for the first time in a bar in Montparnasse November 6th 1925
* Stevie Smith, prompted by the producer's stopwatch, raced through a reading of her poem 'Tenuous and Precarious' for the Dial-A-Poem telephone service, in an apparent attempt to 'beat the record', November 6th 1970

Tenuous and Precarious

Tenuous and Precarious
Were my guardians,
Precarious and Tenuous,
Two Romans.

My father was Hazardous,
Hazardous,
Dear old man,
Three Romans.

There was my brother Spurious,
Spurious Posthumous,
Spurious was spurious
Was four Romans.

My husband was Perfidious,
He was perfidious,
Five Romans.

Surreptitious, our son,
Was surreptitious,
He was six Romans.

Our cat Tedious
Still lives,
Count not Tedious
Yet.

My name is Finis,
Finis, Finis,
I am Finis,
Six, five, four, three, two,
One Roman,
Finis.

Stevie Smith
(September 20th 1902 – March 7th 1971)

By all accounts, Stevie Smith was very fond of this poem. She found it "cheerful, as it is a word-play poem (on Latin endings to adjectives). But there is murder hidden in it, I think she murdered everybody except the cat." According to Lady Lawrence, an erstwhile friend of the poet, Smith wrote the poem whilst visiting her and her husband. Sir John suggested some Latin words and "Stevie just made it up as she went along, almost like a conversation. It was easy but erudite."

320

Deep Sorriness Atonement Song
for missed appointment, BBC North, Manchester

The man who sold Manhattan for a halfway decent bangle,
He had talks with Adolf Hitler and could see it from his angle,
And he could have signed the Quarrymen but didn't think they'd make it
So he bought a cake on Pudding Lane and thought 'Oh well I'll bake it'
    But his chances they were slim,
    And his brothers they were Grimm,
    And he's sorry, very sorry,
    But I'm sorrier than him.

And the drunken plastic surgeon who said 'I know, let's enlarge 'em!'
And the bloke who told the Light Brigade 'Oh what the hell, let's charge 'em,'
The magician with an early evening gig on the *Titanic*,
And the Mayor who told the people of Atlantis not to panic,
    And the Dong about his nose,
    And the Pobble *re* his toes,
    They're all sorry, really sorry,
    But I'm sorrier than those.

And don't forget the Bible, with the Sodomites and Judas,
And Onan who discovered something nothing was as rude as,
And anyone who reckoned it was City's year for Wembley,
And the kid who called Napoleon a shortarse in assembly,
    And the man who always smiles
    'Cause he knows I have his files,
    They're all sorry, truly sorry,
    But I'm sorrier by miles.

And Robert Falcon Scott who lost the race to a Norwegian,
And anyone who's ever spilt the pint of a Glaswegian,
Or told a Finn a joke or spent an hour with a Swiss-German,
Or got a mermaid in the sack and found it was a merman,
    Or him who smelt a rat,
    And got curious as a cat,
    They're all sorry, deeply sorry,
    But I'm sorrier than that.

[Continued]

All the people who were rubbish when we needed them to do it,
Whose wires crossed, whose spirit failed, who ballsed it up or blew it,
All notchers of *nul points* and all who have a problem Houston,
At least they weren't in Kensington when they should have been at Euston.
    For I didn't build the Wall
    And I didn't cause the Fall
    But I'm sorry, Lord I'm sorry,
    I'm the sorriest of all.

Glyn Maxwell
(November 7th 1962 –)

Glyn Maxwell writes: "In the mid-1990s the evening show on Radio 1, hosted by Mark Radcliffe and Mark Riley (aka 'Mark and Lard') started including readings by various poets between the songs. I'd gone up to Manchester about three times to do this gig – which was the biggest audience any British poets have ever been lucky enough to encounter – and was due to go up again. I was at a party in Kensington when the poet David Morley told me I was supposed to be in Manchester that night doing the recording. He was right, I'd got the week wrong. I was pretty mortified, because this was a great gig and I didn't think they'd ask me again. When they eventually did, I figured I'd better write a bloody good apology, and I wrote this on the train going up, which probably accounts for the rhythm. The penultimate line used to be 'Oh and I love Alan Ball', in homage to the manager of the perennially unsuccessful Manchester City, Mark Radcliffe's team of choice. When I published the poem I thought that might be an in-joke too far ... Anyway, this is for Mark and Lard."

Glyn Maxwell was born in 1962 in Welwyn Garden City. He read English at Oxford and subsequently studied on Derek Walcott's Writing Program in Boston. He is currently Visiting Writer at Amherst College, Massachusetts, and is editor of the *Republican*.

• *John Milton died of "gout stuck in" in Chalfont St Giles,*
  Buckinghamshire, November 8th 1674
• *Hungarian poet Miklos Radnóti is thought to have died*
  November 8th 1944

November 8

i carry your heart with me(i carry it in

i carry your heart with me(i carry it in
my heart)i am never without it(anywhere
i go you go,my dear;and whatever is done
by only me is your doing,my darling)
                                        i fear
no fate(for you are my fate,my sweet)i want
no world(for beautiful you are my world,my true)
and it's you are whatever a moon has always meant
and whatever a sun will always sing is you

here is the deepest secret nobody knows
(here is the root of the root and the bud of the bud
and the sky of the sky of a tree called life;which grows
higher than soul can hope or mind can hide)
and this is the wonder that's keeping the stars apart

i carry your heart(i carry it in my heart)

E. E. Cummings
(October 14th 1894 – September 3rd 1962)

Cummings wrote a letter to Ezra Pound's son, Omar, on this day in 1954, congratulating him on his recent marriage. His letter begins "Joy is by far the rarest thing,in or out of every world ... Joy isn't un-anything; Joy IS", and continues, "with regard to the subject of your letter:our nonhero [Cummings always referred to himself in this way] has a single statement to make;not a generality,but a function of his own particular experience – women are always right."

November 9

• French poet Guillaume Apollinaire died of flu November 9th 1918
• Poet James Schuyler born in Chicago November 9th 1923
• Poet Anne Sexton born in Massachusetts November 9th 1928
• Liverpool poet Roger McGough born November 9th 1937
• Dylan Thomas died in a New York hospital November 9th 1953
• Scottish poet Jackie Kay born in Edinburgh November 9th 1961

A Poem Just For Me

Where am I now when I need me
Suddenly where have I gone?
I'm so alone here without me
Tell me please what have I done?

Once I did most things together
I went for walks hand in hand
I shared my life so completely
I met my every demand.

Tell me I'll come back tomorrow
I'll keep my arms open wide
Tell me that I'll never leave me
My place is here at my side.

Maybe I've simply mislaid me
Like an umbrella or key
So until the day that I come my way
Here is a poem just for me.

Roger McGough
(November 9th 1937 –)

Roger McGough writes: "You know the feeling, you wake up one morning and you're just not there..."

Roger McGough, who has been described as "a trickster you can trust", was born in Liverpool and is one of Britain's best known voices. Besides his poetry for adults, he is a popular children's poet and TV presenter. In the 1960s he formed the band The Scaffold with Mike McGear, younger brother of Paul McCartney; they performed sketches, poems and songs, and rose to fame with the number one hit, Lily the Pink. McGough now lives in Twickenham, Surrey.

- Oliver Goldsmith born in Ireland November 10th 1728
- Friedrich von Schiller born in Marbach November 10th 1759
- American poet and artist Vachel Lindsay born in Springfield, Illinois, November 10th 1879
- Arthur Rimbaud died in Marseilles November 10th 1891; having abandoned writing at 20, he became a trader and gunrunner in Africa

Especially When It Snows
(for Boty)

especially when it snows
and every tree
has its dark arms and widespread hands
full of that shining angelfood

especially when it snows
and every footprint
makes a dark lake
among the frozen grass

especially when it snows darling
and tough little robins
beg for crumbs
at golden-spangled windows

ever since we said goodbye to you
in that memorial garden
where nothing grew
except the beautiful blank-eyed snow

and little Caitlin crouched to wave goodbye to you
down in the shadows

especially when it snows
and keeps on snowing

especially when it snows
and down the purple pathways of the sky
the planet staggers like King Lear
with his dead darling in his arms

especially when it snows
and keeps on snowing

Adrian Mitchell
(October 24th 1932 –)

Adrian Mitchell writes: "The poem is for my beloved adopted daughter Boty Goodwin. She was born on February 12th 1966 and died on November 10th 1995. It comes from my book *Blue Coffee, Poems 1985–1996* (Bloodaxe Books). Caitlin is my grand-daughter."

November 11

• "I have a kind of spooniness and delight over married people," wrote Hopkins to Bridges on November 11th 1884, "Especially if they say 'my wife', 'my husband' "
• In a bitter irony, Wilfred Owen's family learned the news of his death the day the Armistice was signed, November 11th 1918
• American poet Alicia Ostriker born November 11th 1937

Dulce Et Decorum Est

Bent double, like old beggars under sacks,
Knock-kneed, coughing like hags, we cursed through sludge,
Till on the haunting flares we turned our backs
And towards our distant rest began to trudge.
Men marched asleep. Many had lost their boots
But limped on, blood-shod. All went lame; all blind;
Drunk with fatigue; deaf even to the hoots
Of tired, outstripped Five-nines[1] that dropped behind.

Gas! GAS! Quick, boys!—An ecstasy of fumbling,
Fitting the clumsy helmets just in time;
But someone still was yelling out and stumbling,
And flound'ring like a man in fire or lime . . .
Dim, through the misty panes and thick green light,
As under a green sea, I saw him drowning.

In all my dreams, before my helpless sight,
He plunges at me, guttering, choking, drowning.

If in some smothering dreams, you too could pace
Behind the wagon that we flung him in,
And watch the white eyes writhing in his face,
His hanging face, like a devil's sick of sin;
If you could hear, at every jolt, the blood
Come gargling from the froth-corrupted lungs,
Obscene as cancer, bitter as the cud
Of vile, incurable sores on innocent tongues,—
My friend, you would not tell with such high zest
To children ardent for some desperate glory,
The old Lie: Dulce et decorum est
Pro patria mori.

Wilfred Owen
(March 18th 1893 – November 4th 1918)

Wilfred Owen drafted this poem in early October while still at Craiglockhart Hospital outside Edinburgh. He enclosed the poem in a letter to his mother, Susan Owen, with the words: "Here is a gas poem, done yesterday ... The famous latin tag [from Horace, Odes, III.ii.13] means of course It is sweet and meet to die for one's country. Sweet! and decorous!' "
The 'friend' addressed in the poem is Jessie Pope, a pro-war poet who wrote gaudily patriotic poems for the tabloids. The poem was originally dedicated to her.

1. 5.9-inch caliber shells.

- *John Bunyan was arrested for "devilishly and perniciously abstaining from coming to Church", November 12th 1660*
- *Milton was buried in St Giles' Cripplegate November 12th 1674. His grave was later raided and locks of his hair stolen*
- *Emily Dickinson's Poems were published posthumously November 12th 1890*

There's a certain Slant of light

There's a certain Slant of light,
Winter Afternoons –
That oppresses, like the Heft
Of Cathedral Tunes –

Heavenly Hurt, it gives us –
We can find no scar,
But internal difference,
Where the Meanings, are –

None may teach it – Any –
'Tis the Seal Despair –
An imperial affliction
Sent us of the Air –

When it comes, the Landscape listens –
Shadows – hold their breath –
When it goes, 'tis like the Distance
On the look of Death –

Emily Dickinson
(December 10th 1830 – May 15th 1886)

The full extent of Emily Dickinson's output was not realised until after her death, when her sister Lavinia found a locked box containing over 1,000 poems in fair copy. The first volume of her poetry, prepared by Mabel Loomis Todd and Thomas Wentworth Higginson, brought Dickinson the fame she had long deserved, and the book went through six imprints in six months. The book was, however, a serious misrepresentation of her art, since the pair had set about rigorously 'normalising' Dickinson's supposed unorthodoxies of syntax and meter. The result was a very different set of poems to those Dickinson had originally written.

November 13

- *St Augustine born in North Africa November 13th 354 AD*
- *Wordsworth and Coleridge began composing 'The Rime of the Ancient Mariner' November 13th 1797*
- *Robert Louis Stevenson born in Edinburgh November 13th 1850*
- *Francis Thompson died November 13th 1907*
- *Edmund Blunden was awarded the military cross after crossing the enemy lines on a raid, November 13th 1916*

I Came to Love You too Late

I came to love you too late,
O Beauty, so long ago and immaculate.
I searched the wide earth's reach and go.
But what, what of that grace did I know?
I could not look into my proper heart or body,
Yet you were in me.

I waged my campaign, a murderous
Fanatic, against all things wondrous,
Each living being, every true person
Of your absolute creation.
You writ me through,
But I, I could not read me in you.

You called out to me and wept to me;
You shattered the brute bowl of my deafness.
You lanced the cleansing rays at me;
You sliced the clouded cataract of my blindness.

You drifted fragrant winds to me
And I drew in the air's sacred delicacy.
And I desired you,
And I tasted you,
And that taste – O the release! –
Famished the starved in me.
You touched me
And I burn, burn for your peace.

St Augustine
(November 13th 354 – August 28th 430)

version by John Stammers

Augustine was born in Tagaste (modern Souk Ahras, Algeria). Fired by his love of the wisdom of Cicero, the young Augustine was a devotee of the religious cult Manichaeism – a rival to Christianity at the time. But after coming under the influence of Bishop Ambrose of Milan, he was baptized in 387 AD. Two years later, while on a visit to Hippo, he was pressed into the priesthood by the local congregation. He broke into tears as they laid hands on him in the church. Augustine became Bishop of Hippo in 395 AD, and remained there until his death.

- *Ben Jonson married Ann Lewis November 14th 1594*
- *Emily Dickinson's mother died November 14th 1882:*
  "[Her] dying almost stunned my spirit"
- *Norman MacCaig born in Edinburgh November 14th 1910*
- *Vicki Feaver born in Nottingham November 14th 1943*

Judith

Wondering how a good woman can murder
I enter the tent of Holofernes,
holding in one hand his long oiled hair
and in the other, raised above
his sleeping, wine-flushed face,
his falchion with its unsheathed
curved blade. And I feel a rush
of tenderness, a longing
to put down my weapon, to lie
sheltered and safe in a warrior's
fumy sweat, under the emerald stars
of his purple and gold canopy,
to melt like a sweet on his tongue
to nothing. And I remember the glare
of the barley field; my husband
pushing away the sponge I pressed
to his burning head; the stubble
puncturing my feet as I ran,
flinging myself on a body
that was already cooling
and stiffening; and the nights
when I lay on the roof – my emptiness
like the emptiness of a temple
with the doors kicked in; and the mornings
when I rolled in the ash of the fire
just to be touched and dirtied
by something. And I bring my blade
down on his neck – and it's easy
like slicing through fish.
And I bring it down again,
cleaving the bone.

Vicki Feaver
(November 14th 1943 –)

Vicki Feaver writes: "Judith is the Jewish heroine who saved her people by cutting off the head of Holofernes, the enemy general. That's well known: but not the fact that in the period before she had shut herself away in mourning for the death of her husband. She used the anger of her grief to give her the courage to act. At the time I wrote the poem, I also felt stuck in grief. Judith's story provided both inspiration for the poem and the stimulus for me to use my anger to write it."

November 15

• William Cowper, hymn-writer and poet, who suffered a crisis of
faith and rejected the chuch, born November 15th 1731
• Marianne Moore born in Missouri November 15th 1887
• Charlotte Mew born in London November 15th 1889

Rooms

I remember rooms that have had their part
  In the steady slowing down of the heart.
The room in Paris, the room at Geneva,
The little damp room with the seaweed smell,
And that ceaseless maddening sound of the tide –
  Rooms where for good or for ill – things died.
But there is the room where we two lie dead,
Though every morning we seem to wake and might just
                        as well seem to sleep again
  As we shall somewhere in the other quieter, dustier bed
  Out there in the sun – in the rain.

Charlotte Mew
(November 15th 1869 – March 24th 1928)

After the death of her brother, Fred, in September 1898, Charlotte Mew decided to spend some
time abroad. She arrived in Paris determined to see an old friend Ella D'Arcy, with whom she
believed she was rather in love. But, as was her custom, she could not find the necessary resolve
to act on her feelings. She wrote home to say "[I]t is a queer uncertain mind this of mine – and
claims are being made on it at the moment which I find difficult to meet."

Over-anxious, desperate to please, and tormented by doubt, it would seem that Mew only
confused Ella D'Arcy, who said to her "One acts foolishly in order to write wisely." Many of the
poems she wrote during her Paris stay strike a note of mild hysteria, though 'Rooms', with its quiet
lyricism, seemingly acknowledges defeat. Charlotte Mew returned to England frustrated, and it is
doubtful she saw Ella D'Arcy again.

• *William Broome, best remembered for his translation of Homer's* Odyssey, *died in Bath November 16th 1745*
• *Following his release from jail, Oscar Wilde wrote on November 16th 1897: "It is curious how vanity helps keep the successful man and wrecks the failure. In old days half my strength was my vanity"*

Slow, Slow, Fresh Fount

Slow, slow, fresh fount, keep time with my salt tears;
Yet slower, yet, O faintly, gentle springs!
List to the heavy part the music bears:
Woe weeps out her division, when she sings.
  Droop herbs and flowers;
  Fall grief in showers;
  Our beauties are not ours.
    O, I could still,
Like melting snow upon some craggy hill,
  Drop, drop, drop, drop,
Since nature's pride is now a withered daffodil.

Ben Jonson
(June 11th 1572 – August 6th 1637)

This lyric is from the first act of *Cynthia's Revels*, an early comedy by Jonson written at the end of the 16th century. The play deals with the sin of self-love, and 'Slow, Slow, Fresh Fount' is a lament sung by Echo for Narcissus, who, entranced by his own reflection in the pool, was eventually transformed into a daffodil (otherwise known as a narcissus).

The play was first performed at the Blackfriars Theatre in early January 1600 by the Children of the Chapel, a theatre company made up solely of boy actors. Such children's companies were in vogue for several years, and gave professional adult theatre companies genuine competition for audiences. Boys were selected for their looks and voices by the masters of the companies, before being trained in acting and singing.

November 17

• *John Dryden anonymously published* Absalom and Achitophel, *a political satire attacking the Earl of Shaftesbury, November 17th 1681*
• *After a 14-year battle with cancer, self-described "Black Lesbian, mother, warrior, poet" Audrey Lorde died in the Virgin Islands November 17th 1992*

Snow

The room was suddenly rich and the great bay-window was
Spawning snow and pink roses against it
Soundlessly collateral and incompatible:
World is suddener than we fancy it.

World is crazier and more of it than we think,
Incorrigibly plural. I peel and portion
A tangerine and spit the pips and feel
The drunkenness of things being various.

And the fire flames with a bubbling sound for world
Is more spiteful and gay than one supposes –
On the tongue on the eyes on the ears in the palms of one's hands –
There is more than glass between the snow and the huge roses.

Louis MacNeice
(September 12th 1907 – September 3rd 1963)

As his reputation grew, Louis MacNeice became grudgingly aware of the possibility of a biography being written about him. On this day in 1940, MacNeice wrote to his friend Professor E. R. Dodds on the subject, saying, "In case any super-mug wants to do a life of me I would warn him against accepting, without careful scrutiny, any alleged information from my family ... The best authorities (though each only from a certain angle) are Graham Shepard, Nancy Coldstream, yourself, Eleanor Clark &, I suppose, Wystan [Auden]. (How mortuary-egotistical all this sounds)."
MacNeice himself wrote an (unfinished) autobiography, which was published posthumously as *The Strings Are False* in 1966.

• Kathleen Morrison (née Johnston), who became Frost's secretary
and lover, born in Nova Scotia November 18th 1898
• Margaret Atwood born in Ottawa November 18th 1939
• Australian poet, critic and novelist W. J. Turner, died
November 18th 1946
• Paul Éluard, poet and founder of the Surrealist Movement, died
of a heart condition in Charenton-le-Pont November 18th 1952

Habitation

Marriage is not
a house or even a tent

it is before that, and colder:

the edge of the forest, the edge
of the desert
                    the unpainted stairs
at the back where we squat
outside, eating popcorn

the edge of the receding glacier

where painfully and with wonder
at having survived even
this far

we are learning to make fire

Margaret Atwood
(November 18th 1939 –)

Margaret Atwood is married to the Canadian writer Graeme Gibson about whom it was once said:
"Every female writer should be married to Graeme Gibson." They live in Toronto and have three
children.

November 19

• Poet Laureate and dramatist Thomas Shadwell died of a
  suspected drug overdose in Chelsea November 19th 1692
• American poet and critic Allen Tate, whose early ambition
  was to be a professional violinist, born November 19th 1899
• W. S. Graham born in Greenock, the son of a shipyard
  engineer, November 19th 1918
• Sharon Olds born in San Francisco November 19th 1942

True Love

In the middle of the night, when we get up
after making love, we look at each other in
complete friendship, we know so fully
what the other has been doing. Bound to each other
like mountaineers coming down from a mountain,
bound with the tie of the delivery-room,
we wander down the hall to the bathroom, I can
hardly walk, I wobble through the granular
shadowless air, I know where you are
with my eyes closed, we are bound to each other
with huge invisible threads, our sexes
muted, exhausted, crushed, the whole
body a sex - surely this
is the most blessed time of my life,
our children asleep in their beds, each fate
like a vein of abiding mineral
not discovered yet. I sit
on the toilet in the night, you are somewhere in the room,
I open the window and snow has fallen in a
steep drift, against the pane, I
look up, into it,
a wall of cold crystals, silent
and glistening, I quietly call to you
and you come and hold my hand and I say
I cannot see beyond it. I cannot see beyond it.

Sharon Olds
(November 19th 1942 –)

Sharon Olds once commented: "I think that love is almost the hardest thing to write about. Not a general state of being in love, but a particular love for a particular person ... It just seems to me if writers can assemble, in language, something that bears any relation to experience – especially important experience, experience we care about, moving and powerful experience – then it is worth trying. The opportunities for offence and failure are always aplenty. They lie all around us."

Sharon Olds' latest collection is *The Unswept Room* (Jonathan Cape, 2003). *The Dead and the Living* (1984), won the Lamont Poetry Prize and the National Book Critics Circle Award. She founded the Writing Program at Goldwater Hospital for the severely physically disabled and is Chair of New York University's Creative Writing Program.

• Thomas Chatterton, the "marvelous boy poet" whose tragic life
and death had a powerful influence on the Romantic imagination,
and inspired Wordsworth and Keats, born November 20th 1752
• Nâzim Hikmet, Turkish poet who spent 28 years in prison, born
November 20th 1902
• Hugging poet John Horder born in Brighton November 20th 1936

Through the Lavatory Window

I see heaven
Through the lavatory window.
I see God
On the tips of the branches
In amongst the leaves of the branches,

I see God
Through the lavatory window.
He is mule-aching about
Amongst the trout
At the bottom of the sea.

He is a skirmisher:
You can see him too
In the flight of the jet
If you poke your head far enough out
Of the lavatory window.

John Horder
(November 20th 1936 –)

John Horder writes: "I meant to convey the unity of all life, the beautiful and the squalid. The
human condition is such that we are always looking outside ourselves for solutions to our
transitoriness, our emptiness. The only way we can embrace it is from within. The poem is about
embracing the smallest details of our life and finding meaning in the most unlikely places."

John Horder is a storyteller, freelance journalist and broadcaster. He has published three collections
of poetry, including *A Sense of Being* (1968) and *Meher Baba and the Nothingness* (1981) and recently
co-edited *Stevie: A Motley Collection*. He has followed Meher Baba's teachings for 34 years and is
a dedicated devotee of writing 'morning pages' as suggested in Julia Cameron's *The Artist's Way*.
He lives in West Hampstead and is passionate about daily walking.

November 21

• Sir Arthur Quiller-Couch, poet, writer and editor of The
  Oxford Book of English Verse, born November 21st 1863
• Oscar Wilde transferred to Reading Gaol November 21st 1895
• Graves gave his first poem to Beryl in secret on November 21st
  1938; Beryl was at this time still married to his friend, the
  writer Alan Hodge

She Tells Her Love While Half Asleep

She tells her love while half asleep,
   In the dark hours,
      With half-words whispered low:
As Earth stirs in her winter sleep
   And puts out grass and flowers
      Despite the snow,
      Despite the falling snow.

Robert Graves
(July 24th 1895 – December 7th 1985)

This poem appeared in a collection published in 1945 when Robert Graves was living with his future wife Beryl. Like several other poems in the collection, 'She tells her love...' displays the new trust, calmness and affection that Beryl inspired in him. They lived together in Majorca until his death in 1985.

Before the serenity of his marriage to Beryl, Graves had been heavily involved in a tempestuous poet-muse relationship with Laura Riding. On one occasion in the spring of 1933, Riding threw herself out of a third-storey window after an argument with another male collaborator, Geoffrey Phibbs, who had spurned her advances. Graves raced down a flight of stairs before flinging himself out of a window in his haste to reach her. Riding fractured her pelvis, crushed several vertebrae and bent her spinal cord, while Graves survived unscathed.

- *John Donne elected Dean of St. Paul's November 22nd 1621*
- *French poet and master of the sonnet, José Maria de Heredia, born in La Fortuna, Cuba, November 22nd 1842*
- *C. S. Lewis's death on November 22nd 1963 was overshadowed by the assassination of President Kennedy on the same day*
- *Erich Fried died November 22nd 1988 and was buried in Kensal Green cemetery*

What It Is

It is madness
says reason
It is what it is
says love

It is unhappiness
says caution
It is nothing but pain
says fear
It has no future
says insight
It is what it is
says love

It is ridiculous
says pride
It is foolish
says caution
It is impossible
says experience
It is what it is
says love

Erich Fried
(May 6th 1921 – November 22nd 1988)

translated by Stuart Hood

Erich Fried was born in Vienna to Jewish parents, but fled Austria for London in 1938, after his father had been beaten to death by the Gestapo. After being involved with various political and refugee groups during the war, Fried joined the BBC in 1952 and worked as a political commentator in the German Service there for 16 years. He was a passionate anti-war campaigner throughout his life: he condemned both the Vietnam War and, more controversially, Israel for its policies towards Palestine. Described by his translator Stuart Hood as a man of "inexhaustible energies and inventiveness", he also found the time to write plays, novels, essays and hundreds of poems, and to translate works by, amongst others, Dylan Thomas, T. S. Eliot and Shakespeare.

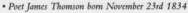

• Poet James Thomson born November 23rd 1834
• Paul Celan born Paul Antschel in Czernowitz (then in
  Romania) November 23rd 1920
• Christopher Logue born in Portsmouth November 23rd 1926
• Poet Derek Mahon born in Belfast November 23rd 1941

Walked Out One Evening

ning,
ol Street,
e pavement
rvest wheat.

And do.   ne brimming river
  I heard a lover sing
Under an arch of the railway:
  'Love has no ending.

'I'll love you, dear, I'll love you
  Till China and Africa meet,
And the river jumps over the mountain
  And the salmon sing in the street.

'I'll love you till the ocean
  Is folded and hung up to dry
And the seven stars go squawking
  Like geese about the sky.

'The years shall run like rabbits,
  For in my arms I hold
The Flower of the Ages,
  And the first love of the world.'

But all the clocks in the city
  Began to whirr and chime:
'O let not Time deceive you,
  You cannot conquer Time.

'In the burrows of the Nightmare
  Where Justice naked is,
Time watches from the shadow
  And coughs when you would kiss.

'In headaches and in worry
  Vaguely life leaks away,
And Time will have his fancy
  To-morrow or to-day.

'Into many a green valley
  Drifts the appalling snow;
Time breaks the threaded dances
  And the diver's brilliant bow.

'O plunge your hands in water,
  Plunge them in up to the wrist;
Stare, stare in the basin
  And wonder what you've missed.

'The glacier knocks in the cupboard,
  The desert sighs in the bed,
And the crack in the tea-cup opens
  A lane to the land of the dead.

'Where the beggars raffle the banknotes
  And the Giant is enchanting to Jack,
And the Lily-white Boy is a Roarer,
  And Jill goes down on her back.

'O look, look in the mirror,
  O look in your distress;
Life remains a blessing
  Although you cannot bless.

O stand, stand at the window
  As the tears scald and start;
You will love your crooked neighbour
  With your crooked heart.'

It was late, late in the evening,
  The lovers they were gone;
The clocks had ceased their chiming,
  And the deep river ran on.

W. H. Auden
(February 21st 1907 – September 29th 1973)

In the summer of 1941, Auden learnt that his partner, Chester Kallman, had been unfaithful. He had believed their relationship to be the 'marriage' he had so long desired, and the revelation left him grief-stricken. At his lowest ebb, Auden threw himself into his writing, and composed this poem in November of that year.

- John Evelyn met the Earl of Rochester at dinner on November 24th 1670, and pronounced him "a very prophane Wit"
- Paul Blackburn born in St Albans, Vermont, November 24th 1926
- Dylan Thomas buried at Laugharne cemetery November 24th 1953, "a passionate day of sorrow ... and drinking ... a time of dignity and farce"

Being but men

Being but men, we walked into the trees
Afraid, letting our syllables be soft
For fear of waking the rooks,
For fear of coming
Noiselessly into a world of wings and cries.

If we were children we might climb,
Catch the rooks sleeping, and break no twig,
And, after the soft ascent,
Thrust our heads above the branches
To wonder at the unfailing stars.

Out of confusion, as the way is,
And the wonder that man knows,
Out of the chaos would come bliss.

That, then, is loveliness, we said,
Children in wonder watching the stars,
Is the aim and the end.

Being but men, we walked into the trees.

Dylan Thomas
(October 27th 1914 – November 9th 1953)

Dylan Thomas was reciting reams of Shakespearean soliloquies by the age of three. He opposed his father's wish for him to study at university and dedicated himself instead to writing. His first job was with a newspaper, but with the publication of his first collection at 20, he was set for the life of a poet – one of notorious character, impoverishment and alcoholism.

Dylan Thomas delighted in his own inimitable self-deprecation. He would frequently refer to his poems as "little lyrical cripples" and himself as "the pig that roots for unconsidered troofles in the reeking wood of his past." But, as both irreverent drunk and incorrigible flirt, Thomas succeeded in amusing and outraging people wherever he went.

339

November 25

• Hymn-writer Isaac Watts died November 25th 1748
• Painter and poet Isaac Rosenberg born in Bristol into a
  working-class Jewish family November 25th 1890
• David Gascoyne died November 25th 2001

To Emilia V

Music, when soft voices die,
Vibrates in the memory—
Odours, when sweet violets sicken,
Live within the sense they quicken.

Rose leaves, when the rose is dead,
Are heaped for the beloved's bed;
And so thy thoughts, when thou art gone,
Love itself shall slumber on . . .

Percy Bysshe Shelley
(August 4th 1792 – July 8th 1822)

In late November 1820, Mary Shelley and her companion Clair Clairmont were introduced to Teresa (Emilia) Viviani, a 19-year-old woman confined in a convent by her parents and awaiting an arranged marriage. Percy Shelley was immediately enchanted by her and indignant at her fate. 'Emilia' was the inspiration for *Epipsychidion*, which Shelley composed in Pisa in early 1820 and published anonymously the following year.

By June 1822, however, Shelley wrote to a John Gisborne: "The *Epipsychidion* I cannot look at; the person whom it celebrates was a cloud instead of a Juno ... I think one is always in love with something or other; the error, and I confess it is not easy for spirits encased in flesh and blood to avoid it, consists in seeking in a mortal image the likeness of what is, perhaps, eternal."

• *Essex-born poet Coventry Patmore, who declared in the preface to his slim* Collected Poems, *"I have written little, but it is all my best", died November 26th 1896*

Aubade

I work all day, and get half-drunk at night.
Waking at four to soundless dark, I stare.
In time the curtain-edges will grow light.
Till then I see what's really always there:
Unresting death, a whole day nearer now,
Making all thought impossible but how
And where and when I shall myself die.
Arid interrogation: yet the dread
Of dying, and being dead,
Flashes afresh to hold and horrify.

The mind blanks at the glare. Not in remorse
—The good not done, the love not given, time
Torn off unused—nor wretchedly because
An only life can take so long to climb
Clear of its wrong beginnings, and may never;
But at the total emptiness for ever,
The sure extinction that we travel to
And shall be lost in always. Not to be here,
Not to be anywhere,
And soon; nothing more terrible, nothing more true.

This is a special way of being afraid
No trick dispels. Religion used to try,
That vast moth-eaten musical brocade
Created to pretend we never die,
And specious stuff that says *No rational being
Can fear a thing it will not feel,* not seeing
That this is what we fear—no sight, no sound,
No touch or taste or smell, nothing to think with,
Nothing to love or link with,
The anaesthetic from which none come round.

[Continued]

And so it stays just on the edge of vision,
A small unfocused blur, a standing chill
That slows each impulse down to indecision.
Most things may never happen: this one will,
And realisation of it rages out
In furnace-fear when we are caught without
People or drink. Courage is no good:
It means not scaring others. Being brave
Lets no one off the grave.
Death is no different whined at than withstood.

Slowly light strengthens, and the room takes shape.
Its stands plain as a wardrobe, what we know,
Have always known, know that we can't escape,
Yet can't accept. One side will have to go.
Meanwhile telephones crouch, getting ready to ring
In locked-up offices, and all the uncaring
Intricate rented world begins to rouse.
The sky is white as clay, with no sun.
Work has to be done.
Postmen like doctors go from house to house.

Philip Larkin
(August 9th 1922 – December 2nd 1985)

'Aubade' was first published in the *Times Literary Supplement* in December 1977. Harold Pinter promptly sent a telegram of congratulation. In fact, as was his wont, Larkin had begun the poem three years previously. The final stanza was written considerably later than the others and an early draft made Larkin's intentions rather more explicit: 'Postmen go / From house to house like doctors to persuade / life to return.'

In a letter to his friend W. G. Runciman written on this day in 1978, Philip Larkin commented on 'Aubade': "It's hard to say whether fear of death is a neurotic condition ... my first impulse is to say that it is simply seeing things clearly ... or that it's simply being more sensitive ... But does one's fear increase in direct ratio to the nearness of death? ... perhaps we can comfort ourselves with the thought that when death is really near, it won't worry us. We shall become as thick-skinned as everyone else ... and personally I should be delighted to live forever (just as I have never thought it would be a dull world if everyone was like me)."

- *Quintus Horactius Flaccus (Horace), Augustan poet whose influential ideas such as 'Carpe diem' have weathered history, died November 27th 8BC*
- *A special licence was issued for the marriage of William Shakespeare to Anne Hathaway November 27th 1582*
- *Alexandre Dumas the Younger, dramatist and poet, died November 27th 1895*
- *Romanian poet Nina Cassian born November 27th 1924*

Anniversary
for Barbara Davis

I love you with the syllables I learned
from Shakespeare's sonnets, burning, never burned.

I love you with the everlasting sounds
of memory, your ups and downs
and calm and frenzy, ecstasy and grief.

I love your life as much as I believe
in elements, in islands under spell,
in howling oceans, magic dew . . .

When once you called me Prospero, you knew
that I am Caliban as well.

Nina Cassian
(November 27th 1924 –)

translated by the poet

Nina Cassian writes: "Life is not only a succession of anniversaries. The in-between times can be difficult and challenging. But I'm not afraid of ageing. I feel rather that advancing through the decades is a kind of triumph, especially if it carries with it some achievements. Anyway, art and poetry proved to be my best investments!"

Nina Cassian was born in Galati, Romania, but lived most of her adult years in Bucharest until 1985, when she was invited to the USA as a visiting professor. Despite the then political unrest, she intended to return home until a friend was arrested by the Romanian secret service for keeping a diary, which happened to include a number of Cassian's satirical poems about the Ceauscescus (then still the reigning dictators). She was forced to remain in exile and was granted political asylum in the States, where she has lived ever since. Cassian has published over 50 books and is also a journalist, film critic, translator and a composer of classical music.

343

November 28

• Preacher and writer John Bunyan baptised November 28th 1628
• In an autograph album kept by his friend and patron, William Upcott, William Blake noted that he was "Born 28. Nov 1757 / & has died several times since"
• On November 28th 1969 Stevie Smith described meeting the Queen as "Rather like meeting the very best sort of headmistress in the very best sort of mood"

My Papa's Waltz

The whiskey on your breath
Could make a small boy dizzy;
But I hung on like death:
Such waltzing was not easy.

We romped until the pans
Slid from the kitchen shelf;
My mother's countenance
Could not unfrown itself.

The hand that held my wrist
Was battered on one knuckle;
At every step you missed
My right ear scraped a buckle.

You beat time on my head
With a palm caked hard by dirt,
Then waltzed me off to bed
Still clinging to your shirt.

Theodore Roethke
(May 25th 1908 – August 1st 1963)

Theodore Roethke's father Otto ran a greenhouse business with his brother Charles in Saginaw, Michigan. The brothers fell out when Charles got the business into financial trouble, a factor which played a part in his eventual suicide in February 1923. Otto died from cancer just two months later.

Three years later Theodore Roethke wrote: "A great story could be written about my father, for in many ways he was a truly great man. I have never found anyone remotely like him in life or literature."

• Tess of the d'Urbervilles published November 29th 1891
• C. S. Lewis born in Belfast November 29th 1898
• George Szirtes, painter, poet and translator, born in Hungary
November 29th 1948

November 29

I Look into My Glass

I look into my glass,
And view my wasting skin,
And say, "Would God it came to pass
My heart had shrunk as thin!"

For then, I, undistrest
By hearts grown cold to me,
Could lonely wait my endless rest
With equanimity.

But Time, to make me grieve,
Part steals, lets part abide;
And shakes this fragile frame at eve
With throbbings of noontide.

Thomas Hardy
(June 2nd 1840 – January 11th 1928)

When Hardy's fifteenth (and final) novel, *Tess of the d'Urbervilles,* was panned by reviewers, Hardy was inclined to say he would "never write another line." Instead, he turned his attentions to poetry. The resulting *Wessex Poems*, which Hardy kept a closely guarded secret, were accompanied by sketches done by the author. Critics were sceptical, if not dismissive, when the collection was published in December 1898, but Hardy himself was happy; poetry was a relief after the constraint of writing to tight deadlines and he had enjoyed the opportunity of exploiting his passion for music and drawing, as well as the freedom to say what he felt.

'I Look into My Glass', the last poem in the collection, was inspired by an experience in October 1892: "Hurt my tooth at breakfast-time. I look in the glass. Am conscious of the humiliating sorriness of my earthly tabernacle, and of the sad fact that the best of parents could do no better for me."

November 30

• Sir Philip Sidney born November 30th 1554
• Poet and satirist Jonathan Swift born November 30th 1667
• Oscar Wilde died of cerebral meningitus in a Paris hotel room
  November 30th 1900
• Fernando Pessoa died in Lisbon November 30th 1935
• Irish poet Patrick Kavanagh died November 30th 1967

From Astrophil and Stella
XXXI

With how sad steps, O Moon, thou climb'st the skies,
　How silently, and with how wan a face!
　What, may it be that even in heavenly place
That busy archer his sharp arrows tries?
Sure, if that long-with-love-aquainted eyes
　Can judge of Love, thou feel'st a Lover's case;
　I read it in thy looks: thy languished grace,
To me that feel the like, thy state descries.
　Then even of fellowship, O Moon, tell me
Is constant *love* deemed there but want of wit?
Are beauties there as proud as here they be?
Do they above love to be loved, and yet
　Those lovers scorn whom that *love* doth possess?
　Do they call *virtue* there ungratefulness?

Sir Philip Sidney
(November 30th 1554 – October 17th 1586)

Philip Sidney was born on this day in 1554. A recent biographer has called Sidney "the ultimate silver-spoon baby": his godparents included King Philip II of Spain, the Earl of Bedford and the Duchess of Northumberland, ensuring Sidney would never be short of well-connected friends.

The poem above is from Sidney's best-known work, the sonnet-sequence *Astrophil and Stella*. Though here the 'archer' primarily refers to Cupid, there are several other references to arrows and arrow-heads in the sequence, which many commentators have linked to the silver arrow-head in the Sidney family coat of arms. This has been taken as further evidence of the likeness between the character Astrophil and Philip Sidney himself.

- Spenser's Faerie Queene *was registered for publication with the Stationers' Company December 1st 1590*
- Leigh Hunt's' 'Young Poets', *published December 1st 1816, named Keats as one of three "young aspirants ... who promise ... to revive Nature and put a new spirit of youth into everything"*

Lines for Winter
for Ros Krauss

Tell yourself
as it gets cold and grey falls from the air
that you will go on
walking, hearing
the same tune no matter where
you find yourself –
inside the dome of dark
or under the cracking white
of the moon's gaze in a valley of snow.
Tonight as it gets cold
tell yourself
what you know which is nothing
but the tune your bones play
as you keep going. And you will be able
for once to lie down under the small fire
of winter stars.
And if it happens that you cannot
go on or turn back
and you find yourself
where you will be at the end,
tell yourself
in that final flowing of cold through your limbs
that you love what you are.

Mark Strand
(April 11th 1934 –)

Mark Strand writes: "I wrote the poem back in 1976 or '77 and dedicated it to a friend, Rosalind Krauss, who was feeling depressed at the time. I was reading lots of Robert Penn Warren and Galway Kinnell and the poem owes something to each of them, although they were very different from each other."

Mark Strand grew up in the States and South America. He spent a year as a Fulbright Lecturer at the University of Brazil, where he was deeply influenced by Latin American poets and he is now regarded as one of the foremost translators of Latin American poetry into English. He is the author of ten books of poetry, including *Blizzard of One* which won the Pulitzer Prize in 1999, as well as a number of prose works. He served as Poet Laureate of the United States from 1990 to 1991.

December 2

• Samuel Pepys was scandalised to hear the King tell of Rochester "having of his clothes stole while with a wench", December 2nd 1668
• Argentine poet José Marmol was born December 2nd 1817
• Poet Jon Silkin born in London December 2nd 1930
• Poet Philip Larkin, who claimed "Deprivation is for me what daffodils were for Wordsworth", died December 2nd 1985

The Winter Palace

Most people know more as they get older:
I give all that the cold shoulder.

I spent my second quarter-century
Losing what I had at university

And refusing to take in what had happened since.
Now I know none of the names in the public prints,

And am starting to give offence by forgetting faces
And swearing I've never been in certain places.

It will be worth it, if in the end I manage
To blank out whatever it is that is doing the damage.

Then there will be nothing I know.
My mind will fold into itself, like fields, like snow.

Philip Larkin
(August 9th 1922 – December 2nd 1985)

Larkin once famously claimed that his biography could begin at 21 and omit nothing of importance. Priding himself on his peculiarly British brand of nihilism, he believed that "nothing like something happens everywhere". In later life he declined the invitation to succeed John Betjeman as Poet Laureate, shunning public and media attention in favour of a quiet life. Eric Hamburger described him as "the saddest heart in the post-war supermarket."

Larkin died on this day at the age of 63; just as he had predicted, the very same age at which his father had died.

• *Following a marriage proposal from Lord Otis Phillips, Emily Dickinson wrote on December 3rd 1882: "You even call me to your Breast with apology! Of what must my poor Heart be made!"*
• *Robert Louis Stevenson died in Samoa December 3rd 1894*
• *Poet and critic Craig Raine born December 3rd 1944*

The Vagabond

Give to me the life I love,
  Let the lave go by me,
Give the jolly heaven above
  And the byway nigh me.
Bed in the bush with stars to see,
  Bread I dip in the river –
There's the life for a man like me,
  There's the life for ever.

Let the blow fall soon or late,
  Let what will be o'er me;
Give the face of earth around
  And the road before me.
Wealth I seek not, hope nor love,
  Nor a friend to know me;
All I seek, the heaven above
  And the road below me.

Or let autumn fall on me
  Where afield I linger,
Silencing the bird on tree,
  Biting the blue finger.
White as meal the frosty field –
  Warm the fireside haven –
Not to autumn will I yield,
  Not to winter even!

Let the blow fall soon or late,
  Let what will be o'er me;
Give the face of earth around,
  And the road before me.
Wealth I ask not, hope nor love,
  Nor a friend to know me;
All I ask, the heaven above
  And the road below me.

Robert Louis Stevenson
(November 13th 1850 – December 3rd 1894)

Much as Stevenson loved his native Scotland, ill-health forced him to seek out warmer climes, and he became in the process a great traveller. This travelling poem is meant to be sung "to an air of Schubert".

December 4

• Scots poet William Drummond died December 4th 1649
• John Gay died December 4th 1732
• Rainer Maria Rilke born in Prague, the son of a railway
  official, December 4th 1875
• Art historian and war poet Sir Herbert Read born in Yorkshire
  December 4th 1893
• Hungarian poet Zsuzsa Rakovszky born December 4th 1950

They Were Burning Dead Leaves

They were burning dead leaves. Must oozed with scent,
    tar bubbled and blew.
The moonlight glow behind the thistle bent
    like a torn rainbow.

The street was a forest, night slid into the heart
    of deepest autumn.
A guilty music blew the house apart
    with its fife and drum.

To have this again, just this, just the once more:
    I would sink below
autumnal earth and place my right hand in your
    hand like a shadow.

Zsuzsa Rakovszky
(December 4th 1950 –)

translated by George Szirtes

Zsuzsa Rakovszky was born in Sopron, Hungary and studied English and Hungarian Literature at the Eötvös University in Budapest. She has received the prestigious József Attila Prize and appeared in the UK at Poetry International. Her work is translated into English by the poet George Szirtes.

December 5

- *Phillis Wheatley, America's first published black poet, died in Boston December 5th 1784*
- *Poet Christina Rossetti born in London December 5th 1830*
- *Poet and writer Flora Thompson born December 5th 1877*
- *American poet Vachel Lindsay committed suicide by drinking Lysol, December 5th 1931*
- *Novelist and poet Adam Thorpe born December 5th 1956*

A Birthday

My heart is like a singing bird
   Whose nest is in a watered shoot;
My heart is like an apple-tree
   Whose boughs are bent with thick-set fruit;
My heart is like a rainbow shell
   That paddles in a halcyon sea;
My heart is gladder than all these
   Because my love is come to me.

Raise me a dais of silk and down;
   Hang it with vair° and purple dyes;   *squirrel fur*
Carve it in doves, and pomegranates,
   And peacocks with a hundred eyes;
Work it in gold and silver grapes,
   In leaves, and silver fleurs-de-lys;
Because the birthday of my life
   Is come, my love is come to me.

Christina Rossetti
(December 5th 1830 – December 29th 1894)

Christina Rossetti was intensely guarded about her private life and emotions. On sending her poems to her publisher she wrote: "I must beg that you will not fix upon any [poems] which the most imaginative person could construe into love personals ... you will feel how more than ever intolerable it would now be to have my verses regarded as outpourings of a wounded spirit."

December 6

• Poet Alfred Joyce Kilmer born December 6th 1886
• Sir Osbert Sitwell, poet and satirist, born December 6th 1892
• Poet, short story writer and novelist Sylvia Townsend Warner, born December 6th 1893
• Ira Gershwin, American songwriter, born December 6th 1896

The Balance Wheel

Where I waved at the sky
And waited your love through a February sleep,
I saw birds swinging in, watched them multiply
Into a tree, weaving on a branch, cradling a keep
In the arms of April, sprung from the south to occupy
This slow lap of land, like cogs of some balance wheel.
I saw them build the air, with that motion birds feel.

Where I wave at the sky
And understand love, knowing our August heat,
I see birds pulling past the dim frosted thigh
Of Autumn, unlatched from the nest, and wing-beat
For the south, making their high dots across the sky,
Like beauty spots marking a still perfect cheek.
I see them bend the air, slipping away, for what birds seek.

Anne Sexton
(November 9th 1928 – October 4th 1974)

In late 1956, a 28-year-old Anne Sexton happened to see a televised lecture about the sonnet form, and eagerly took notes. "I thought, well I could do that. So I went downstairs and wrote one ... I wrote one another day, and I took them to my doctor ... He said they were wonderful." Sexton's doctor was psychiatrist Dr Martin Orne, only one year older than her, and a good friend to her throughout her life. He noticed her latent creative ability early on, and strongly encouraged her to write herself to health. Between January and December 1957 she brought over 60 poems to her therapy sessions, and soon felt confident enough to join a poetry class at a local adult education centre, run by Robert Lowell and attended by Sylvia Plath.

In December 1959, almost three years to the day she penned her first poem, Sexton was invited to give a prestigious reading at Harvard. She had just published her debut collection, *To Bedlam and Part Way Back*. 'Anne Sexton, Poet' had truly arrived.

• American poet and writer Willa Cather born December 7th 1873
• Robert Graves died December 7th 1985. On his gravestone in
 Majorca is written simply, 'Robert Graves, Poetà'

December 7

From The Wreck of the Deutschland[1]

I am soft sift
In an hourglass – at the wall
Fast, but mined with a motion, a drift,
And it crowds and it combs to the fall;
I steady as a water in a well, to a poise, to a pane,
But roped with, always, all the way down from the tall
Fells or flanks of the voel, a vein
Of the gospel proffer, a pressure, a principle, Christ's gift.

I kiss my hand
To the stars, lovely-asunder
Starlight, wafting him out of it; and
Glow, glory in thunder;
Kiss my hand to the dappled-with-damson west;
Since, tho' he is under the world's splendour and wonder,
His mystery must be instressed, stressed;
For I greet him the days I meet him, and bless when I understand.

Gerard Manley Hopkins
(July 28th 1844 – June 8th 1889)

On this day in 1875, the Deutschland, an iron passenger liner, struck shallow ground and sank off the coast of Essex near Harwich. Passenger lists were lost, but estimates at the time put the death toll at about 150, with roughly the same number saved. Amongst the dead were five Franciscan nuns from Westphalia who were on their way to a new life in Missouri.

Hopkins had not written poetry since joining the Jesuits in 1868, considering it inappropriately self-indulgent for a Jesuit priest. It was the sinking of the Deutschland that started him writing again. As Hopkins explained in a letter three years later, "I was affected by the account [of the sinking] and, happening to say so to my rector, he said that he wished someone would write a poem on the subject. On this hint I set to work and, though my hand was out at first, produced one." The resultant poem is the first example of his new 'sprung rhythm' metrical system, upon which Hopkins' uniqueness as a poet rests.

1. Stanzas 4 & 5 of this 35 stanza poem.

December 8

• Roman poet and satirist Horace born near Venusia in Southern
  Italy December 8th 65 BC
• Poet and critic Delmore Schwarz born December 8th 1913
• American surrealist poet James Tate born in Kansas, Missouri,
  December 8th 1943
• Romanian poet Marin Sorescu died December 8th 1996

Musée des Beaux Arts

About suffering they were never wrong,
The Old Masters: how well they understood
Its human position; how it takes place
While someone else is eating or opening a window or just walking dully along;
How, when the aged are reverently, passionately waiting
For the miraculous birth, there always must be
Children who did not specially want it to happen, skating
On a pond at the edge of the wood:
They never forgot
That even the dreadful martyrdom must run its course
Anyhow in a corner, some untidy spot
Where the dogs go on with their doggy life and the torturer's horse
Scratches its innocent behind on a tree.

In Brueghel's *Icarus*, for instance: how everything turns away
Quite leisurely from the disaster; the ploughman may
Have heard the splash, the forsaken cry,
But for him it was not an important failure; the sun shone
As it had to on the white legs disappearing into the green
Water; and the expensive delicate ship that must have seen
Something amazing, a boy falling out of the sky,
Had somewhere to get to and sailed calmly on.

W. H. Auden
(February 21st 1907 – September 29th 1973)

Auden witnessed the Spanish Civil War at first hand. Visiting Spain in 1937, he ostensibly sought
work driving ambulances but proceeded to make propaganda broadcasts on behalf of the
Republican Government. Auden's experiences there had a profound effect on him and lent weight
to his concerns about staying in England during the war.
During a brief trip to Brussels with Christopher Isherwood in December of the following year,
Auden saw a collection of Brueghel paintings and wrote 'Musée des Beaux Arts' shortly afterwards.
Paul Hendon believes the poem can be read as "Auden's attempt to digest his experiences in Spain
while thinking ahead to his imminent move to America", "the mythical Auden/Icarus figure of
the political thirties plunging into the water".

• *The flyleaf of Milton's bible stated: "John Milton was born the 9th of December 1608 die Veneris (Friday) half an hour after 6 in the morning"*
• *Poet and writer James Hogg born December 9th 1770*
• *English poet Stephen Phillips died December 9th 1915*
• *Dame Edith Sitwell died in Hampstead December 9th 1964*

December 9

Methought I Saw My Late Espousèd Saint

Methought I saw my late espousèd saint
  Brought to me like Alcestis[1] from the grave,
  Whom Jove's great son to her glad husband gave,
  Rescued from death by force though pale and faint.
Mine, as whom washed from spot of childbed taint,
  Purification in the old Law[2] did save,
  And such, as yet once more I trust to have
  Full sight of her in Heaven without restraint,
Came vested all in white, pure as her mind.
  Her face was veiled, yet to my fancied sight
  Love, sweetness, goodness, in her person shined
So clear, as in no face with more delight.
  But O, as to embrace me she inclined,
  I waked, she fled, and day brought back my night.

John Milton
(December 9th 1608 – November 8th 1674)

Milton married Katherine Woodcock, his second wife, in 1656, four years after the death of his first wife Mary. The marriage to Katherine was purported to be a happy one, but she, like Mary, died following the loss of a child.

Woodcock is almost undoubtedly the subject of this sonnet; the Greek for Katherine, *katharos*, means pure, and supports the emphasis on purity in the poem. Milton went completely blind in 1651 and thus never saw his wife. After two bereavements, a spell in prison for his passionate advocacy of the Commonwealth, and the burning of his books, Milton married his third and final wife, Elizabeth Minshull, in 1663; Minshull survived him.

1. Apollo prevailed on the Fates to save Admetus from death on the condition that someone die in his stead. His lover Alcestis volunteered herself but Hercules interceded at the last minute and brought her back from the dead.
2. Leviticus 12: 2-5 – for purifying the uncleanness associated with childbirth (40 days for a male child, 80 days for a female)

December 10

- *Poet, novelist and preacher George MacDonald, born in Aberdeenshire December 10th 1824*
- *Emily Dickinson born December 10th 1830*
- *German poet Nellie Sachs born December 10th 1891*
- *American poet Carolyn Kizer born December 10th 1925*
- *Poet Carol Rumens born in London December 10th 1944*
- *Mark Van Doren died December 10th 1972*

He Loves Me

That God should love me is more wonderful
Than that I so imperfectly love him.
My reason is mortality, and dim
Senses; his – oh insupportable –
Is that he sees me. Even when I pull
Dark thoughts about my head, each vein and limb
Delights him, though remembrance in him, grim
With my worst crimes, should prove me horrible.

And he has terrors that he can release.
But when he looks he loves me; which is why
I wonder; and my wonder must increase
Till more of it shall slay me. Yet I live,
I live; and he has never ceased to give
This glance at me that sweetens the whole sky.

Mark Van Doren
(June 13th 1894 – December 10th 1972)

Mark Van Doren, poet, fiction writer, playwright and teacher, first established his reputation as a critic and scholar in the 1920s and '30s. His *Collected Poems* won the Pulitzer Prize in 1940.

One of Van Doren's favourite students at Columbia was Thomas Merton, a budding poet who became a Catholic and entered a Trappist monastery after graduating. Not a Catholic himself, Van Doren was much surprised to learn upon reading Merton's 1948 autobiography, that the classes and conversations they had shared "had been of decisive importance" in helping Merton to decide that he wanted to be a Catholic. Merton was ordained a priest in 1949 – the same year that Van Doren wrote 'He Loves Me' – and died in 1968. He is now considered the most famous Catholic spiritual writer of the 20th century. He once wrote to Van Doren: "You always used your gifts to make people admire and understand poetry and good writing and truth."

- *Colley Cibber, whose appointment to Poet Laureate was widely ridiculed, died December 11th 1757*
- *Robert Louis Stevenson complained of Browning's prolific output: "He floods acres of paper with brackets and inverted commas", December 11th 1875*
- *Poet and pilot John Gillespie Magee, Jr died when his plane nosedived in Tangmere, England, December 11th 1941*

December 11

High Flight (An Airman's Ecstasy)

Oh, I have slipped the surly bonds of earth
And danced the skies on laughter-silvered wings;
Sunward I've climbed and joined the tumbling mirth
Of sun-split clouds – and done a hundred things
You have not dreamed of; wheeled and soared and swung
High in the sun-lit silence. Hovering there
I've chased the shouting wind along, and flung
My eager craft through footless halls of air;
Up, up the long, delirious, burning blue
I've topped the wind-swept heights with easy grace,
Where never lark nor even eagle flew;
And while, with silent lifting mind I've trod
The high untrespassed sanctity of space,
Put out my hand, and touched the face of God.

John Gillespie Magee Jr
(June 9th 1922 – December 11th 1941)

John Gillespie Magee Jr left England under the threat of the Second World War to take up a place at Yale University. Once there, however, he wanted to join the fighting, and crossed the border into Canada in October 1940 to enlist illegally with the Royal Canadian Air Force.

Within a year, Magee had gained his wings and was sent to Wales to complete his advanced training. 'High Flight' was written on September 3rd 1941, when Magee flew a high altitude test flight in a Spitfire. He sent the poem in a letter to his parents with the note, "I am enclosing a verse I wrote the other day. It started at 30,000 feet, and was finished soon after I landed."

December 12

- *Robert Browning died December 12th 1889*
- *Tennyson, whom T. S. Eliot called 'the great master of metric as well as of melancholia', was buried in Westminster Abbey December 12th 1892*
- *Futurist poet and ardent fascist F. T. Marinetti died December 12th 1944*
- *Helen Dunmore born December 12th 1952*

Love

So, the year's done with!
  (Love me for ever!)
All March begun with,
  April's endeavour;
May-wreaths that bound me
  June needs must sever;
Now snows fall round me,
  Quenching June's fever –
  (Love me for ever!)

Robert Browning
(May 7th 1812 – December 12th 1889)

Both Elizabeth Barrett Browning and Robert Browning believed their marriage was eternal. After her death Browning wrote the following quote from Dante into his wife's bible: "I believe and I declare – Certain I am – from this life I pass into a better, there where that lady lives of whom enamoured was my soul."

During her life Elizabeth Barrett Browning conjectured that Browning would indulge in some "feeble bigamy" after her death. Though Browning outlived his wife by 28 years, he never remarried. A certain Lady Ashburton once proposed to him but he declined, assuring her that his heart lay buried in Florence, and any marriage would be for the benefit of his young son.

Browning died of bronchitis on this day in 1889 and was buried in the Poet's Corner at Westminster Abbey.

- *Scots poet William Drummond born December 13th 1585*
- *Samuel Johnson died December 13th 1784*
- *Poet and writer Heinrich Heine born December 13th 1797*
- *Poet Kenneth Patchen born in Ohio December 13th 1911*
- *Poet James Wright born in Ohio December 13th 1927*
- *Ted Hughes became Poet Laureate December 13th 1984*

December 13

A Nocturnal upon Saint Lucy's Day,
Being the Shortest Day

'Tis the year's midnight and it is the day's,
Lucy's, who scarce seven hours herself unmasks;
  The sun is spent, and now his flasks°   *stars*
  Send forth light squibs, no constant rays.
    The world's whole sap is sunk;
The general balm[1] th' hydroptic earth hath drunk,
Whither, as to the bed's feet, life is shrunk,
Dead and interred; yet all these seem to laugh,
Compared with me, who am their epitaph.

Study me, then, you who shall lovers be
At the next world, that is, at the next spring;
  For I am every dead thing
  In whom love wrought new alchemy.
    For his art did express°   *press out*
A quintessence[2] even from nothingness,
From dull privations and lean emptiness.
He ruined° me, and I am re-begot   *distilled*
Of absence, darkness, death: things which are not.

All others from all things draw all that's good,
Life, soul, form, spirit, whence they being have;
  I, by love's limbeck°, am the grave   *distilling apparatus*
  Of all that's nothing. Oft a flood
    Have we two wept, and so
Drowned the whole world, us two; oft did we grow
To be two chaoses when we did show
Care to aught else; and often absences
Withdrew our souls, and made us carcasses.

But I am by her death, (which word wrongs her)
Of the first nothing, the elixir grown;
  Were I a man, that I were one
  I needs must know; I should prefer,
    If I were any beast,
Some ends, some means; yea plants, yea stones detest
And love. All, all some properties invest°.   *clothe*
If I an ordinary nothing were,
As shadow, a light and body must be here.

[Continued]

359

But I am none; nor will my sun renew.
You lovers, for whose sake the lesser sun
    At this time to the Goat³ is run
    To fetch new lust, and give it you,
        Enjoy your summer all;
Since she enjoys her long night's festival,
Let me prepare towards her, and let me call
This hour her vigil and her eve, since this
Both the year's and the day's deep midnight is.

John Donne
(c. June 1572 – March 31st 1631)

December 13th is St Lucy's Day, and was traditionally regarded as the shortest day of the year, the Winter Solstice. St Lucy, the 'queen of light', was believed to lead the way for the sun to bring longer days. A virgin and martyr, she was one of the most popular saints of the Middle Ages.

This poem mourns the death of a loved woman. Some believe that she may have been John Donne's wife, Ann More, who died at the age of 33 in 1617, after giving birth to a stillborn child. However, Donne's favourite daughter, Lucy, also died young, at the age of 17, in early 1627. Donne was grief-stricken. At a sermon he gave shortly after her death, he declared: "I shall have my dead raised to life again." Lucy was named after her godmother – and Donne's patron – Lucy, Countess of Bedford, who died later the same year. This poem was first published in 1633, two years after Donne's own death.

1. Donne believed that, 'In everything there naturally grows / A Balsamum [balm] to keep it fresh and new.'

2. The fifth essence of medieval philosophy and alchemy, latent in all things and the substance of the heavenly bodies.

3. At the Winter Solstice the sun enters Capricorn.

• *Aphra Behn baptised in Kent December 14th 1640*
• *French Surrealist poet Paul Éluard born Paul-Eugène Grindel in Saint-Denis, Paris, December 14th 1952*
• *Spanish poet Vicente Aleixandre, died December 14th 1984*
• *W. G. Sebald, German poet and novelist, died in a car accident in Norwich December 14th 2001*

The earth is blue like an orange

The earth is blue like an orange
Never an error words do not lie
They no longer supply what to sing with
It's up to kisses to get along
Mad ones and lovers
She her wedding mouth
All secrets all smiles
And what indulgent clothing
She looks quite naked.

The wasps are flowering green
Dawn is placing round its neck
A necklace of windows
Wings cover the leaves
You have all the solar joys
All sunshine on the earth
On the paths of your loveliness.

Paul Éluard
(December 14th 1895 – November 11th 1952)

translated by Mary Ann Caws

After being involved with the Dada movement in the early 1920s, Paul Éluard became one of the founding members of the Surrealist movement, signing its first manifesto in 1924, along with Louis Aragon, Antonin Artaud and the leader André Breton. The poem 'The earth is blue like an orange' ('La terre est bleue comme une orange') is often upheld as the archetypal surrealist poem.

In 1938, Éluard left the Surrealist movement to concentrate on politics, rejoining the Communist party. In the Second World War, he was part of the underground resistance, publishing his famous poems 'Liberté' and 'Rendez-vous Allemand'. Due to this clandestine publishing, Éluard and his second wife Maria Benz ('Nusch') were forced to change residences every month, in order to avoid capture by the Gestapo. Éluard continued to write prolifically (publishing over 70 books in his lifetime) up until his death from a stroke at the age of 56.

December 15

• Poet and playwright Margaret Cavendish, Duchess of
  Newcastle, died December 15th 1673
• Acclaimed feminist poet Muriel Rukeyser born in New York
  December 15th 1913

Born in December
for Nancy Marshall

You are like me born at the end of the year;
When in our city day closes blueness comes
We see a beginning in the ritual end.

Never mind: I know it is never what it seems,
That ending: for we are born, we are born there,
There is an entrance we may always find.

They reckon by the wheel of the year. Our birth's before.
From the dark birthday to the young year's first stay
We are the ones who wait and look for ways:

Ways of beginning, ways to be born, ways for
Solvings, turnings, wakings; we are always
A little younger than they think we are.

Muriel Rukeyser
(December 15th 1913 – February 12th 1980)

The eldest daughter of affluent Jewish parents, Muriel Rukeyser was a poet, pilot, journalist, single parent and social activist who remained under FBI surveillance for 40 years. She argued compellingly for poetry's vital role in society, and had an unflinching vision of the world: "Pay attention to what they tell you to forget." Her poetry insists upon the relationship between the world and the individual, and is informed by a life of political engagement. She was arrested at the age of 19 at the trial of the Scottsboro Boys, was present at the Gauley Bridge tragedy in West Virginia (where miners were dying of silicosis due to inadequate protection), and was in Spain during the Civil War in Spain when she was just 22. She travelled to Korea to protest against the imprisonment of a dissident poet, and to Hanoi during the Vietnam War.

In her first collection, *Theory of Flight*, published when she was 21, she wrote, "Breathe-in experience, breathe out poetry", a philosophy that characterises all of her work. Rukeyser influenced generations of female poets from Anne Stevenson to Sharon Olds and was referred to by Anne Sexton as "the mother of everyone".

- *Poet and philospher George Santayana born in Madrid December 16th 1863*
- *Composer, actor playwright and poet Noel Coward born in Teddington December 16th 1899*
- *Dylan Thomas' father died December 16th 1952, with his son at his bedside. Soon afterwards Dylan Thomas wrote 'Do Not Go Gentle Into That Good Night' and 'Elegy'*

December 16

Variation on the Word *Sleep*

I would like to watch you sleeping,
which may not happen.
I would like to watch you,
sleeping. I would like to sleep
with you, to enter
your sleep as its smooth dark wave
slides over my head

and walk with you through that lucent
wavering forest of bluegreen leaves
with its watery sun & three moons
towards the cave where you must descend,
towards your worst fear

I would like to give you the silver
branch, the small white flower, the one
word that will protect you
from the grief at the centre
of your dream, from the grief
at the centre. I would like to follow
you up the long stairway
again & become
the boat that would row you back
carefully, a flame
in two cupped hands
to where your body lies
beside me, and you enter
it as easily as breathing in

I would like to be the air
that inhabits you for a moment
only. I would like to be that unnoticed
& that necessary.

Margaret Atwood
(November 18th 1939 –)

Margaret Atwood is the author of more than 25 books of poetry, fiction and non-fiction, and her work has been translated into more than 30 languages. She won the Booker Prize in 2000 for her novel *The Blind Assassin*.

December 17

• *Andrew Marvell, MP, petitioned the House of Commons for the release of Milton from prison, December 17th 1660*
• *American poet John Greenleaf Whittier born December 17th 1807*
• *Novelist, editor and poet Ford Madox Ford, born in Merton December 17th 1873*

Things

There are worse things than having behaved foolishly in public.
There are worse things than these miniature betrayals,
committed or endured or suspected; there are worse things
than not being able to sleep for thinking about them.
It is 5 a.m. All the worse things come stalking in
and stand icily about the bed looking worse and worse and worse.

Fleur Adcock
(February 10th 1934 –)

Fleur Adcock writes: "I wrote this in December 1973, in the middle of the 'Winter of Discontent'. There were power-cuts, a rail strike, shortages of every kind (a note in my diary on the 15th says that I managed to buy the last oil lamp in East Finchley), I had a cold, an elderly friend had just died, and all was bleak. The occasion for the poem was probably some minor cause for embarrassment that was keeping me awake, but then all the more serious matters came crowding in. I thought other people would recognise the sentiments."

- *Hymn-writer Charles Wesley born December 18th 1707*
- *Francis Thompson born in Preston December 18th 1859*
- *Australian poet Christopher Brennan married the ill-suited German, Elisabeth Werth, December 18th 1897*
- *Verse-dramatist Christopher Fry born December 18th 1907*
- *Dylan Thomas' first collection,* Eighteen Poems, *was published December 18th 1934, when the poet was 20*

December 18

An Arab Love-Song

The hunched camels of the night[1]
Trouble the bright
And silver waters of the moon.
The Maiden of the Morn will soon
Through Heaven stray and sing,
Star gathering.

Now while the dark about our loves is strewn,
Light of my dark, blood of my heart, O come!
And night will catch her breath up, and be dumb.

Leave thy father, leave thy mother
And thy brother;
Leave the black tents of thy tribe apart!
Am I not thy father and thy brother,
And thy mother?
And thou—what needest with thy tribe's black tents
Who hast the red pavilion of my heart?

Francis Thompson
(December 18th 1859 – November 13th 1907)

After abandoning his training as first priest, then doctor, Francis Thompson fled to London where he lived in destitution, scraping a living together where he could. He was still writing, however, and sent an essay and some poems to a new Catholic journal, *Merry England*. The manuscript languished for six months before the editor, Wilfred Meynell, read it and determined to print it. Thompson proved untraceable, so Meynell published the poems anyway, hoping Thompson would get in touch. When he did, giving his contact address as a local chemist, the two became life-long friends.

Under Meynell's supervision, Thompson was treated for his opium addiction (which he had picked up some years earlier under treatment for illness), spending two years at a monastery at Storrington. It was here that he began to write in earnest and he returned to London to publish three collections of poetry within six years, all to considerable critical acclaim. He died of tuberculosis in London aged 44.

1. Cloud shapes observed by travellers in the East.

December 19

- *American poet Philip Freneau died December 19th 1832*
- *Emily Brontë died of tuberculosis aged 30, December 19th 1848*
- *Robert Frost married Elinor White December 19th 1895*
- *Ted Hughes was appointed Poet Laureate in succession to John Betjeman, December 19th 1984*

Reluctance

Out through the fields and the woods
    And over the walls I have wended;
I have climbed the hills of view
    And looked at the world, and descended;
I have come by the highway home,
    And lo, it is ended.

The leaves are all dead on the ground,
    Save those that the oak is keeping
To ravel them one by one
    And let them go scraping and creeping
Out over the crusted snow,
    When others are sleeping.

And the dead leaves lie huddled and still,
    No longer blown hither and thither;
The last lone aster is gone;
    The flowers of the witch hazel wither;
The heart is still aching to seek,
    But the feet question "Whither?"

Ah, when to the heart of man
    Was it ever less than a treason
To go with the drift of things,
    To yield with a grace to reason,
And bow and accept the end
    Of a love or a season?

Robert Frost
(March 26th 1874 – January 29th 1963)

Robert Frost resolved to marry his fiancée, Elinor White, the minute his first poem was accepted for publication in 1894. She, however, wanted to wait until after her own graduation. Frost had two copies of a collection of his poems bound, and delivered one copy to Elinor by hand. In despair at her cool reception, and believing her to be in love with someone else, he destroyed his own copy and headed off in early November into the wilderness. His destination was the auspiciously named Dismal Swamp, a stretch that runs along the Virginia–North Carolina border, favoured by poets through the centuries as a refuge for the hopeless. Frost trudged forlornly though this dark, swampy terrain for many days and found there the inspiration for 'Reluctance'.

The pair were eventually married on this day in 1895. Elinor's father, believing Frost to be incurably lazy and a poor prospect as a son-in-law, refused to attend the wedding.

- *Wordsworth and his sister Dorothy arrived at Dove cottage on December 20th 1799. They lived there for eight years*
- *Nancy ('Mopsy'), E. E. Cummings' daughter with Elaine Orr, born December 20th 1919*
- *Poet and novelist Sheenagh Pugh born December 20th 1950*

December 20

Sometimes

Sometimes things don't go, after all,
from bad to worse. Some years, muscadel
faces down frost; green thrives; the crops don't fail,
sometimes a man aims high, and all goes well.

A people sometimes will step back from war;
elect an honest man; decide they care
enough, that they can't leave a stranger poor.
Some men become what they were born for.

Sometimes our best efforts do not go
amiss; sometimes we do as we meant to.
The sun will sometimes melt a field of sorrow
that seemed hard frozen: may it happen for you.

Sheenagh Pugh
(December 20th 1950 –)

Sheenagh Pugh writes: " 'Sometimes' was originally written about a sportsman who had a drug problem and it expressed the hope that he might eventually get over it – because things do go right sometimes, but not very often ... But it isn't anywhere near skilful or subtle enough and I would cheerfully disown it, if people didn't now and then write to me saying it had helped them. I originally wrote "the sun will sometimes melt a field of snow" (the sportsman's drug of choice was cocaine), but I mistyped "sorrow" for "snow" and then decided I liked that better. I believe in letting the keyboard join in the creative process now and then."

Sheenagh Pugh lives in Cardiff with her husband, two children and cats. She teaches Creative Writing at the University of Glamorgan and has published nine collections of poetry and translations, as well as two novels.

December 21

• Italian poet and novelist Giovanni Boccaccio, whose work was
influential to Chaucer, died December 21st 1375
• Portuguese poet Manuel Bocage died December 21st 1805
• French symbolist poet Gustave Kahn born December 21st1859
• Poet Richard Hugo born December 21st 1923
• Poet and artist Adrian Henri died December 21st 2001

Wedding

From time to time our love is like a sail
and when the sail begins to alternate
from tack to tack, it's like a swallowtail
and when the swallow flies it's like a coat;
and if the coat is yours, it has a tear
like a wide mouth and when the mouth begins
to draw the wind, it's like a trumpeter
and when the trumpet blows, it blows like millions . . .
and this, my love, when millions come and go
beyond the needs of us, is like a trick;
and when the trick begins, it's like a toe
tip-toeing on a rope, which is like luck;
and when the luck begins, it's like a wedding,
which is like love, which is like everything.

Alice Oswald
(August 31st 1966 –)

Alice Oswald comments: "I like the way the poem moves sideways through similes instead of
forwards through time."
Alice Oswald's husband, Peter Oswald, to whom the poem is addressed, was born on this day in
1965.

- *Emily Brontë was buried December 22nd 1848*
- *American poet Edwin Arlington Robinson born in Maine December 22nd 1869*
- *George Eliot, whom Henry James described as "magnificently, awe-inspiringly ugly", died December 22nd 1880*
- *Kenneth Rexroth, poet and translator (from Chinese and Japanese), born December 22nd 1905*

December 22

Remembrance

Cold in the earth—and the deep snow piled above thee,
Far, far, removed, cold in the dreary grave!
Have I forgot, my only Love, to love thee,
Severed at last by Time's all-severing wave?

Now, when alone, do my thoughts no longer hover
Over the mountains, on that northern shore,
Resting their wings where heath and fern-leaves cover
Thy noble heart for ever, ever more?

Cold in the earth—and fifteen wild Decembers,
From those brown hills, have melted into spring:
Faithful, indeed, is the spirit that remembers
After such years of change and suffering!

Sweet Love of youth, forgive, if I forget thee,
While the world's tide is bearing me along;
Other desires and other hopes beset me,
Hopes which obscure, but cannot do thee wrong!

No later light has lightened up my heaven,
No second morn has ever shone for me;
All my life's bliss from thy dear life was given,
All my life's bliss is in the grave with thee.

But, when the days of golden dreams had perished,
And even Despair was powerless to destroy;
Then did I learn how existence could be cherished,
Strengthened, and fed without the aid of joy.

Then did I check the tears of useless passion—
Weaned my young soul from yearning after thine;
Sternly denied its burning wish to hasten
Down to that tomb already more than mine.

And, even yet, I dare not let it languish,
Dare not indulge in memory's rapturous pain;
Once drinking deep of that divinest anguish,
How could I seek the empty world again?

Emily Brontë
(July 30th 1818 – December 19th 1848)

This poem derives from the saga Emily wrote with her sister Anne about life on an imaginary Pacific island, Gondal. In the story, it was intended to be the heroine's lament for the hero's death.

December 23

- 'Idea' poet Michael Drayton died December 23rd 1631
- Harriet Monroe, founder and longtime editor of Poetry magazine, born in Chicago December 23rd 1860
- Poet and translator Robert Bly, who won't get out of bed until he has written a poem, born December 23rd 1926
- Poet and playwright Carol Ann Duffy born in Glasgow December 23rd 1955

Prayer

Some days, although we cannot pray, a prayer
utters itself. So, a woman will lift
her head from the sieve of her hands and stare
at the minims sung by a tree, a sudden gift.

Some nights, although we are faithless, the truth
enters our hearts, that small familiar pain;
then a man will stand stock-still, hearing his youth
in the distant Latin chanting of a train.

Pray for us now. Grade I piano scales
console the lodger looking out across
a Midlands town. Then dusk, and someone calls
a child's name as though they named their loss.

Darkness outside. Inside, the radio's prayer –
Rockall. Malin. Dogger. Finisterre.

Carol Ann Duffy
(December 23rd 1955 –)

Carol Ann Duffy has written: "[P]erhaps poetry can articulate ordinary people's feelings and worries and in some small way be a form of consolation or utterance for common humanity – very much in that way as a form of unholy prayer."

- Poet George Crabbe born December 24th 1754
- Poet and critic Matthew Arnold born December 24th 1822
- William Makepeace Thackeray died December 24th 1863
- Poet Juan Ramón Jiménez born in Helva, Spain,
  December 24th 1881
- Tristan Tzara died in Paris December 24th 1963

December 24

Out in the Dark

Out in the dark over the snow
The fallow fawns invisible go
With the fallow doe;
And the winds blow
Fast as the stars are slow.

Stealthily the dark haunts round
And, when the lamp goes, without sound
At a swifter bound
Than the swiftest hound,
Arrives, and all else is drowned;

And star and I and wind and deer,
Are in the dark together, — near,
Yet far, — and fear
Drums on my ear
In the sage company drear.

How weak and little is the light,
All the universe of sight,
Love and delight,
Before the might,
If you love it not, of night.

Edward Thomas
(March 3rd 1878 – April 9th 1917)

This poem, composed on Christmas Eve 1917, is one of the 'household poems' that Thomas wrote about the Thomas' last home in High Beech, near Loughton.

After his death, Edward Thomas' wife Helen wrote in a farewell to him: "Beloved, there have been many weeks and now I have come to today. The way has been very difficult for me, but even through darkness and despair and just nothingness and fear, just as ever when these things came before, all has been well at last because of our love."

December 25

• *Poet William Collins born in Chichester December 25th 1721*
• *Dorothy Wordsworth, sister of William Wordsworth, born December 25th 1771*
• *Keats became engaged to Fanny Brawne December 25th 1819*
• *Poet Isabella Crawford born in Dublin December 25th 1850*

From A Christmas Carol[1]

In the bleak mid-winter
    Frosty wind made moan,
Earth stood hard as iron,
    Water like a stone;
Snow had fallen, snow on snow,
    Snow on snow,
In the bleak mid-winter
    Long ago.

Our God, Heaven cannot hold Him,
    Nor earth sustain,
Heaven and earth shall flee away
    When He comes to reign:
In the bleak mid-winter
    A stable-place sufficed
The Lord God Almighty
    Jesus Christ.

Angels and archangels
    May have gathered there,
Cherubim and seraphim
    Thronged the air;
But only His mother
    In her maiden bliss
Worshipped the Beloved
    With a kiss.

What can I give Him,
    Poor as I am?
If I were a shepherd
    I would bring a lamb,
If I were a Wise Man
    I would do my part, —
But what I can I give Him,
    Give my heart.

Christina Rossetti
(December 5th 1830 – December 29th 1894)

1. Stanzas 1, 2, 4 & 5 of this 5 stanza poem.

• Poet Thomas Gray born in London December 26th 1716, the fifth and only surviving child of twelve
• Depressive First World War poet Ivor Gurney, who struggled to make a living as a writer and worked as a farm labourer, cinema pianist and clerk, died of TB December 26th 1937
• Scottish poet and dramatist Liz Lochhead born in Lanarkshire December 26th 1947
• Lancashire poet Rod Riesco born December 26th 1949

December 26

Announcement

The 10.19 will call at Sideways Glance,
Eye Junction, Smile, and Unexpected Chance,
Then Disco, Party, Pub, and Country Walk,
And on to Intimacy, Bed and Talk,
Commitment, Mortgage, Offspring, Menopause,
Where it divides; passengers for Divorce
Should travel in the front. Any passenger
For Widowhood should travel in the rear.
A hot and cold service will be supplied
Throughout. We wish you all a pleasant ride.

Rod Riesco
(December 26th 1949 –)

Rod Riesco writes: "I wrote this poem in early middle age, after being widowed twice and remarried twice, so I suppose I'm now on the third stage of the journey. I have been accused of being cynical but, looking back, I'm glad I bought the ticket. And I like trains as well."

Rod Riesco works as a freelance translator, and became interested in poetry after attending a local creative writing class. He has been published in various collections and magazines and is Secretary of Bank Street Writers.

December 27

• *Poet Charles Lamb died December 27th 1834*
• *Charles Olson born in Massachusetts December 27th 1910*
• *Elizabeth Smart born in Ottawa, Canada, December 27th 1913*
• *Osip Mandelstam died in a transit camp December 27th 1938*
• *Kay Boyle died December 27th 1992, aged 90*
• *Ian Hamilton, the notable poet, biographer, critic and editor, died December 27th 2001*

Advice to the Old (Including Myself)

Do not speak of yourself (for God's sake) even when asked.
Do not dwell on other times as different from the time
Whose air we breathe; or recall books with broken spines
Whose titles died with the old dreams. Do not resort to
An alphabet of gnarled pain, but speak of the lark's wing
Unbroken, still fluent as the tongue. Call out the names of stars
Until their metal clangs in the enormous dark. Yodel your way
Through fields where the dew weeps, but not you, not you.
Have no communion with despair; and, at the end,
Take the old fury in your empty arms, sever its veins,
And bear it fiercely, fiercely to the wild beast's lair.

Kay Boyle
(February 19th 1902 – December 27th 1992)

Kay Boyle was born in Minnesota but moved to France after marrying a French man, living for many years as one of the 'lost generation' of American emigrés in avant-garde Paris. She was a committed social activist as much as a writer, and believed above all that "the writer must recognize and must accept his commitment to his times". Her poetry and short stories bear witness to the injustices she observed. Boyle was twice imprisoned in her seventies for protesting against US involvement in the Vietnam war and continued to support social causes even at an advanced age. Late in life she joked that she saw herself "as a dangerous 'radical' cleverly disguised as a perfect lady."

• Robert Burns first wrote to Mrs McLehose ('Clarinda') with whom he had a passionate but unconsummated relationship, on December 28th 1787, describing himself as "a strange willo' wisp being; the victim too frequently of much impudence and many follies"
• American poets' biographer and novelist Henry Allen died in Coconut Grove, Florida, December 28th 1949

December 28

The Pobble Who Has No Toes

The Pobble who has no toes
    Had once as many as we;
When they said, "Some day you may lose them all;" –
    He replied, – "Fish fiddle de-dee!"
And his Aunt Jobiska made him drink,
Lavender water tinged with pink,
For she said, "The World in general knows
There's nothing so good for a Pobble's toes!"

The Pobble who has no toes,
    Swam across the Bristol Channel;
But before he set out he wrapped his nose,
    In a piece of scarlet flannel.
For his Aunt Jobiska said, "No harm
Can come to his toes if his nose is warm;
And it's perfectly known that a Pobble's toes
Are safe, – provided he minds his nose."

The Pobble swam fast and well
    And when boats or ships came near him
He tinkledy-binkledy-winkled a bell
    So that all the world could hear him.
And all the Sailors and Admirals cried,
When they saw him nearing the further side, –
"He has gone to fish, for his Aunt Jobiska's
Runcible Cat with crimson whiskers!"

But before he touched the shore,
    The shore of the Bristol Channel,
A sea-green Porpoise carried away
    His wrapper of scarlet flannel.
And when he came to observe his feet
Formerly garnished with toes so neat
His face at once became forlorn
On perceiving that all his toes were gone!

[Continued]

And nobody ever knew
    From that dark day to the present,
Whoso had taken the Pobble's toes,
    In a manner so far from pleasant.
Whether the shrimps or crawfish gray,
Or crafty Mermaids stole them away –
Nobody knew; and nobody knows
How the Pobble was robbed of his twice five toes!

The Pobble who has no toes
    Was placed in a friendly Bark,
And they rowed him back, and carried him up,
    To his Aunt Jobiska's Park.
And she made him a feast at his earnest wish
Of eggs and buttercups fried with fish; –
And she said,– "It's a fact the whole world knows,
That Pobbles are happier without their toes."

Edward Lear
(May 12th 1812 – January 29th 1888)

'The Pobble Who Has No Toes' was included in the fourth and last book of Lear's nonsense verse that was released in his lifetime, *Laughable Lyrics*, published in December 1876.

For the final years of his life, Lear lived in a specially built villa on the Swiss-Italian border, named 'Villa Tennyson' after his good friend, the Poet Laureate, whom he met in 1851. Indeed, the final project of his life was a collection of illustrations to accompany Tennyson's poems, but this was abandoned shortly before his death. An accomplished painter and musician, Lear had previously set some of Tennyson's poems to music, and Tennyson had written his poem 'To E. L., on His Travels in Greece' after receiving Lear's travel book *Journal of a Landscape Painter in Greece and Albania*.

- *Christina Rossetti died of Graves disease, "in the act of inarticulate prayer", December 29th 1894*
- *Austrian lyric poet Rainer Maria Rilke died in Switzerland December 29th 1926*
- *Novelist, poet and dramatist Eden Phillpotts, died in Devon December 29th 1960*

Garden tenderly darkened, almost

Garden tenderly darkened, almost, by nearness of rain or thunder,
garden under hesitant hands.
As though in their beds more earnestly plants now must wonder
how it could be that a gardener invented their kinds.

For it's of him they are thinking; admixed to pure freedom, their trueness,
to them his laborious care, or acceptance of failure, clings.
Even they feel the pull of our curious tutor, that twoness;
we awaken the counterweight in the very lightest of things.

Rainer Maria Rilke
(December 4th 1875 – December 29th 1926)

translated by Michael Hamburger

Rilke endured a difficult upbringing. His mother, compensating for the earlier loss of a baby girl, insisted on called him Sophia, and dressed him in girl's clothes until he was five. He was sent to military academy and business school against his will but nonetheless found his poetic voice early, publishing his first collection at the age of 19. He became one of the most influential poets of the 20th century and an important mentor to many younger poets.

Rilke was already suffering from leukaemia when a prick from a rose thorn became infected, causing his death on this day in 1926.

December 30

- *Shelley married his second wife, Mary Godwin (author of Frankenstein), December 30th 1816*
- *Rudyard Kipling born in Bombay December 30th 1865*
- *Wilfred Owen, Second Lieutenant of the Manchester Regiment, left England for the Western Front December 30th 1916*
- *Al Purdy born in Wooler, Ontario, December 30th 1918*
- *Patti Smith born in Chicago December 30th 1946*

Burning Roses

Father I am burning roses
father only God shall know
what the secret heart discloses
the ancient dances with the doe

Father I have sorely wounded
father I shall wound no more
I have waltzed among the thorns
where roses burn upon the floor

Daughter may you turn in laughter
a candle dreams a candle draws
the heart that burns
shall burn thereafter
may you turn as roses fall

Patti Smith
(December 30th 1946 –)

Whilst working at a toy factory after her graduation in 1964, Patti Smith came across a volume of Rimbaud's poetry, which inspired her to follow her own creative path. Combining the influence of Rimbaud with that of contemporaries such as Bob Dylan and the Rolling Stones, Smith devoted herself first to painting and then writing. She emerged in New York in the early 1970s as a feminist punk poet of huge presence and talent. She followed this with the seminal album, *Horses*, in 1975, which many people consider a key precursor to the punk records of a few years later.

After relationships with photographer Robert Mapplethorpe and playwright Sam Shepard, she settled down with husband Fred 'Sonic' Smith (a member of the band MC5) in 1979 and disappeared from the music and poetry scenes until his death in 1994. She has since made something of a comeback, and is as influential today as ever.

- *Poet and critic Holbrook Jackson born December 31st 1910*
- *The Stray Dog Café in St Petersburg, where Akhmatova and Mandelstam recited their poetry, opened December 31st 1911*
- *T.S. Eliot wrote to Conrad Aiken from London, December 31st 1914: "I have been going through one of those nervous sexual attacks which I suffer from when alone in a big city"*
- *African poet Franciso José Tenreiro died December 31st 1963*

I Stood on a Tower

I stood on a tower in the wet,
And New Year and Old Year met,
And winds were roaring and blowing;
And I said, 'O years, that meet in tears,
Have you all that is worth the knowing?
Science enough and exploring,
Wanderers coming and going,
Matter enough for deploring,
But aught that is worth the knowing?'
Seas at my feet were flowing,
Waves on the shingle pouring,
Old year roaring and blowing,
And New Year blowing and roaring.

Alfred Lord Tennyson
(August 6th 1809 – October 6th 1892)

'I Stood on the Tower' was written on this day in 1865. That same day, Tennyson wrote to his lifelong friend Francis Turner Palgrave, editor of the famous Victorian poetry anthology *The Golden Treasury*: "What a season! The wind is roaring here like thunder, and all my ilexes[1] rolling and whitening. Indeed, we have had whole weeks of wind!"

1. Holly trees

Acknowledgements

The editors are very grateful to all those friends and family who so kindly suggested poems, including Heather Albery, Josefine Speyer, Yvonne Malik, Carol de Vaughn, Olivia Davies, Kathy Lacy, Molly Mackey, Peggy Poole, Claudia Boulton, Katie Whiting, Angelika Wienrich, China Williams, Sinead Wilson, Kate Weinberg, Lawrence Rampling, Jason Locke, Valerie Grove, Dr Stephen Bryans, Hugh Kelly, all the participants at the annual Poetry Challenge, and especially to John Stammers, whose suggestions were invaluable: heartfelt thanks.

Enormous thanks are also due to those who helped with research or made helpful suggestions on the book, especially Kate Weinberg, Billy Magner, Danny Barrett, Sandra Howgate, Jason Locke, John Stammers, Sarah Sheldon, Rupert Bowen, Rebekah Lattin-Rawstrone, and Sarah Cuddon. Many thanks also to Briony Everroad at Random House.

Much of the source material that provided biographical information on the poets was collected from books too numerous to list here, but those most frequently consulted were *Contemporary Poets* edited by James Vinson and D. L. Kirkpatric (St Martin's Press, New York, 1985), *Lives of the Poets* by Michael Schmidt (Vintage, 2000), *The Hand of the Poet* by Rodney Phillips (Rizzoli, New York, 1997) and *The Oxford Companion to Twentieth Century Poetry in English* by Ian Hamilton (Oxford University Press, 1994). We also gratefully acknowledge the assistance from librarians at the British Library and Poetry Library, Level 5, Royal Festival Hall.

The editors also wish to thank to all the Copyright holders cited below for their patient assistance, and often very generous permission.

DANNIE ABSE: 'Thankyou Note' from *New and Collected Poems* (Hutchinson, 2002), by kind permission of the author; FLEUR ADCOCK: 'Things' and 'For a Five Year Old' from *Poems 1960-2000* (Bloodaxe Books, 2000), by kind permission of the publisher; JOHN AGARD: 'Rainbow' from *Mangoes and Bullets* (Serpent's Tail, 1990), by kind permission of the publisher and John Agard; ANNA AKHMATOVA: 'Death' from *The Complete Poems of Anna Akhmatova* (Canongate Books Ltd., 1992), by kind permission of the publisher; 'You will hear thunder and remember me' and 'Let any, who will, still bask in the south' from *Selected Poems* by Anna Akhmatova, translated by D. M. Thomas (Penguin, 1988), published by Secker & Warburg. Reprinted by kind permission of the Random House Group Ltd.; NICHOLAS ALBERY: 'To Know a Poem by Heart' Copyright © 1999 Nicholas Albery, reprinted by permission of Josefine Speyer; MONIZA ALVI: 'A Bowl of Warm Air' from *A Bowl of Warm Air* (Bloodaxe Books, 1996); LOUIS ARAGON: 'The Lilacs and the Roses' from *Collected Poems* of Louis MacNeice (Faber & Faber, 1965), by permission from David Higham Associates Ltd.; SIMON ARMITAGE: 'Kid' from *Kid* (Faber & Faber, 1991), by permission of the publisher; JOHN ASHBERY: 'Some Trees' from *The Mooring of Starting Out: The First Five Books of Poetry* (Carcanet, 1997), by permission of the publisher; MAYA ANGELOU: 'Come. And Be My Baby' from *The Complete Collected Poems* (Virago Press, 1995), by kind permission of the publisher; YEHUDA AMICHAI: 'Near the Wall of a House' from *The Selected Poetry of Yehuda Amichai*, edited and translated by Chana and Stephen Bloch (University of California Press, 1996). Copyright © 1996 The Regents of the University of California, by kind permission of the publisher; MARGARET ATWOOD: 'Habitation' and 'Variation on the Word *Sleep*' from *Selected Poems II: Poems Selected and New, 1976-1986*, by permission of Time Warner Books, UK; W. H. AUDEN: 'If I Could Tell You', 'Calypso', 'As I Walked Out One Evening' and 'Museé des Beaux Arts' from *Collected Poems* (Faber & Faber, 1976), by

ING HAMILTON: 'Along the Road' by kind permission of Virginia Hamilton Adair; SOPHIE HANNAH: 'Leaving and Leaving You' from *Leaving and Leaving You* (Carcanet Press, 1999), by permission of the publisher; TONY HARRISON: 'The Icing Hand' from *Gaze of the Gorgon* (Bloodaxe, 1992), by kind permission of the author; SEAMUS HEANEY: 'Postscript' and 'Glanmore Sonnet VIII' from *Opened Ground: Poems 1966-1996* (Faber & Faber, 1998), by permission of the publisher; NÂZIM HIKMET: 'Maybe I' from *Nâzim Hikmet: Beyond the Walls: Selected Poems* translated by Ruth Christie, Richard McKane & Talât Sait Halman. Published by Anvil Press Poetry in association with Yapi Kredi Yayinlari in 2002; SELIMA HILL: 'Nuage Argente' from *Violet* (Bloodaxe Books, 1997), by kind permission of the author; JOHN HOLLANDER: 'An Old-Fashioned Song' from *Tesserae and Other Poems* published by Alfred A. Knopf Inc. Copyright © 1993 by John Hollander; by permission of the publisher; MIROSLAV HOLUB: 'The Door' from *Poems Before and After: Collected English Translations* by Miroslav Holub (Bloodaxe Books, 1990), by kind permission of the publisher; A. D. HOPE: 'The Gateway' from *Selected Poems* (Carcanet Press, 1986), by permission of the publisher; JOHN HORDER: 'Through The Lavatory Window' from *Meher Baba and the Nothingness* (Menard Press, I98I) by kind permission of John Horder; FRANCES HOROVITZ: 'New Year Snow' and 'Poem of Absence' from *Collected Poems* (Bloodaxe, 1985), by permission of the publisher; A. E. HOUSMAN: 'Stars, I have seen them fall', 'Into my heart an air that kills' and 'Loveliest of Trees' from *A Shropshire Lad*, by permission of The Society of Authors as the Literary Representative of the Estate of A. E. Housman; LANGSTON HUGHES: 'I, too' and 'Harlem' from *The Collected Poems of Langston Hughes* (Alfred A. Knopf, 1994), by permission of David Higham Associates Ltd.; TED HUGHES: 'Song' and 'Full Moon and Little Frieda' from *New Selected Poems 1957-1994* (Faber & Faber, 1995); EMYR HUMPHREYS: 'From Father to Son' from *Collected Poems: Emyr Humphreys* (The University of Wales Press, 1999), by kind permission of the author; KATHLEEN JAMIE: 'Skeins o' Geese', from *Mr and Mrs Scotland are Dead: Poems 1980-1994* (Bloodaxe Books, 2002), by kind permission of the publisher; ELIZABETH JENNINGS: 'Light' and 'Into the Hour' from *Collected Poems* (Carcanet Press, 1987), by kind permission of David Higham Associates Ltd; GALWAY KINNELL: 'When One Has Lived a Long Time Alone', 'After Making Love We Hear Footsteps' and 'St Francis and the Sow' from *Selected Poems* (Bloodaxe, 2001), by permission of the publisher; MAXINE KUMIN: 'After Love' from *Selected Poems 1960-1990*. Copyright © 1996 by Maxine Kumin, by permission of W. W. Norton & Company, Inc.; PHILIP LARKIN: 'The Trees', 'Aubade' 'The Winter Palace', 'Solar' and 'Coming' from *Collected Poems* (Faber & Faber, 1993, with The Marvell Press) by permission of the publisher; DENISE LEVERTOV: 'Variation on a Theme by Rilke' from *Selected Poems* (Bloodaxe Books, 1986) by permission of Laurence Pollinger Ltd; PRIMO LEVI: '25 February 1944' from *Collected Poems* (Faber & Faber, 1988), by permission of the publisher; ALUN LEWIS: 'The Sentry' and 'Raiders' Dawn' from *Collected Poems* (Seren, 2001), by permission of the publisher; MICHAEL LONGLEY: 'The Linen Industry' from *Selected Poems* (Jonathan Cape, 1998), by permission of The Random House Group Ltd.; FEDERICO GARCIA LORCA: 'The Moon Sails Out', from *Lorca and Jimenez: Selected Poems*, translated by Robert Bly (Beacon Press, 1997), by kind permission of Robert Bly; ROBERT LOWELL: 'Will Not Come Back' from *History* (Faber & Faber, 1973), by permission of the publisher; NORMAN MACCAIG: 'Toad' from *Collected Poems*, (Chatto & Windus, 1993), by kind permission of The Random House Group Ltd.; ANTONIO MACHADO: 'Is My Soul Asleep?' from *The Soul is Here for its Own Joy: Sacred Poems from Many Cultures* edited by Robert Bly (Ecco Press, 1997), by kind permission of Robert Bly; HUGH MACDIARMID: 'Skald's Death' from *Complete Poems* (Carcanet Press, 1994) by permission of the publisher; ARCHIBALD MACLEISH: 'You, Andrew Marvell' from *Collected Poems: 1917-1982*, Copyright © 1985 The Estate of Archibald MacLeish, by

from *Love Poems* (HarperCollins, 1991), by permission of the publisher; TOM PAULIN: 'A Lyric Afterwards' from *Selected Poems 1972-1990* (Faber & Faber, 1993), by permission of the publisher; OCTAVIO PAZ: 'Letter of Testimony' from *Collected Poems 1957-1987* (Carcanet Press, 1988), by permission of the publisher; FERNANDO PESSOA: 'In the Dead Afternoon's Gold More' and 'The Gods Do Not Consent to More Than Life' from *Fernando Pessoa: Selected Poems* (Penguin Books, 1974, second edition 1982). Copyright © L. M. Rosa, 1974; translation Copyright © Jonathan Griffin, 1974, 1982; ROBERT PINSKY: 'Lair' from *The Figured Wheel: New and Selected Poems* (Noonday Press, Princeton University Press, 1997), by kind permission of the publisher; SYLVIA PLATH: 'You're' and 'Morning Song' from *Collected Poems*, (Faber & Faber, 1981), by permission of the publisher; EZRA POUND: 'The Garret' from *Selected Poems, 1908-1969: Selected Poems 1908-1959* (Faber & Faber, 1975), by permission of the publisher; SHEENAGH PUGH: 'Sometimes' from *Selected Poems* (Seren, 1990), by kind permission of the publisher; MIKLOS RADNÓTI: 'O Ancient Prisons' from *Foamy Sky: The Major Poems of Miklos Radnóti*, (Princeton University Press, 1992), by kind permission of the publisher; ZSUZSA RAKOVSZKY: 'They Were Burning Dead Leaves' from *New Life: Selected Poems* (OUP, 1994), by kind permission of George Szirtes and the publisher; A. K. RAMANUJAN: 'A Hindu to His Body' from *The Collected Poems of A. K. Ramanujan* (Oxford University Press, India, 1998), by kind permission of the Estate of A. K. Ramanujan; 'In Those Years' Copyright © 2002, 1995 by Adrienne Rich, 'Song' Copyright © 2002 by Adrienne Rich. Copyright © 1973 by W. W. Norton & Company, Inc., from *The Fact of a Doorframe: Selected Poems 1950-2001* by Adrienne Rich, by permission of the author and W. W. Norton & Company, Inc.; ROD RIESCO: 'Announcement' from *Marigolds Grow Wild on Platforms* (Cassell, 1996), by kind permission of the author; DENISE RILEY: 'Lyric' from *Selected Poems* (Reality Street, 2000), by kind permission of Denise Riley; RAINER MARIA RILKE: 'Evening' and 'The Panther' from *The Selected Poetry of Rainer Maria Rilke*, (Picador, 1980), by kind permission of D. G. Snell; 'Garden tenderly darkened, almost' from *An Unofficial Rilke* translated by Michael Hamburger (Anvil, 1981), by permission of Anvil Press Poetry; MICHÈLE ROBERTS: 'Lacrimae rerum' from *All the Selves I Was: New and Selected Poems* (Virago Press), by kind permission of the publisher; ROBIN ROBERTSON: 'Fall' from *Slow Air* (Picador, 2002), by kind permission of Robin Robertson and Pan Macmillan Ltd.; THEODORE ROETHKE: 'The Sloth', 'My Papa's Waltz', 'The Shape of the Fire' from *Collected Poems of Theodore Roethke* (Faber & Faber, 1968), by permission of the publisher; ISAAC ROSENBERG: 'August 1914' from *The Collected Works of Isaac Rosenberg* (Chatto & Windus, 1979), by kind permission of the Random House Group Ltd.; TADEUSZ ROZEWICZ: 'Busy with Many Jobs' from *Tadeusz Rozewicz: They Came to See a Poet* (Anvil Press Poetry, 1995), translated by Adam Czerniawski, by permission of the publisher; MURIEL RUKEYSER: 'Born in December' from *Collected Poems* (McGraw-Hill, 1982), by permission of International Creative Management, Inc. Copyright © 2002 by William Rukeyser; CAROL RUMENS: 'Prayer for Belfast' from *Best China Sky* (Bloodaxe Books, 1995), by permission of the publisher; SIEGFRIED SASSOON: 'Invocation' and 'The Power and the Glory' from *Collected Poems* (Faber & Faber, 2002), © Siegfried Sassoon by kind permission of George Sassoon; F. R. SCOTT: 'Caring' from *The Collected Poems of F. R. Scott* (McClelland & Stewart, 1981) by kind permission of William Toye, Literary Executor for the Estate of F. R. Scott; GEORGE SEFERIS: 'Interlude of Joy' from *Complete Poems*, translated by Edmund Keeley & Philip Sherrard (Anvil Press Poetry, 1995), by permission of the publisher; ANNE SEXTON: 'Her Kind', 'The Balance Wheel' and 'The Truth the Dead Know' from *Selected Poems of Anne Sexton* (Mariner Books/Houghton Mifflin Co., New York, 2000) by permission of Stirling Lord Literistic Inc., New York, Copyright © Anne Sexton; JO SHAPCOTT: 'Northern Lights' and 'Muse' from *Her Book: Poems 1988-1998* (Faber & Faber, 2000), by permission of the publisher; JOE SHEERIN: 'Diaries' from *Oxford Poets 2000*

Index of Poets

Index of First Lines and Titles

The Poetry Challenge

Organise a Poetry Challenge in *your* school

• A Poetry Challenge is an event in which pupils (and teachers) are sponsored to recite a poem they have learned by heart in order to raise money for charity
• It can be any poem, and any charity, and the event can happen at any time in the school year. It is a flexible idea that can be moulded and altered to whatever suits, be it a week-long festival of poetry or a single assembly of recitals
• Hundreds of successful challenges are run every year, not only raising funds for many worthy causes, but also bringing poetry alive for students in a hugely enjoyable event

Excerpts from recent Challenge reports:

"We have again held a very successful challenge involving the whole school which we completed in an assembly ... We send the money raised to our local children's hospice every year. May the Poetry Challenge always continue!" *Wendy Boulton, Manor House School, Surrey.*

"The act of committing a poem to heart and memory has inspired pupils to not only appreciate the power of the spoken word, but delivering the poem in a public way has endowed the words with a personal reinterpretation." *Kerrie Conlon, Head of English, Woodford Lodge High School, Cheshire.*

"Each class or year group chose a poem and asked family and friends to sponsor them to learn the poem – a skill which many staff agreed was in danger of being lost! The poems were performed at a special Harvest Assembly, at which we also handed over a cheque to Macmillan Cancer Relief for £5600! Thank you for the idea – it's an event we will repeat." *Carol Mairs, Vice-Principal, Antrim Primary School, Northern Ireland.*

"The event we ran was a huge success. We are a school located a 'stone's throw' away from New York City. All of us knew someone who was touched by the tragedy of September 11th. The Poetry Challenge was a wonderful way for our students to reach out and help others. We all loved listening to the variety of poems memorized. We are proud of the $2292 we have earned, which has been donated to the New York Times Neediest Cases 9/11 Fund. Our thanks for a wonderful idea – we are proud to have accepted The Poetry Challenge." *Linda Carlson, Teacher, Prospect Hill Elementary School, Pelham, New York.*

"The Poetry Challenge inspired me because it allowed me to do things I never thought I could do. Before at our school's annual Christmas review, I was always watching or not really taking part. Now, though, I had enough courage to recite my poem in front of just under two hundred people." *Rowan Martin, Pupil (Year 7), Denmead School, Middlesex.*

For further information and resources, write to the Poetry Challenge, 6 Blackstock Mews, Blackstock Road, London N4 2BT (tel 020 7359 8391; e-mail: poetry@alberyfoundation.org) or see www.poetrychallenge.org.uk where sample certificates, posters and sponsorship forms can be downloaded.

The Nicholas Albery Foundation

The Nicholas Albery Foundation is an umbrella charity for a number of innovative projects which aim to improve society with creative solutions to real-world problems. The Foundation is named after its visionary founder and chairman of 20 years, Nicholas Albery, who instigated many of the projects and wrote many of the publications which help support the charity, including the original volume of *Poem for the Day* and its companion book *Seize the Day*. He sadly died in 2001, and the Foundation is a living memorial to him and his work, aiming to both continue and build upon his legacy.

The present projects of the Foundation include:

The Institute for Social Inventions – the central project of the Foundation, the Institute promotes and disseminates good ideas to improve society around the world, and encourages public participation in the creative problem-solving process. To this end, it publishes an annual compendium of the year's best ideas, gives annual innovation awards and runs the popular Global Ideas Bank website (www.globalideasbank.org).

The Natural Death Centre – the Centre advises on alternative funerals, woodland burials, biodegradable coffins, and private land burial, and educates more widely on the subject of death and dying with workshops, seminars and an annual Day of the Dead. For more information, see the Natural Death Centre website (www.naturaldeath.org.uk), which also has a list of publications available to order online.

The Poetry Challenge – this project provides information and resources (sponsor forms, certificates, tips etc) to schools and other organisations wishing to hold a challenge; a Poetry Challenge is an event in which participants are sponsored to learn poems by heart to raise money for charity. For more on this project, see previous page.

The ApprenticeMaster Alliance – this online directory matches up apprentices looking to learn a trade with masters willing to teach it. In the ideal apprenticeship, there is a beneficial exchange of skills, knowledge and time. It is ideal for school-leavers, recent graduates or those out of work. For the current list of available apprenticeships and more information see the ApprenticeMaster Alliance website at www.apprentice.org.uk

www.DoBe.org – DoBe.org is a website for listing participatory events in every city in the world, in order to foster real-world interaction and to combat urban isolation. It aims to retribalise the cities using the power of the internet. Log on at www.DoBe.org to find out more.

To learn more about any of the projects above, or how you can support them through donations or buying publications, please contact The Nicholas Albery Foundation, 6 Blackstock Mews, Blackstock Road, London N4 2BT (tel 020 7359 8391; fax 020 7354 3831; e-mail: info@alberyfoundation.org; web: www.alberyfoundation.org).

Poem for the Day One

The original and best-selling *Poem for the Day*

"The book is a dream, a revivalist campaign, a challenge, a fundraising vehicle, a book of days and an anthology, all in one"
The Guardian

"It's a brilliant concept and should give a lot of pleasure to all ages"
Antonia Fraser, Daily Mail

366 inspirational poems from around the world, old favourites and new discoveries, one for each day of the year, chosen for their resonance, magic and ease of learning. Poets included range from Yeats, Shakespeare, Housman and Kipling, to contemporary poets such as Wendy Cope, Carol Ann Duffy, Maya Angelou and Thom Gunn.

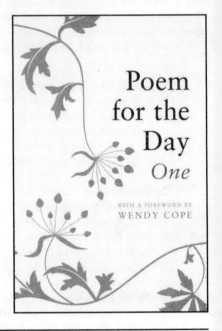

Poem
for the
Day
One

WITH A FOREWORD BY
WENDY COPE

'This splendid anthology collects 366 poems, each short enough to learn in a day, each rich enough to repay the effort' *(Annals)*

'Poetry is for me one of the great peripheral pleasures in life, but I have never encountered a volume which has given me such a frisson of joy and excitement as this' *(Fourth World Review)*

'I am writing to express my delight in *Poem for the Day* ... Each poem is a joy to read – even if not learnt by heart – and your notes add to the pleasure ... I am learning three or four poems a week and my enthusiasm has passed to friends who are also taking up the challenge' *(Ash Faith)*

• *All royalties from this 400-page book go to the Nicholas Albery Foundation, so please buy copies for your friends! To order copies for £11.97 (inc p&p), call the Nicholas Albery Foundation on 020 7359 8391, or send a cheque made payable to 'ISI' to NAF, 6 Blackstock Mews, Blackstock Road, London N4 2BT.*